Enactments

EDITED BY RICHARD SCHECHNER

To perform is to imagine, represent, live and enact present
circumstances, past events and future possibilities. Performance takes
place across a very broad range of venues from city streets to the
countryside, in theatres and in offices, on battlefields and in hospital
operating rooms. The genres of performance are many, from the arts to
the myriad performances of everyday life, from courtrooms to legislative
chambers, from theatres to wars to circuses.

ENACTMENTS will encompass performance in as many of its aspects and
realities as there are authors able to write about them.

ENACTMENTS will include active scholarship, readable thought and
engaged analysis across the broad spectrum of performance studies.

DANCING ODISSI

Paratopic Performances of Gender and State

Anurima Banerji

LONDON NEW YORK CALCUTTA

Seagull Books, 2019

© Anurima Banerji, 2019

ISBN   978 0 8574 2 553 9

Portions of the Indrani Rahman interview by Genevieve Oswald (dated 11 December 1975) are reprinted here with the kind permission of Sukanya Rahman and the New York Public Library for the Performing Arts, New York.

British Library Cataloguing-in-Publication Data
A catalogue record for this book is available from the British Library

Typeset by Seagull Books, Calcutta, India
Printed and bound by Maple Press, York, Pennsylvania, USA

Dedicated to my mother and father,
who put me in Odissi classes when I was a child
and cultivated my love of dance

How could we know the history of nations but for the ever-lasting monuments of the pen?

—Alberuni

We need a history that does not save in any sense of the word; we need a history that performs.

—Jane Blocker

CONTENTS

ACKNOWLEDGEMENTS

So many people deserve thanks for accompanying me on this journey through the world of Odissi. This work started as a dissertation at NYU's Department of Performance Studies, and I was honoured that Profs Richard Schechner and Barbara Kirshenblatt-Gimblett agreed to co-direct that project. I am deeply grateful for their superb mentorship; at every step of the process, they gave me the gift of their invaluable intellectual and moral support. They continue to inspire me with their generosity, their innovative scholarship and creative projects.

Many of the ideas in this book developed first in dance studies classes I took at NYU with Profs Barbara Browning and André Lepecki, both of whom helped me refine my initial thoughts into cogent ideas and frameworks. Prof. Arti Dhand at McGill University introduced me to subtle ways of thinking through the relationship between South Asian religions and gender, while Profs Marike Finlay-de-Monchy, Karin Cope, Judith Whitehead, Kristen Norget, George Szanto and Will Straw sparked my initial thinking on many of the theoretical questions that inform this book.

I thank the faculty at NYU's Department of Performance Studies for their intellectual guidance, especially Profs Diana Taylor, Ann Pellegrini, Tavia N'yongo, Karen Shimakawa, and the late José Muñoz. The department staff—Noel Rodriguez, Patty Jang, Jason Beckerman, and Laura Fortes—provided wonderful support on the administrative side. I benefitted from the insights of my colleagues in the doctoral program, especially Shayoni Mitra, Joshua Chambers-Letson, Mila Aponte-Gonzalez, Brigitte Sion, Joseph Shahadi and Tina Majkowski. Jill Gellerman offered her vital support by reading every draft, providing detailed comments and suggestions, and helping me organize concepts and arguments—at the earliest stages of developing the manuscript.

UCLA has provided a most congenial and vibrant atmosphere for pursuing this research. I am privileged to work with the faculty and staff at the Department of World Arts and Cultures/Dance— Kyle Abraham, Bryonn Bain, Dan Froot, David Gere, Angelia Leung, Victoria Marks, Peter Nabokov, Janet O'Shea, Lionel Popkin, Al Roberts, the late Polly Roberts, David Roussève, Peter Sellars, David Shorter, Christopher Waterman, Cheng-Chieh Yu and Tria Blu Wakpa. Aparna Sharma sustained me through this project with her great camaraderie, wit and collaborative spirit— not to mention a mutual love of Odissi and cinema. My deepest appreciation is reserved for Susan Leigh Foster, to whom I owe bountiful thanks for her exceptional mentorship, her intellectual leadership and for opening up valuable opportunities to advance my scholarship. Her help on this project has been indispensable.

I wish to thank the participants in the UC-Santa Cruz Dance Theory Workshop organized by Mark Franko (January 2013) and the UCLA Postcolonial Colloquium coordinated by Yogita Goyal (February 2014) for their comments on Chapter Two. Profs Bishnupriya Dutt and Urmimala Sarkar kindly invited me to share portions of my research at JNU's School of Art and Aesthetics while Meera Das did the same at the Gunjan Dance Academy as did the UCLA's Center for India and South Asia. My fellow members of the Ritual and Performance project at the Asia Institute and the How Art Does Politics Network, especially Profs Violaine Roussel, Bin Wong and Andrea Goldman, have enriched my thinking greatly.

It was a gratifying experience to work with a range of senior scholars at the Dr. Penny Kanner Manuscript Workshop, facilitated by the UCLA Center for the Study of Women (CSW), at a critical stage in the writing process. Profs Akhil Gupta, Rachel Lee, Saloni Mathur, Sean Metzger, Aamir Mufti, Jenny Sharpe and Jasmine Nadua Trice offered valuable suggestions for sharpening my arguments and analytics. It is my good fortune that two eminent outside readers, Profs Partha Chatterjee and Parama Roy, graciously agreed to engage with my work. I appreciate the considerable time and care they devoted to a close reading of the manuscript, as their input indelibly strengthened the ideas developed here.

I owe a debt of gratitude to Shyamhari Chakra, Sahadev Dhala, Kedar Mishra, Jagabandhu Jena and Raja Panda in Odisha, without whose help I simply could not have conducted the in-depth research required for this project. They directed me to significant resources essential for my analysis, accompanied me on visits to key research sites and enriched my knowledge of the culture and landscape of Odisha. They deserve a great deal of credit for the energy and enthusiasm they dedicated to guiding me. I also want to acknowledge Beena Keum's help in this regard. D. C. Panda took me on two fascinating tours of Bhubaneshwar's temples and archaeological sites and shared his considerable knowledge of Odisha's architectural heritage. Devadutta Samantasinghar guided me to significant sites for mahari and gotipua history in Puri on a day-long visit. I am grateful to Madhavi Puranam for hosting me in Hyderabad, for taking me to Kuchipudi village, for setting up interviews with scholars at Central Hyderabad University and for providing crucial access to her archive of *Nartanam* journals. The hospitality extended by Bijayini Satpathy, Surupa Sen, Pavithra Reddy and Lynne Fernandez at Nrityagram made my visit there memorable.

Dr Sunil Kothari put me in touch with important contacts and led me to scholarly materials that advanced my work. Conversations with Aloka Kanungo, Kapila Vatsyayan, Aruna Mohanty, Rahul Acharya, Nandini Sikand, Rachel McDermott and Uttara Asha Coorlawala proved important for my meditations on Indian performance. Profs Carol Martin and Richard Schechner allowed me access to an original manuscript on Seraikella Chhau from their private collection. Meena Murugesan and Lorenzo Perillo provided expert research assistance.

For their extraordinary help in locating resources for this project, I wish to acknowledge Dr Helen Acharya and the library personnel at Sangeet Natak Akademi, New Delhi; David Hogge at the Freer and Sackler Galleries, the Smithsonian Institution, Washington DC; Ashim Mukhopadhaya at the National Library and

Gargi Gangopadhyay of Jadavpur University, Kolkata. I'm also grate-
ful to the staff at the India Office of the British Library (London,
UK); the Library of Congress (Washington DC); UC-Berkeley's
Bancroft Library and the Art Museum and Pacific Film Archive
(Berkeley); NYU's Bobst Library, the Institute for the Study of
the Ancient World (ISAW), and the New York Public Library of the
Performing Arts (New York); Shriram Bharatiya Kala Kendra, Triveni
Kala Sangam, Nehru Memorial Library, and the Center for Cultural
Resources and Training (New Delhi); the Madras Music Academy
and *Sruti Magazine* (Chennai); Guru Kelucharan Mohapatra Odissi
Research Center, the Odisha State Archives, and the Odisha State
Museum (Bhubaneshwar); and UCLA's Young Research Library (Los
Angeles). The Odisha Tourism Office provided photos, maps, and
guides to key sites and assisted with access to dance festivals. Dr
Swarnamalya Ganesh and Prof. Raman Siva Kumar shared important visual resources with me. Thanks also to everyone who imparted
their insights in interviews and meetings—I am privileged that they
gave me their precious time.

It is no exaggeration to say that I could not have completed this
project without the love of my parents, Dilip and Pubali Banerji.
They always encouraged me in my dance endeavours, and came to
stay with me at a crucial moment to take care of domestic matters
in Los Angeles, giving me the luxury of concentrating fully on
writing. Their support means more than they'll ever know.

Joy Banerji, Susana Cook, Maneesha Deckha, Faizal Deen,
Anjula Gogia, Marcia James, Ronak Kapadia, Devaki Panini, Shahin
Parhami, Harsha Ram and Shanti Pillai sustained me with their
encouragement and affection through the arduous writing process.
I want to give a special thanks to F. K. in this regard. My aunt and
uncle Dr M. N. and Sucheta Roy, cousin Priyadarshini Roy, along
with Rachna Pathak and her family in Delhi, were ever-generous in
hosting me during frequent stays in Kolkata and Delhi.

I am much obliged to my Odissi gurus, who made it possible
for me to enter the world of dance: Guru Dibakar Khuntia, who
taught me in my childhood; the late Guru Muralidhar Majhi, who,
with his wife, and children Bapi and Tapi, took me on my first trip

through Odisha in 1991; and Guru Bichitrananda Swain, under whose tutelage I took up advanced training. I thank them for the joy they brought to their creative endeavours, and for sharing their talents and wisdom with me.

Sadly, several pioneers of Odissi passed away during the time I was working on this book. Renowned scholar D. N. Patnaik was deeply involved in the revival of Odissi dance as a performer and writer, and authored the first in-depth history of Odissi in 1954. Guru Maguni Das resurrected gotipua dance at a time in history when it could have disappeared for good. Guru Gangadhar Pradhan, Ritha Devi, and Muralidhar Majhi's tireless efforts to promote Odissi in India and abroad won them respect and recognition. Shashimoni Devadasi was one of the last group of female ritual specialists to serve at the Jagannath temple. Dinanath Pathy pushed us to think about Odissi practice with critical verve. Odissi would simply not be what it is today without the contribution of these great figures. Their words and memories are gifts I will cherish. And while I did not have the chance to meet Guru Surendranath Jena in person when he was alive, I am lucky to have learnt about his work through his daughter Pratibha, who continues to carry on the tradition on his behalf.

During the course of researching and preparing this book, I was fortunate to receive support from the Corrigan Fellowship, Paulette Goddard Scholarship, Dean's Predoctoral Summer Fellowship, and Dean's Dissertation Fellowship at NYU; an International Dissertation Fellowship from the American Association for University Women; and funding from the UCLA Dean's Office, the Academic Senate's Research Enabling and Faculty Research Grants, a CSW Fellowship for Junior Scholars, a Faculty Career Development Award, and a Hellman Fellowship. This book could not have been completed without this generous assistance.

*

Earlier versions of Chapter 2 appeared as 'Dance and the Distributed Body: Odissi, Ritual Practice, and Mahari Performance' in *About Performance* 11 (In-Between Moves special issue, co-edited by

Amanda Card and Justine Shih Pearson) (2012): 7–39; and 'Dance and the Distributed Body: Odissi and Mahari Performance' in Mark Franko (ed.), *The Oxford Handbook of Dance and Reenactment* (New York: Oxford University Press, 2017, pp. 413–48).

A NOTE ON THE TEXT

In the text, I have elected to use conventional phonetic spellings of Indian-language terms in translation and transliteration rather than incorporating diacritical marks that assist with their pronunciation in the original language. The latter approach requires specialized knowledge of the original language (and its nuances of speech) as well as familiarity with the system of linguistic marks, complicating matters for the general reader. Thus, I use *shastra* rather than *sastra*, *chari* instead of *cari*, *rishi* instead of *rsi*, *nritta* instead of *nrtta*, Krishna instead of Krsna, Jagannath instead of Jagannatha, etc.

The dance Odissi, the name of the state in which it flowered, and related regional terms have changed spellings in the last 60 years—Odissi is often listed as Odishi or Orissi. The state officially changed its name from Orissa to Odisha on 4 November 2011. The language known as Oriya is now called Odia (and was granted classical status by the Indian government in 2013). Variations of these terms are used, when appropriate, for historical referencing, in the contexts specified below.

Please note that in their English translations/transliterations, different authors use variant spellings or phrases for the same concept, name or term. Examples include: *Natya Shastra, Natyashastra, Natya Sastra; nritya* and *nrutya; Shabda Swarup* and *Shabda Nritya; Gita Govinda, Gitagovinda, Geeta Govinda, Geetagovindam; Pattanaik, Pattnaik, Patnaik, Patnayak; Prataparudradeva, Pratapa Rudra Deva,* etc. In all instances, I have kept intact the conventions used by the specific authors when I quote or cite them but opt for the standard phonetic spelling or officially accepted terms otherwise.

PART I

MANGALACHARAN
BEGINNINGS

THE BEADS OF HISTORY

Beginnings often conceal the desire for other beginnings.
—Paul Carter, *The Lie of the Land* (1994)

This book traces the transformation of Odissi, a South Asian classical dance style, from its historical role as a regional practice to its modern incarnation as national spectacle, with a focus on the state's regulation of the dance and performances of gender embedded in it. It constructs new histories of Odissi by analysing the wide spectrum of discourses to which it has been affiliated, both normative and transgressive. Specifically, it considers the arc of Odissi's chronologies by highlighting its engagements with the state in the ancient, medieval, colonial and postcolonial periods of South Asian history. It suggests that, throughout Odissi's changing pasts, two threads have remained constant: one, the subversive potential of the dance in creating distinct visions for extraordinary performances of gender and sexuality which transcend quotidian social norms; and two, the idea of the state not only as a prohibitive agent that regulates bodily practice but also as a choreographic agent that generates and prescribes idealized movements of the body and social relations, both inside and outside the zone of dance. Tying these threads together, I will call for an identification of Odissi as a 'paratopic performance'—a practice that creates a space of alterity for reimagining orthodoxies of gender against the normalizing mandates of the state and what is scripted in social law.

Commonly perceived as the oldest classical dance in India, Odissi originated in the eastern state of Odisha. Presented as a

3

traditional style in discourses of Indian art, Odissi is in fact the modern appellation for an amalgam of Odishan forms. The earliest-known signs of Odissi's antecedents can be traced to ancient India (around the first century BCE) in the dance style known as Odra-Magadhi, a form of professional entertainment, interweaving dimensions of the secular and the sacred.[1] In the eleventh century CE, Mahari Naach (dance of the maharis or female ritual specialists) was introduced as a devotional practice in Odisha, performed to honour the Hindu divine,[2] and this temple style is conventionally considered the authentic progenitor of contemporary Odissi. Denounced by British imperialists and indigenous elites, allegedly for its ties to prostitution, Mahari Naach was forced underground during the British Raj.

Earlier, in the sixteenth century, with the advent of the Bhakti movement in eastern India, another lineage emerged—the gotipua tradition, of young boys embodying the feminine in public dance performance. Unlike the Mahari Naach, this tradition escaped colo-

---

1 Throughout this book, I use the term 'secular' in two ways: first, in contrast to the sacred, as in 'areligious'; and second, to identify the uniquely Indian view, articulated by Rajeev Bhargava (2006), in which the governing state recognizes that religion cannot be relegated to the private domain, and claims to recognize plural religions in the public sphere in a relatively egalitarian or neutral mode. I realize that the secular, in my usage, indexes both the separation and integration of the religious and nonreligious, and that this may be a confusing point. I hope each meaning will be made clear in context.

2 I recognize that Hinduism is a composite formation and that originally there was no such homogenous or unitary religious tradition in India. Autonomous sects such as Vedic Brahmanism, Shakti, Bhakti, Puranic cults, Vaishnavism and Shaivism predominated in early India. These disparate lineages were homogenized into a single category over time. Adherents of Hinduism often position themselves as followers of Sanatana Dharma (loosely translated as the 'eternal way' that directs one's religious or moral duties and practices). It is generally agreed that the designation 'Hindu' first came about in the eighth century CE to mark a geographically based identity referring to the inhabitants of the Indian subcontinent. Later, in the medieval and colonial periods, it became a political and religious signifier. I use 'Hindu' as a shorthand to refer to a consolidated religious identity and as a synonym for the different sects that predated its emergence.

nial scrutiny and survived into the early decades of the twentieth century.

By the 1930s, the dance scene in Odisha aligned with a new cultural environment. As Mahari Naach diminished in stature, concert dances crafted in indigenous idioms began to emerge in the context of Indian nationalism. Inspired by prominent choreographers like Rabindranath Tagore and Uday Shankar, innovators in modern Indian dance, and Rukmini Devi, a pioneering figure in classical Bharatanatyam, dancers in Odisha began to develop their own novel styles for the stage. Prior to its installation as a classical form in the twentieth century, this style was simply called Odra or Odia Naach (Odia dance).

Postcolonial architects of the dance composed a new genre, based on the principles of ancient texts like the *Natyashastra*, the *Abhinaya Darpanam* and the *Abhinaya Chandrika* (collectively known as the Shastras); imagery drawn from sculpture and visual art, profuse in Odisha; the rich poetic and musical repertoires of the region, especially the *Geeta Govinda*; syncretic religious influences, from Jainism and Shaivism, to Shakti, Bhakti and the cult of Jagannath; the combined streams of Odra-Magadhi, and Mahari Naach and Odia Naach; and theatrical genres like Jatra, Rasleela and local dance drama. The reconstruction, fusion and refinement of these congeries of forms culminated in the dance aesthetic we brand classical 'Odissi' today.[3]

---

3 The question of what constitutes the 'classical' in the Indian context is quite politically charged; this is a subject I discuss in Chapter 6, but an in-depth treatment of the subject is out of the scope of this project. Notably, ancient Indian theory never made a strict distinction between classical and popular forms; these are designations that were superimposed on dance in the twentieth century. The need for a discourse of the 'classical' came about in the colonial context and then became so embedded that it is impossible to situate Odissi outside that discourse today. The 'classical' idea was an imported Western concept with a universalist pretence, used as a measure of cultural sophistication and civilizational accomplishment. By contrast, in the world of Indian performance, classical forms today generally refer to those that actively construct a link to the Shastras—they conform to the idioms, rules and formulas set out in ancient Indian texts. The prime example in performance

After its revival in postcolonial India, Odissi was exported to national and international venues as a marker of South Asian art and heritage. Odissi only began its ascent as a popular form in the 1960s, peaking in the 1990s and establishing itself as a significant classical dance ever since.

Pioneering scholars like Ileana Citarasti, Charles Fabri, Priyambada Mohanty Hejmadi, Ashish Khokar and Mohan Khokar, Sunil Kothari, Jiwan Pani, Dhirendra Nath Patnaik, Kali Charan Patnaik, Ratna Roy and Kapila Vatsyayan have made valuable contributions to the study of Odissi's history and technique.[4]

---

is the *Natyashastra*, a work on dance and drama attributed to the sage Bharatmuni, dated between the second century BCE and second century CE. Its recensions were rediscovered by scholars in the late nineteenth–early twentieth centuries and subsequently used as the basis of reconstructing many of the dances in India that collectively became canonized as classical. (The irony here is that the *Natyashastra* itself is a recension, and only partial manuscripts exist; there is also controversy about its authorship, and the degree to which it is fully prescriptive or open to multiple interpretations.) The *Shilpa Shastra*, a treatise on sculpture, is another example of such a text. Thus, while the Western notion of the 'classical' (the best of the heritage, the apex of a style, an exemplary cultural landmark that transcends time and place) holds very different meanings from the Indian idea of the Shastric, for historical reasons, the two terms tend to overlap in meaning and are viewed as close enough in their careers and connotations to serve as rough equivalents. Given this background, and for the sake of precision, I use the term Shastric to specifically refer to performances based on ancient Indian codes; where appropriate in other contexts, I use the term Shastric and classical interchangeably. For more, see Kapila Vatsyayan (1967, 1974, 1983, 1996, 1997 and 2007a).

4 Classics in the field include Dhirendra Nath Patnaik's indispensable *Odissi Dance* (1971, 1990), a pioneering history of the form; Kapila Vatsyayan's scholarship on Odissi in *Indian Classical Dance* (1974), *Classical Indian Dance in Literature and the Arts* (1977) and *Incredible India* (2007b); Mohan Khokar's *Traditions of Indian Classical Dance* (1984); Frédrérique Apffel Marglin's *Wives of the God-King* (1985b), an in-depth ethnography of the devadasis of Puri; Sunil Kothari's *Odissi* (1990); and Jiwan Pani's *Back to the Roots* (2004). Significant recent additions include Dinanath Pathy's *Rethinking Odissi* (2007); Priyambada Mohanty Hejmadi and Ahalya Hejmadi Patnaik's *Odissi* (2007); Alessandra Lopez y Royo's *ReConstructing and RePresenting Dance* (2008); Ratna Roy's *Neo Classical Odissi Dance* (2009); Ashish Khokar and

Among them, the consensus appears to be that Odissi originated as a form of religious worship and eventually moved to the concert stage as a 'neo-classical' form. The aesthetic philosophies of the *Natyashastra*, the *Abhinaya Darpanam* and the *Abhinaya Chandrika*, and the role of Hindu temple culture in cultivating the dance are prominent in this telling, and a linear progression from ancient Odra-Magadhi to present-day Odissi organizes this historical trajectory.

For another group of scholars, Odissi is the product of modern nationalism, and its proponents deploy its heritage politics ideologically to legitimize the form as a cultural emblem. Alessandra Lopez y Royo (2007a and 2008), for instance, has delivered a strong argument that Odissi is an invention of postcolonial India; that from one perspective, it is a thoroughly modern dance whose claims of historicity only obfuscate its recent origins. Ananya Chatterjea has critiqued the manner in which dominant constructs of Odissi imagine its 'logically continuous' link with Odra-Magadhi for the purpose of rarefaction and reification (2004a: 152). Dinanath Pathy (2007) argues that this focus on the

Mohan Khokar's *The Dance Orissi* (2011); and Nandini Sikand's *Languid Bodies, Grounded Stances* (2016).

The definitive biographies of Kelucharan Mahapatra (*The Making of a Guru* by Ileana Citarasti, 2001); Deba Prasad Das (*Icon of Odissi* by Gayatri Chand, 2012); Indrani Rahman (*Dancing in the Family* by daughter Sukanya Rahman, 2004); and Mayadhar Raut (*Odissi Yaatra* by Aadya Kaktikar, 2011) are other notable works.

Rahul Acharya, Sharmila Biswas, Ananya Chatterjea, Bidut Kumari Choudhury, Uttara Asha Coorlawala, Ragini Devi, Charles Louis Fabri, Ranjana Gauhar, Sharon Lowen, Sitakant Mahapatra, Shovana Narayan, Kshirod Prosad, Madhumita Raut, Richard Schechner, Vidya Suresh and Leela Venkataraman have all contributed to the small, specialized but substantial body of research on Odissi.

Films like *Odissi Dance* by Ghanashyam Mohapatra (1971); *Given to Dance* by Ron Hess (1985); *Vibrant Sculpture/Frozen Dance* by Ritha Devi (1987); *Bhavantarana* by Kumar Shahani (1991); *Bandha Nritya* by the Centre for Cultural Resources and Training (2004); *Performing Konarak, Performing Hirapur* by Alessandra Lopez y Royo (2007b); and *Odissi* by Rekha Tandon (2016) are important visual documents.

past keeps Odissi stagnant, and wants choreographers of Odissi to open up its borders and create new repertoires, to repudiate traditional themes steeped in religion and conservative worldviews in order to refashion a *navya* (new or modern) Odissi 'in the present world'. All three scholars suggest that this particular telling of Odissi's past is tied to the cultural agenda of elevating the dance through its association with ancient religiosities. These are persuasive arguments, and in my eyes, very valid ones, for there is ample evidence to support the claim that Odissi is an entirely contemporary invention which draws on the rhetoric and repositories of tradition and religious symbology for its authentication and authorization.

Although the two scholarly constellations to which I have referred appear to be incompatible on the surface, they are complementary at the core. They both accept the significance of historical narrative in shaping the dance, even as they argue for distinct versions of it and place the point of origin at different junctures—one in the scene of the golden past, and the other in the milieu of modernity. In each case, Odissi becomes an argument for mobilizing, or countering, a particular vision of history.

My project subscribes to similar claims but from a different angle. As a dancer trained in Odissi, I repeatedly encountered the story of its hallowed genesis as a temple ritual—in studio classes, at performances and festivals, in media representations, in popular cultural narratives and in dance scholarship. The protocols surrounding Odissi's pedagogy and performance reinforced its ritual identity, and the mythological themes governing its narratives emphasized its devotional dimension. At the same time, the experimental spirit of choreographers who used the framework of classical Odissi to explore contemporary aesthetics and ideas challenged the precepts and premises surrounding its purported essence.

These explorations posed a predicament. If Odissi's identity fundamentally belonged to the domain of the sacred, then working outside a religious aesthetic seemed to betray its core principles. On the other hand, to argue for its status as a modern invention opened up the possibility of contesting its representations as religious fetish but minimized the role of the manifold forms that contributed to its making. A close and critical look at Odissi's principles, themes and techniques made it apparent to me that the dancing body performed a complex politic and aesthetic—it propagated a kinetic knowledge that defied appropriations of the traditional, the modern and the national; it choreographed an identity that existed *parallel* to dominant discourses and values; and it acted as a somatic repository of a past which held importance for the artistic and cultural communities it represented.

What, then, are these pasts? What do they signify and perform? If we provisionally accept Odissi's ancient status, what are its possible social and political histories? And what kinds of discourses and bodies does it produce? What is the relationship between dance and the cultural and political environments in which it resides? To use Susan Leigh Foster's terms, how does Odissi dance choreograph history? (1995)

A tangled picture emerges. For entrenched alongside the story of Odissi as a temple dance lies a history of alternatives—and it is these paratopic expressions that are the subject of my research. As a living tradition, Odissi is an accumulation of past discourses brought into the present through the dancing body, and a collection of a plural set of values: conservative and progressive, stereotypical and liberatory expressions of gender, a praxis of piety and an ethos of eros. It is both a construction of modern regionalism and nationalism as well as rooted in the past.

I argue that Odissi harbours a distinct regional epistemology, that it conjures a contrapuntal discourse of gender and religious expression and that it has mobilized this alterity throughout its jagged history. Here, I set out to trace the dance's trajectory from Odra-Magadhi to Mahari Naach, gotipua and Odia Naach, to its arrival as Odissi. Perhaps controversially, I use Odissi interchangeably with each of these terms. All the forms that make up Odissi have their *own* histories and refuse homogenization, but these different streams intermingle in the contemporary dancing body. My intent in co-naming them 'Odissi' is to acknowledge the

integrity of each form while highlighting the composition of
Odissi as a mosaic without a defining essence. I deliberately claim
each strand as an integral part of Odissi, as witnessed in its
contemporary aesthetic, and suggest that one is as, or no more,
authentic than the other. In doing so, I specifically contest dominant narratives in which Odissi is presented as a discrete and
hermetically sealed form, almost uninterrupted in its travels
from Odra-Magadhi to Odissi. Specifically, I contest the privileged
place of Mahari Naach in Odissi's history, and seek to explore its
imbrications and interplays with traditions established *outside* the
temple. And I contend that, historically, the role of governmentality
has deeply imprinted Odissi's configurations of gender and
ultimately affected its performance aesthetic.

Odissi holds a privileged place in the South Asian cultural
imaginary today, regarded as a powerful performance of art and
identity with a range of ideological and affective attachments. My
goal is to expand Odissi's genealogies instead of perpetuating its
present narrative or interrogating its position as a dance with deep
historical roots. In other words, my project is one of simultaneously deconstructing Odissi's mystique, and reconstructing its
paratopic historical claims. I begin with the premises of Odissi's
standard history and critically examine them; reinterpret and
recontextualize evidence of its past; address significant gaps in the
narrative; offer new materials for analysis; and assemble a fresh
set of histories for consideration. By expanding the definition of
the dance, this project argues for a broad vision of Odissi, where
innovations and experiments that contest Odissi's conventional
techniques and challenge its religious claims can legitimately
coexist with its traditional repertoire. For opening up Odissi's
possible histories also opens up its possible futures.[5]

Odissi's Aesthetics

Odissi's plural histories are embedded in its movement vocabularies and choreographic principles. Representing a striking

---

5 I thank Barbara Kirshenblatt-Gimblett for this important insight.

balance of softness and strength, an alchemy of geometry and grace, for me it has always been a compelling aesthetic of beauty and power. Odissi's paradox is that it contains these opposites and still portrays a serene harmony and lyrical languor.

Odissi's modern inventors designed it to conform to the codes of the Shastras (Patnaik 2008). Like other classical dances, Odissi combines *nritta* (formalist expressions displaying technical, abstract and decorative qualities of dance) and *nritya* or *abhinaya* (expressive qualities of dance, the evocative display of emotion). In an *abhinaya*, the *rasa* (the taste, mood or atmosphere emanating from the performance) is created by the dancer's *bhava* (the emotional state she embodies) and ideally migrates to the spectator, producing a powerful affective experience.[6] With its evocative and poetic lineages, its unique corporealities and its immersion in a cultural landscape where the sacred commingles with the sensual, Odissi epitomizes *shringara*, the shades and nuances of the erotic.

Odissi's technique valorizes body positions rooted in the ground rather than aiming for an air of lightness (Vatsyayan 1967). Grace comes from mobilizing the strength of the spine to control the subtlest of movements. In its groundedness, the Odissi body works with shifts of weight and principles of balance and symmetry in order to create time and shape in space, both linear and curvaceous.

Kapila Vatsyayan has elaborated on two principal ideas that anchor classical Indian dance: the circle and the square (1983), reflected in the composition of spaces of performance, arranged around the figure of the *mandala*, as well as in the dancer's own biograms.[7] Odissi's two signature stances reproduce this complementary duality: Chowk, which literally means square,

6 On the nuances of *rasa* theory, see the well-developed literature of the *Natyashastra*, *Abhinavabharati* and *Bhaktirasamritasindhu* and respective commentaries. See also Hari Ram Mishra (1964); B. M. Chaturvedi (1996); Kailash Pati Mishra (2006); S. C. Pande (2009); and Venkatarama Raghavan (2010).

7 Brian Massumi describes 'biograms' as ingrained patterns of bodily movement that organize one's proprioception (2002).

FIGURES 0.1–0.4. Bijayini Satpathy in (CLOCKWISE FROM TOP LEFT) Odissi Chowk, Tribhangi, Samabhanga and Abhanga positions. Outside Odissi Gurukul, Nrityagram, 4 January 2017. In the Abhanga position, the dancer is echoing the figural motifs found on the walls of Odishan temples, as in Figure 0.5. Photographs by the author.

FIGURE 0.5 (LEFT). An Abhanga stance represented at Konark temple. Ganga period, thirteenth century CE. Konark, Odisha, 21 February 2008. Photoby the author.

FIGURE 0.6 (RIGHT). Sanjukta Panigrahi in a 1989 performance, recreating a graceful pose reminiscent of dancers depicted on temple walls. Photo courtesy of Sangeet Natak Akademi, New Delhi.

and the sinuous Tribhangi, representing the curvilinear dimension. Another two positions featured in the style are Samabhanga, where the dancer stands upright, feet parallel; and Abhanga, an asymmetrical stance, with one knee slightly bent, opposite hip curved, and the weight shifted to the straight leg.

In Odissi compositions, the dancer usually inhabits one of the three bended-knee postures and is rarely in an austere vertical stance. The body tends to alternate between the two central positions of Chowk and Tribhangi, separated by pauses that punctuate the beauty of its 'cadences of movement' (Vatsyayan 1967).

In Chowk, the spine is strong and straight, the chest open, the upper body elevated while the legs are firmly fixed to the ground; the torso controls all the subtle movements of the dance. The swinging of the hip is restrained by the deep bend in the knees, which are turned out gently in opposite directions. The neck is long, the shoulders relaxed, the core engaged. The lower back and pelvis are released (without tucking in), the weight particularly concentrated in the thighs. The forearms, bent at the elbows, are held perpendicular to the body on each side and stay in the same taut position when the hands flick and turn in various mudras. The eyes move side to side, in concert with the lilt of the neck and often follow the pathway of the arms. While the torso shifts, the hips are meant to be constrained or immobilized. This is a symmetrical stance, with the body's energies distributed equally across its vertical and horizontal positionings.

In the Tribhangi, one foot is placed in front of the other so that the heel in the foreground appears in a slight diagonal against the arch of the foot in the back; the knees are bent and lightly turned out, one hip deflected, with the body's weight dispersed unequally and shifted to the back thigh. This position frees up the front leg, allowing it to direct the body's movement from one posture into another while the back leg serves as anchor. The torso juts out opposite to the curved hip, creating a diagonal line from shoulder to waist. The head and the gaze of the eye tilt softly in the same direction as the front foot. The full position resembles an 'S'-shaped curve. These three breaks, at the knee, the torso and the neck, create a series of undulations in the body, highlighting Odissi's elegant architecture.

In both Chowk and Tribhangi, the feet execute ornate patterns in a tightly bound sphere without radically shifting the body's height, planes or place yet convey a sense of dynamic extension. The body is open and fills the space, rather than folding into itself, concave. In the language of the *Natyashastra*, each 'major' or 'minor' limb—the head, the foot, the torso, the hand, the eye—is trained individually and then harmonized into an ensemble that highlights the parts as well as the whole in performance. This complex fragmentation and command over each segment of the body allows the dancer to replicate the *bhangis*, the postures aligned with the poses depicted in Odisha's visual and architectural history, and to navigate the shifts between individual stance and phrase. The attention to several sites of the body produces a multicentric frame for locating sources of movement.

Odissi is also characterized by asymmetric times governing the two divisions of the body, demarcated at the navel (or *nabhi*, the centre of the body in many Indian philosophies; see Vatsyayan 1991: 381). The deliberate lack of simultaneity between the movements of the upper and lower halves manifests as a pleasing polytemporality. Sometimes even the eyes follow their own time, differentiated at moments from the other limbs. The languid delay between the time when the foot instigates a movement and rests on the ground, and the upper body finishes its correlated phrase, with the gaze resting at its fleeting destination, enhances Odissi's mellifluous quality of movement. Yogic notions of balance and equilibrium are essential: whatever happens on one side of the body must be repeated on the other. Such sequences and transitions, with the dancer proceeding from one sculpturesque posture into another, organize Odissi's choreography.

Constant flows of energy and weight, oscillations between asymmetry and symmetry, the shift from one shape into another, and the lag in time between the completion of lower-body movements and the arc of the upper-body patterns, are hallmarks of Odissi. Along with the lyrical parabolas and lines, the artful isolation of transversal torso movements and the fluid *hastas* making soft patterns in the air with delicate turns of the wrists all create the impression of grace.

The sphere within which the performer sculpts her dance is intimate rather than expansive; covering space is secondary to articulating rhythm and situating the body in time. In this, Odissi mirrors other styles of Indian classical dance, many of which share this interest in explorations of temporality as opposed to spatial extension or conquest (Vatsyayan 1967). Indeed, Odissi's action concentrates on reaching *into* the ground rather than *across* it. The dancer's virtuosity is exhibited in her negotiation of the relationship between the velocity of movement and 'moments of arrest': 'the dancer is constantly trying to achieve the perfect pose, which will convey a sense of timelessness,' an idea that dovetails with the characterizations of classicism itself as transhistorical and transcendent (ibid.: 233).

In many Odissi pieces, the performer becomes an embodiment of the rhythmic patterns represented in the musical score, particularly in formal explorations like Pallavis, where the dancer follows the raga (musical melody), and the feet, its *taal* (rhythm) in the form of *bols* (syllables of sound). Odissi songs and instrumental arrangements reflect a blend of North Indian Hindustani and South Indian Carnatic music and use the melodic and rhythmic structures of both systems (Sahoo 2009). Spontaneous plays of movement can unfold within preset musical parameters but, rather than rupturing the tempos, they ultimately come back to align with the principal beats. This is especially true of *abhinaya* items which allow for infinite improvisations.

The Pallavi, as a danced expression of raga and taal, fully emblematizes this departure from and return to the musical structure—the dancer plays with off-beats, working inside and outside syncopation and abrupt shifts in rhythm, then returns to echo the refrain. The body, captured in a moment of stillness, might suddenly erupt into movement. And so the contradictions between creating time, playing with it, filling it, emptying or transcending it, are reflected in Odissi's repertoire.

Odissi's corporeal philosophy and aesthetic developed through the conjunction of myriad sources, layered over time (I explore this subject in more detail in Chapter 1). In its body language, the Chowk includes a double reference to the square principle while invoking the iconography of Jagannath, considered the presiding deity of Odissi dance, and the tribhangi evokes the favoured stance of Krishna at the same time as it conjures images of the female figures replete in Odisha's visual and sculptural heritage. Indeed, many believe the principal aim of the Odissi dancer is to replicate the body positions found in the Shastras, in the palm-leaf illustrations and in Odisha's temple art (see Chapters 1 and 2). The preponderance of imagery centred on Shiva, Devi (the great goddess) and Radha and Krishna also points to the strong influence of Shaivism, Shaktism and Vaishnavism respectively (see Chapters 2, 3 and 4).

By wide consensus, a dance is fully accepted as 'traditional Odissi' if it meets all the following criteria: it adheres to the aesthetic principles set out by authoritative performance treatises as interpreted and standardized by the major architects of Odissi dance in the 1950s (especially *rasa bhava* and *angika abhinaya*); it is inspired by the literary, sculptural and visual-art history of Odisha; it is set to Odissi music—that is, it uses instruments considered indigenous to Odisha, and lyrics (*vachika abhinaya*) primarily in Sanskrit or Odia; its performers wear the sanctioned Odissi costumes, the sari, jewellery and make-up all reflecting Odisha's cultural heritage (*aharya abhinaya*); it forfeits the liberal use of props (a directive for dance, issuing from the *Natyashastra* and related sources, that encourages the imaginative depiction of objects through physical expression alone); and it abides by the vocabulary, grammar, structure, themes and designations set up by the founding gurus in each recognized *gharana* or school/style. If any rule is broken, if any determinant or condition is violated, then the dance is ineligible for consideration as 'classical', perhaps excluded from the realm of 'Odissi' altogether. Not all dance exponents agree with this schema and have amended or introduced their own understandings of Odissi presentation, but the contours and measures of the 'traditional' definition are clear.

The structure of a traditional Odissi concert borrows largely from elements of Odia theatre and gotipua performance; individual dances are adapted from Mahari Naach and gotipua repertoires as well as Odia Naach (see Chapters 2, 4 and 6). The dance melds elements of devotional practice (expressed in the dancer's *bhava*, and in the narration of myths venerating religious figures) and artistic formalism (expressed through proficiencies of technique). It coalesces Odisha's histories and embodies several of its aesthetic and ritual traditions.

Theories and Outlines

In this project, I locate critical histories of Odissi through a close consideration of its discontinuities—the breaks, shifts and ruptures that have governed the dance's metamorphoses under regional, imperialist and nationalist regimes. Against this account of Odissi's attachment to prevailing state discourses, I focus on its subversive power in the arena of gender through an analysis of its cosmologies, its role in producing social identities and the possibilities it offers in terms of troubling normative ideologies and the practices they inform. For subtending the history of the dance as it is tied to dominant ideals is an equally compelling discourse on gender that lies parallel to the hegemonic norms inducted by the state.

Odissi, in its embodiment as Mahari Naach, was formally institutionalized in the twelfth century as a religious dance performed by female temple servitors, In that context, there is a strong argument that the dance is based on a female-centred cosmology, foregrounding the diversity of South Asian feminine expressions and narrativizing Hindu mythologies through a highly gendered perspective. The stories conveyed in its representational form are derived from Jayadeva's *Geeta Govinda*, the celebrated poetic epic dedicated to the archetypal divine lovers, Radha and Krishna. Its eminent practitioners were and are women, or boys and men trained in gotipua performance who exalt/ed the feminine. Odissi is also associated with the category of *lasya*, a term conjuring grace in classical Indian dance. Yet despite its highly feminized aesthetic, I believe that the form was appropriated by patriarchal forces, especially in the colonial and postcolonial periods, when male custodians of culture marginalized the maharis and, in the process of reconstructing Odissi, attempted to sanitize its overt sexuality and recast it as part of a high Hindu classical tradition.[8] I investigate this phenomenon while paying attention to how Odissi performers carved out ways of marshalling the feminized sexuality inherent in the form, and negotiating conservative masculinist cooptations.

---

8 My analysis aligns here with many critical scholars of South Asian dance, such as Amrit Srinivasan (1985, 1990), Janet O'Shea (2007) and Urmimala Sarkar (2010, 2014) who have made the same point about patriarchal effects on Indian classical dance genres.

A related gendered dimension of Odissi's history can be found in the gotipua tradition. With the rise of Gaudiya Vaishnavism, an eastern Indian mystical movement dedicated to Krishna, the feminine figure, representing his consort Radha, came to epitomize the passion of the devotee. Cross-gender performance then emerged as a religious ideal of Bhakti adherents in Odisha. Interestingly, this model of gender impersonation did not instigate a crisis around prevailing concepts of masculinity; its proponents naturalized and contained the practice within the performance event, and the gotipua boys oscillated between ritual expression and the everyday socius where they resumed their normative masculine identities. The fluidity of gender in a ritual context was already normalized in Odisha's cultural atmosphere, given the discourse surrounding migrations of gender across sexed identities. In fact, many in the current crop of established male dance gurus began their careers as gotipuas, publicly reporting no conflict between their self-image as 'male' versus their performance as 'female'. Instead, their ability to embody and portray another gender was often considered a mark of high artistry.

An advantage of the gotipua tradition for male dancers is the flexibility of gender performance that it both energizes and valorizes. This situates the dance's extraordinary dimensions— Odissi becomes a space that offers the potential of embodying a proliferation of genders, and the possibility of enacting multiple identities. Thus, my project is impelled by an interest in Odissi as a form not only produced by the historical masquerades of regionalism, nationalism and imperialism but also as a paratopic force that contains the possibility to challenge dominant discourse and power.

Conceived in interdisciplinary terms, this study lies at the nexus of dance/performance studies, South Asian studies and gender studies. Through it, I propose to build on the existing literature in the field and offer new perspectives on Odissi's praxis. Much of the scholarship on Odissi elaborates its formal techniques and aesthetics. This study is dedicated to fully exploring the specific social histories and political contexts of Odissi's foundations and formations. I hope my work will provide a valuable addition to the existing *oeuvre* on Odissi, as it treats its historical and contemporary status; its gendering potencies; its regional, national, intercultural and interdisciplinary expressions; and its relation to the state's performance of power.

In these dance histories, I mine performances of extraordinary gender. At first, it might appear that the term 'extraordinary gender' is simply a reconstitution of the 'queer,' in that it signals non-normative identities and acts. Yet the 'queer' appellation, however expansive and generatively deployed, is ultimately moored in Western notions of essentially deviant and stigmatized sexualities, and, even when reclaimed, I believe it does not—cannot—encompass the complexity of South Asian ideals of gender that configure(d) sexual difference and ambiguity differently.

As a universalizing construct, the 'queer' can activate global political coalitions and solidarities, but it also risks effacing the specificity of gender expression in diverse cultural fields. Broadly construed, the idea of the 'queer' productively destabilizes hegemonic concepts of proper sexuality in secular terms. The category 'queer' brings to the central questions of sexual identity, sexual practices and non-normative gender expressions that are abjured and pathologized in dominant Western paradigms. However, the devadasi and gotipua practices, for instance, held a different set of significations in the regional imaginary. Emerging from localized religious practices, they embodied a sense of beneficence, specialness and auspiciousness that exceeds the Western conception of the 'queer'. To reposition them as queer, I argue, is to collapse them into systems of valuation that completely deny their rootedness in their particular cultural and historical spheres. So how do we contend with minoritized gender enactments configured as propitious within their own cultural logics, which stand apart from the associations of 'queer' as abnormal, as dissident, as strange? How do we conceptualize the 'non-normative' when it is valorized rather than vilified, exalted instead of disparaged, condoned and not condemned? How do we position maharis and gotipuas, who were culturally rewarded rather than punished for their social difference? I believe the existence of such gendered identifications—out of the ordinary but socially esteemed—requires us to rethink the 'queer' category as a legacy of colonial modernity in the South Asian context; it also calls for us to produce new theoretical models and nomenclatures capable of addressing the nuances of such practices that cannot be easily folded into the global 'queer' embrace and, in fact, pose a significant challenge to its transnational relevance and reach.

Moreover, queer discourse is associated deeply with Western liberal narratives of the 'subject', 'progress' and 'sexual liberation' (Foucault 1988); it often appropriates or homogenizes histories of gender difference suppressed by the forces of Western colonialism and modern nationalism. Through the act of 'queering', Western discourse seeks to name, claim and 'emancipate' the colonial subjects it once ironically sought to subjugate—implicating much of queer liberal discourse in the matrix of imperialism.[9] Critically, while 'queer' refers to both counter-hegemonic enactments of gender and sexuality, in the case of maharis and gotipuas, their performance of (non-normative) gender is separate from the performance of (often-normative) sexuality, complicating the meaning of the category. This kind of specificity requires attention being paid to local ideals and formulations. It is in this context that I propose using the concept of 'extraordinary gender', recognizing its special valence in apprehending and comprehending the multiplicity of performances surrounding ideas of masculinity and femininity in Odissi histories.

I argue that Odissi's gender enactments produce a *paratopia*, a term I coined to refer to the parallel ground carved out by dancing

---

9 The postcolonial predicament of the 'queer' has been taken up by a range of scholars. On the productive possibilities of queer theorizing for South Asian subjects specifically and people of colour generally, see José Muñoz (1999, 2009); Ruth Vanita and Salim Kidwai (2000); Ruth Vanita (2002b); Gayatri Gopinath (2005); and Anjali Arondekar (2009). On the dangers of homogenization, exclusion and imperialism in mainstream queer discourse, see especially the critiques by Joseph Massad (2002, 2008); Jasbir Puar (2007, 2013); and Rustom Bharucha (2014).

bodies. The paratopia is the corporeal realization and material manifestation of a space of alterity, produced by its subjects on their own terms, without reference to dominant valuations and refracted by a constant politics of difference. Paratopic performances refer to those political and cultural enactments engendered by dance *in the contemporary moment and which exist adjacent to the prevailing norm.*[10]

Performance forms carrying within them local histories and philosophies which live alongside hegemonic orders, and which sanction extraordinary enactments that are otherwise unsanctioned by dominant logics, qualify as paratopic. As a theoretical construct, the paratopia can be distinguished from Michel Foucault's heterotopia which speaks 'of other spaces' as geographical or architectural sites (the theatre, the garden, the library, the fairground, the ship . . .) but does not refer to the active structuring of topos by the human bodies moving through them. Formally separated from the built environments encompassed by 'heterotopia', the paratopia indexes a temporal chiselling and physicalization of space that occurs synchronously with the movements of the performing body, registering discrete political effects. For Foucault, the heterotopia presupposes crisis or deviation; as such, it 'has a precise and determined function' within the social system, connected to and reinforcing what is normative in relation to it, rather than operating outside dominative circuits, as I argue the paratopia does (see Foucault 1984: n.p.).[11] Yet it is neither escape, nor refuge, nor counterpart in its juxtapositions. While the paratopia takes shape as a marginal spatial formation against the presiding order, the 'against' here is disentangled from the logics of rebellion or reconciliation, supplementation or negation, agonistics or apposition.[12] For the paratopia is defined by difference, not dissent.

---

10 I have theorized the paratopia concept extensively in my essay 'Paratopias of Performance: The Choreographic Practices of Chandralekha' (Banerji 2009b).

11 In this sense, Foucault's ideas of heterotopia as crisis relate closely to Victor Turner's (1969) notion of liminality.

12 Through this list of associations, I also invoke Jacques Derrida's notion of the 'parergon', defined as an element of an artistic object that 'comes against,

Its force emanates from its disjunctive identifications. The space it marks is evocative, conceptual, and material at once—in contrast to the heterotopia and its associated edifices, secured clearly by engineered boundaries and enclosures (ibid.). Thus while the heterotopia is a place endowed with 'openings' and 'closures', the paratopia is a space created and sustained by choreographic labours that may begin, end, remain suspended or remain iterative, since its borders are configured exclusively by dancing bodies and their gestural or spatial pathways. The paratopia signifies the body's presence, substantively, and presenting, temporally.

The paratopic construct may be considered the opposite of the theory of 'atopia' or 'placelessness', as the paratopia is, by defini-tion, rooted in a particular location and time. For Roland Barthes, the atopia represents the poetic conceit 'of a drifting habitation' while for Jacques Derrida it bluntly signals 'a lack of place' (Barthes 2010: 49; Derrida 1982: 68–9). Harmony Bench theorizes the 'no-place' of dance as 'an abstracted space, a blank or evacuated site' that proliferates in digital media and operates 'by erasing topological specificities' (2008: 37). For Vittorio Gregotti, the 'atopic typology' instead indicates the 'non-place' of uninhabitable areas as well as 'residual' regions—kindred to the heterotopic sensibility, perhaps?—such prototypical sites being highway service stations, exit roads, junkyards, emptied structures and unused land (1996: 79–80). The critical point here is that as abandoned or dessicated topoi, 'they offer none of the spontaneous and temporary gathering' opportunities afforded by other locales, regulated as they are by laws of the market, and 'the social fabric

beside, and in addition to the *ergon* or primary work, 'but it does not fall to one side, it touches and cooperates within the operation' (1987: 54). Crucially, it is an '[n]either simply inside nor simply outside' it, but an appurtenance, the key example being that of the frame (54–5). The description of the parergon as parallel space is thus somewhat reminiscent of the paratopic idea. However, I suggest the paratopia remains clearly outside the dominant-subsidiary stratification, and generates its own logics in place of regularly 'cooperating' with the normative aesthetic operation: less a frame and more an independent, original work. For another discussion of the parergon, see Shannon Jackson (2011: 15).

that encompasses solidarities, contrasts, and a sense of belonging no longer exists for such nonplaces' (ibid.: 80).

I distinguish the paratopic paradigm also from Michel de Certeau's influential notion of 'tactics' which posits specific modes of action (like pedestrian acts which 'give shape to spaces', which 'weave places together' and unfurl 'the long poem of walking,' for instance) as resistance, although the two ideas share an affinity in asserting that corporeal activities, through intentionality and momentum, *produce* space rather than simply being in or of it: for 'space is composed of intersections of mobile elements' (2011: 97, 101, 117).

The perspective that conditions my discussion of the paratopia—that space is socially manufactured rather than perennially existing as an inert entity—is powerfully enunciated and elaborated by José Gil and Henri Lefebvre. 'We know that the dancer evolves in a particular space,' Gil confides to the reader in 'Paradoxical Body': 'The dancer does not move in space; rather, the dancer secretes, creates space with his [sic] movement.' Through the body's multiple operations, attentions and extensions, 'a new space emerges'—'the space of the body' or a 'territory' identified by the 'corporification of space'. The practice of dance is represented as the body's extraversion, a procedure for the performer that involves the imperative of 'tightly imbricat[ing] interior space and exterior space, the inside of the body invested with energy, and the outside where gestures of the dance unfold' (2009: 85–8).

While Gil concentrates particularly on dance, Lefebvre probes the contingencies of space and the subject in more generalized terms. Though Lefebvre's work precedes Gil's, the two are remarkably coordinated in their employment of a language of incorporated space, the body's 'energy' and 'paradox', the generativity of the gestural, the ideation of spatial difference. Lefebvre's primary motive is to disturb the illusion of space 'as luminous, as intelligible, as giving action free rein' (1991: 27), to disassemble the governing impression of a subject simply interpellated or inserted in a static field. His famous dictum, '(social) space is a (social) product'—complementing de Certeau's proposition that 'space is a practiced place' (2011: 117)—sits in counterpoint to the model of space as an otherwise amorphous ambience in which bodily movement just happens, just *takes place*, so to speak. The somatic, the social, and spatial, instead, Lefebvre insists, are always imbricated, and this recognition instigates his call for shifting the order of analysis 'from *things in space* to the actual *production of space*' (2009: 37; original emphasis).

In further reflections Lefebvre takes up the relationship between corporeality and spatial politics. What, for him, is the body? 'A focusing of active (productive) energies.' The 'enigma of the body—its secret at once banal and profound—is its ability, beyond "subject" and "object" [. . .] to produce differences "unconsciously" out of repetitions,' repetitions composed of gestures or rhythms (ibid.: 399, 395). I take his reference here to the 'unconscious' as an allusion to naturalized patterns of movement or techniques of the body, inculcated in a given habitus, as outlined in the work of Pierre Bourdieu (1977) and Marcel Mauss (2006). If we extend his thinking to consider the circumstances where such 'unconscious' patterns become 'conscious' and deliberate, we can suggest a link to dance, as it may be argued that these operations of patterns of difference and repetition align with choreographic technique. 'In the misapprehended *space of the body*,' Lefebvre notes, 'this *paradoxical junction* of *repetitive and differential*—this most basic form of "production"—is forever occurring' (2009: 395; emphasis added, indicating links to Gil).

Importing key ideas from political theorists Gilles Deleuze and Felix Guattari (1988, 1994), Lefebvre deploys the idea of 'differential space' as an attack on what he views as the violent principle of homogenization found in dominant theories and modalities of organizing abstract space, contending that its chimerical uniformity is broken up in its confrontation with actual bodily relations and their promise of an emancipating heterogeneity:[13]

---

13 There are several parallels here with Paul Carter's thinking in *Lie of the Land* (1994), and Gilles Deleuze and Félix Guattari's in *Thousand Plateaus* (1988). Carter argues that colonial projects operate by clearing and occupying the

Abstract space (or those for whom it is a tool) makes the relationship between repetition and difference a more antagonistic one. It reduces differences to induced differences: that is, to differences internally acceptable to a set of 'systems' that are planned as such, prefabricated as such—and which are completely redundant. [. . .]

Just like the fleshly body of the living being, the spatial body of the society and the social body of needs differ from an 'abstract corpus' or 'body of signs' [. . .]: they cannot live without generating, without producing, without creating differences (2009: 396)

These twin ideas of 'social space' and 'differentiality' repudiate the representations of the spatial as a field of stasis, installing in its place a vision of space as kinetically formed and transmogrified by vibrant subjects. Recall that Gil, too, is occupied with interrupting any notion of singularity when he suggests, in almost identical terms, that dance may be defined as 'the art of constructing series' and generates 'the space of doubles, of multiplicities of bodies and bodily movements' (2009: 91). Together Lefebvre and Gil perform these constant refrains: difference and repetition, difference in repetition, difference of repetition, difference from repetition, difference with repetition. After all: 'There is an infinity appropriate to danced gestures that only the space of the body is able to engender,' as Gil proffers (ibid.).

In the convergence of these streams of thinking lies the realization that dance as a corporeal act is fundamentally generative; it does not just happen in a nebulous somewhere but catalyses and composes space, a space marked by the difference promulgated by multiplicity (difference through gestural repetition, and difference through the construction of myriad spaces that decentre the

---

space of land in the name of taming the wilds and civilizing it while Deleuze and Guattari theorize two notions of smooth space (regulated, consolidated, and homogenous, occupied by the sedentarized subject of the state), and striated space (heterogeneous, counter-hegemonic, belonging to the figure of the nomad opposing the state).

hegemonic, interrogate singularity, shelter bodies of marginality, permit minoritarian expressions, invent novel worlds).

I situate the paratopia as a conjunctural analytic that mirrors and extends these foundational proposals, focusing on *how* the body of Odissi dance accomplishes this spatial poesis. Like Gil and Lefebvre, I am interested in the nexus between the anatomical and the architectonic, the power of the dancing body to sculpt a 'new' or 'differential' milieu. Unlike Gil, however, I see dance also in the complex of internalized and interlaid discourses, physical-cultural training and muscle memory residing within the body's chambers, where they may remain indefinitely and transfigure it, rather than answering to the imperative of externalizing as gesture and thus submitting to an 'ocular hegemony', privileging visibility and spectatorship in place of the dancer's experience (Schneider 2011: 98; see also Vatsyayan 1997 and Zarilli 1984). For in alignment with many Indian theories of corporeality, dance may be simultaneously constructed in the internal and external realms of the body, given that space is a common and uniting element of the human form and its outside, captured in the *akash* postulate (Vatsyayan 1991: *xi–xii*; see also Pillai 1991: 437–9 and Holdrege 1998). According to Vatsyayan, *akash* spans bodily, psychic, natural, metaphysical and transcendental space, and these 'diverse levels of meaning are not insulated categories, each merges with the other'. Space 'is thus the first and last element, the beginning and the end, the void and the all-pervasive' in much of Indian thought (1991: *xi*, *xviii*). If *akash* 'denotes the movement from the inner to the outer and vice versa', then we can expansively conceive of dance as belonging to the inside and outside of the bodily stratum (Vatsyayan 1991: xii). Continuing in the same vein, unlike Lefebvre, I see the (Odissi) dancing body as immediately decipherable, intelligible and revelatory, especially for a *rasika* or discerning beholder—as opposed to viewing dance as an esoteric enterprise, mystified 'enigma' or romanticized 'secret' due to its sheer complexity and paradoxical dimensions. That Odissi dance may be ambiguous doesn't defy its power to construct meaning.

Paratopic performance signals an inalienable difference from the norm that is expressed in the moment in which it is executed. It is the material rendering of politics in present time. Temporally, then, it diverges from the idea of utopia which focuses on the vista of futurity for articulating radical change, and is definitely distinct from the despairing mood of dystopia.[14] The question is: Why look only to the future for transformative visions of the political order, when they exist everywhere now, readily distinguishable in certain genres of dance performance?[15] Instead, the idea of the paratopia is premised on the claim that enactments of heterogeneity are abundant and proliferate in perpetual contemporaneity.[16]

Critically, I argue paratopic performances are intrinsically marked by alterity. They are not intentionally resistive, reactive, alternative or counter-hegemonic; rather, they challenge dominant discourses by their very ontology and may be *perceived* as oppositional as they produce political and artistic tenets related to the minoritized communities and collectives from which they emerge.

---

14 See, for instance, Dragan Klaic's *The Plot of the Future* (1992); Jill Dolan's *Utopia in Performance* (2005); Fredric Jameson's *Archaeologies of the Future* (2005); José Muñoz's *Cruising Utopia* (2009); and Barnita Bagchi (ed.), *The Politics of the (Im)Possible* (2012). See also Daniel Sack, *After Live* (2015).

15 Given his statement that 'atopia is superior to utopia' (2010: 49), it may appear that Barthes' view and my own on paratopia are united in their embrace of presentism. However, they are differentiated in that I do not claim the paratopia is of surpassing value. Further, some models of utopia, like Dolan's (2005), make the novel suggestion that its guiding impulse of hope can be found in the present in aesthetic performances, wresting it away from purely futurist orientations. While our frameworks also share certain overlaps, my claim branches away from hers in arguing that the utopic is necessarily anticipatory and belongs to the future—reiterating, in concert with its original sensibility Thomas More (1965) and José Muñoz's (2009) positions that it captures what is 'not yet here'.

16 I refer to the 'present' in Henri Bergson's terms, as a long duration that folds the past into contemporaneity, into a single stretch of time (1990). I also follow Walter Benjamin's directive in 'Theses on the Philosophy of History', where he argues that the critical historian must 'grasp the constellation which [her] own era has formed with a definite earlier one. Thus [she] establishes a conception of the present as the "time of the now" ' (1968: 263).

The aura of alterity that belongs to the paratopia construct derives from the English connotation of the prefix 'para', indexing that which is collateral to a regnant force. Complementarily, 'para' in Sanskrit, in its adjectival form, embraces dispersed meanings— 'another', 'highest', 'last', 'distant', 'after' or 'beyond'—yielding a set of rich symbolisms that imaginatively situates the paratopic as: a *sui generis* phenomenon; in remote relation to a governing precept; that which occupies the final spatial frontier; a privileged vantage point; a prime placement, *in situ*; a process of constant serialization in space; edging towards or exceeding given parameters; a sphere of novelty, in terms of what succeeds or comes after the familiar; what is eternally new or next; or one position, *a* position, among many conditions of possibility.

As I theorize it, paratopic performances embody a state of being and becoming towards what is *distinct* from the dominant, the exceptional from the norm, another way of being. In creating space through kinesthetic engagement, paratopic enactments become forms of political mobilization (Martin 1998). Odissi's paratopic histories also show how traditions contain, perform and provoke their own transgressions, and create an ambience for the expression of values and visions that open up our idea of what is possible in the present, instead of resting in imminency.[17]

One of the principal aims of this study is to initiate a productive dialogue between dance studies and critical political theory in the Indian context, using the concept of choreography as a link.[18]

---

17 I provide a fuller discussion of this point in 'Nrityagram: Tradition and the Aesthetics of Transgression' (Banerji 2017b).

18 Global perspectives on the link between dance and 'political institutions'— which in this context largely covers the strategies of the state apparatus and responses to it—have been explored in writings by Susan Leigh Foster (1998a, 2003); Susan Manning (1993); Randy Martin (1998); Naima Prevots (1998); Mark Franko (2002, 2006, 2012); Anthony Shay (2002); Francesca Castaldi (2006); André Lepecki (2006); Jacqueline Shea Murphy (2007); Christopher T. Nelson (2008); Danielle Goldman (2010); Nicholas Rowe (2010); Ruth Hellier-Tinoco (2011); Christina Ezrahi (2012); Jens Richard Giersdorf (2013); Rachmi Diya Larasati (2013); Hélène Neveu Kringelbach (2013); Stacy Prickett (2013); Susan Reed (2013); Paul Scolieri (2013); Claire Croft (2015); Anthea

I wish to demonstrate how the state and dance are intimately connected—they are not entirely separate institutions in terms of their workings; indeed, what choreography does to the individual body, the state does to the social corpus.

By 'state' I mean a centralized system of government that claims or bears the authority to rule over a given territory and population; in my study, the state encompasses the varied institutions of monarchy, imperialism and parliamentary democracy alike, at the levels of city, region and nation. Where relevant, I discuss 'governance' in relation to 'governmentality', a capacious concept defined by Foucault as the encounter between 'techniques of domination and techniques of the self', an analytic that affords an investigation of individual and state 'conduct'; it is a form of rationality and 'art' of organization that may be exercised in the orbit of the political, the spiritual, the economic, the cultural (1993: 203–04; Burchell et al. 1991: 87–104). These ideas shape much of my analysis, although I grant primacy to the dimension of governmentality as an expansion of political anatomy, an assemblage of sovereign state procedures—manifest in structures of policy-making, as well as legislative and juridical domains—designed to regulate the movement of populations (Foucault 2008; Burchell et al. 1991: 102–03). Following and extending Foucault's thought, I argue that 'governance' and 'governmentality' are conjoined in the colonial modern moment, continuing into the realm of the postcolonial. If governance refers to the exercise of state power over

Kraut (2015); Janice Ross (2015); and Ida Meftahi (2016).

See also the edited volumes *From the Royal to the Republican Body* (Melzer and Norberg 1998); *Dance, Human Rights, and Social Justice* (Jackson and Shapiro Phim 2008); *Choreographies of 21st Century Wars* (Gay and Giersdorf 2016); *The Oxford Handbook of Dance and Politics* (Kowal, Giersdorf and Martin 2017); and *How to Do Politics with Art* (Roussel and Banerji 2017).

Karl Toepfer (1997); Mona Ouzof (1988); John Protevi (2009); Janette Dillon (2010); Shannon Jackson (2011); Sara Brady (2012); Jen Harvie (2013); Rustom Bharucha (2014); and Sara Ahmed (2015) also consider the relationship between the broader spheres of performance and politics. See also the *Dance Research Journal* issue on choreography and state violence (August 2016).

a place and its people, governmentality is diffusely concerned with the ways that the populace conducts itself and is conducted: how it moves within, across, between, beyond and in the interstices of state-controlled space, and, concomitantly, how the state sustains its position of domination through the production of legitimating knowledge, using the alibi of political security to justify and rationalize its actions.

By 'choreography' I mean a set of instructions for arranging the body in time and space, in patterns of stillness and movement, according to an established regime of techniques.[19] My contention is that both choreography and the state are centrally concerned with the body and its orchestrations, and imposing prescriptions and proscriptions for its exemplary movements in space. While dance organizes the body in an aesthetic milieu, the state scripts and arranges corporeal relations in the social. I cannot propose a one-to-one or isomorphic relationship between choreographic and state practices, since their goals, scope and mechanisms differ— achieving virtuosity in a delimited dance sphere in one case versus achieving power and control over entire populations by marshalling a complex of institutions on the other. For the purposes of this study, I concentrate on the analogical value and structural correspondences between the two operations to reveal how Odissi is configured through their intersection, layering, contest and mutual interactions at the same time as it retains its paratopic power.

Choreography typically sets out axioms of movement for the dancing body to make it conform to given aesthetic ideals; the state also carries out this function of disciplining the body and aligning it with its systems in an effort to consolidate its power and control over the polity, often using law as its instrument. Thus, choreography shares a metonymic and metaphoric relationship with the

---

19 I will note here that this definition differs from the prevailing model of 'chorcography' in Indian classical dance communities, where the term refers largely to the work of designing group formations and compositions presented on stage and to works created outside received repertoire, but is not applied to solo performance. This is a topic I discuss at length in Chapter 6.

state, as what happens in the aesthetic space becomes a mirror, model and microcosm for what happens in the social. Through a choreographic prism, dance and state become sites of scripted, embodied performance. With this analysis, I hope to both extend the domain of study for Indian dance and provide a new lens through which the state's actions can be interpreted.

The themes I chronicle here and the intimacies I explore between Odissi, the politics of gender and the choreographic agencies of the state are aptly embodied by the image of Indrani Rahman on the cover. Of course, Odissi cannot be allied to a single historical subject, since a conglomeration of genres and personalities contributed to its making. Nevertheless, Rahman was a unique contributor to Odissi's history—she was the icon who, in the 1950s, first took Odissi from its regional platform to the national and international, and was integral to the effort of persuading the authorities to give Odissi classical status. Less known is the fact that she respected the maharis, insisting on meeting them and watching their dances during a state-sponsored trip to Odisha. As 'Miss India' 1952, she literally embodied the nation; thus the state-and-gender connection evoked in the book title is implicit in her figure. As this study ends precisely at the moment Odissi was formalized as classical dance, Rahman's image consolidates the narrative arc of its project. And she seems absorbed in 'dancing Odissi', the joy apparent in her facial expression, her gaze riveted on the Alapadma hand gesture—and averting the eye of the putative spectator.

Methodologies

The methodology employed in my meditations on Odissi is based on the conjunction of historiography, ethnography, discourse analysis based on written and visual sources, and choreographic analysis. My objective was to rigorously assess the reigning narrative of Odissi and offer new histories based on fieldwork and a critical study of ritual, text, material culture and dance repertoire. A significant element of the process was to draw out the theory from a deep study of the dance phenomenon itself. For the object is its own mediation, as Raymond Williams has taught us (1977: 95–100), and in that sense Odissi dance is a hermeneutic, a mutable container of meaning and knowledge, enunciating a set of politics in its praxis. The propositions offered in this book are thus embedded and derived from Odissi performances, their aesthetics, their histories and their representations.

I have analysed multiple media: literature, websites, videos, films, photographs, music, the material objects used in dance (jewellery, costumes, musical instruments), religious ritual and the places linked to Odissi training and performance. I have obtained primary data through a mix of interviews (in Bengali, Odia, Hindi and English); fieldwork; epigraphic and archaeological evidence; archival documents; legal research; empirical historiography; and cultural policy analysis. Visits to temples, archaeological sites and performance venues in Bhubaneshwar, Cuttack, Dhauli, Kolkata, Konark, New Delhi, Puri, Raghurajpur and Udaygiri and Khandagiri allowed me to explore firsthand the culture of Odissi in India, both past and present. I attended dance conferences, concerts and festivals in Canada, India, the United Kingdom and the United States to stay current with artistic developments in Odissi and obtain a panoramic view of its expressions.

Exploring the dance as phenomenological experience was also important, and insights derived from my training as a disciple of Odissi constituted a significant part of my research process—I was interested not only as a scholar but also as a dancer in the inter-relationship between history, theory and practice. I call this position that of the temporal insider rather than subscribing to the claims of mutually exclusive etic and emic positions—the familiar tropes of standard ethnography. The position of the temporal insider comes from participating in a practice rather than being rooted in an essentialized identity. Thus practice constitutes a claim and framework for investigation instead of naturalized positions of identitarian belonging or exclusion, which are more projections than actual embeddings. It was through my position as a temporal insider, as a student of Odissi, that I was able to establish a

common ground with other Odissi specialists, negotiate relationships in the field and locate myself as a researcher approaching the
subject from an intimate perspective.[20]

I also reflected on a methodology for constructing dance
histories and theories. By now, my attribution of agency and
autonomy to the abstracted entity of 'dance' or the 'dancing body'
(rather than to an individuated 'dancer') may invite the reader's
scepticism. I assert this agency purposefully, taking my cues from
the theoretical interventions proposed by Susan Leigh Foster
(1986, 1997, 1998a and 1998b, 1995). In her work, the dancing
body refers to a corporeal figure shaped and 'know[n] . . . through
its response to methods and techniques used to cultivate it'
(1997: 235). It is a body of performance as well as a 'body-of-ideas'
produced through the confluences of power, discourse and
phenomenological experience (ibid.). The body trained under a
certain regime of movement contains and cultivates particular
kinetic philosophies and arguments. Dance is an outward projection of a subjective cognitive process and corporeal condition—
enacted, transformed, performed. In a circular fashion, these
modes of thought relate to a larger cultural and political field in
which dancing bodies are located.

Foster's ideas led me to a methodology in which I centred the
dancing body and an 'analysis of discourses and practices that
instruct it' (ibid.). My extraction of the 'dancing body' and the
'dance' as autonomous entities reflects an interest in isolating,
prying apart and critically interrogating the ideals and norms
produced (and reproduced) in an assemblage of discourses,
practices and systems—the apparatus of Odissi.[21]

---

20 In a related vein, I enter into a fuller discussion of dance ethnography and
what it means to negotiate the positions of insider and outsider in Banerji
(2009a).

21 When speaking of the 'apparatus,' whether in the domain of the state or
dance, I am referring to Foucault's definition of the term as a translation of
'dispositif'. In *Power/Knowledge,* Foucault describes the apparatus as:

  a thoroughly heterogeneous ensemble consisting of discourses,
  institutions, architectural forms, regulatory decisions, laws, administrative measures, scientific statements, philosophical, moral and

By focusing on individual dancers, this project would, perhaps, veer into the territory of hagiography. While individual contributions are valuable indeed, I subscribe to the view that art is the product of a social process, and so my work focuses on the social relations engendered in and through Odissi dance but identifies 'dance' and the 'dancing body' as conceptually separable from the performer alone. Dance is performed in human bodies but it also lives in texts and images, narratives and memory, representations and ideologies. While dancers cultivate traces of the past and bring them into the world of the present, I am interested in the collective picture, the unfurling of Odissi at particular moments in its history. By its nature, this approach excludes a focus on any single actor. However, I do not wish to propose that either Odissi 'dance' or the 'dancing body' constitutes a unitary transhistorical entity that floats above or across time and space. At definitive historical moments, the dance and its exponents transform, take on different shapes, and the discussion informs what 'dance' and 'dancing bodies' conjure in given temporal and social locations. The method entails an examination of the historical processes that lead to what Foster calls 'the formation of dancing bodily consciousness' (ibid.: 236).

It is in this spirit that I ask: What are the bodily patterns and philosophies evident in Odissi performance, taken as a whole,

---

philanthropic propositions—in short, the said and the unsaid. Such are the elements of the apparatus. The apparatus itself is the system of relations that can be established between these elements. Secondly, what I am trying to identify in this apparatus is precisely the nature of the connection that can exist between these heterogeneous elements. [. . .] whether discursive or non-discursive, there is a sort of interplay of shifts of position and modifications of function which can also vary very widely. Thirdly, I understand the term 'apparatus' [as a] formation which has at its given historical moment that of responding to an *urgent need*. The apparatus thus has a dominant strategic function (1980: 194–228; original emphasis).

I also rely on Foucault's notion of 'discourse' which is 'constituted by a group of sequences of signs, in so far as they are statements, that is, in so far as they can be assigned particular modalities of existence [. . . D]iscourse can be defined as the group of statements that belong to a single system of formation' (*Archaeology of Knowledge*, 1972: 121).

beyond the life of a single dancer? What are the dominant 'techniques' of shaping bodies in Odissi dance? What, or who, are the ideal figures imagined and promulgated in Odissi dance? Which forces shape the bodies of Odissi, and how? Concentrating on 'dancing body' and the 'dance' enables a consideration of these movement techniques, regimes and archetypes, of Odissi as a bodily 'discipline' in the Foucauldian (1979) frame, yet as an entity ever-dynamic and unfolding—hence the title of the book, *dancing Odissi*.

To situate my analysis, I devise a provisional definition of dance as a circuit of relations, highlighting the dialectical relationships between the dancing body, the philosophies and ideologies that govern its aesthetics, and the objects, spaces and institutions that influence its performance and reception. Collectively, this triumvirate of the embodied action, the discourse, and the material culture of objects and architectures constitute the collective corpus of the classical dance that serves as the composite object of analysis. Constructing the history of Odissi in this light means attending to the transitions that occur in each of the three areas that compose the dance, as it travels through various stages and phases—its ascent, alterings, resurrections and crystallizations.

Dance History, Genealogy, and the Politics of 'Origins'

Any serious work of dance history, as a host of performance scholars have shown, must also acknowledge the central tension evoked by the pairing of what appear to be oppositional terms: 'dance' as a mobile, unfixed and evanescent practice, and 'historiography', in its standard Western form, as a logocentric mode of fixing linear narratives about events or objects through the assembly of materials marked by apparent durability and framed as legitimate 'evidence' of a phenomenon. Salient issues regarding this relationship are delineated by Foster in *Choreographing History* (1995). Historiography, she argues, involves an authorized set of protocols and techniques that appear to resolve the predicament of fixing events in time. Dance in general, perceived as ungraspable art, brings up the problem of providing definitive proof that can act as a reliable basis for producing historical knowledge. Another reason for its exclusion from conventional analytical focus is its inescapable corporeality; because of the Cartesian bias against bodily knowing, dance's resistance to fixed objecthood situates it as a problematic for history. Further, because its effects are rarely perceived as epic, it fails to count as part of the idealist schemas of history that order important political and social events of an era into grand narrative.[22]

The task of creating dance history, then, appears to be a paradox. Characterized by temporal compression and physical volatility, an inherent instability, dance seems incapable of providing adequate materials and resources for historicization. This understanding also has the effect of fetishizing dance, imbuing it with a rarefied aura that suggests it cannot be apprehended except at the very moment of its occurrence. A textual bias suggests the writing of the body would enable its conversion from event into object, subsequently enabling its retrieval—supporting its entry into, and visibility within, a historical frame. Even then, dance becomes subsidiary to history, assuming a kind of marginal or renegade identity requiring salvage. In this scenario, dance history could be viewed as a project dedicated to the restoration of an originary past through a resurrection of the 'dead body' lost to history, lost to the text (ibid.: 6). However, as Foster underscores, dance is performed by real, labouring, carnal bodies. It *does* leaves traces, and it is through these traces that its power can be located as a discrete cultural category meriting critical historical attention.

As valid as Foster's arguments may be for a range of dance phenomena, especially those with Western affinities, it is abundantly clear that Indian performance praxis generally refutes the claims of 'ahistoricity', providing a contrasting view and confounding the premises of Western historical approaches relative to the study of corporeality—given the existence of a robust and long-established tradition in the subcontinent that situated dance as a subject of

---

22 On idealist histories, see Foucault (1977).

intense reflection, experimentation and debate (Vatsyayan 1996, 1997, 2007a). In effect, many performance genres have reconciled the value of categories of practice and their documentation or narrativization, what Diana Taylor names the 'repertoire' and 'archive' respectively (2003). Crucially, Taylor calls for us to resist the binarization of the two epistemologies and instead recognize their fundamental interdependence in shaping each other— as does Rebecca Schneider, when she calls on us to remember that 'performance remains' even if it remains *differently* than the usual ephemera of history (2011). Indeed, these intricate inter-connections, as the reader will see, are amply demonstrated in Odissi's praxis; for in the world of Indian aesthetics, inscribed knowledge, the spoken word and customary activity were held in equal esteem for centuries, and continue to command reverence in domains of classical dance and music (*sruti and smriti, lakshana jnanam* and *lakshya sadhana* in Indian philosophical parlance; see Vatsyayan 1982b and Bharatmuni 2007). In this sense, a study of Odissi is methodologically valuable as a paratopic exercise of rehearsing dance history 'differently' compared to the Eurocentric norm.

My method also owes an uneven debt to Foucault's notion of 'genealogy' (1977) and the theoretical procedures of critical historians of South Asia (Thapar 1970, 1989; Sangari and Vaid 1989; Guha 1998, 2005; Kosambi 2002, 2008; and Chatterjee 2013;). Foucault's genealogical approach rejects narratives that locate a single, privileged origin point for the development of any historical phenomenon, and rightly endorses a view that emphasizes the jagged, the fragmented, the multiplicitous and the nonlinear in the making of an event. Essentially, the reductive monocausal and sequentially ordered treatments of any given cultural phenomenon are displaced by an emphasis on the textured, multifactorial and intersectional forces that contribute to the appearance of a historical episode and its afterlives. Many scholars, following Foucault, might advocate a position that diminishes the legitimacy of looking for 'origins', since such a polemical manoeuvre bears the potential for essentializing the phenomenon under discussion through recourse to the dreaded discourse of 'authenticity'.[23]

In the context of Indian dance, the theoretical significance of this genealogical approach is valuable, without doubt, but is equally complicated by limits engendered in the current political environment. Today in India, the question of the 'origins' of a variety of cultural phenomena is virtually unavoidable, as vital as it is for conservative and right-wing ideologues who have devoted considerable resources towards weaponizing cultural history and practice, especially those forms they view as irredeemably belonging—in reality or in the public imaginary—to the majoritarian Hindu realm, and therefore can be deployed for divisive and dominative aims.[24] History becomes a spatializing act in this regard, instrumentalized by agents of Hindutva. Thus an academic argument that disavows the validity of the 'origins' issue by resorting fully to the poststructuralist Foucauldian method risks ignoring the salience of ongoing cultural debates in India and their political utility and volatility. In my opinion, this indifference would be inexcusable in current circumstances, where classical dance is 'owned' by Hinduism in profound ways. It might even perpetuate a false model of disinterested scholarship, whereas the model I seek to emulate is the Gramscian one of the 'organic intellectual'. I am also committed to a perspective informed by the insights of postcolonialism, feminist standpoint epistemology, and the Hindu Left, arguing that critical analysis is never neutral but socially situated and subjective.[25] So I partly embrace Foucault's technique for the value

23 A good journalistic summary of this position is found in Keerthik Sasi-dharan's 'True Authorship is Often a Mirage', *The Hindu*, 17 December 2017 (available at: https://goo.gl/MPhaF2; last accessed on 12 June 2018).

24 See, on this point, Ashish Nandy (1995); Jyotirmaya Sharma (2003); and Partha Chatterjee (2010).

25 A good overview of postcolonial thought is available in Patrick Williams and Laura Chrisman (1994). For a compendium of viewpoints on feminist standpoint theory, see Sandra Harding (2004). On the Hindu Left, see Vanita (2002a) and critiques of academic and political secularism by Ashish Nandy (1997; 2002). I am particularly convinced by Vanita's observation that 'the

it brings to the historical enterprise by dislodging singular narratives, but, in acknowledging the epistemic violence of political Hindutva, I do not wish to abandon the project of grappling with the 'origins' of Odissi in the first place, even as I seek to unsettle and trouble them. Of course, mine is not a unique position or predicament by any means; many progressive scholars who address India as archive contend with this need to negotiate between the theoretical ideal and the political exigencies of the present.

A unique situation in Odissi scholarship is that the current form of the dance is of fairly recent vintage, and we are at a point proximate enough in history where we have access to the dynamics of its making as a twentieth-century classical practice, one that is concurrently citational and new. This is not habitually the case with other genres of dance, whose 'origins' may indeed be mystified, obscured, even lost by the time they reach renown as established forms—thus, a definitive accounting of their pasts is logically impossible, as Richard Schechner has argued (1985: 35–116). Without totally disputing his famous pronouncement that performance is 'twice-behaved behaviour' and never happens for the first time (36), I do want to suggest that there are moments which permit us the rare luxury of serving as close witnesses to the formation of a major cultural practice. Agreeing with Schechner that ' "ancient classical dance" is a projection backward in time' (69), I simultaneously maintain that with Odissi's present-day concert form, at least, we have a wealth of materials drawn from archive and repertoire that lay bare its originary foundations, allowing us the privilege of contemplating its modern inceptions.

social agenda of the secular left and the Hindu one-time left was in large part the same, despite the use of very different theories, language and terminology. To a considerable extent, it continues to be the same even today' (2002a: n.p.). Given the contemporary political environment, I further agree with her that the right wing should not have a monopoly on 'defining and interpreting Hindu heritage', and that progressives 'have an equal right and perhaps even an obligation now to claim that heritage before it gets eroded and destroyed by its self-styled champions' (ibid.: n.p.).

While the approaches of critical historians of India are too diverse to be branded monolithically, what unites them discursively is a commitment to demystifying dominant narratives and assertions attached to conservative and right-wing agendas. My project embraces these progressive initiatives, yet in proposing to build a paratopic history—one that sits adjacent to the reigning narrative—inevitably there is some risk of reifying Odissi as entity and institution. I move freely between these double manoeuvres of epistemic deconstruction and (re)construction, employing the tactic of disclosing these methodological procedures and making them transparent in an effort to enable the reader to consider the preponderance of evidence affirming or denying the validity of a given perspective.

This is the approach I use for tracing the life of Odissi, its trajectory through time and space—its shifts and metamorphoses, its lineages and influences, its transformations both in its own intimate domain and in the larger history of the cultural context in which it is located. I argue that Odissi dance is not only a surface for the imprint of ideology, or an object of manipulation by external forces, but also that it negotiates and mutually constitutes them. It not only reflects and mediates but further contributes to *constructing* the socius. In these capacities, Odissi dance engages with social history and acts as an agent of change as much as it is circumscribed by temporal and spatial circumstance.

Book Structure and Chapter Outlines

The first part of this book, 'Mangalacharan: Beginnings', invokes the story of Odissi's emergence; it reflects on the genesis of dance and the historical and political contingencies of its birth. I relate this to Mangalacharan since it heralds auspicious beginnings as the opening item of the conventional Odissi repertoire.[26]

---

26 In homage to the subject of my book, I have named each part to correspond to the structure of an Odissi performance. Fortuitously, the arc of an Odissi concert dovetails with the way in which the writing of this genre unfolds—an introduction, followed by detailed elaborations and a conclusion.

I suggest that it is in the precolonial period that the main motifs and traits signifying Odissi's distinctiveness are introduced: its aesthetic principles and movement vocabularies; its interstitial status as elite and democratic, ritual and entertainment; its plural religious dimensions; its production of a distributed body that is simultaneously divine; and the entry of the state as a mediating power that seeks to influence the practices of dance.

Odissi claims to have a special position as India's most ancient classical dance, and this claim will be critically explored through a consideration of the social systems and sites which contributed to its formations in Chapter 1, 'Roots, Sources, and Narratives: Multiple Histories, Multiple Genealogies'.

In virtually every narrative related to Odissi, images in the Udaygiri caves are mentioned as the earliest representations of the movement style.[27] Of this history, I ask: What was the Jain context of the images? And if these are Jain images, how does it complicate or complement the story of the dance's exclusively Hindu provenance, and what does it say about Odissi's framing as a temple dance?

Part II, 'Pallavi: Flourishings', is an exploration of Odissi's shifts in the medieval, early modern, and colonial periods, and the attendant political controversies that ensued when power shifted from the regional royal rulers to the Mughal empire and the British colonial state. I examine the legal regimes organizing Odissi's performance, analysing customary laws and written codes, both of which acquired social authority. However, I argue that it is under British imperialism that the law reaches its apotheosis as an instrument of the state and finds its fullest expression as choreographic agent, ironically as a suppressive apparatus. I examine the practices of colonial signification in India, which introduced new legal and social concepts of identity at the national scale and resulted in unprecedented surveillance of Odisha's dance traditions.

---

27 See, for example, Charles Louis Fabri (1974); Kapila Vatsyayan (1974: 34); Mohan Khokar (1984: 175); Sunil Kothari (1990: 1); and Ranjana Gauhar (2007: 35), among others.

In Chapter 2, 'Divining the Distributed Body: Mahari Naach and Ritual Performance', I discuss how Odissi was established institutionally when the king Chodangangadeva built the Jagannath temple at Puri and formalized Odissi as a sacred dance to be performed by the maharis, cast as the consorts of the god. Considered auspicious, the mahari order offered an alternative model of femininity to the social roles afforded to women under quotidian patriarchal strictures. Maharis held positions of religious importance in Hindu society; they were the only women with access to education, esoteric knowledge and specialized training in the arts.

Interestingly, the Jagannath cult emerged from tribal communities whose cosmologies were autonomous of orthodox Hinduism but who were gradually absorbed into its pantheon through a contested process of social assimilation. The temple culture merged tribal practices with religious traditions such as Vaishnavism, Shaivism, Shaktism, Tantrism and Buddhism. Thus, Odissi is unusual in that it was a syncretic expression as cultivated in the confines of the temple, becoming an index of high Brahmanism by the twelfth century, when it became enshrined as a temple practice.

Looking at the mahari context, I suggest there is a distinctive mapping of the body in Odisha, manifest in its architecture, religious praxis and Mahari Naach, which Odissi today aims to magnify. This transindividual body conjoins the abstract and the palpable, the divine and the worldly, the visible and the ineffable. Through a specific philosophy of corporeality mined from the iconography of the Jagannath cult, the dancing body, the deity and the temple all link concentrically into composite corporeal geographies. I excavate the idea of the 'distributed body', drawing from Alfred Gell (1988), as embedded in these histories of Odissi dance.

The decline of the devadasi in the 'Muslim' period is a potent trope in Odissi's prevailing narrative. I focus on this theme in Chapter 3, 'Dominant Historiographies: Dance and the Muslim Thesis', contesting the trope while identifying the ideological agendas behind the construction of Hindu–Muslim binaries in South Asian dance histories. Looking at the mahari system, and the performance forms with which it coexisted, I argue that the 'Muslim thesis' is predicated on the idea of locating the Hindu as native and the Muslim as estranged in the Indian context. I critically interrogate the notion that the entry of Islam in Odisha curtailed Odissi, or that it had uniform effects; instead, I argue for specificity in understanding the relationship between religion and the arts, suggesting that new forms of political governance produced new categories of performance while analysing the status of dance under the Mughal empire.

In Chapter 4, 'Ecstasy and Madness: Gotipuas, Gender Perform-ance, and the Body in Bhakti', I analyse ideations of the body as imagined in the gotipua tradition. Challenging the prevailing view that gotipua dance replaced Mahari Naach in public performance, I discuss it as an autonomous form which complemented, rather than displaced, women's ritual dancing. I then look at how the dancing gotipua body inhabits a tentative, precarious space, poised on the edge of normativity and transgression—a transgression reframed as devotional ritual, which provides the conservative alibi for its radical expressivity. I suggest that, through its oppositional choreographies of gender, Odissi illustrates the gap between modes of aesthetic performance and everyday life, creating a space of alterity in which regional practices of masculinity/femininity challenge 'modern' gender narratives normalized by the Indian state while reinforcing masculinist appropriations of the feminized body.

The shift from the discourse of exceptional genders to the discourse of deviance under imperialism forms the subject of Chapter 5, '"Oh, the Horror of It!" The Scandal of Temple Dance in Colonial Odisha'. The British Raj, in an effort to secure power through policies of divide and rule, contributed in major ways to the accentuation of existing social differences in India based on class, region, caste, religion and gender. The conflation of Victorian morality, social Darwinism, Western concepts of masculinity and femininity, evangelical Christianity and notions of racial supremacy produced a colonial discourse which resulted in the devaluation of renegade South Asian subjects, including the maharis, as degenerate bodies (see also Banerji 2018).

After centralizing the doctrines of law, colonial forces converted the Odissi dancer into the 'prostitute' and then instituted restrictions on temple dancing along with implementing the Contagious Diseases Act (1865) to regulate native women's sexuality. What changed dramatically in this time was the *scale* of the state's control over dance, magnified from the space of the regional to the national-imperial; its *modes* of control, with the colonizers narrowly focusing on managing dancers' bodies and behaviours rather than the dance aesthetic alone;[28] and the *intensification* of control, through policies adopted by government agencies, the enactment of countrywide laws and interventions in dance matters by the courts. Thus, while the dance domain had previously served as the object of *spatialization* and *legislation* by precolonial regimes, its *nationalization* and *judicialization* were novel developments under British rule. The colonial authorities also put into place several measures designed to constrain both the quotidian and aesthetic movement practices of the native populace, launching the 'anti-nautch' campaign that essentially banned performances of Odissi's precedent dances. British colonizers and native elites imposed a notion of pathologized subjectivity on dancers, targeting them as objects of moral reform. No longer divined but profaned, the meaning and context of mahari performance changed monumentally—as it did with devadasis across india, especially those linked to Bharatnatyam, a situation described in depth by scholars like Amrit Srinivasan (1985, 1990), Avanthi Meduri (1996), Janet O'Shea (2007) and Davesh Soneji (2012). Dance in Odisha was similarly affected, but with the added liability of personifying a marginal polity within a colonized landscape— what I call the trope of double savagery.

In Part III, 'Moksha: Conclusions', I investigate the revival, reconstruction and institutionalization of Odissi as a classical dance

---

28 This is in contrast to the Dramatic Performances Act (1876), for instance, which prohibited the public presentation of certain theatre genres.

representative of a national Hindu heritage in post-Independence India. In this era, there were a number of legal acts implemented to ban the devadasi system in India, though the laws were typically enforced in certain regions of the nation. However, despite the castigation of the dancer, devadasi dance itself was not outlawed. In Chapter 6, 'A Museum of Movement: The Postcolonial State of Classical Odissi', I discuss how a number of cultural policy initiatives, institutions and venues sprang up so the dance could enjoy continuity beyond the devadasi/temple order as a secular spectacle, newly nationalized and allegorized. The government also encouraged the revivification of traditions that had been suppressed during colonial times, as a testament to the vitality and resilience of South Asian cultural forms. Thus Odissi became an index of cultural purity and patrimony.

I look at how patriarchal authorities took over the project of codifying Odissi and imbuing it with a classical aura, by assembling a formal movement vocabulary diminished of its original eros, and authorizing it by inscribing the new tenets of the dance style in textual form and inaugurating a new dance repertoire. This nascent version of Odissi bore little resemblance to its antecedents. Although the maharis who had kept their *naach* alive underground were still accessible, they were deliberately excluded and distanced in this process, as they bore the stigma of prostitution and were associated with cultural deprecation. The effort to classicize Odissi was very much tied to purifying it of an explicitly erotic history in order to ensure its lasting appeal to the elite and to seal its status as an authentic symbol of nationhood. The superseding of customary and social laws by written legal acts, policies and choreographic directives was also rendered complete in this moment of Odissi's new spatialization and canonization.

'Tehai, Unfinished' represents the conclusion of this project. The *tehai* is a triple refrain that signals the end of an Odissi dance performance. Or, in cyclical fashion, the beginning of a new one. In recognition of this trope, I offer summative thoughts on the choreography of the state, and reiterate key arguments for rethinking Odissi as a performance practice, its repercussions and effects.

Despite attempts at its appropriation, I maintain that Odissi exudes a paratopic force with the opalescent histories of gender and region it expresses in its choreographies, its refusal to be ultimately constrained by state agents and dispositifs.

In arguing for these perspectives, I am inspired by the formidable Walter Benjamin, whose words about the task of the critical historian invigorate my work:

> Historicism contents itself with establishing a causal connection between various moments in history. But no fact that is a cause is for that reason historical. It became historical posthumously, as it were, through events that may be separated from it by thousands of years. A historian who takes this as [her] point of departure stops telling the sequence of events like the beads of a rosary (1968: 263).

She replaces the beads of history with redolent gestures: baroque, abstract, semiotic. Odissi's narrative, like all *abhinaya* elaborations, is infinitely repeatable, revealing new shades and nuances in each telling. Opening up the narrative to these multiplicities is an urgent maneuver, for so often the narrative about the dance *becomes* the dance, controlling its creative possibilities.

And so we circle back to the start, to the centre, to the thought that opened this inscribed Mangalacharan—that beginnings often conceal the desire for other beginnings; and endings always reveal the desire for endlessness.

Their story begins on ground level, with footsteps.[29]

---

29 Michel de Certeau (2011: 97).

Chapter 1

ROOTS, SOURCES AND NARRATIVES

MULTIPLE HISTORIES, MULTIPLE GENEALOGIES

The discovery of Odissi should be hailed as one of the great events in recovering a much lost heritage.

—Charles Fabri,
in the special Odissi issue of *Marg* (1960)

The classical dance Art of Orissa is one more manifestation, among our classical dances, of a tree which grew in the eastern region, put on many fresh leaves, decayed and blossomed again, almost to collapse with the illwinds that blew, but which is now resurgent with new shoots upon its tender branches.

—Mulk Raj Anand,
Introduction to the Odissi special issue of *Marg* (1960)

The root is not important. Movement is.
—Édouard Glissant
Poetics of Relation (1997: 14)

Odisha lies nestled at the crossroads between north and south on the eastern side of the Indian peninsula, bordered by West Bengal above it and Andhra Pradesh below, with Chhattisgarh and Jharkhand on its western horizons.[1] Full of hills and forests, deltas

---

1 Historically, Odisha has shared geographic as well as 'political-cultural alignment' with the contiguous Bengal and Assam regions, notes Chandra Tripathi (2008).

FIGURE 1.1 (ABOVE). A contemporary map of the states of India. Courtesy of MapsOfIndia.com.
FIGURE 1.2 (BELOW). A map of present-day Odisha. Courtesy of MapsofIndia.com.

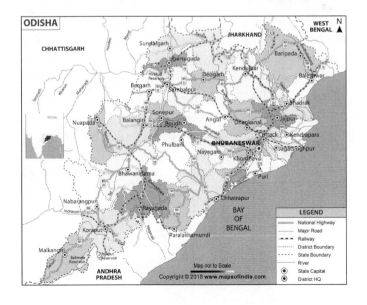

and plains, rivers, lakes and waterfalls, its landscape is lush from endless seasons of tropical monsoons. Rich in natural resources, the land is filled with villages in dense jungles and a medley of urban centres, along with seaside settlements that connect it, via maritime trade and voyages across sea routes, to Southeast Asia. Odisha's coastline is dotted with beaches sitting at the edge of the Bay of Bengal, the spray of cold saltwater rising in strong blue waves and eventually folding into the immense Indian Ocean. This propinquity to the sea opens Odisha to lands beyond, but it also leaves it vulnerable to the furies of water, as the region is prone to devastating cyclones.

Artistically, Odisha has an equally evocative ethos, distinguished for its painting, music and literature, for its gorgeous temples and shrines, and for its unique expressive culture of performances, festivals and religious rituals. The presence of a large number of lineage-based groups—tribals or adivasis, first settlers—with their own devotional practices, aesthetics and social structures contributes another element to Odisha's unique character; its culture is defined by the coexistence and fusion of these forest-dwelling communities with those based in the countryside and cities. For millennia, Odisha has also been home to a range of religions, including Hinduism, Buddhism, Jainism, Islam and Christianity as well as several indigenous faiths. This open mélange of cultures, beliefs and practices—often in harmony, often in friction—is an especially arresting characteristic of Odishan society.

Its regional distinctiveness has always been an important part of its identity, even though parts of Odisha were periodically subsumed by rulers hailing from the north and south; for much of its past, many of its areas were assimilated into Bengal and Bihar or annexed by South Indian regimes, making its boundaries malleable. The struggle to attain sovereignty—political, cultural and territorial—has been a recurring theme in Odisha's history. With its ever-shifting divisions and borders, the region has known many names: Kalinga, Kosala, Udra, Odra Desh, Odraka, Ushin and Utkal are among some of its past appellations (Panigrahi 2008: 3–7).[2] It was only in the last half of the twentieth century, after prolonged and passionate agitation, that Odisha was formally recognized as a separate state in post-Independence India.[3]

Dance today is a special signifier asserting Odisha's regional identity, and Odissi thus holds a privileged place in the state's history. Regarded by scholars everywhere as one of the classical dances of India, Odissi is considered so largely because of its alignment with the aesthetic principles of the *Natyashastra*, an ancient Indian (*c*.second century BCE–second century CE) Sanskrit treatise on performance. The standard narrative associated with Odissi goes something like this: the dance, which has ancient roots— mentioned in textual tradition, depicted in paintings and sculptures, found in inscriptions and friezes—enjoyed full efflorescence as a Hindu temple ritual in the 'golden age' of Odisha under the Ganga dynasty, encompassing the twelfth to the early fifteenth centuries (1110–1434 CE). Upon the arrival of Muslim rulers, the art went into decline, especially as the maharis who had performed within the temple precincts as an act of worship started branching out into courts and salons and became associated with prostitution, while public ceremonies tied to temple festivals were taken over by the gotipuas. The dance then virtually disappeared under British rule as a result of anti-nautch moral-reform campaigns, mounted by colonial authorities and zealous Indian activists, but was fortunately salvaged by cultural revivalists in the post-Independence

---

2 Many communities in the region still use some of these names to refer to Odisha, although most of these allusions are found in historical literature, according to K. C. Panigrahi (1981).

3 Under the nineteenth-century British colonial regime, parts of Odisha were annexed to the Bengal, Bihar and Madras Presidencies between 1803 and 1935. Odisha regained some territory and first received official political recognition as a province on 1 April 1936, on the grounds of Odia-speakers qualifying as a distinct linguistic community; it then acquired full status as a state in 1950 as part of the newly independent Republic of India (see Das and Huke 2009). For more on the politics of twentieth-century Odisha, see Chapter 6.

period. In its reconstructive phase, Odissi emerged as a neoclassical form, shaped through the union of mahari and gotipua dance, a retroactive alignment with aesthetic principles laid out in texts such as the *Natyashastra*, *Abhinaya Darpanam* and *Abhinaya Chandrika*, and a movement vocabulary derived from Odisha's traditions of sculpture and visual art.[4]

A dedicated group of gurus, dancers and scholars crafted a new Odissi repertoire—transformed from its temple roots, newly designed for display on the concert stage— synthesizing elements from these various sources.[5] The Mahari Naach infused qualities of grace and flow into the Odissi repertoire while the gotipua tradition lent its vigour and theatricality. Jayadeva's great twelfth-century literary work, the *Geeta Govinda*, inspired the lyrical and mimetic expressivity of Odissi's *abhinayas* (dances based on narratives or poems in Sanskrit and Odia literature/orature[6]) while

---

4 The standard narrative associated with Odissi is found in numerous texts outlining its history; a sampling of well-regarded works in the field include: Charles Fabri, 'Introduction to Orissa Dance' in *Marg* (1960: 4–5); D. N. Patnaik, *Odissi Dance* (1971, 1990 and 2006); Mohan Khokar, *Traditions of Indian Classical Dance* (1984); Kali Charan Patnaik, 'The Shastric Basis of Odissi Dance' in Gandharva Mahavidyalai (1985); Sunil Kothari, *Odissi: Indian Classical Dance Art* (1990); Kapila Vatsyayan, *Indian Classical Dance*, (1997) and *Classical Indian Dance in Literature and the Arts* (2007); Jiwan Pani, *Back to the Roots* (2004); and Priyambada Mohanty Hejmadi and Ahalya Hejmadi, *Odissi: An Indian Classical Form* (2007).

See also Enakshi Bhavnani (1970); Sitakant Mahapatra (1979b); Bidut Choudhury (1999); Sharon Lowen (2004); Madhumita Raut (2007); Ritha Devi (2008); and Ranjana Gauhar (2008). Other resources include Kala Vikash Kendra's *Dance and Music of Orissa Souvenir* (1958) and the special issue of *Marg* (1960).

5 In Chapter 6, I discuss details of the stylistic differences among the various Odissi schools, and also address the process of Odissi's reconstruction.

6 I draw on Pio Zirimu's coinage of 'orature'—meant to bridge the gulf between literature and oral art forms— which he defined as 'the use of utterance as an aesthetic means of expression' (cited in Ngugi wa Thiong'o, 1998: 111). See also Thiong'o's chapter 'Oral Power and Europhone Glory: Orature, Literature, and Stolen Legacies' from *Penpoints, Gunpoints, and Dreams* (1998: 103–28), and his essay 'Notes Towards a Theory of Orature' (2007).

the melodies and rhythmic syllables of Odissi music's ragas and *talas* accompanied its Pallavis (abstract dances, free of narrative content, which explore the formal and structural properties of Odissi movement).[7] From the texts on aesthetic philosophy came tenets and techniques of performance, including the qualities of *rasa* and *bhava*, those predominant sentiments that suffuse Indian performance, connecting artist and spectator viscerally in a nuanced landscape of emotions, intimated in and through the body. The profusion of statues in Odishan temples presented a visual and tactile lexicon of gestures and postures for Odissi choreography, so much so that its distinction among the Indian classical styles rests on its emblematically sculpturesque qualities.[8] In addition to spearheading its renewal, Odissi's exponents and proponents sought and received inclusion of the dance into the classical canons. The gurus and their disciples were then able to popularize Odissi regionally, nationally and globally, in India and its diasporas.

This picture may be vastly oversimplified, but it draws from the existing scholarship to give an idea of the leitmotifs governing its history. The narrative arc neatly encapsulates several critical ideas: that the 'Hindu' period contributed to Odissi's rise while the 'Muslim' period contributed to its fall; the nail in the coffin was delivered by the British, but they were merely witnesses and occasionally accomplices to the derogation of the dance, the *real* cause of which was Muslim rule.[9] It was up to the modern (Hindu?) revivalists to rescue Odissi and restore the original glory it had once enjoyed, even as it was reframed under seemingly

---

7 See Itishree Sahoo's *Odissi Music: Evolution, Revival, and Technique* (2009), especially Chapter 6, 'Odissi Music: As Cognate of Odissi Dance'.

8 The transposition of sculpture into the dancing body, and vice versa, is a theme beautifully explored in two notable film works: Ritha Devi's *Vibrant Sculpture/Frozen Dance* (1987) and Alessandra Lopez y Royo's *Performing Konarak, Performing Hirapur* (2007).

9 See Chapter 3 for an extended discussion of this issue—how the standard narrative associated with Odissi mirrors conservative interpretations of Indian history, coinciding with broader Hindutva claims about the negative impact of Muslim cultures on Indian society.

secular norms.[10] The role of Jain, Buddhist, Muslim, Christian and lineage-based groups in Odissi's formation, and the impact of the broader public sphere, are neatly effaced and rendered unproblematic in this perspective. Another theme is the scandal of sexuality associated with the history of Odissi, which, to many eyes, has tarnished its contemporary image, culminating in a quest to purify the dance of these allegedly immoral influences in order to elevate its authentically pure and pristine past.[11] While these assumptions are rarely stated explicitly, they do provide a subtext—sometimes subtle, sometimes strong—to the prevailing story of Odissi, and dovetail with larger debates in Indian history about religion, culture, gender, regionalism, nationalism and power. These discourses need to be examined to locate alternative visions of Odissi, to situate some of the dissonances, disjunctions and disturbances in the historical account that is almost universally promulgated by eminent scholars. Selected clues have been assembled to support their narrative, but other traces lie still hidden and contain different echoes, promising a different telling.

Odissi: A Paratopic Perspective

Let me offer, briefly—to be expanded throughout this book—my own interpretation of the dance. Odissi is a regional performance tradition which reflects a variety and confluence of cultural practices. From its beginnings, Odissi has been interdisciplinary, interreligious and intercultural. Its past is a microcosm of Odisha's history. As a composite form, the dance encompasses a breathtaking multiplicity of roots and sources: text, sculpture, literature,

---

10 The famous danseuse Indrani Rahman and her mother Ragini Devi, both of whom played a part in Odissi's revival, are exceptions to this narrative. See Rahman (2004).

11 The stigma of sexuality surfaces most frequently in debates about the position of maharis and devadasis in Odissi and Bharatanatyam, especially in the context of modern revivals of the dance forms. See, for example, Patnaik (1971, 1990, 2006); Mahapatra (1979); Marglin (1985b); A. Srinivasan (1990); Meduri (1996); Nair (1996a, 1996b); Kersenboom (1998); and R. Roy (2004). I pursue this topic further in Chapters 4 and 5.

painting, theatre, music, martial arts, religion, mythology, philosophy. The *Natyashastra, Shilpa Shastra, Abhinaya Darpanam and Abhinaya Chandrika.*[12] The *rasa* and *bhava* of *abhinaya*. Shaba Swarup and Bandha Nritya. Jain monuments, Shaivite and Shakti temple iconography, Vaishnav rituals and festivals. The culture surrounding the Jagannath temple. Maharis and gotipuas, kings and priests, today's gurus and disciples. Vedic Brahmanism, Tantrism, Buddhism and Bhakti. Tribal cosmologies. Ashtapadis from Jayadeva's *Geeta Govinda.*[13] Pattachitra paintings and illustrated manuscripts.[14] Folk dance, Jatra, dance drama. Champu and Chhanda, Odia poetry and song. The culture of the royal courts, society salons, public festivals, the professional stage. All of these contributed to the dance—some at its putative genesis and some over time—but some of them have been excised while others have been emphasized in its modern form. Odissi's multiple genealogies attest to its multiple framings as prayer, as art, as spectacle, as *shringara*. Far from being an exclusively Hindu temple dance, Odissi represents a rich amalgam of religious and secular histories, manifold genres and disciplines, myriad traditions and practices.

This is no original observation on my part—the quality of heterogeneity inherent to Odissi was the subject of a landmark 2003 conference.[15] Organized by the Sangeet Natak Akademi

---

12 For a description of all of these terms, see Appendix A, 'Notes on Allied Forms of Odisha'.

13 Ashtapadis are poetic verses composed of eight lines, and Jayadeva's twelfth-century *Geeta Govinda* is considered the best representative of this literary form.

14 The Odisha State Museum (OSM) possesses a treasure trove of original palm-leaf manuscripts in Sanskrit and Oriya, depicting the poetry and art of the *Geeta Govinda*; some gems from its outstanding collection are published in its *Descriptive Catalogue of Illustrated Manuscripts* (2007). For English translations of the *Geeta Govinda*, see Mohanty (2005) and Tripathy and Tripathy (2006), and Stoler Miller's classic 2004 commentary.

15 I am thankful to Dr Helen Acharya of the Dance Division at the Sangeet Natak Akademi in Delhi (personal conversation, September 2007) for pointing out this interdisciplinary dimension of Odissi, an insight I built on in my research inquiries.

(SNA), India's national institute of the performing arts, it brought together a number of scholars, critics, artists, presenters and lovers of Odissi (and for many attendees, several of these identities were not discrete but overlapping). Through various presentations, participants productively explored connections between Odissi and an array of performing arts, including Pala, Prahlad Natak, Geeti Nritya, Sahi Jatra, Sakhipila . . . This proved to be a revelation. Insights from that conference, combined with my ethnographic and archival research, dance training, personal observations and accidental stumbling, led me toward a new ideation of Odissi beyond the grounds of the temple and into alternative arenas. What emerged is that Odissi is less a discrete practice than a deep repository of ancillary Odishan traditions and forms. A dialectical dance in continuous flux. This plurality is aptly reflected in the name of the genre, as Odissi 'literally means anything belonging to Orissa' (Patnaik 2006: 75). Yet somehow, given its synthetic histories, this acknowledgement of its hybrid character lies latent in general public discourse in favour of the impression that Odissi is a stable classical entity.[16]

The creation of Odissi as a classical form in the 1950s involved selective practices of inclusion, exclusion and distillation. The assignment of a classical status usually suggests that the art in question embodies qualities of excellence and represents the best of its heritage (Williams 1986; Cherian 2009). In the world of dance, the art is appraised also for its adherence to ancient norms and aesthetic codes, which gives it a timeless glow. It is on this basis that Odissi attained classical designation. Yet, in my view, its true character lies in the fusion of forms—as Sitakant Mahapatra writes of Odisha, 'there is a remarkable continuity between classical, folk and tribal art-forms . . . This is true of Orissi as a classical dance' (1985: 15). The link between the varying performance styles is apparent when we compare their movement lexicons and notice their mutually visible imprints. After witnessing the performances,

---

16 I draw on Chris Ballard's work in referring to 'synthetic histories,' defined as 'broad narratives of historical process that critically combine the insights and perspectives of research from multiple disciplines' (2010: 232).

it becomes difficult to make a strong demarcation between 'folk', 'classical' and 'ritual' dances, for instance, or to make claims about the inherent aesthetic superiority of Odissi in its concert form.[17]

In the revival period, an alchemy of forms was still perceptible in Odissi's techniques and movement vocabularies, but, over time, the presiding schools deleted certain influences and emphasized others, deconstructing the dance in the name of aesthetic refinement and purification, expressing allegiance to the textual and temple-based tradition on which the model of classicism was founded; other schools actively experimented with a range of sources in their repertoires, resulting in prolonged debates over authentic representations of the dance which continue to hold power today.[18]

---

17 Interestingly, two of the key texts that serve as Odissi's foundation make no distinction between 'classical' and 'folk' performances. In the *Natyashastra*, the terms *margi* and *desi* are often cited as synonyms for 'classical' and 'folk' respectively; however, in a different reading, *margi* seems to suggest a pan-Indian aesthetic, while *desi* suggests local inflections of dance practice (P. Shah 2002). The *Abhinaya Chandrika* mentions several Odishan dances which we could call 'folk' in today's dance parlance, but which did not have such an association in the time the text was written. In the *Brihaddeshi* (*c.*sixth century CE), Matanga Muni provides a deep theorization of *margi* and *desi* music, ideas which have found resonance in dance theory. *Desi*, which conjures links to 'space or region or location,' is defined as: 'That which is sung by women, children, cowherds and kings out of their own will with love (and pleasure) in their own (respective) regions' (Matanga Muni 1992: 147n5 and 5).

Prem Lata Sharma observes that '[t]he so-called folk and the elite (represented by kings) have been clubbed together here, on purpose, because the *desi* music that is the object of description our text is not "folk" in the western sense, nor is it "classical" in the same sense' (in ibid.: 150n27, original emphasis). *Margi* is cited in two ways: as a general musical system, and as a special type of music under the *desi* umbrella (ibid.: 5, 150n28 and n29).

Mandakranta Bose argues that in dance, *margi* and *desi* should not be seen as 'exclusive of one another in terms of their components. They should rather be seen as different stylistic approaches that grew through time into separate traditions of the same basic art form'; and that *desi* forms place 'emphasis on the style of presentation rather than on the content of the composition' and integrate 'more acrobatic movements' than *margi* types (2007: 217).

18 Lively debates and discussions around divergent choreographic strategies

I argue that Odissi is a regional, syncretic dance that first achieved pre-eminence in the cultural centres of Odisha through the active patronage of the ruling regimes. Several of the afore-mentioned performance traditions contributed to Odissi's forma-tion, but on their own they never became fully emblematic of the region, nor were they associated with the historical sites and rites that eventually contributed to Odissi's ascendance among the movement arts. In addition, they eventually failed to acquire Shastric sanction and status as idealized forms. (Chhau is the single exception.)[19] Yet, their influences flowed into the classical form so indelibly that Odissi cannot claim to have originated as an autonomous dance style, as it contains within it the history of both the collision and coalescence of several (trans)local traditions, revealing its making through a panoply of art forms. With such fluid and permeable boundaries, the dance manifests the cultural hybridity of Odisha itself.

Nevertheless, despite the evidence to the contrary, the idea that Odissi's origins lie in Hindu temple dance continues unabated. Several of the interviews I conducted confirmed the potency of this narrative, ingrained within Odishan history and myth; the narrative abounds in dance scholarship as well. A fresh look at the evidence excavates another story which exposes what is already tacitly acknowledged about the history of cultural forms, *especially* those in Odisha: that they are often richly textured as a result of incorpo-rating multiple influences. So why does the temple myth persist?

Given Odissi's relatively recent revival, its deliberate recon-struction through modern and historical sources, and its innovative engagements with tradition, the dance can be considered just as 'contemporary' as it is 'classical'.[20] Its flourishing in today's

are taken up, for instance, in online discussion forums devoted to Odissi, at Odissi festivals in India and abroad, and in regional and national symposia that regularly take place in cultural centres across India. I discuss the major styles of Odissi in Chapter 6.

19 See Appendix A for more on Chhau.

20 Alessandra Lopez y Royo makes a strong case on behalf of this claim in her 2008 analysis.

international dance scene, its continuing transformations in India and beyond would seem to support such a qualification. But the investment in its antiquity often overshadows this reading. The temple narrative enables the dance to be linked to religious ritual, giving it divine sanction as a Hindu tradition—the foundation on which its legitimacy rests and replicates itself. Mohan Khokar's words are representative of the reigning view:

> The temple dancing girls, then, have been the earliest performers of Orissi dance [. . .] The legacy of Indian classical dance has, indeed, been bequeathed by the temple. And for this one has to be thankful to those who built the temples, and even more so to those who had the genius to recognise the dance as a path of spiritual exaltation of highest potency (1984: 175, 181).

The temple myth also creates an asymmetry between the sacred and the secular, with the assumption that forms utterly suffused with Hindu religiosity are somehow the purest and most sophisticated in Indian performance.

The ascription of the classical designation is predicated largely on a theological meaning. In this model, 'religious' is conflated with 'classical', such that other forms rarely qualify as 'serious'; arts emanating from 'folk', 'social', 'street', 'modern', 'political', 'secular' and 'popular' sources are often discursively placed in opposition to 'religious' performance.[21] Negatively distinguished from the sacred, the public and profane are realms in which the cultural position of a form erodes, disqualifying it as a proper sign of heritage. In a self-perpetuating cycle, the classical becomes sacred and the sacred becomes classical, while the arbitrary divisions between the classical and other categories are sustained, conceptually sequestered *from* each other, even though in practice they spill *into* each other.

These tautologies and concatenations of meaning emerged rather recently. Undeniably, Odissi *does* have a historical link

---

21 On the arbitrary categorizations of traditional performances in India, see Bharucha (1993: 192–210) and Cherian (2009). On the folk roots of classical culture, see Maury (1969), Chandralekha (1980) and Kramrisch (1983).

with the sacred; but the significance attached to spirituality in classical performance largely reflects the aftermath of India's colonial legacy. In a neat reversal of an Orientalist construct, spirituality as a marker of India's primitivism and irrationalism is transformed into a positive signifier capable of countering Western modernity and its materialism—the burden of religion thus becomes a boon. And this inverted meaning is then transposed to the world of classical dance. Nonetheless, even as asymmetries shift, the construct itself lies intact, largely due to the preponderance of 'over-ritualization.' This dynamic has its roots in a dominant pattern where India is discursively overidentified with excessive religiosity, its cultural praxis misapprehended in an act of pareidolia rather than astute interpretation.[22]

Beyond Over-Ritualization

The analysis of the early history of Indian classical dance, including Odissi, is marked by what Mundoli Narayanan calls 'over-ritualization' (2006). Discussing approaches used primarily by Western scholars to interpret Kutiyattam, a genre of Sanskrit theatre from Kerala, Narayanan suggests that its ritual purposes and principles have been accentuated to the extent that appraisals of the aesthetic and secular aspects of the form are nullified:

> [T]here has developed a tendency when it comes to non-Western theatres—especially traditional Asian theatres—to overemphasize the importance of ritual in performance. Sometimes this is done even to the exclusion of other aspects that are equally or more vital to the understanding of performance. This inclination has also led some to explain away many features of performance by interpreting them as rituals, while obviously ignoring their value as tech-

---

22 See Said (1978), Mohanty (1991) and Inden (2006: 13–60) on the Orientalist strategy of associating the Indian ethos with superstitious belief and primitive religiosity.

niques or conventions of theatre . . . implicitly assuming [them] to be totally religious and ritualistic in nature (2006: 137).

Narayanan argues for an evaluative approach that considers the performative codes and non-religious, or at least extra-religious, interdisciplinary aspects embedded in Kutiyattam—a method that vitally enhances our comprehension of such classical styles.

Narayanan's generative critique can be applied to a broader set of writings on Indian classical dance and drama ('Western' or otherwise), especially Odissi, where 'over-ritualization' is conspicuously at play as the prevailing interpretive framework. There are some notable exceptions to this tendency, but, over all, the dominant narrative pattern supports the 'over-ritualization' thesis.[23] As such, there seems to be a widespread agreement among scholars that Odissi's roots are self-evidently religious and that it espoused ritual functions affiliated to Hindu worship. The writings of Ragini Devi—an American-born dancer who devoted her life to learning Indian classical dances in the 1930s, and who wrote the first English-language book on the subject, *Nrityanjali* (1928)— typify this understanding:

> In the East art has been developed and sustained through the ages by pure devotion [. . .] The dances of the ancients were essentially a sacred rite. In India, where all forms of art were united to religion, the art of representing the inner experience of the human soul found its highest expression in music and dancing [. . .] The Hindu conception of the dance, as the visible representation of the mystic rhythm of the Universe, is in a sense symbolic of the *race-spirit* of India (1980: 62–3; original emphasis).

Mirroring her view, Odissi scholar D. N. Patnaik proffers, '[s]pirituality is the core of Indian Art. Evolved out of spiritual passions, art in India has gone hand in hand with religion since

---

23 Exceptions to, and critiques of, the standard narrative can be found in Chatterjea (2004); R. Roy (2004); Schechner (2004); Pathy (2007); Lopez y Royo (2008); and Gandhi (2009).

time immemorial [. . .] From a very early time the dance found its spiritual home in the holy caves, temples and religious institutions as an essential religious practice' (2006: 6)—a sentiment strongly echoed across the works of influential cultural theorist, translator and historian Kapila Vatsyayan (1997, 2007a).[24] Mohan Khokar, former secretary of the Sangeet Natak Akademi, concurs that 'the temple has played a vital role in the genesis and growth of all forms of the Indian classical dance arts,' reiterating that 'Orissi is a dance which has from the outset been wedded to religion. It is not surprising, therefore, that most of the items in its repertoire have a devotional bias' (1984: 179). Dance critic Sunil Kothari agrees that 'Odissi dance, its growth, development, support, and existence have been inseparably linked with the temple rituals' (1990: 1).

Subscribing wholly to the over-ritualization thesis, scholar Susan Schwartz even goes as far as to say that besides dance, *all* Indian embodied arts are religious in nature, contending that:

> performance itself is central to the way the varied cultures within India understand their world, interact with it, and thus produce an active dynamic. This dynamic may be identified as proceeding from a *religious* sensibility, how-ever diffuse the term 'religion' may be. The sources of performative inspiration have been religious from the beginning [. . .] Most Indians go to performances of whatever type and experience devotion, wonder, and the like [. . .] Whether the art form is classical, that is, derived from the formal textual tradition, or a form of folk art, as in the numberless theatrical presentations across South Asia, the potential for religious transformation is inherent (2004: 1, 3).

Then, doing away with the divide between religion and philosophy (and repeating Devi's sentiments), she makes this bold assertion:

---

24 Vatsyayan's research and translations of key Sanskrit texts are unsurpassed contributions to contemporary conversations on Indian aesthetics. For a list of her major works, see Works Cited.

Both religion and philosophy take their inspiration and application from a worldview that combines them. It is more fruitful to state that *the goal of aestheticians, from Bharatamuni onward, has been to facilitate a transformation— of the artist, audience, and ultimately the world—that may only be understandable from the perspective of religion.* So central has the religious context been to understanding and achieving the goals of performance that it is possible to study the religions of India through her performing arts. The forms performance takes and the ways it is studied, learned, and experienced reveal ways in which *religion* may be understood in India. To push the point further, it is obvious that there is religion in the performing arts of India: *the ageless mythology, as well as the references to religious paths toward ultimate spiritual goals, have formed the narrative, structural, and teleological goals of music, dance, and drama since ancient times* (ibid.: 3; emphasis added).

This focus on religiosity and 'the ageless mythology' as the originary and structuring conditions of Indian performance is seductive, reductive and problematic. Numerous artistic traditions in India cannot be defined in (solely) religious terms, a fact that troubles Schwartz and others' generalizations about the role of religiosity in Indian enactments.[25] Many classical forms include

---

25 A short and random list of such nonreligious examples might include Bhangra, Bollywood dance, Rabindra-*nritya*, forms of Jatra, leftist political street theatre, popular music, contemporary Indian concert dance by artists like Astad Deboo, Padmini Chettur, Daksha Seth and Ranjabati and Manjushri Chaki Sircar. Even forms supposedly attached to religious sources, from Kathak to Bharatanatyam, integrate areligious influences—economic, political, aesthetic. As Narayanan says of the diverse ideas encompassed in Kutiyattam, 'the specific themes of the plays themselves are far more complex and varied: some are indebted to the main themes of the epics, some are far removed from any concerns of devotion or morality, and some others have nothing to do with epics at all.' Instead, he reaffirms that the 'critical attention of the initiated audience is then on the actual theatrical circumstance and proficiency and the virtuosity of the actor(s) in rendering that particular situation [. . .] it is not on any 'religious' concerns[.]' (2006: 140).

worldly motifs in expressions of both *nritya* and *nritta*. Most crucially, the idea of art as an instrument of *bhakti*, or eliciting religious devotion, emerged in the tenth century CE, when the Kashmiri scholar-*sant* Abhinavagupta introduced the ninth *rasa*, *shanti* (peace), and encouraged art as a mode of spiritual contemplation.[26] Prior to this, the existence of religious iconography in media like theatre and dance did not necessarily imply or correspond with an interest on the part of the artist in cultivating the spectator's religious sentiments.[27]

The key question is: Why is the religious dimension deemed primary in so many discussions of Indian performance? In effect, it repeats an Orientalist strategy of imbricating 'Indianness' with religiosity, to the exclusion or subordination of other layers of experience. Looking at the sheer multiplicity of performance forms in India, an *aesthetic* sensibility, an *expressive* sensibility or a *moral* sensibility could just as easily supplant or supplement the 'religious' one.[28] More straightforwardly, the proliferation of performance in India could simply reveal a desire for leisure, an interest in experiencing art in a public setting, an engagement with sensory pleasure—a deeply social or scopophilic sensibility. Indeed, at the time of the *Natyashastra*'s writing, there was little to no mention of drama as an instrument of religious propitiation, since performance was primarily imagined and instrumentalized as a mode of disseminating dominant values to mass audiences who relied on orature for the twin purposes of education and entertainment.[29]

---

26 Abhinavagupta expounded on the theory of *rasa* in his *Abhinavabharati* (*c.*tenth century CE), a commentary on Bharatmuni's *Natyashastra* and a landmark in Indian aesthetic philosophy. See also K. P. Mishra (2006).

27 I thank Arti Dhand for sharing her expertise on this point in a personal conversation (June 2010).

28 For a discussion of the complexities between 'sacred' and 'profane' interpretations of ancient dance, see P. Banerji (1942: 47); Sarkar Munsi (2010: 165–84); S. Nair (2015); C. Rajendran (2016); and Chakravarti (2018).

29 Anand Coomaraswamy supports this point in his introduction to the *Abhinaya Darpanam*, noting that the appeal of performance historically extended beyond 'an academic circle' and 'corresponded to the common and

To propose religion as the genesis of all performance consolidates stereotypical colonial and nativist ideas of India, in which the national essence is identified with religion, with religion constraining the advent of 'progress' or 'modernization'.[30] Such a gesture is implicated in denying India's culture contemporaneity, denying its 'habitations of modernity', [31] imparting a certain changeless and timeless quality to its essence—a vision of India in inertia, in perpetua.

This disentangling of the sacred and secular, and the total supercession of the latter by the former, promulgates a myth of an inherent and natural partition between the two realms. In this vein, 'religious symbols are sui generis, marking out an independent religious domain' (Asad 1993: 52). However, as Talal Asad reminds us, religious signs

> cannot be understood independently of their historical relations with nonreligious symbols or of their articulations in and of social life, in which work and power are always crucial . . . [D]ifferent kinds of practice and discourse are intrinsic to the field in which religious representations (like any representation) acquire their identity and their truthfulness. From this it does not follow that the meanings of religious practices and utterances are to be sought in social phenomena, but only that their possibility and their authoritative status are to be explained as products of historically distinctive disciplines and forces (53–4).

To state the obvious: the existence of religious symbologies in dance does not necessarily impute religious meaning nor imply a religious purpose to the performance. The presence of sacred imagery might instead be significant in a given cultural lexicon, deployed as referent to ensure the legibility of the event to diverse

---

collective need of the folk'. It was such a vital part of the social fabric that even as a specialized activity, it was 'understood by everyone' (in Nandikesvara 1936: 20–1).

30 On the relationship between religion and modernity, see Talal Asad (2003).

31 The phrase is from Dipesh Chakrabarty's 2002 book of the same name.

onlookers. Assigning an immediate mystical meaning to this gesture flattens the complexity involved in contemplations of performance, in deciphering patterns of authorial intention and audience reception.

To be clear, I am not denying Hindu praxis its place as a major influence on Odissi. But to propose it as the *only* influence is to collapse its diffuse influences into a single frame and to advance the narrative of religious overdetermination. In this book, I argue that Odissi has multiple roots—I speculate on its developments in the public sphere, outside the precincts of the Hindu temple, and contend that it acquired strong religious hues largely because of its attachments to the devadasi system.

In the story of Odissi's formation, one piece of the puzzle is rarely considered—the tale of Jain representations of Odra-Magadhi dance at the Udaygiri monuments (*c.*first century BCE), an essential part of Odissi's past and pointing to evidence that bears the potential to unravel the myth of Odissi's genesis and identity as a Hindu temple ritual.

The Udaygiri Monuments

Calm and still, but somehow lively, she is on the verge of movement. She looks out with stony eyes and full lips opening into a small smile, an expression of perpetual serenity on her face. The hair is set into two braids, gently swinging at the back of her head as she moves. A diaphanous cloth, following the shape of her ample hips, flows down in soft pleats along her left leg, angled on a diagonal and moored to the ground. Her torso shifts ever so subtly—almost imperceptibly—to the right, and on this side of her body, she presses her bent knee against an arch festooned with floral patterns, her foot just skimming the surface of the floor in its curved position. Her figure is decorated with a splendid array of jewels—bracelets and bands circling her arms, feet adorned with heavy anklets. Her hands form mysterious mudras: Is this a Pataka gesture? A mirror? A bow and arrow? A flower? She isn't telling. Yet.

She has been standing in this same posture for over two thousand years. In her idealized figure, she represents the conventions of her

FIGURE 1.3. Detail of *nartaki* (dancer) in the upper-storey reliefs of Ranigumpha (Queen's Cave). Bhubaneshwar, Odisha, 7 February 2008. Photograph by the author.

time. In this depiction, her image is immortalized, though not immobile. She inaugurates the contested history of Odissi. This kind of vibrant representation reflects the potency of stone: its power to catalyse movements—both aesthetic and social. Infused with legends and myths of origin, the image invokes a cultural past inevitably intermingled with the social life of the present.

This nameless figure, dancing on through time, has been the subject of endless interest and fascination in Indian classical dance circles. She is called the *nartaki*, dancer—a rather generic name for such a consequential character. Her image can be found in the Udaygiri–Khandagiri rock caves, some miles outside Bhubaneshwar, an ancient city of temples and Odisha's modern capital since 1948. The Udaygiri monuments, dating back to the first century BCE, appear to contain the earliest representation of a dance form connected to contemporary Odissi, proving its antique

FIGURE 1.4. A court scene of dancers and musicians entertaining the Rani (Queen). The caves are her namesake. Bhubaneshwar, Odisha, 7 February 2008.

provenance.³² In a series of magnificent panels and friezes in the Ranigumpha (Queen's Cave), dancers and musicians are shown displaying their art at a royal court, cavorting outside around a tree, under the leafy umbrella of its shade, and performing a duet to the beat of drums and the melody of stringed instruments. Crowded close together in these tableaux, the exuberance of these dancing bodies resonates through rock. The archetypal view is held by Kapila Vatsyayan, who suggests: 'Orissa may well claim to be the earliest classical Indian dance style on the basis of archeological evidence [. . .] certainly these caves are the first specimens of a dance scene with full orchestration found in sculptures of the historical period.' The Udaygiri monuments, she writes, 'are the first records in stone' of that era (1997: 49).

32 Several dance scholars have suggested this; see, for example, Fabri (1974); Khokar (1984: 175); Vatsyayan (1974: 34); Kothari (1990:1); and Gauhar (2007: 35), among others. More than one has suggested the dances depicted in the Ranigumpha resemble the Odra-Magadhi form listed in the *Natyashastra*, dated to the same period or shortly thereafter.

FIGURE 1.5. A relief of dancers revelling in a pastoral setting at Ranigumpha. Bhubaneshwar, Odisha, 7 February 2008. Photograph by the author.

The appearance of dance in the Ranigumpha is not a total mystery, thanks to the revealing Hathigumpha (Elephant's Cave) inscription found in an adjacent cavern, indicating that these elaborate rock-cut pavilions were originally built by the Jain king Kharavela of Kalinga to shelter wandering Jain monks.[33] Considered important in the history of India as one of the oldest surviving royal inscriptions, it provides a glimpse of Odisha as an autonomous region under a Jain monarch. Previously, Odisha had come into the orbit of Ashoka's vast empire in the third century BCE during the famous battle of Kalinga, and achieved liberation only after the decline of the Mauryans.[34] Kharavela presided over a

33 Kharavela ruled Kalinga around the second half of the first century BCE.

34 Historians of India generally agree the Mauryan dynasty was responsible for creating India's first empire. The last of the Mauryans, Emperor Ashoka, ruled from the central region of Magadha in a city identified with modern-day Patna in the state of Bihar. Ashoka famously converted from Hinduism to Buddhism as a gesture of profound remorse after witnessing the carnage his army unleashed in the bloody battle of Kalinga in 261 BCE. Renouncing

brief era of Kalinga's independence and oversaw the expansion of
its boundaries, largely through military campaigns, and released
the region from Magadhan rule.[35]

The Hathigumpha inscription is one of the most intriguing
documents available in Indian historiography. Because it 'permits
of alternative readings,' the interpretation of the epigraph has
long been the subject of controversy and conjecture, and several
scholars have devoted years to deciphering its precise meanings

---

violence, Ashoka then propagated the Buddhist message of dhamma, or the
righteous path, through rock inscriptions and his religious emissaries, while
espousing a stance of respect for all other faiths. Ashoka is often hailed as
India's first true 'secularist,' an honour that has to do with the unique valences
of secularism in India. Rather than suggesting the separation of religion and
state, such that religious expression occurs in privatized space, secularism
alludes to the aspiration of treating all major faiths equally in the public
sphere. In epochal terms, the Mauryan period also ushered in the first great
challenge to Vedic supremacy. The beginnings of Odishan history, in the
conventional sense, are attributed to the Ashokan era. For more on Indian
approaches to secularism, see Bhargava (1994, 2005); Sen (2005); Thapar
(2000b, 2002); Vanita (2002a); and Sen (2005).

35 After Kharavela, little is documented about the cultural life of Odisha until
the later part of the first millenium. Jainism declined in the region, experiencing
a brief revival several centuries later. N. K. Sahu suggests this was due to the
rise of Puranic religions from the first to tenth centuries CE, along with 'the collapse of commercial activities of the trading communities who were its chief
patrons on the eastern coast' (1996: 627). Further, Buddhism, another heterodox tradition, enjoyed an ascending profile in Odisha and gradually edged out
Jainism in popularity and influence. Diminishing royal patronage eventually
sealed Jainism's status as a minor faith in the Odishan religious landscape until
its resurgence in the eighth century CE. Ultimately, however, historians agree it
was the perceived or actual dilution of Jain practice that led to its disappearance
from Odisha; after assimilating several elements of the Brahmanical faith into
its own structures of worship, Jainism couldn't sustain enough of a distinction
from the Hindu order to justify its existence as a separate tradition (635). However, Jains continued to thrive largely in Delhi and western India—Rajasthan,
Gujarat, and parts of Maharashtra. Today they make up a small but prominent
religious community, numbering 4,200,000, accounting for less than 1 per
cent of the total Indian population; see Census of India 2010. On 20 January
2014, Jains were given minority status by the central government.

(Thapar 2002: 211).[36] Composed in the Prakrit language and rendered in Brahmi script, the inscription is a 17-line paean to Kharavela's deeds and accomplishments.[37] Romila Thapar suggests that the text's importance can be attributed to its status as one of 'the early biographical sketches of a king,' one which 'represents the beginnings of a style of royal eulogy' (ibid.). B. M. Barua adds that its significance 'lies in the fact that up till now there is no other record which can vie with it in antiquity as an epigraph in the ancient kingdom of Kalinga set up by its own independent king' (1938: 260), a statement which still holds true today.

The Hathigumpha inscription offers a précis of significant events in Kharavela's life and also contains a tribute to Jain saints. It indicates the king belongs to the Chedi dynasty, which replaced the Mauryans after their empire disintegrated and Kalinga once again proclaimed its sovereignty. It speaks of Kharavela's triumphal reclamation of a Jain image stolen by a Magadhan monarch whose descendants he claims to have easily vanquished. Additionally, the engraving takes note of Kharavela's unusual solicitude towards his subjects.[38]

The fifth, sixteenth and seventeenth lines are of special import for scholars of performance: the fifth speaks of Kharavela arranging

36 See note 41 for a full list of such scholars who have debated the meanings and interpretations of the inscription since the last century, when it was first mentioned by Andrew Stirling in 1825. See Appendix B for the full English translation, adapted from R. D. Banerji and K. P. Jayaswal, 'The Hathigumpha Inscription of Kharavela', *Epigraphia Indica, Volume 20* (1929–30): 71–89. This is considered the authoritative translation in the literature on the inscription, and provides the basis of most of the commentaries and modifications by successive scholars.

37 Prakrit was the vernacular language of the time, and used widely by communities of Buddhists and Jains to communicate with a range of social groups. Sanskrit was carefully guarded as the 'language of the gods'. In its exclusivity, it was less accessible to the public, restricted to study by Brahmans and select Kshatriyas, who sat at the apex of the caste system in the Vedic Brahmanical system. Prakrit then became the language of the heterodox groups who challenged Vedic authority.

38 See lines 3, 9 and 17 of the epigraph on this point.

spectacles of dance, acrobatics and music which turned the whole city into a site of revelry and celebratory play in the third year of his reign; the sixteenth and seventeenth reaffirm the king's position as patron and preserver of the arts while avowing his religious orientation. An English transliteration of the fifth line reads: *Tatiye puna vase / Gamdhava-vedha-budho dapa-nata-gita-vadita-samdamsanahi usava-samaja-karapanahi cha kidapayati nagarim* (Banerji and Jayaswal 1929–30: 79). This translates into: 'Again, in the third year [of his reign] / [His Majesty], who was well-versed in the science of music, caused the capital to be entertained by the display of combats, dancing, singing, and instrumental music, and by the arrangement made for festivities and convivial gatherings.'[39] Kharavela is described as having restored Tauryatrika, or three performance forms, alluding to dance, instrumental music and songs—artistic endeavours that were apparently suppressed by the previous Mauryan regime (D. B. Mishra 2006: 23).

---

39 I have provided this translation after comparing and combining elements, verbatim, from three sources: R. D. Banerji and K. P. Jayaswal (1933: 87); the commentary on this text by B. M. Barua (1938: 275); and D. B. Mishra (2006: 22). I have relied mostly on the Barua translation as it offers the smoothest reading of the original script. Banerji and Jayaswal's text, while the most accurate, is also the most literal (see Appendix B). Important individual components of the inscription based on translations by Rajendra Lal Mitra (2007: 16–26), and D. B. Mishra (2006), are as follows: *Gandhava-veda-budha*: 'well-versed (*budha*) in the art (*veda*, Sanskrit *vidya*) of music' (*gandhava*); *dapa-nata-gita-vadita*: acrobatics (*dapa*), dance (*nata*), song (*gita*), musical instruments (*vadita*); *samdasanahi* (Sanskrit *sandarsanhara*): 'worthy of being beheld'; *usava* (Sanskrit *Utsava*), entertainment or festivals, *samaja*: social gathering; *kidapayati* (Sanskrit *kridayati*): 'causes to be played', *nagarim*: 'in the capital city'. The word *dapa* is a source of some pondering. While Banerji and Jayaswal have not ventured to give a translation, leaving it as it is, they suggest its connection to dance, theatre, and 'antics', B. M. Barua calls it 'combat' (1938: 275) while Ragini Devi has interpreted *dapa-nata* and *vadita* to mean 'forceful' and 'lyrical' dances, basically equivalents to the *tandava* (vigorous) and *lasya* (soft) characterizations of dance set out in the *Natyashastra*. See Ragini Devi (2002: 138). D. N. Patnaik and Mishra agree that *dapa* in fact means 'acrobatics' (see D. N. Patnaik 2006). For more commentaries on the history of the inscription and to compare various transliterations/translations, see Romila Thapar (2002: 211–13) and K. C. Panigrahi (1981: 17–28).

Dance and Politics

What I find most intriguing about this inscription is its juxta-position of wildly disparate themes: the king's magnanimity, his religious devotion, the well-being of his subjects, his military conquests, his dedication to social harmony, realized through the performing arts—elements that appear to have held equal weight and importance in the monarch's biography. The encomium devotes several passages to describing the king's own artistic endeavours, reserving a whole line to record his munificence in arranging performances for his subjects. I infer from this emphasis that the arts visibly served a political purpose—they were taken seriously enough to warrant mention in a monument designed to stand as a record of the king's honorific achievements. The mention is neither casual nor incidental, and has been included deliberately as an index of the king's own aesthetic sensibilities while giving a glimpse into the connections between statecraft and stagecraft.

At the Udaygiri caves, the intimate relationship between dance and the state is, through inscription and relief, literally carved in stone. Taking the dance sculptures and epigraph together, it seems that performance held a privileged position in relation to the state. This association of dance with power connects to the idea of dance as a spatializing art, a symbolic and material analogy for the actual expansionist ambitions of kings.[40] I argue that dance was not just a way for the royal authorities to demonstrate their benevolence, sophistication and cultivation but also a mode of displaying royal authority by means of 'conquering' and 'subjugating' space. That dance is mentioned in concert with religious activity and military

40 I borrow here from James Ferguson and Akhil Gupta's influential idea of the 'spatializing state' (2002). Noting that states 'are not simply functional bureaucractic apparatuses, but powerful sites of symbolic and cultural repre-sentations,' they go on to argue that 'states represent themselves as reified entitites with particular *spatial* properties [. . .] By doing so, they help to secure their legitimacy, to naturalize their authority, and to represent themselves as superior to, and encompassing of, other institutions and centers of power' (981–2). It's abundantly clear that Kharavela engaging in such a politics of spatialization by engaging dance as one mode of expressing his power.

exploits—both forms of monarchical power—lends credence to this claim. At Udaygiri, images of dance are as central as images of royal processions.

That dance in specific features prominently both in the Hathigumpha inscription and in the surrounding Ranigumpha reliefs suggests that it held an important place in the cultural life of Odisha in Kharavela's time. But to understand the context of dance in this period, we need to understand the commonalities and contrasts between Jain and Hindu approaches to art. If indeed the relics at Udaygiri contain the first known representations of Odissi, then we need to consider the specific world these relics inhabited, and the meanings of dance in that world. Mandakranta Bose's critical work on early Jain ideas of performance is crucial here. She considers the significance of the *Rajaprasniya Sutra* in particular, a Jain text collated by Bhadrabahu and dated to *c.*fourth century BCE, possibly predating the *Natyashastra*, in which are detailed 32 varieties of *natyavidhis* ('dance dramas or musical plays') performed by *devakumaras* and *devakumaris* (male and female dancers in the Jain tradition) and depicting episodes of Mahavira's life (2001: 83, 90–3, 96). The *Rajaprasniya Sutra* is, then, 'an important record as much of the cultural tradition of Jainas as of a particular phase in the evolution of the performing arts of India' (83). Dance is additionally a subject of concern in other related literature, like the *Nisitha Bhasya, Jnatadharmakatha* and *Rayapaseniyasutta* which point to its dual purposes as entertainment and veneration in the period of antiquity (93–4, 96).[41]

---

41 Another text of interest here is the *Dattilam*, a treatise dedicated to explicating the *gandharva* concept and practice, connected to the *purvaranga* (a play's prologue) which incorporated musical and dance performances (Dattila 1988: *xii*; Bharatmuni 2007). The *Natyashastra* also addressed *gandharva* as a subject, although its sources are unknown. Some speculate that its authors may have borrowed insights from the *Dattilam*. However, this guess is complicated by the difficulty of assigning accurate dates to either text; both are placed somewhere between the first century BCE and first to second century CE (Dattila 1970: 2; Dattila 1988: *xiv*). In his *Dattilam* translation, Mukund Lath explains that it might predate the *Natyashastra*, or be contemporaneous to it; at any rate, 'the Dattilam cannot post-date the Natyasastra by

Was there any correlation between these early Jain texts and traditions, and the traces of dance found at Udaygiri? This is a question which remains to be explored, and is outside the scope of my project. Instead, I offer a series of meditations on the openings that might be created for a speculative history of Odissi by contemplating the content of the Hathigumpha epigraph and Ranigumpha dance representations.

Jainism in Odisha's History

The Hathigumpha inscription states that in the thirteenth year of his reign, King Kharavela excavated the rock shelter at Udaygiri as a resting place for itinerant Jain monks, undertaking considerable expense to make it a place that would elicit the delight of weary travellers through its myriad ornamental elements—decorative pillars, sculptural depictions of the performing arts and the creation of a beautifully appointed courtyard, allowing the ascetics to sleep and linger in the inviting surrounds. The Jains, despite their austerities, used the rich aesthetic milieu promoted by the king, reconciling it with the belief that aestheticizing the space would advance their spiritual experience (Barua 1938: 280–1). This created an interesting paradox of providing ascetics with a luxurious setting, but, in the prevailing Jain worldview, beautification and beatification were conceptually aligned (Dehejia 2009).

Kharavela's piety was not directed solely at Jains—the inscription ends with a remarkable passage asserting his respect for all faiths, and characterizes Kharavela as unusually liberal in his religious approach, calling him *sava-pasanda-pujako-savadevay-atana-sankar-karako* or 'the repairer of all abodes of the gods, the worshipper of all sects, accomplished by virtue of the possession

---

any significant margin' (1988: *xiii*). Thus the questions of whether the *Dattilam* influenced the *Natyashastra*, or vice versa, remains open. For other notable ancient texts that mention dance, pre-*Natyashastra*, the Vedas include several references to entertainment culture, and grammarian Panini in his *Ashtadhyayi* refers to two texts on performance: the *Nata-Sutra* of Shilalin, and Krishasva (Panini 1891–98: IV.3.110, 111).

of certain special qualities' (Barua 1938: 282). This passage mirrors the emperor Ashoka's views; it resembles the language of his rock edicts at Dhauli, near Hathigumpha. Possibly Kharavela was attempting to leave a similar legacy by continuing Ashoka's generous policies of embracing an egalitarian approach to various expressions of the sacred (Thapar 2002: 211).

Both Ashoka and Kharavela seem to have put this notion of pluralism into practice and are celebrated historical figures partly for this reason (Panigrahi 1981: 19; Sen 2005). Here we see early evidence of a practice of this peculiarly Indian philosophy, one that doesn't necessarily separate religion and politics nor make religion absent from the public sphere but, rather, declares its theoretical intent to treat all religious groups equally (Bhargava 2005). This expression of a pluralist ideal persists rhetorically in the present as an aspiration of the Indian state, even as it is constantly destabilized, constantly in crisis and constantly redefined. As many scholars have argued, the basic tenets of such a pluralist model can be traced to the pre-Christian era, and the Hathigumpha inscription provides impressive support for this claim.[42] It is possible that Kharavela's statement is designed to strategically camouflage a sectarian bias, although this seems highly unlikely, given that missives about defeating religious rivals at the time were far more common and proved the leader's allegiance to a single professed faith. In the eyes of their subjects, such communal expressions would generally have been received as an important indication of religious loyalty and increased kingly prestige. In other words, Kharavela could not hope to extract major political benefits from announcing his tolerant and generous outlook and appears to have been a genuine believer in the pluralist model, a perspective that seems to dovetail with broader Jain ethics of venerating other belief systems (Panigrahi 1981: 19).

---

42 On the history of Indian ideas of religious pluralism, see Rajeev Bhargava (1995, 2005, 2006); Amartya Sen (2005); Romila Thapar in Anuradha Needham and Rajeshwari Sunder Rajan (2007). For critiques of Indian secularism and religious fundamentalism, see Aijaz Ahmad (1999, 2000); Madhu Kishwar (2002); and Angana P. Chatterji (2009).

Kharavela's egalitarian approach is all the more interesting given the tensions and hostilities that marked encounters between orthodox Vedic sects, who enjoyed domination in other regions outside Odisha, and the heterodox Jain community. Jainism emerged in India around the sixth century BCE as a dissenting movement against the dominant Vedic religion, as part of the Shramanic (ascetic) orders, coinciding with the beginnings of Buddhism. Shramanic traditions underscore individual austerity and ethical living as modes of gaining spiritual truth and nirvana, rather than relying on the performance of elaborate rituals mediated by Brahman priests. This orientation is reflected in the sect's very name—Jain is a modification of *jina*, meaning 'conqueror,' and alludes to the saint Mahavira as well as other prophets of the order or tirthankars, revered for achieving victory in the spiritual realm through their demanding physical and metaphysical disciplines (Basham 1967: 287–96; Shah 1998; von Glasenapp 1999).

Jainism was born as an oppositional discourse to the basic tenets of Vedic thought. In contrast to the Brahmanic worldview, Jainism proselytized on the basis of universal admission, preaching against enforced hierarchies; people from any social rank or origin could join the order. This was a crucial distinction, as Jains advanced a philosophical position that ultimately meant spiritual liberation for all, not only for dominant elites. The idea of spirituality was universalized as well—Jains believe the soul is not the sole property of humans but can be extended to other species, in addition to entities usually considered inanimate, like fire and water, which they perceived as full of essential, life-sustaining energies. Out of respect for all sentient beings, Jains advocated vegetarianism and abided by a strict doctrine of non-harm (ahimsa). They openly opposed animal sacrifice, once a central part of Vedic ritual.[43]

---

43 Animal sacrifices were believed to consolidate royal power and propitiate goddesses and gods, the Ashwamedha Yagna horse killings and Rig Vedic cow sacrifice being two major instantiations. The 'sacred cow' is the enduring symbol of Hinduism. In early Vedic times, however, cow slaughter was not forbidden and there was no injunction against eating beef. On rituals involving cows in sacrifices, see, for instance, the sacred scriptures of the *Rig*

Jain ethical and belief systems were similar, though not identical, to those of the Buddhists. And like Buddhism, Jainism's egalitarianism, non-violence and universalist doctrine attracted a wide following across India, especially in Odisha, from the sixth century BCE onwards. This is not surprising, given the great variety of social groups populating the region who were looking to subvert the power of the dominant castes by exiting the Vedic caste system and converting en masse to the heterodox orders. According to myth, the great Jina, Mahavira, came to preach in Odisha, another reason for its early popularity there.[44]

Given the pervasive nature of caste and its promiscuous hold, Jainism and Buddhism managed to modify the social system to an appreciable extent. It is against this complex social background that the first representations of dance in Odissa emerged.

Images of Odissi's Antiquity

Whether the images at Udaygiri faithfully represent or correspond to what we call Odissi today is, of course, unknowable. One strong possibility that needs to be entertained is that these images are not actually connected to Odissi at all, that the link between the image and the dance is wholly fabricated, that it has been invented to invest the dance form with an antiquity it never had. The Udaygiri images could be stylized renderings of local dances instead. Kapila Vatsyayan (1997), D. N. Patnaik (2006) and other dance scholars have correlated some of the Udaygiri body postures with those of

---

Veda (1896: VIII.43.11) in which it is said: 'Let us serve Agni with our hymns, Disposer, fed on ox and cow/ Who bears the Soma on his back'. The embrace of vegetarianism among Brahmans and the abhorrence of cow-killings became widespread after the ascent of Shramanic sects; it was under their influence that animal sacrifice and meat-eating were prohibited especially for orthodox upper castes. These beliefs were adopted widely by Hindus over time and many today continue to abide by them.

44 As scholars have noted, Jainism changed over time and, in the medieval period, became institutionalized while integrating elements of caste (see Chanchreek and Jain [2004] on this point). This is one of the reasons given for its declining popularity in Odisha at that time.

present-day Odissi, suggesting for example that Odissi's signature Chowk is portrayed in the caves, showing the dance's unbroken continuity. The truth of this is difficult to ascertain and remains speculative at best. And it may be the other way round: the modern inventors of Odissi modelled its *bhangis* on these ancient depictions.

Some of the Udaygiri *bhangis* and *mudras* may bear affinity to the techniques catalogued in the *Natyashastra*. Seeing that the treatise mentions Odra-Magadhi and Dakshinatya as two established dance styles (from Odra and Kalinga respectively—both areas connected to modern-day Odisha),[45] and seeing that the *Natyashastra* and Udaygiri images were perhaps contemporaneous (since the former is dated sometime between *c*.second century BCE–second century CE), a strong case can be made that the images portray a Shastric style of dance from the region (Bharatmuni 2007: 246–8). The *Natyashastra* identified four principal styles—classified as verbal (*bharati*), grand (*sattvati*), graceful (*kaisiki*), and violent (*arabhati*)—each corresponding, in isolated or combinatory form, with a specific region. The Dakshinatya style of the South featured 'an abundance of the Graceful (*kaisiki*) Style, and clever and graceful gestures' and Odra-Magadhi from the East was marked by both *bharati* and *kaisiki* qualities (Bharatmuni 2007: 247–8). Specifications for entering the stage also differ for each type: from the right in Dakshinatya, from the left in Odra-Magadhi (ibid.: 249). Despite the overlapping geographies of Odisha historically conjured by the two genres, most dance histories favour Odra-Magadhi as the type correlated with Odissi. '[T]he tradition codified in the *Natyashastra* took cognisance of the particular regional style known in eastern India' called Odra-Magadha, 'which can be identified as the earliest precursor of the present Orissi,' asserts Kapila Vatsyayan (1974: 34).

A popular narrative claims the Udaygiri cave images prove Odissi's status as India's oldest dance form and attest to its durability in the present. D. N. Patnaik, who pioneered the study of Odissi,

---

45 Adya Rangacharya mentions the same point in his *Natyashastra* translation, that Dakshinatya and Odramagadhi both refer to dance in Odisha (Bharatmuni 1996: 113).

writes: 'These representations of dancers [. . .] have been inter-preted by scholars as the earliest representation of human beings dancing in our country. If this be so, Odisha furnishes the earliest evidence of dance in India' (1990: 8–12). The idea that Odisha (and therefore, Odissi) has the 'most ancient' classical dance of India is evoked regularly in popular histories of the form, in tourist litera-ture, at festivals, on the internet and among the worldwide comu-nity of Odissi scholars, critics, gurus, choreographers, performers and audiences.

Contrary to this chorus of claims, there is contesting evidence displacing the notion of the Udaygiri caves being the earliest depictions of Indian dance. An earlier sculpting is that of a 'the dancing girl', one hand resting on her waist, standing nude in a stylized posture. Currently on display in the National Museum in Delhi, the figure is from Mohenjodaro, dated to c.2500 BCE, and so presumably precedes the Udaygiri *nartaki* by at least two millennia (that is, if we accept her status as a dancer at all). Very little is known about dance in the intervening years, and nothing is known about Mohenjadoro movement vocabulary or how it was socially regarded, but the very existence of this much-celebrated bronze figure and its latent dance histories naturally challenges narratives in which Odissi can stake a claim as the 'oldest' Indian classical dance based on its purported performance remains.

The impulse to infuse Odissi dance with antiquity speaks to a desire, simultaneously affective and political, to create an unbreakable line between the tenses of past and present, threading them together seamlessly and lending an historical weight to contemporary practice. I have often surrendered to this impulse myself, and found that the question of truth or illusion remains less important than pondering the reasons for sustaining such different narratives: some mystical, some mythical, some empirical, some fictive, some explicitly ideological, some implicitly so. All poesis. Every analysis, every rationale, every hermeneutic act, is moored in a specific worldview and thus assumes validity in its own way, coexisting with a host of confluent or conflicting perspectives (White 1990, 2010). To deny the status of 'truth' to certain claims potentially denies the force of the multiple histories in which dance is entangled. At the same time, these divergent framings are never innocent or neutral; understanding each position in the context of the perspective, philosophy or agenda to which it is linked enables an appreciation of how interpretations of culture are ineluctably caught up in constellations of power.

Initially, I saw the Udaygiri–Khandagiri caves on my first visit to Odisha in the summer of 1991 while travelling through the state with my guru, Muralidhar Majhi, and his family. Before embarking on the tour, I had eagerly read about Odissi and learned as much about its history as I could, so I was awestruck when I finally saw the Ranigumpha reliefs and took in their status, without question, as the ancient traces of my art. I wanted to feel a connection between the dance I performed and the images preserved in those carvings. For me, they held the enchantments of history and silence, ambivalence and mystery. On my second visit to Udaygiri—years later in 2008—I was curious to see whether these famous dancers could indeed be connected to Odissi, looking at them through new eyes, subjecting them to a critical gaze. Seeing them again only resurrected the romance. Undoubtedly, there is something thrilling and humbling in seeing the possibility of the permanence of a form, however it has changed through the centuries, and finding a small piece of a collective past in which you may be intimately embedded. Implicated? Linking a current practice to a past laces it with significance. At the same time, closely attending to the images, to the enunciations of stone, opens up the potential for an alternative dance history.

We will never know for certain if the Ranigumpha dances are linked to Odissi or its antecedents. But we need to consider the context of the images and what they reveal. If we accept that these are indeed depictions of Odra-Magadhi, then what this means for the story of Odissi needs to be fully explored, its insinuations in history fully excavated. And if we do not accept that thread, then it involves choosing different routes: we need to revisit Odissi's position as an ancient art, or appraise other evidence closely in order to make a fine-grained argument about the correspondences between Odra-Magadhi and Odissi today.

Udaygiri: City and Stage

The Ranigumpha images attest to the worldly, non-religious aspects of dance. The images act partly as illustrations of Kharavela's putative accomplishments, inscribed around the corner at Hathi-gumpha. The sites of performance shown in the images are telling. Dancers and musicians perform for the king and queen in a royal court; a solo *narthaki* moves on a small stage; an ensemble of dancers move together in a pastoral setting. No deities are visible in these representations. In their vivacious movements, the dancers make graceful patterns with their bodies which appear to be in the mode of *nritta*; there is no pronounced religious iconog-raphy in their gestures.[46] Instead, as Thapar writes, 'attributes of royalty such as conquest, patronage, and the welfare of subjects are accentuated, with royalty being emphasized in the sculptures and reliefs in the surrounding caves' (2002: 213).

Read in concert with the Hathigumpha inscription, the images show that, under the reign of the Jain king, dance may have func-tioned as a symbol of royal power. Perhaps it embraced the purpose of promoting sociality and engendering cultural capital. In the process, it strengthened the monarchy and sealed the position of the king as one possessed of profound elegance and taste. Looking at the dancing images correlated with the inscription, then, we can see that dance under Kharavela engendered sparse religious meanings but embodied clear areligious political purposes.

D. B. Mishra points out that 'the Hathigumpha inscription provides us with a fairly good idea about the practice, nature and

---

46 The *Natyashastra* and *Shilpa Shastra* denote the ways in which deities should be represented in danced and figural representations, through *mudras* and *hastas*, specific body positions, and *bhavas*, moods or facial expressions (Dehejia 1979; Bharatmuni 2007; Mohanty Hejmadi and Hejmadi Patnaik 2007). Many of the Jain conventions of representation in dance and drama followed or complemented Hindu aesthetics (M. Bose 2001). These icono-graphic gestures are absent in the Ranigumpha caves.

development of music, dance, and dramaturgy' (2006: 22). One of Kharavela's aims was to set himself apart from his predecessors by resurrecting the arts of the region, says Mishra, and the inscription lays emphasis on the king's identity as an aesthete, erudite in musical matters (*Gandharva-veda*), thus linking his proficiency and passion to his patronage.[47] Certainly, there is nothing in the Hathigumpha inscription to suggest that dance had assumed a specifically religious character at this stage, purely intended to stir the devotional sentiments of the audience, or even that the status of dance was closely tied to ritualization. They do, however, show that dance enjoyed a public life outside the context of Hindu worship.

This brings us to the point that in Kharavela's time, religion did not have an autonomous status but was interwoven with other realms of life; thus, if there was a theological intent behind the images, it would have overlapped with other transparently articulated aims linked to aesthetic refinement, conviviality, popular entertainment and political consolidation. However, the carvings do not appear to express a set of explicit religious values.

Some nationalist historians have called Kharavela the greatest king of Odisha and consider his rule particularly exemplary, as Kalinga recovered its sovereignty under his reign. His kingdom was expansive, stretching from central India into the eastern peninsula. From the epigraphic and historical evidence that survives, it seems appropriate to speculate that just as Odisha was asserting its independence politically, culturally Kharavala's rule enabled the Kalingans to explore local customs and practices suppressed by previous rulers and to develop new artistic traditions or recover older forms. [48]

---

47 D. N. Patnaik supports Mishra's view: 'It is believed that [Kharavela] revived the cultural trends of ancient Kalinga in dance, song and instrumental music and by his sincere patronage immensely contributed to the development of these performing arts' (1990: 9).

48 To be clear, I do not intend to suggest that Odissi began at this point—this is impossible to know—but I wish to emphasize that if we choose to accept the evidence discussed by other dance scholars as legitimate, and believe that

From the inscription, it seems that the king arranged dance performances to delight his subjects and enhance his own image as a refined and benevolent monarch. Dance seems to be presented for pure enjoyment, as a social activity that binds together the polity. It consolidates royal power by creating an atmosphere of goodwill between the people and the monarch, underscoring the king's beneficence and increasing popular trust in the ruling political institution.

The dancing body, migrating through space, further illustrates the spatializing power of performance, connecting the king to his territory and illuminating his position of dominance. The engravings give the impression that Kharavela staged a cornucopia of performances, converting the urban milieu into a site of spectacle; the whole city became a stage for performances of dance, music and monarchical authority, projections of royal charisma, a spatialization of aesthetic performance that amplified both the king's auspiciousness and authority.

Ideals of Governance—'King Is State'

The Hathigumpha inscriptions and Ranigumpha images offer a small glimpse into the early cultural and social life in Odisha. While it is difficult to paint a complete picture of the society over which Kharavela ruled, a partial one does emerge from the interpretation of extant evidence. Placed in the context of broader Indian history, they give a sense of the prevailing values at the time, especially regarding the relationship between dance and the state.

Like other regions in the subcontinent, the Odishan state developed and changed according to the types of political organization dominant in a specific period. It emerged from a lineage-based form of rule (where collective decision-making by representatives of families and households was the norm), morphing into a system

it convincingly points to a shared aesthetic between the dance depicted at Udaygiri, Odra-Magadhi and contemporary Odissi, then its patronage by and development under a Jain monarch and the possible imprint of Shramanic influences on the form cannot be ignored.

of chieftainship (where authority resided in a single post), eventually leading to a system of hereditary monarchy based on the idea of divine kingship, well-established by Kharavela's time.[49] These newer state formations never wholly succeeded in supplanting the pre-existing systems, and so, instead, they gradually incorporated them into their structures while preserving their essential features at the local levels (Mohanty 2002). This was done openly in order to allow the state to establish its legitimacy and retain the support of a wide range of constituents in its quest to centralize power.

This 'integrative' model of the state required, as in any hegemony, the constant negotiation of power between the leadership and the people (Panda 1995; Kulke 2006). Newer state systems were superimposed onto the preceding ones, only to be dissolved or changed in the light of fresh political exigencies, in an incremental dance of centripetal and centrifugal movement over time. This layered political model proved both resilient and relevant; to this day in Odisha, lineage-based systems co-exist with community-based, regional, and national models of governance (see Kulke 2006 and Tanabe 2006).

Ancient Jain principles of government adhered largely to those enshrined in Kautilya's *Arthashastra* (*c*.fourth century BCE). Penned as a basically secular text on the science of statecraft, the *Arthashastra* sets out strategems for rulers to attain power within the borders of their territory, and win wars against foreign powers beyond. It propounds the belief that the 'king is state:' the total identification of the monarch with the land, the populace and the apparatus of authority—the entire body politic—is expressed in this formulation, accentuating his supreme position of command (Kautilya 1976).

As a political text, the *Arthashastra* served as a handbook for rulers interested in securing and protecting their status, including Jain aspirants to the throne. 'It is in accordance with its royal origin when the political philosophy of Jainas equates the governance

---

49 See John W. Spellman (1964); A. L. Basham (1967: 83–8); Romila Thapar (2002: 211); and Basanta Kumar Mallik (2004).

completely with the king,' states Helmuth von Glasenapp.⁵⁰ It
appears that Jain kings like Kharavela upheld principles of rule
aligned with the *Arthashastra* and followed its doctrines. Shyam
Singh Shashi provides further insight into the role of the Jain
monarch: 'The king was always surrounded by exceptional pomp
and decorum. [. . . He] was the sovereign head in performing the
military, judicial, legislative, and executive functions of the State.
[. . .] The laws of the country were formulated by the king in accordance with the customs of the land' (1996: 543). The concept of
'king-as-state' found justification here, and extended to theological
affairs as well.⁵¹

Jainism had taken root in Odisha very early in its history and
rose as the favoured faith under Kharavela's rule, though not to
the exclusion of other groups. As Shashi explains, 'It was firmly
believed that the subjects "follow the king in every matter including
religion." It may, however, be said that leaving aside a few exceptions, the kings of this age were not sectarians or hostile to religions
other than their own' (ibid.: 544). While welcoming diverging
beliefs into the fold of his kingdom, Kharavela did of course nurture
his own, with Jainism sanctioned as the state religion.⁵²

Worship of the *jinas*, the protection of temples and ensuring
the welfare of saints and monks were also duties of the broader
Jain community, of which the king was the head. Shashi elaborates
on this ideal of the Jain ruler as one

---

50 In von Glasenapp's analysis, '[li]ke political science, [the] jurisprudence of
Jainas also agrees with the one of the Hindus in its main features' (1999: 364).

51 More research needs to be done on the specific manifestation of divine
kingship in the Jain context. Jainism is often considered an atheist movement;
however, as John Cort points out, the tradition acknowledged deities from the
Hindu pantheon as sacred figures in addition to their own *tirthankars*, or the
enlightened ones, and Jinas, the ones who have conquered desire, and are
'collectively [. . .] the God of the Jains' (2001: 23).

52 N. K. Sahu argues 'the involvement of the royal personnel activity acceler-
ated and helped the [Jain] faith to secure a prime and predominate position
in the religious history of Odisha just before the closing of the pre-Christian
era' (1996: 626).

responsible for the overall social, cultural and moral well-being of his subjects. Very often we find the kings . . . arranging various festivals and also taking a lively part in the social functions . . . It can thus be visualized that the duties and functions of the king were as varied as his powers, and that a high moral and spiritual standard must have been expected of him (ibid.).

Thus, one of the characteristics of a good and ethical monarch is that he supports the arts, and conducts his duties by arranging performances and spectacles for public consumption.

This is an idea congruent with the philosophy of the *Natyashastra* as well. The sage Bharatmuni, attributed as its author, makes mention of the monarch's orchestration of performance as an expression of philanthropy, of virtuous rulership: 'Of all duties of the king, this has been proclaimed as possessing the best result (*mahaphala*). Of all kinds of charities, allowing people to enjoy a dramatic show without payment, has been praised most' (2007: 237). 'The king who is well-educated and disciplined in sciences [*shastras*], and bent on doing good to all people will enjoy the earth unopposed,' declares Kautilya (1976: 10). Judging from the historical evidence, it seems that Kharavela fulfilled his obligations concerning the ideal behaviour of a king, as set out in the Jain literature as well as the *Arthashastra*, aesthetic treatises, and other sources; the execution of performance was contiguous with the execution of overall royal responsibility, a sign of largesse and leadership.

Dance served as an instrument of hegemony—as one of the modes of actualizing the 'social, cultural and moral well-being' of the kingdom's populace (Shashi 1996: 544). Under Kharavela's rule, dance had had the translucent purpose of establishing links between elites and commoners, of establishing important social bonds that were aimed at stabilizing relations between the king and his polity, supporting his vision of social unity and reiterating his personal authority. The king-as-state philosophy worked as analogy by linking together the body of the monarch, the body of the people and the body of the territory. Dance acted to symbolize and spatialize the matrix of these relations, displaying the unified body of the kingdom and its power.

Circling Back to Udaygiri, Again

Returning to the scene at Udaygiri: the relationship between dance and the state is made tangible and visible by the Hathigumpha inscription and Ranigumpha reliefs. Judging from the text and images, no overtly religious meaning is intended, assigned or ascribed. The cave sculptures were commissioned by an avowedly pluralist Jain king, and they depict court scenes and bucolic settings—not the surrounds of a temple.[53] The dancers are not shown performing any religious duty in service to a deity. Apparently revelling in the presence of mortal rather than divine beings, they assume gestures and positions that correspond to 'worldly' movements and eschew the purely religious context, instead using the formal vocabulary of *nritta*.

The positioning of the dancers depicted in the Ranigumpha caves corresponds to broader sensibilities about performance in this specific historical situation. Dance at the time was an activity attached to a variety of venues: courts, festivals, public stages, private salons and religious establishments. A class of professional dancers existed, and, significantly, were able to cross spatial boundaries and perform in different places without inviting stigma, as few distinctions or restrictions existed between groups of artists based

---

53 Anand Coomarswamy ventures that the Ranigumpha *narthaki* is shown dancing in a *natyashala*, or dance hall (cited in Kothari 1990: 93). It is quite likely that the cave sculptures portray dances on a theatrical stage specially built for the purpose of performance. This practice of setting up a temporary stage was common even in the time of the *Natyashastra*, and into the early millennium until more durable materials for temple-building emerged. Notably, formal dance pavilions, crafted as stone structures and designed to showcase devadasi performances for public festivals, started being built as permanent edifices on temple grounds in the 10th century in Odisha (see Donaldson 1981). I discuss the specifics of Odishan temples in Chapter 2.

on their affiliation with a particular institution.[54] In time, however, site-specific designations of dance came to be articulated in India, and regulations on religious choreography emerged in Odisha as the nascent devadasi system took root.

Dance was a highly gendered profession in the early era, performed mostly by female artists. Representations of dance in this period, as seen at Udaygiri, confirm this.[55] The *Arthashastra* (which predates Kharavela's reign) also spoke favorably of female artists and mentioned that they were to be protected under the king's patronage. A 'superintendent of prostitutes' oversaw the employment and maintenance of female courtesans selected for their 'beauty, youth, and accomplishments'; they doubled as artists, since the law decreed 'from the age of eight years, a prostitute shall hold musical performance before the king' (Kautilya 1976: 139). Further, instructors of courtesans and other performing artists were entitled to payment from the state's coffers. An entire system of government-based arts sponsorship had been set up, then, in antiquity. We see here the germination of the idea of 'extraordinary genders'—a specifically gendered category of artists, who held exceptional duties and roles compared to ordinary subjects, and whose dance activities were sanctioned by the state, though in a setting where performance served multiple purposes—sometimes as entertainment, sometimes as religious ritual, sometimes as an assertion of governmental power. The ability of artists to combine

54 Scholarship by Sukumari Bhattacharji (1987), Romila Thapar (2002) and Monika Saxena (2006), and sources such as the *Kama Sutra* and *Arthashastra* show, for instance, that a category of prostitutes called *ganikas* served as professional artists at temples and other sites. Others suggest that there was also a class of devadasis who did not overlap with ganikas, that they 'belonged' to the temples (little more than free-standing structures at this historical juncture) and that they enjoyed an elevated ritual status, unlike areligious performers (see Varadpande 1983: 51–6).

55 Manohar Laxman Varadpande finds that except for representations of the deities associated with dance (such as Shiva in his Nataraj form, and Ganesh in his dancing mood), prevailing images foreground women almost exclusively (1983: 45–76).

or shift their professional roles translated into the mobility of dance across various platforms at a time when there were scarce constraints on the performing arts in terms of their assignments to the domains of the sacred or profane.

That a broad ideal of performance prevailed at this time is corroborated by the Udaygiri monuments themselves. The Hathigumpha engravings make mention of *dapa* (or 'acrobatics') as well as *nata* ('dance'), and in parallel, the sculptures portray styles of movement that are at once vigorous and graceful (Devi 1990: 138; D. B. Mishra 2006). D. N. Patnaik reports:

> Among the elaborate forms of the sculptural representations and epigraphic records it is evident that there was a particular mode of dancing and professional female musicians and dancers were there to dance for the entertainment of kings, courtiers, and the general public. [. . .] In ancient Orissa there were specific caste-groups of Natas and Gandharvas whose profession it was to dance and sing (2006: 10).

These groups could perform in diverse situations, including *but not exclusively limited to* the context of the Hindu temple. As mentioned earlier, even the *Natyashastra* makes no mention of a religious mandate as such and speaks of performance as public art and spectacle, designed to address worldly themes as much as religious ones. And though there is recorded proof of devadasi systems in other regions like Madhya Pradesh and South India, there is sparse evidence of its formation in Odisha in this ancient moment.

A salient feature of ancient Odra-Magadhi dance is its democratized status as a *sovereign spectacle*—in a double sense. It departs from the general classical Hindu pattern where dance is linked to associative rituals, defined by Mundoli Narayanan as 'those conducted in connection with other practices or activities and [. . .] peformed primarily for the successful conduct and completion of those particular practices and activities' (2006: 143). Rather, in this historical juncture, it seems that dance events could be framed as 'self-contained rituals,' marked as 'independent, stand-alone practices in themselves, not associated with or dependent on any other activity, and conducted for some specific purpose that is built into the structure of ritual itself' (ibid.). If we extend Narayanan's argument, and shift the reading of ritual such that it is pried loose from its Hindu context, we can see how dance may have functioned as an areligious practice in Kharavela's time. In the Hathigumpha inscription and Ranigumpha reliefs, it appears that dance is produced and consumed as an autonomous form of artistic labour rather than being synechodically connected to religiosity. Another force unambiguously projects its importance instead—politics.

Dance as Political Dynamic

The monuments at Udaygiri offer proof of the coexistence of elements of the sacred and the profane in ancient times, dislodging the notion that dance in antiquity was shrouded in religiosity. The invocation of Odissi's primordial genesis by the community of scholars, artists and audiences today has a legible purpose, however: the dance's exalted identity emanates from its alleged appearance under the auspices of the sacred.

If we admit the premise that the Udaygiri monuments embody Odissi/Odra-Magadhi while symbolizing its myriad roots and sources, then we might meditate on what this insinuates about the relationship between dance, religion and politics in the public sphere.[56] I have drawn three conclusions from the Udaygiri evidence: specifically, that there is an analogous relationship between dance and governance; that religious indexes are conspicuously absent in the inscriptions and images related to dance; and that a Jain king committed to pluralism was responsible for producing the epigraph and reliefs.

The juxtaposition of these elements, arranged in my perspective, implies two directions of thought. Given the profuse images

---

56 As I hope my discussion makes clear, I do not mean to exclude religion from the realms of dance, state, or public sphere. However, for analytical clarity, I do wish to address them as separate domains with separate primary purposes.

of choreographed bodies in the Udaygiri caves, Kharavela's profes-
sions of faith and the content of the Hathigumpha inscription—
and given that the historicity of Odissi is based on these
representations—it can be argued that Jain political thought was
one of the influences that shaped the form. Indeed, we might go
as far as saying that the story of Odissi is *inseparable* from Jain
history and politics. It is equally plausible to suggest that the
images at Udaygiri attest to development of the style as neither
exclusively 'Hindu' nor religious but as a hybrid and secular art.
Both arguments counterpose the prevailing storyline associated
with Odissi, in which its telling is linked to a devotional trajectory
and follows this singular narrative arc. Udaygiri's eloquent dancing
bodies, evoked in writing and carving, articulate other possible
histories.

In the Ranigumpha caves, then, we see images perhaps linked
to Odissi—and we see the choreography of the body as a choreography of power, etched into stone. From the beginning, then, if we
consider as persuasive the sources offered as proof of Odissi's
origins, then we can also see a discernible link between dance
formations and state formations.

If we read the evidence generously, there is another implica-
tion here about the position dance holds as political force. Looking
at the links between dance and governmentality, we might presume that certain genres like Odra-Magadhi depended on the state
to ensure their survival; but what is doubly intriguing is that the
state is equally dependent on dance to derive a form of legitimacy.
Often this takes the shape of negotiating with dancing communities to ensure that their art articulates the logics, values and ideological programmes of the state; just as often, the reverse is true,
as the dance form influences the state and produces new significations. Saturated with ideological meaning and sutured to power,
dance is neither an inconsequential form, nor apolitical, as often
contended.[57] Dance is a crucial instrument for securing the state's

---

57 For engaging critiques of the argument that dance is an apolitical art, see
Jane Desmond (1997); Susan Leigh Foster (1998); Randy Martin (1998);
Diana Taylor (2003); and Mark Franko (2006).

hegemony, as the governing regime disperses and displays its power through performance. That dance is chosen as a symbol for commemorating the king at Udaygiri is no accident, for the value of choreography exceeds the aesthetic. Dance embodies power.

A New History of Odissi?

The Udaygiri caves are said to be the oldest representations associated with Odissi. While several scholars have written about these early images and their import, they have largely been silent on the question of who is represented here, in what context and why. I have sought to address some of the gaps in this history by suggesting that dance is clearly tied to the state as an enactment of its sovereign power, rather than religiosity (alone).

The cave sculptures were commissioned by a Jain king. They depict dancing bodies in courtly and pastoral scenarios. The inscriptions also shed some light on the framing of dance in worldly terms. While the monuments themselves hold some religious significance, the delineations of dance escapes a monolithic reading. For Kharavela, dance apparently bore no direct religious purpose or import, but held an expressly political status and bolstered the powers of the state. Even as the Udaygiri monuments are held up as proof of Odissi's longstanding existence, they also challenge the idea that it emerged as a proto-Hindu, temple-based dance. This thesis is supported by the *Natyashastra*, in which we find mention of Odra-Magadhi as a well-developed art. The *Natayashastra* deals specifically with *staged* performances—indicating that the dance had a public life; it wasn't confined to temples. The traces of dance at Udaygiri, along with the characterizations of Odra-Magadhi in the *Natyashastra*, intimate that Odissi had secular roots, in the sense of being 'worldly' rather than 'spiritual', or at least raise the possibility that it was shaped in an interreligious political matrix. [58]

---

58 In Odisha, since oral history and other types of historically 'verifiable' evidence dated prior to the Christian era are not available for review, it may be difficult to analyse exactly how other cultural and religious groups left their

An obvious consequence of this reading is that, either way, we cannot hold on to the idea that Odissi emerged only within a Hindu crucible. Looking at the archaeological and literary evidence linking Odissi to dance at Udaygiri and Odra-Magadhi in the *Natyashastra* challenges the widely disseminated view that

> Orissi, in fact, was never performed publicly, as a piece of entertainment, outside the temple: it always was confined to the precincts of the gods, and formed part of sacred ritual [. . . I]f Orissi was danced at any time as a public spectacle, or an entertainment of kings and courtiers, we have so far no evidence of it [. . .] It is now for the first time [in the twentieth century] that Orissi has come out of the temple and appears on the theatrical stage' (Fabri 1960: 4).

Even if we reject the attenuated claim that Udaygiri relates to Odra-Magadhi/Odissi, it is still important to engage the contesting discursive position that suggests it is so. From the perspective of a critical history, this is a productive act, as a rigorous examination of the claim leads to a path that makes it necessary to analyse diachronically the influence of a mixed range of religions on the dance, and understand how Odissi burgeoned on the stage, in the courts and in spaces emblematizing the state.[59] While many agree that the 'antiquity of Odissi dance has been traced to an early

---

imprints on Odra-Magadhi dance. This poses a challenge, but it is one that may be met imaginatively. Susan Leigh Foster's *Choreographing History* (1995), Diana Taylor's *The Archive and the Repertoire* (2003) and Paul Scolieri's *Dancing the New World* (2013) all offer models for conjuring dance in its articulate absence from the conventional record, and for constructing or retrieving nontextual evidence using performance historiography.

59 In his important book *Unfinished Gestures* (2012), Davesh Soneji reorients the reading of Bharatanatyam by analysing its historical development both within and outside the temple milieu. He argues, for instance, that devadasi performers associated with Bharatanatyam and its antecedents presented their art in salons, courts, processions, and other public settings. This kind of work is yet to be fully realized, historicized, and theorized in Odissi dance scholarship.

sculptural representation' at Udaygiri (Kothari 1990: 1), and that the images have 'become a landmark of the ancient-in-contemporary continuum of Odissi' (Gauhar 2007: 35), it seems surprising to discuss these images without considering their social and political matrix. I have argued that to discover the true relevance of these images in the history of Odissi, we need to place them in their proper context and comprehend how dance was situated within and across specific cosmologies and sociopolitical frameworks, especially given that Odisha represents a synthesis of cultures and religions which shaped its performance traditions.

The paratopic narrative I propose complicates the story of Odissi's unilateral progression 'from the *devasabha* to the *janasabha*', from the interior of the Hindu temple to the exterior of the proscenium stage (Kothari 2001: 93). It indicates a disruption of Odissi's dominant historical arc, as it moves *between* worldly and the sacred sites over time. Consequently, my hypothesis militates against the entrenched idea that Odissi had singularly divine origins, with the aim of releasing it from a purely devotional imperative, and delinking questions of its authenticity from its religiosity. Contrary to the discourse of over-ritualization, Odra-Magadhi/Odissi dance can be framed as secular practice. In other words, I argue it is more true to say that Odissi's ancient history resides outside the temple than within its sacred bounds, and more accurate to frame the dance's jagged itinerary as proceeding from stage–court–temple–street and back to the stage, than simply from temple to stage.

Perhaps predictably, debates about Odissi continue to rely on the story of its sanctified Hindu origins to appraise and (in)validate its authenticity in terms of its contemporary practices. Yet, as I have emphasized, in its imputed incipient forms, Odissi didn't follow a seamless religious trajectory; metaphorically, its beginnings can be imagined as spirals, mazes, labyrinths, messy and unruly roots, never traceable to a single point of origin. Its remnants may be deciphered in Jain history as much as a Hindu one; in the theatre as much as the temple; and in the realms of the worldly as much as the sacred. Once we look closely at inflections of the past in Odissi dance, we see a skein of stories: a chronicle of hybridity and interdisciplinarity, an intertwining of the political, the aesthetic and the ineffable, and multiple imprints, multiple histories, multiple genealogies.

PART II

PALLAVI
FLOURISHINGS

Chapter 2

DIVINING THE DISTRIBUTED BODY

MAHARI NAACH AND RITUAL PERFORMANCE

> Over the centuries, the sensuous bodily form, female and
> male, human and divine, has been a dominant feature in
> the vast and varied canvas of the Indian artistic tradition.
> The human figure—complete, elegant, adorned, and eye-
> catching—was, indeed, the leitmotif.
>
> —Vidya Dehejia, *The Body Adorned* (2009: 1)

Images of the body proliferate in the cultural landscape of Odisha.
Lavishly depicted in painting and stone, poetry and song, in drama,
flesh and myth, the body as a motif is etched deep in its aesthetic
terrain. Ideations of the body are manifest in multiple milieus,
such as temple architecture, sculpture and Mahari Naach.[1] Taken

---

[1] For an excellent ethnography on the Puri maharis, see Frédérique Apffel
Marglin's *Wives of the God-King* (1985b). There is by now a vast literature on
the history and context of devadasi performances across India; see, for
instance, L. A. K. Iyer (1927), Santosh Kumar Chatterjee (1945); Govind
Vidyarthi (1958); Projesh Banerjee (1982); Amrit Srinivasan (1985, 1988);
Jogan Shankar (1990); S. Anandhi (1991); A.K. Prasad (1991); Anne-Marie
Gaston (1992); Avanthi Meduri (1996); Janaki Nair (1994 and 1996); Pran
Neville (1996); Matthew Harp Allen (1997); Saskia C. Kersenboom (1998);
Kunal Parker (1998); Kakolee Chakraborthy (2000); Kali Prasad Goswami
(2000); Leslie C. Orr (2000); Judith Whitehead (1998, 2001); Anil Chawla
(2002); Selina Thieleman (2002); Kay K. Jordan (2003); Priyadarshini Vijaisri
(2004); Ratna Roy (2004, 2006, 2009); Uttara Asha Coorlawala (2005); Janet
O'Shea (2007); Vakulabharanam Lalitha (2011); S. Jeevananadam and Rekha
Pande (2012); Davesh Soneji (2012); Lucinda Ramberg (2014); and Uma
Chakravarti (2018).

together, they propose a unique somatic archive and reveal concepts of the body embedded in Odisha's artistic heritage.

Mahari performance is aesthetically and ideologically linked to Odissi classical dance. For many, the mahari tradition is *the* source of an authentic Odissi while for many others the culture of the Jagannath temple and its presiding deity are equally significant factors in its history. Here, my intention is to explore the discourses of embodiment and the hermeneutics of the corporeal subject subtending and surrounding mahari dance. To excavate the body of dance in this sense involves looking at the spaces surrounding it and examining its relationship to divinity.

With this in mind, I mine three layers of the body illuminated in Odissi's history: the body of the deity, the body of the temple, and the body of the dancer. I use the metaphor of 'divining' the body to allude to a double set of meanings. To 'divine' is to prophesy, to find something hidden, obscured from everyday view. In the second association, 'divining' is used in place of 'divinizing' and suggests consecration. The twinning of these meanings implies 'divining' as a mode of both probing and intuiting the varying valences of embodiment and its sacralization.

I ask: What kind of body was proposed in mahari dance? Was there a singular ideal or expression? What were the regional philosophies of the body, and how were they revealed? What are the layers and genealogies of such corporealities? I pose these questions in the context of the ascent of mahari dancing at Puri's Jagannath temple by the twelfth century CE, and its continuity into the 1950s.

I explore the relationship between the bodies of the dancers, the deity and the architectures within which they were conceived, framed and culturally comprehended, and reflect on the ways in which concepts of the body are generated and perpetuated by spatial, sacred and artistic forms in this context. For in Odishan cultural logics, the temple and the deity constituted 'bodies' in themselves. I argue that mahari dance represents an intersubjective encounter between the ritual performer, the material space and the religious icon, producing a '*distributed body*' (Gell 1998). As I will discuss, the distributed body thus emerges in- between these performative entities.

The value of the distributed body lies in hinting at a parallel economy of the subject that lies at the centre of mahari dance. It contests dominant ideas of liberal subjectivity which have come to serve as the harbingers and hallmarks of the ethos of modernity, and which are apparent today in Odissi dance. In contrast, the distributed body shows how ritual practices contain and reenact the values of a local epistemology, opening up new possibilities for imagining notions of the subject on grounds different than those offered by the conventional narratives of Western modernity or dominant Indian paradigms. The distributed body of ritual dance thus generates and reenacts a voluptuous history that is otherwise lost to what Foucault calls 'subjugated knowledge' (1980: 81).

From Odra-Magadhi to Mahari Naach

As discussed in the previous chapter, Odissi is often called the oldest classical dance form in India, based on claims of its consonance with Odra-Magadhi, a style described in the *Natyashastra*. Noted scholars have also analysed sculptural images in Odisha's Udaygiri caves, dating to the first century BCE and commissioned by the Jain monarch Kharavela; these relics, in concert with the *Natyashastra* references, they claim, serve as the earliest known evidence of the Odra-Magadhi form.

Representations of dance in Odisha are difficult to trace after this historical moment (Patnaik 2006). Buddhist sculptures at Ratnagiri and Lalitagiri indicate the presence of a regional dance style.[2] Early Shaivite temples in Odisha, like the seventh-century Parashurameshwara, also depict choreographic imagery. These fragmentary histories point to a thin aesthetic link which has yet to be fully explored, though they allow us to speculate that Odra-Magadhi, or some of its traces and variations, continued to thrive in the region well into the first millennium and incorporated Shaivite and Buddhist influences. Dance rose to prominence again

---

2 D. N. Patnaik (2006) briefly mentions this link in his history of Odissi dance. For more on the Buddhist iconography at Lalitagiri and Ratnagiri, see Donaldson (2001b: 52–9).

in early medieval Odisha, between the sixth and tenth centuries CE, with the emergence of four historical changes: the origination of stone temples; the popularization of Vaishnavism through the Jagannath cult; the advent of the mahari system; and the development of new state formations.

Whatever happened to the Odra-Magadhi style in this scenario? Did it lie dormant, disappear or disperse into new forms? Jasobanta Narayan Dhar offers a reading that suggests that 'this secular dance later named as Odissi dance was first originated as a court dance and in due course of time became associated with Jaina monasteries as patronised and performed by royal presence, later on also performed in all religious places including Buddhist monasteries' (2008: 17). My hypothesis, yet to be conclusively proven, is that mahari dance appropriated elements of Odra-Magadhi and successive iterations, sanctified them, institutionalized them and sustained them through their transformations in a Hindu ritual context. Adaptations of South Indian dance later contributed to the creation of a hybrid, localized tradition.[3]

Dominant narratives of Odissi tend to emphasize its past links to ritual dance to validate its long lineage and sacred status. Indeed, several scholars, artists, critics and members of the viewing public locate the authentic identity of Odissi in Mahari Naach.[4]

This premise organizes the story of Odissi's temple–stage trajectory, suppressing the form's eclectic influences in favour of an

---

3 My hypothesis is based on an analysis of Buddhist dance images and early Hindu temples in Odisha, and scholarship on the process of cultural change in the region, which emphasizes the appropriation of local forms as the basis of temple ritual. For instance, Jagannath himself was a Sabara tribal deity, Nilmadhava, assimilated into the Hindu pantheon. I would suggest that in line with this pattern, existing dance practices could have also been absorbed into temple service, and adapted to meet the new ritual requirements. See Eschmann et al. (2005); see also R. Sathyanarayan's extended commentary on the links between dance in Odisha and South India (1998: *Nartana-Nirnaya*, 3.273–80).

4 See, for example, Mohan Khokar (1984); Sunil Kothari (1990 and 2001); and Kapila Vatsyayan (1997 and 2007).

exclusive identification with Hindu ritual. It promotes the reinterpretation of Odissi as a purely devotional dance, problematically
positing texts and practices appropriated in its historical telling—
like the *Natyashastra* and Odra-Magadhi—as religious in nature,
despite their contested status. Alessandra Lopez y Royo has argued
that, at the time of its 1950s revival, 'Odissi was being created anew
as a re-imagined mahari ritual' even as the link between the two
styles 'remains open to controversy', and that 'Odissi as the-dance-
of-the-mahari-of-Lord-Jagannath continues to play on the ambiguity
and ambivalence of a ritual and exotic spectacle' (2008: 11–12, 15).
This is largely because Odissi's reconfiguration as a 'classical'
dance was heavily predicated on its identification with precolonial
religious tradition.

The move further connects the dance to other classical
forms—like Bharatanatyam and Kathakali—that claim to trace
their genesis to the temple order, and magnifies the links between
dance and religiosity to elevate Odissi's special position among
Odisha's myriad performing arts.

At the same time, we cannot overlook the role of Hindu praxis
as a vital force in Odissi's formation. Mahari performance, the
Jagannath cult which supported its growth and the Puri temple
were all essential components in shaping the history and aesthetics
of the dance style (though not exclusively so). The temple's centrality in Odishan culture, the significance of its iconography and ritual
system absolutely account for the privileged position of Mahari
Naach in Odissi's narrative. The strength and pre-eminence of the
dance/temple nexus thus merits close attention.

The City of Jagannath-Puri and the Body of the Deity

The maharis are significant figures as purveyors and protectors
of a cultural tradition that thrived within the precincts of the
Jagannath temple in Puri, publicly embraced as the hallowed
ancestral site of Odissi dance. I vividly recall hearing the origin
myths of the god, the temple and the devadasi tradition from my
dance gurus, especially Muralidhar Majhi, and from people I met

during my travels through Odisha, like Babaji and Raja Panda. Religious texts like the *Kapila Samhita* and *Skanda Purana*, along with the *Madala Panji* (literally, the 'drum chronicle' or chronicle of the Jagannath temple) also contain stories about Jagannath and his provenance.[5] Here is one telling of how the bodies of the deity and temple came into being at Puri:

The vision of Nilmadhava (blue-bodied Krishna) haunted King Indradyumna in his dreams, and so he sent a trusted advisor, Vidyap-ati, on a search for the elusive dark god.[6] Vidyapati journeyed to the east and finally entered Utkala where he was welcomed by Vishwavasu, the king of the Sabara village where Vidyapati landed after his wander-ings. For the king's shy daughter, Lalita, it was love at first sight when she laid eyes on the new visitor who sought rest in their tribal settlement.

---

5 The palm-leaf manuscript of the *Madala Panji* is kept at Puri's Jagannath Temple. An Odia book with selections of the text was published by Prachi Samiti in 1960 (see Mohanty 1960). See also the excerpts of royal chronicles from the *Madala Panji* in Behera and Parida (2009).

6 The story of Nilmadhava evinces the importance of Sabara tribal history to the Jagannath cult. The contributions of the Daita or Daita-pati (non-Brahmin priests), a class of servitors who self-identify as the descendants of Vishwavasu and Lalita and known as the first worshippers of Nilmadhava/Jagannath, are essential for the fulfillment of key Jagannath-Puri rituals, such as the process of making the new bodies of the deities during Nabakalebar and serving the deities during Snan Yatra and Rath Yatra (see K. C. Mishra 1984; Eschmann et. al. 2005). The dynamic of elevating the status of non-Brahmins during the festival season reminds us of Victor Turner's observation about liminal occa-sions and their reversal of social hierarchies (1995[1969]). There is an active Nilmadhava shrine in Kanthila built recently, near Sabarapalli (or Kaliapalli), the ancient home of the Sabaras by the holy Dengeni Pahad (mountain). In homage to its heritage and its links to the Jagannath temple, the Kanthila area is variously called *pratham* Puri (first Puri) or *dwithiya* Puri (second Puri), illus-trating its importance as a sacred site. During my visit there on 27 June 2012, the *panda* Lakhana Mishra told me that earlier temples in the area had once integrated mahari practice; however, they were women assigned by the Khondpara raja to serve as devadasis without receiving any income or land but enjoying the social prestige that came with their position. Otherwise they lived ordinary lives, able to marry and live in their own households—in con-trast to Puri's mahari system.

For his part, the canny Brahman intuited the presence of Nilmadhava in his new surroundings and romanced Lalita purely as a ploy to find his god.

Knowing that in the early light of dawn, Vishwavasu would go to a secret place only known as Nilakandar (the blue cave/the dark cave) for his daily prayers, Vidyapati asked Lalita—by now his wife—to intercede on his behalf, asking for darshan with Nilmadhava. Unable to turn down his daughter's request, Vishwavasu reluctantly agreed, but arranged for Vidyapati to be blindfolded along the route so he could never divulge the mysterious place of worship. Vidyapati then enlisted his wife in a clandestine plot to defy the king by leaving a trail of seeds that would grow into saplings, later making a green pathway leading back to shrine. Lalita consented. Vidyapathi then visited the shrine dutifully with his father-in-law, but, to their surprise, Nilmadhava refused the king's offerings that day. Mystified, they both suddenly heard an oracle announcing that the Nilmadhava would no longer belong to the Sabaras as their deity, and that the god was to assume a new name, a new form and a new temple abode through which he would become the object of devotion for Indradyumna and his followers.

Leaving Lalita behind, Vidyapati left the Sabara village and recounted his story to Indradyumna who set out on a visit to the shrine himself to seek Nilmadhav's blessings. Much to his disappointment, he found no one there. But he heard a divine whisper telling him to build a temple dedicated to Nilmadhava at Nilasaila (blue mountain).

Afterwards, in his dreams that night, the divine voice spoke again and told him that the idols for his temple would be made from daru (a piece of neem wood) floating in the sea. Soon this wood with an unusual aura appeared out of nowhere, drifting along the waves. Recognizing a sign from heaven, the sage Narada advised Indradyumna to carve out three images from the tree for installation in the new temple. The king faithfully followed his command.

Indradyumna then set out to find an artist capable of making the sacred idols, but could find none with the right skills or talents. Finally, Krishna arrived in disguise as a gifted carpenter and offered to make the carvings, on the condition that he should be left completely alone in the room where he was working, with the door closed at all times, so that

FIGURE 2.1. An antique Chitropathi of Jagannath, Subhadra, and Balaram in the Puri temple. From author's private collection.

he could concentrate fully on his craft. While the king initially obliged, he was left uncertain and became more so when the queen expressed her nervousness about their guest. The royal pair sprang a surprise on the carpenter by abruptly flinging the door of his room open; Krishna, revealed as the secret artist, immediately vanished, leaving the half-finished idols behind. Nevertheless, the divine voice spoke again at the scene, telling Indradyumna to present the three images at the temple.

The heavens were filled with jubilation when the prathishta *(installation ceremony) took place for the sibling trio, Balabhadra, Subhadra and Jagannath. All the gods, goddesses and* gandharvas *descended to the new temple—which the divine architect, Vishwakarma, had built himself—for the auspicious event. Apsaras entertained the assembled crowd. Rambha and Menaka danced especially to honour Jagannath. The devadasis call the apsaras their ancestors, situating themselves as part of an exalted artistic and spiritual lineage. As direct descendants of the apsaras, the devadasis continue this tradition of venerating the gods through devotional dancing and singing in Puri.*

A place that combines both pleasure and pilgrimage, the city of Puri is a magnet for pilgrims and seekers, sadhus and *sants*, tourists and devotees, those in search of the healing waters of the Bay of Bengal and those coming to be blessed by Jagannath, lord of the universe, and his sister and brother, Subhadra and Balaram.[7] Puri is one of the *char dham*—that quartet of supremely holy places in India, where Hindu pilgrims flock for a vision of the deity and a blessing (Bharati 1963). Each of these four *kshetras*, or revered places, corresponds to one of the four directions: Badrinath to the north, Rameshwaram to the south, Dwarka to the west and Puri to the east.[8] Travelling to the *char dham* is considered to be the sacred duty of every faithful Hindu.

Many Hindus consider Puri to be the holiest among these abodes of the divine. Some say it is because Puri was a favoured *kshetra* of Adi Shankaracharya (788–820 CE), the great philosopher who initiated the *char dham* concept as a way of inculcating a spiritual 'all-India' unity among his followers, inspiring a sense of cultural, geographical and religious connection. Others say it is because of the unique traditions that have sprung up around the cult of Jagannath, and the power associated with the god's paramount position as lord of the universe.[9] Still others say Puri

---

7 Sadhus and sants are holy mendicants and saints who have left worldly life to wander in search of spiritual liberation.

8 The list of *char dhams* may vary, depending on the perspectives of specific Hindu sects. For instance, other formulations of *char dham* include Benares and Vrindaban instead of Dwarka or Badrinath.

9 The deity Jagannath is a cognate of Vishnu and Krishna. In Hindu mythology, the gods have multiple incarnations. Krishna is popular all over India as

holds an esteemed position because of its location on the eastern peninsula. Since the sun first rises in the east, it gives us light, both literally and metaphorically, dispelling the darkness of night and the darkness of ignorance, and bathes the world in its incandescent wisdom. The primacy of the east as cardinal point is also recognized in many Hindu scriptures; in the *Shilpa Shastra*, for instance, it is decreed that a temple should always face east to intensify its propitious qualities (Muralidhar Rao 1995: 31–2). In popular tellings, the word Puri itself is derived from *purba*, 'east', evoking all of the beneficial aspects linked to this placement (Babaji 2008).

Many other meanings are ensconced in the city's name. The most well-known ascription is 'Jagannath Puri, the city where Jagannath lives'. Here, Puri is taken as a variation of *pur*, a common suffix used to refer to a city (as in Kanpur, Sambhalpur, Kolhapur, etc.); it is also considered an equivalent of *nibashashthan* or *bashasthali*, or dwelling place. In a related mode, Puri is said to be derived from Purushottam, or 'supreme being', a reference to both Jagannath and Vishnu (Choudhury 2008: 5).[10]

A connection between spatiality and corporeality is embedded in the very name Puri: etymologically it is linked to the Hindu concept of *purusha*, indicating a place where the soul has taken root. The concept is also linked to a sense of fullness, abundance and plenitude, as both the human body and the home are called *pura* (Babaji 2008). Puri thus represents a place of sacred wholeness.[11]

---

one form of Vishnu. When Jagannath became part of the Hindu pantheon, he was identified with Krishna/Vishnu. Jagannath is worshipped exclusively in Odisha, unlike other gods whose worship is widespread in other regions of India.

10 In Hindu philosophy, *purush* refers to the masculine force, and *uttam* means highest or greatest among all. K. C. Panigrahi explains that Purushottama means 'the best of men' as well as 'the city of Purushottama' (1981: 58).

11 Janmejay Choudhury elucidates on Puri's position in sacred literature: 'Purusottam Ksetra-Puri has been described in the Puranas as the most sacred place in Bharata Varsa [India]. It is the ksetra where the God Purusottama made his perpetual abode, Vaikuntha Bhubana. The sacred place, according to the tradition, existed even during the great universal deluge and also in

Puri is often considered the spiritual home of Odissi dance, as the site of the Jagannath temple where mahari service was formalized. The temple, built in the twelfth century CE by King Anantavarman Chodaganga Deva of the Ganga dynasty, became a significant space of power and worship (Eschmann et al. 2005). The king formalized three institutions long identified with the culture of the temple—the association of the royal ruler as an embodiment of Jagannath, and the god's reciprocal position as the 'king of the kingdom of Odisha'; Rath Yatra, the annual Chariot Festival; and mahari service, based on pre-existing traditions of dancing girls performing at Odisha's temples (P. Kanungo 2003).

The Jagannath cult developed in Odisha with the rise of Vaishnavism in the region. The deity is an unusual figure in the Hindu pantheon. He is considered to be a living entity, thus all the rituals of the temple are designed to attend to him and his family's needs. Every day, Jagannath is awakened from sleep; he is bathed, dressed and offered food. Before the evening prayer, he takes rest and so will not meet his worshippers. He grants *darshan* to his followers at specified times of the day, and at night he falls into a restful sleep; the next day, the cycle begins all over again.[12] His consort, Laxmi, lives in the same temple complex, but Jagannath is always depicted as part of a trio of siblings. The gods leave the temple precincts to meet the faithful at special festivals, most famously the Rath Yatra. They even ritually fall ill once a year after the Snan Yatra (Bathing Festival), when they are sequestered from their devotees. At auspicious intervals, in the years when two full moons appear in the month of Ashadha,[13] they are said to die. On the occasion of Nabakalebar, then, the gods are given new bodies

the beginning of this creation. Its greatness is unparalleled, its importance is unique and its sanctity is unquestionable'. Puri is known as a place of purification, a place that 'takes away sin' (2008: 6).

12 *Darshan*, literally 'sight', is the term in Hinduism for paying tribute to the divine by visiting a temple and meeting the gaze of the deity (Eck 1998). *Darshan* also bears haptic implications, as looking is a form of 'touching' and 'being touched' by the divine figure.

13 This is June–July in the Gregorian calendar.

and change souls through the Brahma Paribartan ceremony, resurrected in refashioned images made of *daru brahma* (sacred neem wood, selected specially by a priest), at the centre of which is placed a sacred element, the *brahma padartha*,[14] that is said to bestow them with a life force; and the old idols are buried in the temple courtyard. These elaborate daily and ceremonial rituals, it is said, mark a thousand-year tradition, and are carried out by local servitors assigned to their special tasks on a hereditary basis (Mishra 1984; Jagannath Temple 2011).

The Body of the Temple

Walking through the temple now, a pilgrim can imagine what it might have been like, all those centuries ago, to travel through the same domain and behold the trinity of gods.

FIELD NOTES: PURI, ODISHA, MARCH 2008

You walk towards the eastern gate of the Jagannath temple, feet bare. To reach this holy place at the edge of the street, you dodge everything from garbage and piles of dung, to cows, rickshaws, dogs, bicycles, cars, scooters and buses along with peddlers, performers and pedestrians. As you step inside, you immerse your feet in cool water, cleansing them of the outside elements. You veil your face with the pallu *of your sari, and watch other women do the same with the dupattas of their salwar kameez.[15] You follow the stairs, lined with scores of pilgrims, leading up to the temple courtyard. A magnificent white edifice housing the trinity of Jagannath, Subhadra and Balaram sits at the centre, surrounded by a series of smaller shrines dedicated to a pantheon of other gods.*

---

14 The *brahma padartha* is a *shaligram* (sacred stone) wrapped in seven layers of materials, each of which represents an aspect of the human body (Rahul Acharya, personal conversation, 18 February 2015; see also Acharya and Devi 2008: 318–22, 450).

15 The *pallu* is the part of the sari that drapes over the shoulder, or covers the head. Dupattas are scarves worn with a salwar and kameez to make a complete outfit.

It seems as if all seekers and wanderers have arrived in this place. Some hold rudramalas *(rosaries), praying and meditating, some are lost in a trance, some whisper secret mantras to themselves, speaking in tongues, swaying their bodies, lifting their arms up to the sky, eyes closed in ecstasy. The air is redolent with the sounds of devotees yearning for Jagannath's blessings, and, if you are a seeker too, your voice joins their jagged music of shrieks and cries. You walk with them, pierced by magical incantations.*

The moment of darshan, *that sacred look from the deity and at the deity, is sublime. Darshan unleashes the fullest power of the gaze: a mutual witnessing, a powerful conjunction of looking. You possess and are possessed, grateful for a glimpse of Jagannath and his intensely potent gaze. Then you bow down, touch the crown of your head to the earth. To complete the act of worship, you walk through the crowd up near the altar where you can pass your hands over the sacred flame. And as you meander among the others, you realize that you are just a single drop in the endless river of worshippers, flowing constantly through the thresholds of temple and time, purified by the presence of the deities. And you feel the metamorphosis happening—the divining of the body* (Banerji 2008).

To enter the great temple is to not only to enter an exalted place but also an exalted religious and aesthetic history, for Jagannath-Puri is a magnificent exemplar and embodiment of Kalingan temple design.

Kalingan temples are marked by a set of traits—conceptual and architectural—that differentiate them from other Indian forms.[16] Stone temples began to emerge in the fifth century CE, and

---

16 The Kalingan style was first isolated by scholars in a temple inscription from Karnataka which mentions it in conjunction with the more well-known Nagara, Dravida, Bhumaja, and Vesara types, and in Sanskrit texts such as the twelfth-century CE *Kamikagama* (Linda 1990: 87; Dhaky 1977: 1). Odishan shrines are more or less derived from the northern pattern but exemplify one of the most 'distinct variations of the *Nagara* style of temple construction' (Donaldson 1985: *ix*). Stone temples proliferated under the auspices of the Gupta dynasty (c.320–550 CE) during what is typically regarded as the birth of the classical age in north India. The Gupta period is often referred to as the 'golden era' when

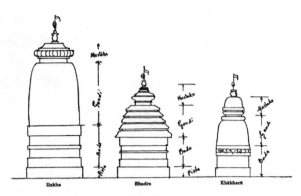

FIGURE 2.2. Illustration of various styles of Kalingan architecture. From N. K. Bose, *Canons of Orissan Architecture* (1932), n.p.

were broadly categorized into three general types—the northern Nagara, the Deccan Vesara and the southern Dravida varieties—based on a combination of their geographical genealogies and architectural traits. Odisha temples constitute a fourth kind, the Kalingan style, which thrived between the sixth and sixteenth centuries (Donaldson 1985: *ix*). Often, Kalingan architecture combines elements of the first three dominant types as well as artistic motifs from neighbouring regions, exhibiting the hybrid impulse so evident in several of Odisha's cultural forms. [17]

Hindu art and culture blossomed under royal patronage, representing the pinnacle of aesthetic sophistication (Desai 1990). However, this was primarily a North Indian experience. The 'golden age' of the South and the East came about in the post-Gupta era, producing a new artistic ethos. Undeniably, many of the Gupta aesthetic codes and blueprints influenced other localities and periods; these artistic ideas and imprimaturs were borrowed, adapted, recast, and reshaped in other regions to suit their own specific cultural circumstances. This heritage of heterogeneity is especially visible in temple art.

17 The development of an indigenous brand is attributed to the system of royal patronage, which historically 'inspired the Oriya architects to carry on the spirit of creating their own style of architectural temple representations' (Chand 2005: 49). Further, it attests to the broad regionalization of the arts in early medieval India. Shankar Goyal suggests that specifically 'towards the end of the seventh century AD a regional spirit began to assert itself' as a response to 'the tendency of regionalization in political life' (1993: 143). See also Dei (1998) on this point.

FIGURE 2.3. View of eastern gate of Jagannath temple on Bada Danda (Grand Road), Puri, Odisha, 7 March 2008. Photograph by the author.

Famous for their bold and intricate style, Kalingan monuments can be immediately identified by the *rekha* (curved tower), *bhadra* or *pila* (horizontal courses) and *khakara* (spherical shape) structures (Linda 1990: 87; Bose 1932). Once installed as stark and simple single-edifice shrines, they gradually developed into compounds featuring the *deul* (main shrine), the *jagmohan* (audience hall), the *bhoga-mandap* (dining hall) and the *nata-mandap* (dance hall) (Donaldson 1981).

The outer walls of Kalingan temples tend to be exquisitely embellished with images of gods and goddesses, their vehicles and symbols, semi-celestial beings like *yakshas* and *yakshis* (protectors of nature), *nagas* and *naginis* (human-serpent hybrids), *apsaras* and *gandharvas* (heavenly dancers and musicians), legendary creatures (often lions, elephants, birds), as well as *mithuna* (erotic couples), *nayikas* and *kanyas* (women), yogis and yoginis and royal figures. The carvings are placed in a stunning aesthetic universe, where every surface is richly adorned with abstract patterns accented by *jali* or filigree work.[18]

---

18 Soma Chand (2006) points out this type of embellishment is another feature distinguishing Kalingan architecture. According to her, the decorative

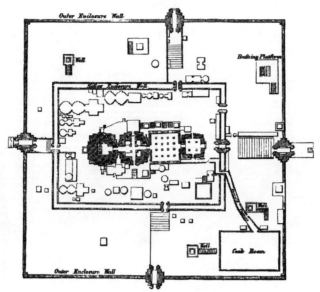

PLAN OF TEMPLE OF JUGGERNAUT.

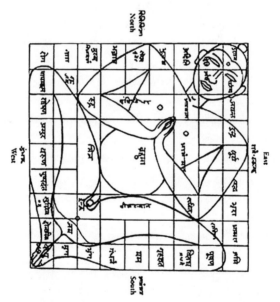

FIGURE 2.4 (TOP). Plan of the Jagannath Temple. From *Harper's New Monthly Magazine* (1878: 226).

FIGURE 2.5 (BOTTOM). *Purusha-mandala*, according to the *Vastu Shastra*. The plan of the Jagannath temple follows this model and accordingly faces east (*purab*), considered the most auspicious direction in Hindu thought. Public-domain image.

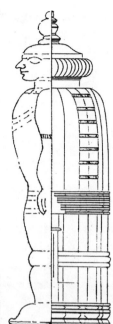

FIGURE 2.6. An illustration of the correspondence between the parts of the human body and linked sections of the temple in Kalingan architecture. Image courtesy of D. C. Panda.

Most importantly, the Kalingan temple has a specific foundational philosophy, illuminated in its form. In standard Hindu architectural works, the earth's surface is represented as a mandala—a square diagram signifying cosmic order, infused with sacred meaning—permeated by the male principle of *purusha*. (In Hindu philosophy, the square is the emblem of perfection.) A potent sign, the Purusha Mandala is used as the basis of architectural planning and positioning to maximize the circulation of positive energies in a space and impede negative forces (Vatsyayan 1983; Muralidhar Rao 1995). Thus the Purusha Mandala is used to construct and orient the *devalaya* (literally, 'home of the gods'), serving as the abstract anchor of its architecture. With the mandala as its model,

programmes can be classified into three types—the constructive, representative and ornamental—in conformance with the *Shilpa Shastra*. Thomas Donaldson argues the exterior ornamentation also expresses shifts in Odisha's cultural make-up, as it 'continuously changes and reflects a peculiar propensity for religious synthesis on part of the indigenous people' (1981: 35). See also Goswami (1950) and Dehejia (1979).

the sacred space ultimately signifies the universe over which an all-powerful deity reigns. Axioms of Odishan architecture align closely with the precepts of the *Shilpa Shastra* but with a unique twist—the Kalingan temple is specially designed so that its contours and silhouettes correspond to parts of the human body (D. C. Panda 2008, 2010).[19] In this sense, it enacts and enlivens the concept of *sharira yantra* (body diagram). While other Hindu temple styles are based on *principles* of the human body, the Kalingan style moves towards the architectural *personification* of that body.

The Odishan temple's metaphorical and metonymic transformation into a corporeal entity is directly evinced in the naming of each segment: 'architects perceived the temple in the form of a human male figure or *purusha*. Like human physical divisions of leg, thigh, waist, chest, neck, and head, the temple had similar shapes and structures' (Chand 2005: 50). In this physicalization, the base mouldings and plinth are known as *pabhaga*, or foot division. The vertical portion of the wall is called *jangha*, or legs (further split into *tala* and *upar jangha*, or calf and thigh, linked by another class of mouldings called *bandhana*, which literally means 'binding' or 'tying together'). The *bada*, or perpendicular wall, constitutes the rest of the body. The *baranda* (lower torso, or 'belt region') are upper mouldings that separate the *bada* from the *gandi*, the latter signifying the main torso, the curvilinear spine. Above this portion, the structure proceeds on a gradual upward gradient, so that the four walls slope inward, pyramid-like, meeting at a point known as the *mastaka*—the crowning element, or head—which consists of the *beki* (neck), *amala* (top of the neck) and *khapuri*

---

19 D. C. Panda, a renowned scholar of Odishan architecture, first explained to me how the Kalingan temple is conceived in terms of a human body. In March 2008 and December 2010, he was my guide on a tour of the Mahamaya temple in Hirapur, the Udaygiri caves, and 18 Bhubaneshwar temples: Ananta-Vasudev, Brahmeshwar, Bharateshwar, Bhaskareshwar, Jameshwar, Kedar-Gauri, Lingaraj, Markandeshwar, Megheshwar, Mukt-eshwar, Parashurameshwar, Paschimeshwar, Rajarani, Shatrughaneshwar, Shishireshwar, Siddheshwar, Swarnajaleshwar and Vaitul Deul. I am deeply indebted to him for sharing his knowledge with me.

(skull), capped by the *kalasa*, a decorative element (D. C. Panda, 2008, 2010).[20]

All in all, the temple is structured as a human body. D. K. Ganguly elaborates on this association:

> The temple has always been conceived in India as the 'visible outer encasement of the invisible deity, a visible image which is installed in it as an emblem of the invisible spirit which pervades all nature. It is, like the human body, the outer visible shape of the shapeless. This explains why the various parts of a temple in Odisha or elsewhere in India are designated by names which correspond to various parts or limbs of the human body (1984: 56).

The spatial relationship between the human body and the divine is immediately and irrevocably established in this schema. Most importantly, the temple ceases being an inanimate object—it is refashioned as a religious agent, underscored by the idea that the five organic elements that make up the human body and the temple are one and the same: *bhumi* (earth), *jal* (water), *vayu* (wind), *agni* (fire) and *akash* (space). In this perspective, the essence and substance of each personified entity is indistinguishable from the other, and the Kalingan temple acts as both body and abode. Thus the temple exceeds its role as a dwelling or site of representation, housing the deity and bearing sculptural depictions of human, celestial and otherwordly beings, and, instead, *becomes* a body, attaining a kind of cosmic corporeality, anointed and animated with the energy of the *purusha* principle. Layers and layers of embodiment reveal themselves, blurring and coalescing together: the temple is a body; the body of the deity lives here;

---

20 On the general correspondence between temple and body in Indian architecture and performance, Vatsyayan explains that 'in artistic form temple architecture invokes in its massive proportions the "figure of Man", and is closely related to the rhythm and movement of Indian music, dance and sculpture. Conversely, the compositions of classical dance are seen as the different sections of the Indian temple and its parts become the imagery for describing the structure of a dance recital' (1983: 80).

sculpted bodies adorn the larger body of the temple; all witness
the migration of flesh-and-blood bodies coming in and out of the
vivified place. In a relational cycle, bodies of human devotees
pass through the body of the temple for a glimpse of the body of
the deity, surrounded by bodies carved in stone. In a mutual
manifestation, the human figure is newly spatialized in the bones
and scaffolds of the religious structure. The architecture of the
temple and the anatomy of the human body dissolve into a single
harmonious entity, bound within a sacred geography.

The Dancing Body: Mahari Rituals

The concern with corporeality and the relation between the human
and the divine body are key tropes of foundational Hindu myths.
Maharis and other devadasis are regarded as the descendants of
apsaras, celestial beings who dance in the heavenly courts to enter-
tain gods and mesmerize mortals.[21] Historically speaking, the
Mahari tradition's existence in Odisha is recorded as far back as
the eleventh century CE. Of this there is ample proof, in the form
of inscriptions and images on the Brahmeshwar temple (*c.*1058 CE)
describing how Queen Kolavati Devi brought with her a troupe of
dancing girls as part of her wedding trousseau and dedicated the
artists to the temple as an offering. The epigraph reads:

> By her were dedicated to God Shiva some beautiful women,
> whose limbs were adorned with ornaments set in gems and
> thus appearing as the everlasting but playful lightning, and
> who were restless with the weight of their loins and breasts,
> and whose eyes were fickle and extended up to their ears
> and who looked lovely like the pupils of the eyes of men.
> (S. N. Rajguru, quoted in Patnaik 2006: 31)

The related image is the earliest known depiction of devadasis of
Odisha:[22]

---

21 In Puranic legend, the *apsaras* were born during the Samudramanthan, the
great churning of the ocean that created the universe.

22 There is some debate as to whether this image represents a dancing
girl or Queen Kolavati herself. Thomas Donaldson (1981) argues the former,

FIGURE 2.7. Dancer surrounded by musicians, Brahmeshwar temple, Somavamsi period, eleventh century CE. This is considered the first image of a devadasi, or female ritual specialist, in Odisha. Bhubaneshwar, Odisha, 26 December 2014. Photograph by the author.

All eyes are on the woman in the extravagant pose on the walls of the Brahmeshwar. She is in Nupurpada *(one foot touching the anklet of the other), her figure simultaneously angular and curved, surrounded by a bevy of joyous musicians entranced equally by her movement and their own melodious sounds. Two celestial figures look on delighted from*

---

while K. C. Panigrahi (2008) has argued the latter. Judging from the body lines and stylization of the image, the profusion of other dance images in the Brahmeshwar's decorative program, and viewed in the context of the commemorative inscription praising Kolavati Devi's act of dedicating dancers to the temple, Donaldson's argument appears to have a stronger claim. The image also reveals that the devadasi system, otherwise well-entrenched in India by this point, was still nascent here, confirmed by the fact that the dance pavilion was not yet a feature of the temple complex. According to Donaldson, the dancer on the wall of the Brahmeshwar appears to be performing in the *jagamohan*, not a *natamandir*, which would be integrated much later (1981: 37). He also argues the twelfth-century Shobhaneshwar temple in Niali was likely the first one in which the performance space was built coterminously with the main structure, and contains 'possibly the earliest known inscription that explicitly states that *devadasis* performed in a *nata-mandira*' (39). For details of the evidence at Shobhaneshwar, see Rajguru (1966: II, 3.2, 338).

above, hovering in flight. They might be tiny dancers themselves in their yoga-like postures, their feet nearly touching their own heads as they float in space on opposite sides of a temple spire, improbably held up by the dancer's delicate hand. Or, perhaps, the space simply cannot contain the devadasi's exuberant dancing. Each limb on her body is beautifully carved: the fingertips on her left hand brush the ceiling in an almost-mudra while her right hand stretches down and drops at the wrist, bending into a circular hasta just beyond the knee. Thin garments, folded into tight pleats, follow the shape of her strong thighs. She has arms full of bangles, a heavy belt at her waist, long earrings dangling down to her chin, a sweetheart necklace grazing the top of her décolletage. Her face leans into one shoulder, revealing a stylish chignon. The combination of her head turning away from the rest of her upper body, the triangles of her bent knees and the swerve of her torso create the extreme S-curve that conveys both athletic virtuosity and the paradoxical impression of shyness. Seductive and languid, her bejewelled body at the centre of the scene commands the viewer's eye—but as much as we search for her gaze, she doesn't look back directly at us, perhaps lost in the rhythms of her own dance.[23]

The *Madala Panji* (twelfth century CE) suggests the continuity of the women's performance tradition into the next century, stating that Raja Raja Dev II (r.1170–94) commissioned 20 dancing girls for devadasi service at Jagannath-Puri. The claim is tentative, since the credibility of the *Madala Panji* as a historical source is precarious, but discursively it suggests that devadasis were acknowledged as significant contributors to the ritual life of the region.[24]

---

23 The similarity of this image to the one at Udaygiri—with both dancers in a defined and confined space, in a dynamic posture at the centre of the scene, appreciative musicians off to the side—is quite striking (see Chapter 1).

24 While the *Madala Panji* is held in great esteem by religious authorities, due to the provenance of the text and its multiple interpolations, scholars have cast doubt on its legitimacy as a historical document. Thus its contents are subject to corroboration. See K. C. Panigrahi (1984). Also of interest, the Orissa Research Project (1999–2005), sponsored by Heidelberg University, held a symposium on the *Madala Panji and Orissan Historiography* in Bhubaneshwar, 18–19 September 2006.

The roots of the mahari system in Odisha are difficult to disentangle and the question is subject to great contest. The most likely scenario is that in a departure from dominant or orthodox Brahmanical custom, the devadasi system came about as a way of including women in temple service.

Odisha was governed by various clans and dynasties after the end of Kharavela's rule. In the intermediary years, a splintered picture of the past suggests Odisha segmented into small kingdoms and principalities with a variety of political actors vying for control—the Shailodhbhavas, the Bhauma-Karas and the Somavamsi-kesaris being some of the most important players who successively ruled portions of the state (Panigrahi 2008). These rulers allied themselves to a whole spectrum of religious beliefs as the influence of Buddhism and Jainism slowly receded, with Shaivite and Shakti cults dominating (Goyal 1993: 144–5).

Based on the set of images and inscriptions at Brahmeshwar, scholars have concluded that '[i]t is the Somavamsi-kesaris who appear to have introduced the system into Orissa' (Donaldson 1981: 36) and borrowed the tradition from the South, given the ubiquity of its practice there and comparing the substantive elements of the regional rituals. D. K. Ganguly avers: 'It is not unlikely that the institution of *devadasis* was of South Indian inspiration. That *devadasis* for different Orissan temples were sometimes recruited from South India even in later centuries is evidenced by a fifteenth-century inscription of King Kapilendradeva, recording the presence of Telugu dancers in the Jagannatha Temple at Puri' (1984: 87n19).[25] In any case, it seems the devadasi institution was alien to Odisha until the rise of the Somavamsi-kesaris, and became indigenized only thereafter.[26]

---

25 Donaldson suggests the mahari system 'most likely was influenced by the popularity of this custom in Central India rather than South India,' departing from the general consensus (1981: 36).

26 While many attribute its beginnings to the Ganga dynasty (1110–1434 CE), others suggest the previous Somavamsi regime (931–1110 CE) (Donaldson 1981). This historical misapprehension is mostly likely due to the fact that the maharis are best known as servitors of the Jagannath temple, built during the

The migration of devadasis from Telangana in particular
had a major impact on precursors of Odissi dance; it is quite
plausible that they contributed extensively to shaping the Mahari
Naach technique, which I speculate as eventually emerging from a
combination of existing regional-dance vocabularies and the
imported Andhra-based lexicon. The Chennai-based choreographer,
dancer and scholar Dr Swarnamalya Ganesh, who has extensively
researched the history of medieval South Indian dance, points
out that in the Chowk we find a strong resemblance to a body position used in early antecedents of Bharatanatyam;[27] and that the
Ardhamandi position central to Bharatanatyam today, which
emphasizes the geometry of the triangle, actually began with a leg
position akin to that of Chowk or Mandala.[28] In fact, the name of
this Nayak-period dance position in South India was Chaturasra, or
square, and can be correlated to the earlier Mandala. Ganesh suggests that the term Chaturasra emerged in the post–*Abhinaya
Darpanam* period, when dance was treated as an autonomous art
and started to develop its own theoretical and technical language.
Ganesh's investigation has yielded the important finding that a
variation of what we know as Chowk today was called Chaturasra
or Mandala in aesthetic treatises as authoritative as the *Natyashastra*, the *Sangita Darpana* (dated to 1625; authored by Damodar
Misra) and the *Nartana-Nirnaya* (by Pandarika Vitthala, dated to
the late sixteenth century CE).

The last of these deserves a special mention, as the text was
authored under the Mughal emperor Akbar's reign, with his support,
and provides the dance lexicon of the time. A translator of this work,

---

Ganga period, which is also considered the 'golden age' of Odisha. However,
current interpretations of archaeological evidence point to the Somavamsis
as inaugurators of the mahari order.

27 See Swarnamalya Ganesh (2012). I am also relying on information gleaned
from a talk and lecture-demonstration she gave at UCLA ('From the Attic') on
10 November 2014, and a conversation we had on 14 November 2014. In
Ganesh's reconstructions of early Nayak-period Bharatnatyam repertoire, she
emphasizes the Chaturasra body posture.

28 Mandala is the first foot position noted in the *Natyashastra*; Ganesh posits
thus that Ardhamandi refers to Ardha Mandala, or 'half-mandala'.

R. Sathyanarayana, writes that originally it 'was composed during a cultural watershed when a distinct polarization was emerging in the art forms on a South-North axis in India. This contribution consisted of refocusing them on a national canvas' (1994: 1.*viii*). Additionally, with a full section devoted to dance as an independent art, the *Nartana-Nirnaya* comprises 'much that may be interpreted as partial germinations in our dancescape what came to be called Bharatanatya, Kathak, Odissi, etc. in course of time. Yet another major contribution of this treatise is the descriptions of actual dance compositions from contemporary practice'—particularly, the terms *bandha* (denoting closed, fixed or established movement sequence) and *anibandha* (open movement within a set of rules) are introduced by Pandarika Vitthala as frames for understanding dance syntax and constitute 'a major departure from earlier textual convention' (Pandarika Vitthala 1998: 3.*vii–viii*). Mandakranta Bose, who has examined the relationship between the *Nartana-Nirnaya* and Odissi in specific, elaborates that '*Bandhanrittas* are set pieces with every movement in their structured sequences clearly specified and unalterably prescribed for the dancer,' and notes they permit 'no variations, no straying from the rigidly determined choreography' (1992: 213).[29] Anibandhanritta is complementary but has a diverging function as an improvisational practice, its content and form in flux rather than fixed by any prevailing aesthetic template.[30]

Bandha scores in the *Nartana-Nirnaya* depended on careful arrangements of *karanas*, or movement units. Pandarika Vitthala's opus indicates that of the 108 *karanas*, just 16 were actively applied in choreographies of the day (1998: 3). Vatsyayan speculates that, by the late sixteenth century, 'many movements must have gone

29 For an example, see Chapter 4 and the discussion of Bandha Nritya in gotipua dance, as well as Chapter 6 in the discussion of Batu.

30 Bose offers this assessment of the *Nartana-Nirnaya*'s innovations: 'There can be little doubt that the categories *bandha* and *anibandha* mark a historical point in the evolution of Indian dancing at which established traditions and new forms existed side by side. The *bandha* category encompassed the styles that had been firmly defined and codified by long usage. Other styles, still fluid and evolving, were placed within the *anibandha* category' (1992: 217).

FIGURE 2.8. A sculpture series from Sesharaya Mandapam, Srirangam Temple, Tamil Nadu. Here the dancers are wearing Yakshagana head-gear and perhaps performing Yakshagana. This stance is still used in Yakshagana today. Swarnamalya Ganesh notes that the feet of the dancers in these South Indian illustrations can be compared to Chowk, and are, in the terminology of dance treatises, in either *aalidam* or *prathyalidam* and *Vaishnavam* position. Photograph courtesy of Swarnamalya Ganesh.

out of vogue and many new forms may have come into being' (in Pandarika Vitthala 1994: 1.*ix*), a suggestion which makes the retention and materialization of Chaturasra in the movement vocabulary of the region all the more significant. Odissi's *bhangi* and the *Nartana-Nirnaya*'s *bandhanritta* are indeed kindred systems, as an analysis by Bose reveals: Chaturasra/Mandala/Chowk corresponds to Vaishakha-sthana (and perhaps Chinna); Samabhanga resonates with Samanakha; Tribhangi looks like Agratalasancara-pada (1992: 219–20).

The Chaturasra position emerged as a corporeal motif common to both Odisha and South Indian traditions, as exemplified in their respective visual and sculptural histories and as manifested in their performance techniques. In Odisha, early renderings of Chaturasra/Mandala are found at Udaygiri and Parashurameshwar temple; and in Tamil Nadu, at Srirangam and Bodinayakanur in illustrations of Sangita Melam, Bharatanatyam, and, putatively, the dance-drama Yakshagana. Ganesh affirms that 'the preeminence of mandala/chaturasra can be observed in almost all the sculptures of the Nayak times' in South India—from about 1529 to 1736, when the titular royal family ruled Thanjavur and presided over a period during which Bharatnatyam developed part of its repertoire.[31] Complementary evidence of cross-cultural pollination is provided in prior chronicles like the *Kalingathu Parani*, an eleventh–twelfth century CE Tamil epic authored by the poet Jayamkondar, extolling the heroism of South Indian king Kulottunga Chola during his conquest of Kalinga and containing documentation of Odisha's dance and musical traditions.[32] Considering the prevalance of physical techniques like Chaturasra/Mandala and the accounts of intraregional interaction in the *Nartana-Nirnaya* and *Kalingathu Parani*, it is unsurprising that Odissi's Chowk would mimic or correlate with similar stances in dances from South India, that they would share a common aesthetic and cultural foundation.[33]

The advent of the mahari order does, however, indicate a more complex history than the simple migration and importation of the

---

31 Ganesh emphasizes that Chaturasra 'has a long history. [. . .] It is my view that the depictions of all the Nayak dancers in paintings and sculptures [are] in either chaturasra or its variations. [. . .] In fact, the patronage yakshagana as a literary work received in the Nayak courts (in the Tamil country) and the patronage the dance form found with them, lead us to understand how the chaturasra position is universal' (Email correspondence, 16 February 2016).

32 Ganesh kindly alerted me to this epic in a conversation on 14 November 2014. The Tamil text of *Kalingathu Parani* is available from Project Madurai (2001), an online initiative that prepares and distributes literary works for free. There is also a prose version of the epic in Tamil, titled *Cayankontar Kalinkattu Parani: Kata Cankirakam* (Chennai: T. Celvakesavaroya Mudali, 1920), housed in the British Library, and another version (Chennai: Virpanai urimai Tirunelveli Tennintiya Caivacittanta Nurpatippuk Kalakam, 1928) located in the US Library of Congress. I have not been able to find a copy in English or Hindi translation, but rely on Ganesh's research ascertaining its contents.

33 Other evidence suggests these aesthetic frameworks may have had an even broader reach; the Jain Kalpasutras, for instance, which were written in Gujarat in western India around the fourteenth century CE, indicate the interaction between different regions of the subcontinent as they depict dance positions reminiscent of Odissi's *bhangi* system. Kapila Vatsyayan highlights 'the *Devasano Pada Kalpasutra*, where the marginal figures all pertain to musicians and dancers. The style of the movement illustrated has a marked affinity with what we today identify as Odissi' (in Misra 2009: 1.iv).

devadasi system and its techniques from the South to Odisha. While the mahari order may have had southern roots, there were some essential differences that contributed to its eventual status as a separate Odishan practice.

Given its intercultural influences, the preeminence of Odissi as a discrete dance style poses a historical puzzle. If the earliest devadasis came to Odisha from the South with their own developed artistic practices, why didn't this migration simply lead to the transplantation and dissemination of their own special dance forms? That is, why didn't variants of early Bharatanatyam and Kuchipudi simply spread to Odisha instead? I believe that the persistence of regional dance styles in the pre-mahari period explains why Odissi today is stylistically individuated. In Chapter 1, I put forward the claim that Odissi developed as a distillation and refinement of several performance traditions. I suggest that by the time devadasis arrived from the South, their practice changed to integrate elements of the existing dance repertoires replete in Odisha, and through its enshrinement at the temple as a ritual service, Odissi further consolidated its difference from Southern dance forms, becoming a new dance style altogether. Odissi's uniqueness derived from the strength and influence of its regional foundations, and its past incarnations outside the temple. The dance became a symptom and symbol of Odisha's cultural landscape, a strong embodiment of its pluralities and a character that set it apart from the South.

Another order of difference is plainly evident in the nomenclature. The terms *mahari* and *devadasi* are often used interchangeably, but *mahari* is exclusively reserved for female ritual specialists in Odisha. The roots of the word give us some clues to its history. Shashimoni Devadasi, one of the last maharis of the Jagannath temple, told me the word is a compressed form of *mahan* ('great') and *nari* ('woman'); others suggest that it is a shorthand or variation for *mangala nari* ('auspicious woman'), *ma-iri ortri* ('mother'),, *mohan nari* ('a woman who belongs to god'), *maha ripu nari* ('one who conquers her enemies'), or simply, *maharani* ('queen').[34] It

---

34 Sharmila Biswas (2003–04/2007); Marglin (1985b: 77); and Mohanty Hejmadi and Hejmadi Patnaik (2007: 34–5) discuss some of these meanings.

could also be another version of *mahattari*, a title used in the *Natyashastra* for a woman who performed service at the temple with her songs.[35] Jibananda Pani surmised that the word stemmed from the Vishnu Purana and refers to female inhabitants of *mahar-lok*, a mythical place where those faithful to Vishnu found refuge at a time of universal turbulence.[36]

But why was the category 'devadasi' supplanted by the local term 'mahari' at all, especially when the title of 'devadasi' was the reigning term for female dancers in the Southern regions? I would argue that the existence of a distinct name in Odisha is evidence of a distinct practice. At the very least, the use of the term 'mahari' seems to indicate some desire for differentiation, but it goes beyond this surface level—the designation actually seems to distinguish the religious affinities and rituals of Odisha from its Southern counterparts, affinities that seem bound up with the worship of Jagannath and the conception of the mahari as his consort: she is Laxmi incarnate, she is Radha, she is Devi (Marglin 1985b; Citarasti 1987).

Strikingly, the devadasis were introduced to Odisha by Shaivite rulers, and were first affiliated to Shaivite temples like Brahmeshwar and Megheshwar.[37] Gradually, they came to be exclusively identified with the worship of Vishnu:

Over the centuries, the legends connected with Lord Jagannath underwent a progressive Vishnu-ization and

Biswas cites Pankaj Charan Das on the *mohan nari* reference. Mohanty Hejmadi and Hejmadi Patnaik cite an article about the 'Mairi' from the *Star of Utkal*, reprinted in their book (2007: 34–6, 49; see also Anonymous 2012).

35 According to Manmohan Ghosh's translation, the *Natyashastra* states: 'Women who, for the protection of the entire harem and for [the king's] prosperity, take pleasure in singing hymns [to gods], and in performing auspicious ceremonies, are known as Mahattaris (matrons)' (Bharatmuni 2007: 207).

36 Cited in Ratna Roy (2007: n.p., note 1).

37 A link with Devi worship is suggested by D. N. Patnaik, who writes that maharis 'were also attached to the Shakti shrines of Mangala at Kakatpur in Puri district and a temple at Khambakul in Cuttack district. They were popularly known as "*Dari*" (Darika) or prostitutes. They not only danced in the temples but also danced on social and religious festive occasions' (2006: 63).

Jagannath came to be identified more and more with Krishna. As a result, a servitor who in the temples of the South was known as devadasi underwent a transformation in Odisha to emerge as Radhadasi, symbolising the highest degree of pure and disinterested love towards Jagannath-Krishna (Citarasti 1987: 51).

The history of the term mahari proffered by Pani also specifies it as a practice bound to Vaishnavism. Certainly, this is the dominative association of the maharis and speaks to an Odishan religious sensibility that centres on the cult of Jagannath and the city of Puri. As I have previously discussed, the mahari role may have been based on pre-existing traditions of dancing girls performing at Odisha's shrines, and, until the 1950s, mahari performance was the only category of ritual service taken up exclusively by women.

Mahari rituals have been well documented by a number of scholars, most notably Frédérique Apffel Marglin, and so I do not dwell on them at length here.[38] I will note that the rituals described here pertain largely to the practices of twentieth-century maharis.[39]

---

38 In the past three decades, there has been an ongoing debate as to whether the mahari order, and devadasi expressions in general, can be viewed from a feminist lens as a mode of women's empowerment, or, oppositionally, as a symptom of patriachal exploitation and violence. This debate, while extremely important, is outside the scope of this chapter and I do not address it here. See Chapters 5 and 6 for a discussion of this issue.

39 My discussion here is based on an analysis of the ethnographic literature, documentation of mahari rituals (such as in Ron Hess's film, *Given to Dance* [1985]), my interviews with specialists in the field, including Shashimoni Devadasi (2008) and Parashmoni Devadasi (2012), and studies of the related repertoire. Ileana Citarasti (1987); Sunil Kothari (1990); Sharmila Biswas (2003–04, 2008); and Ratna Roy (2004, 2006, 2009) have conducted extensive research on mahari practices; and Biswas developed a project to re-present several items from the mahari repertoire (see Sangeet Natak Akademi 2003). Sarat Das, the son of Guru Pankaj Charan Das, has taken on the mission of preserving the choreographer's repertoire through his eponymous Odissi Research Foundation (GPCDORF 2012). Rupashree Mohapatra, who studied with Guru Pankaj Charan Das and Haripriya Devadasi, has established Kala Mandir, her Puri-based institute dedicated to presenting mahari dances in concert form (Mohapatra 2012; see also *Hindu* [2009] and Namita Panda [2011a and 2011b]).

While accounts of mahari practices preceding the twentieth century cannot be fully verified, the extant epigraphic, ethnographic and textual evidence offers a glimpse of a tradition that suggests at least some resonance with the recent forms, if not absolute consonance. It is, of course, impossible to tell definitively.

It appears that the mahari system was identified with cultivating extraordinary expressions of gender. The young girls, usually nine years of age when they joined the order, were often dedicated by their families to the temple, typically as a sign of gratitude for receiving divine blessings, or as a mode of appeasing the deity in fulfillment of a wish (to avoid a calamity or seek a good marriage alliance in the family, for instance). A girl could also be chosen independently by a mahari for adoption. Although her social background held relatively little importance, the girl's beauty, bodily proportions, devotional intensity and artistic aptitude were all appraised before she could be accepted into the system.[40]

The emphasis on a girl's outward appearance and (potential) talents were just as important as her inner spiritual leanings. The construction of an ideal body in these circumstances was contingent on both these factors rather than being mutually exclusive— the cultivation of art and the cultivation of religious character held equal import within a worldview that regarded beauty as inextricably linked to the moral and the good (Dehejia 2009: 65). Beauty was taken as a symbol of the devadasi's innate, essential nature, and the presence of the devadasis in the temples both beautified and beatified the surrounds.

---

40 Historically, the maharis became 'casteless' when they entered temple service and achieved equivalence in status, since they received a new identity through their profession. However, the girls chosen for adoption generally had to belong to 'water-giving' castes, which included most caste groups except the Dalits, or untouchables, and tribals, who existed outside the caste system but whose presence in the temple was nevertheless considered polluting. Shashimoni Devadasi said in an interview with dancer/scholar Rahul Acharya that at the time of her dedication in the early twentieth century, 'it was a norm to choose either Brahmin, Karana, or Khandayat, girls' for the service (2003; translated from Odia by Acharya).

Temple inscriptions illustrate the premium placed on the mahari's attractiveness; at Megheshwar (*c.*1195–1198 CE), for example, the poet Udayan praised the dancing girls 'whose eye-lashes constitute the very essence of captivating the whole world, whose very gait brings about a complete stillness in the activities of the three worlds, whose bangles bejewelled with precious stones serve as unarranged candles during the dance; those deer-eyed maidens are offered in devotion to Him—Lord Shiva' (cited in Patnaik 2006: 32). [41]

The *sari-bandhan* or *gopa sari* ritual marking the girl's dedication to the temple mirrored the marriage ceremony (Citarasti 1987; Roy 2007). First, her outer body was purified with turmeric and her inner body cleansed through fasting. Freshly bathed and dressed in a new sari, bedecked with jewels, she was taken to the temple by her female relatives and the elder maharis for the momentous occasion. Receiving *dikshya* (instruction) from the principal guru signaled her official entry into the mahari order. She then was taken to see the deity. A special sari was tied around her head; she received a fragrant flower garland, signifying eternal union with Jagannath; and the part of her hair was marked with sindoor, vermilion, the red paste symbolizing her newly married status. After performing circumambulations, the newly consecrated devadasi celebrated the occasion with a gathering of her family and friends, where she was welcomed with *arati*[42] and given the gift of a special silk sari, reserved for ceremonial performance. All at the event received *mahaprashad* from the temple.[43] The presence and very

---

41 See also the inscriptions at the Shobhaneshwar and Ananta Basudeva temples, in which similar language is used to describe the dancers and the role of the arts in ritual service (Rajguru 1992: 335–46; Patnaik 2006: 32–4).

42 *Arati* refers to an act of worship in which the devotee venerates the deity using the purifying element of fire, usually by waving oil lamps in front of the image.

43 *Mahaprashad* is the food prepared under the supervision of Laxmi and consecrated by Jagannath and Vimala Devi at the Puri temple, then distributed to devotees. In Hindu thought, partaking *mahaprashad* leads to the expiation of all negative deeds. Importantly, unlike ordinary food, it is never considered *jutha*, a Hindu dietary law relating to food or drink tainted by another's touch or taste. On Hindu concepts of purity and pollution, see Marglin (1985a).

sight of the devadasi promised auspiciousness to all who congre-
gated at this transformative event (Marglin 1985a; Citarasti 1987).

At dusk, the new devadasi was taken to visit the king. As part
of the *palanka-seva* (bed rituals), she symbolically touched his bed
(*sheja meda*) and the two met each other's gaze (*chakshyu milan*).
D. N. Patnaik notes that the palace ritual 'is observed as the Raja
of Puri is venerated as the moving image of Vishnu or Jagannath'
(2006: 56). The mahari became his female counterpart and
consort and was herself known as Chalanti Devi, or 'walking
goddess' (Marglin 1985b, 1990). Disturbingly, there are also firsthand reports provided in Marglin's ethnography, suggesting that
the touching was more than symbolic, and actually carnal in
nature—some kings sexually exploited even very young maharis
in the early twentieth century, reflecting social mores regarding the
age of consent at the time. Indeed, many progressive activists
highlighted the sexual abuse of women and girls in their
campaigns to abolish devadasi systems all across India; though this
was not a uniform experience, it was sufficiently embedded in the
system to elicit urgent calls for social and moral reform.[44]

After her initiation, the acolyte lived with her compatriots in
quarters close to the temple and began a life of religious service.
Along with her new status came the privileges of property owner-
ship, education, artistic training, access to royalty and elevated
ritual status. As a novice, she was given training in dance and
music—depending on her particular skill—by the other devadasis
and their guru, and instructed in religious and political protocols
by the *rajguru* (the head priest representing the king). Following
this period of immersion in aesthetic and devotional disciplines,
she could make her debut as part of a formal temple ritual.

Maharis were subdivided into four broad categories: Bhitara
Gauni, Bahara Gauni, Nachuni, and Pathuari or Sampradanijoga.
Each subgroup was identified closely with a space and time in
which the performance took place—as part of the daily temple ritual

---

44 On this, see the in-depth discussions by Amrit Srinivasan (1990); Avanthi
Meduri (1996); Judith Whitehead (2001); and G. Chandrikha (2009).

or during the festival season. The highest prestige belonged to the Bhitara Gauni who had the greatest physical proximity to the deity as the 'inside singer', and presided over the nocturnal ritual of singing Jagannath to sleep in the innermost quarters of the temple. The Bahara Gauni was literally the 'one who sings outside' the main shrine. The Nachuni, or dancer, also performed outside the sanctum sanctorum, generally in the *nata-mandir* built specially for this purpose but also in the *jagamohan* under the *rajguru*'s supervision (K. C. Mishra 1984: 108). The Pathuari or 'the one of the road', also called Sampradanijoga, aptly held a more public role as her name suggests, performing at religious processions and ceremonies.[45] Different groups of devadasis came together on important occasions like Chandan Yatra (Sandalwood Festival), Rath Yatra (Chariot Festival), Jhulan Yatra (Swing festival), Nabakalebar (installation of new idols), Snan Purnima (Bathing Festival), Janmashtami (Krishna's birth anniversary) and Dola Yatra (Spring Festival). [46]

Although the mahari enjoyed a high status compared to ordinary women, she still had to conform to a disciplinary regime full of rules specific to the religious habitus. These binding regulations, both written and customary, governed the full continuum of her social conduct outside the temple and bodily comportment inside it. On the days that she was to perform at the temple, she was forbidden from speaking to any man. She bathed and dressed in her special sari and followed *habisa*.[47] Generally, once she reached

---

45 D. N. Patnaik states the Pathuaris were once known as Sampradanijoga (2006: 58), and the *Record of Rights* confirms this (see Appendix E and Government of Orissa 1956).

46 Details of devadasi rituals in Odisha, and the occasions when they are performed, are provided in excellent accounts by Frédérique Apffel Marglin (1985a and 1985b); D. N. Patnaik (2006); Ileana Citarasti (1987); and Ratna Roy (2007, 2009). See also Appendix E; Government of Orissa (1956); K. C. Mishra (1984); and Yamini Mubayi (2005). For a comprehensive discussion of the rituals of the Jagannath temple, see Hermann Kulke (1981); Anncharlott Eschmann et. al. (2005); Rahul Acharya and Parama Karuna Devi (2008).

47 *Habisa* is a special Hindu vegetarian diet. Odia cuisine prepared according to its rules avoids the use of stimulating spices (including turmeric), chilis,

the age of consent, she would be seen as sexually available to the king as well as temple priests. These were unconventional sexual mores and relations, outside everyday social norms, but regarded as a part of ritual life to reinforce the special status of the mahari, the deity and the king as intermediaries between the celestial and terrestrial.[48] At the same time, to protect her privileged status, a *mina nahak* or *sahi nahak* (guard) accompanied the mahari to and from the temple. This regulation precluded the possibility of the mahari entering into contact with ordinary men and thus risking her status by mingling with them socially or sexually. Certainly this was intended as a form of sexual control, but it was also imposed in recognition of the mahari's extraordinary status, to guard against public contaminations when she was summoned for ritual occasions and required to manifest a state of purity as defined by the moral and social codes outlined by temple authorities.[49]

The regulation of mahari movements occurred both inside and outside the temple. Rahul Acharya and Parama Karuna Devi (2008) have unearthed the customary laws pertaining to dance in the *Niladri Mahodaya*, a text delineating temple *niti* (rituals). Relying on a mythological frame, the *Niladri Mahodaya* attributes the implementation of the service at Puri to the god Brahma advising Indradyumna: 'Oh King! During the ritual proceedings, daily, there should be arrangement for the playing of the Ghanta (brass-plate instrument), Mardala (percussion) and for dance. This should continue till the Puja (worship) is over.' A second verse declares '[t]he arrangement for a performance of dance and music is a must when the Lord [Jagannath] is being adorned with garlands' during

---

onions and garlic, along with tomatoes, lemons and sugar. Widows following orthodox Hindu tenets largely observe *habisa*, but devotees also accept these food austerities for religious occasions.

48 I should note that many authorities dispute this account of the mahari's sexual availability to the raja and *rajguru*; see, for instance, Acharya and Devi (2008: 332).

49 See Frédérique Appfel Marglin (1985b); Ileana Citarasti (1987); and Buli Mahari, cited in D. N. Patnaik (2006).

Bada Singara, the evening ceremony (*Niladri Mahodaya* 7.17 and 8.49, translated and cited in Acharya and Devi 2008: 333).

At the edge of the fifteenth century CE, the royal authorities issued a legal proclamation, setting the choreographic limits of the devadasi repertoire. This inscription, once on the western wall of the Jagannath temple near the Jayavijaya door, states:[50]

> [T]he mighty Prataparudradeva Maharaja orders: Dancing will be performed thus at the Bhoga time of the elder *thakura* Balarama and *Gitagovinda Thakura* (Jagannath). This dancing will be held from the end of the evening *dhupa* upto the time of *Barasingar dhupa*. The batch (of dancing girls) of Bada Thakura, the fixed female dancers of Kapilesvara thakur, the old batch, the Telanga batch, all will learn no other song than *Gitagovinda* of *Bara Thakur*. They will not sing any other song. No other kind of dancing should be performed before the god. Besides the dancing, there are four Vaisnava singers: they will sing only Gitagovinda. Hearing in one tone from them, those who are ignorant will learn the Gitagovinda song; they should not learn any other song. That Superintendent who

---

50 This is the original old-Odia-language inscription in English transliteration, from the *Journal of the Asiatic Society of Bengal* (Chakravarti 1893: 96–7):

> *Vira Sri Gajapati Gaudesvara navaoki Karnata Kalavargesvara Birabra Sri Prataprudra Maharajankara Samsta anka srahi kakada su budhabare abadharita agayan pramane Bada thakuranka sri Gitagovinda thakuranka bhogabele e nata hoiba. Sanghadhupa Sailatharu e nata hoiba. Badathakura samparada Kapilesvara thakuranka bandha nachunimane puruna samparada telengi samparada emane savihen badathakuranka Gitagovindam ana gita na sikhibe. Ana gita na gaibe ana gita hoi paramesvaranka chhamure na haba. E nata bitarake Vaisnava gaana charijana acchanti, emane Gitagovinda gitahi gaibe. Ehankatharu asiksita mane ekasvarare suni Gitagovinda gitahin sikhibe. Ana gita na sikhibe. Eha je parksa ana gita nata karaile jani se Jagannthanka droha karai.*

The order is dated to Wednesday, the tenth day of the fortnight during the month of Ashadha, on the occasion of Bahuda Jatra, when the chariot returns to the Jagannath temple during the Rath Yatra festivities.

knowingly allows other songs to be sung, and other dancing to be performed, rebels against Jagannatha (translated
and cited in K. C. Mishra 1984: 54–5).

In recognition of its beauty, its *rasa*, its *shringara* and as a sign of
his own allegiance to Vaishnavism, King Prataparudradeva made
it mandatory to use the *Geeta Govinda* as the source of all mahari
rituals. Dance is compulsory—*nata hoiba*, in the original Odia—
as is song from the authorized text: *Ana gita na sikhibe. Ana gita
na gaibe ana gita hoi parameshvaranka cchamure na haba.*[51] Any
other performance constituted a serious violation—*droha karai.*
Dance thus became a powerful sign of the state, and the integration
of the *Geeta Govinda* in the repertoire both represented and
reinforced the auspiciousness of the maharis and the god-king.
Only later in time, the maharis were able to experiment with
vernacular musical and poetic forms for their dance compositions
(Shashimoni Devadasi 2008).

Dance as Puja, Dance as Gift

Field Notes: Puri, Odisha, March 2008

*The mahari is wrapped in a aubergine cotton sari with a white-and-
gold patterned border, the* pallu *draped around her head, A row of red
bangles adorns her arms. She wears several rings on her fingers; a small
diamond decorates her nose. The bright red* sindoor *on her forehead,
marking the part of her hair, announces her married, auspicious status.
Singing a popular Odia song, 'Bansi teji hela', Shashimoni Devadasi
begins to perform a playful* abhinaya.

---

51 The *Madala Panji* credits King Narasimhadeva (r.1278–1309) with
introducing *Geeta Govinda seva* in the temple, though not as legal decree:
'*E uttaru kavi Narasingha Deva raja hoile, Gitagovinda siloukale*' (in old
Odia; cited in Tripathy 2009: 21; see also Dhar 2008: 17–18). However, S. N.
Rajguru maintains there is evidence that Anangabhima earlier appointed a
party of Telangana Sampradaya at the temple in 1230 CE (1992: 148). While
different versions of the *Geeta Govinda* had been used in temple service,
Prataparudradeva's directive made Jayadeva's poetic masterpiece the official
text (Rajguru 1992: 148–9; Tripathy 2009: 24).

FIGURE 2.9. Shashimoni Devadasi performing an *abhinaya* sequence. Puri, Odisha, 7 March 2008. Photograph by the author.

In an earlier time, her dress would have been different—she would have worn the ceremonial garb that we see in pictures of Suhasini Mahari, frozen in time c.1960: an embroidered velvety blouse, short-sleeved, dark in colour, tucked into the waist of a lighter-hued sari, body covered with heavy gold ornaments (see fig. 6.6).

Still, in those few and fragmented moments, Shashimoni Devadasi transports us to another world. With her vivid facial expressions, she poignantly evokes the rasa *of* shringara *contained in the melancholy music. After the phrase* gada-padma-hasta, *she bursts into a short nritta sequence, reciting the* bols *so familiar in Odissi:* 'thei ta thei ta thei / thei ta thei ta thei / thei ta thei ta thei / na kiri kiri . . . diguna thei / diguna thei / diguna thei.' *She sits in a loose Chowk position, her knees slightly bent and turned out. Then she moves her feet into Kunchita Pada and alternately stamps them lightly, her hands lyrically displaying* mudras—now Pataka, now Mayura, now Hansasya. *The movements are abrupt but soft, not sharp. She follows up with a Sanskrit song from the* Geeta Govinda, 'Lalita labanga', *accompanying it with fine, nuanced expressions. She keeps the* tala and laya *of the music steady with claps of her hand. Quick and eager and animated in her*

FIGURE 2.10. Parashmoni Devi, the last surviving mahari to date, at her home in Puri Odisha, December 3, 2012. Photograph by the author.

movements, we would never know she is in her eighties. Through her dance, she confers a blessing on those in her presence.

When I met her in 2008, Shashimoni Devadasi was one of two surviving maharis in Puri.[52] Sadly, she has since passed away.[53] Today, Parashmoni Devi is the sole carrier of the tradition. Faithfully, she makes a daily effort to go to the temple and sing with a group in the *Devasabha mandapa* (pavilion). I had the privilege of meeting her at her humble home and attending her evening ritual on 23 December 2014, where, despite her fragile health, she sat clad in an elegant cotton sandalwood-coloured sari, and sang two solos

---

52 After mahari service was discontinued in Odisha, Shashimoni negotiated a liminal identity, where she was revered for her ritual status but could not take up a regular livelihood or lifestyle as a bride of Jagannath. In recognition of her service, she received a modest sum of 1,000 rupees per month from the state government (Avinash Sharma 2015). She lived with her guardian, an adopted son, Somnath Panda, in a house on Narayana Chowk, located in a lane adjacent to the Jagannath temple.

53 Shashimoni Devadasi left this world at the age of 92 on 19 March 2015; see Ellen Barry (2015); Avinash Sharma (2015); and Leela Venkataraman (2015a).

followed by chorals in a two-hour set from 7 to 9 p.m. Song selections included a lullaby for the infant Krishna by his mother, Yashoda; Radha anticipating a visit from a youthful Krishna, in the Rasleela genre; and Odia and Sanskrit lyrics based on the *Geeta Govinda* and other sources. The *Record of Rights* (1956) states that Parashmoni had the title of Bhitara Gauni while Shashimoni is listed as a Sampradanijoga, who performed at the Sakaladhupa (morning service) and took part in public processions like Chandan Yatra,[54] as a dancer on the boat (*chapa*) decorated for the ceremony; during Bahuda Yatra;[55] and for Rukmini Bibaha, the wedding celebration of Krishna and Rukmini, the god's principal wife.

Shashimoni learnt dance (*naacha-bhava*), from her adoptive mahari mothers and Shri Mohan Mahapatra, one of the last gurus affiliated with the Jagannath temple (interview with author 2008). The training emphasized the qualities of *bhava*, or feeling: 'We never had any strict grammar for dance. All lessons were quite spontaneous and we were supposed to feel the dance rather than doing it mechanically' (interview with Acharya 2003). Though the learning style was flexible, there were still set pieces to memorize in the mahari dance routine. For her inaugural temple performance at Sakaladhupa, she 'performed to the accompaniment of mardala (percussion) and gini (cymbals), quite oblivious of the surrounding. [. . .] The dance was a *nritta* (pure dance) without any song accompanying it. The second performance took place during Bada Singara (the god's bedtime) and this was performed behind closed doors. During this time the dance was supposed to be expressional and the songs accompanying the dance were from the *Geeta Govinda* alone' (2003).

Shashimoni Devadasi became a mahari at the age of eight. From what she remembers, she conducted her ritual service every day for 40 years after the *sari-bandhan*, and 'enjoyed performing

---

54 A major festival where the deities are taken on a public procession to specially decorated boats for a series of 21 days.

55 Bahuda Yatra is the day when the chariot returns to the Jagannath temple during the Rath Yatra festivities.

for the Lord. Each day was a divine experience for me and I used to become ecstatic during my performances' (2003). She continued to perform her duties well after the time after mahari service formally declined, yet her role during festival occasions was not at all ornamental. On the occasion of Janamashtami, celebrating the birth of Krishna, she acted as mother Nandarani, and during Nabakalebar, she took on the essential role of singing outside the door of the room where the new bodies of the deities were being carved, until the carpenters finished their work with providential care. Her specialty songs included 'Chalo chalo natha, he jiba mandira' and 'Nata kori chalu kette range, je keya phullo' (Venkataraman 2015a: n.p.).

It is interesting to note that when some Odissi revivalists and dancers speak of reconstructing the dance, they downplay or disavow the role of the maharis, claiming that they simply embellished their songs with *mudras* and *bhava*.[56] Yet, from mahari descriptions, demonstrations and existing documentation, it appears that there was, in fact, a strong *nritta* component in Mahari Naach.[57] Rather

---

56 For examples of this tendency, see the discussions by Sri Gopal (2005) and Alessandra Lopez y Royo (2008: 12–13). Leela Venkataraman suggests 'any dance the post-1945 mahari clan claimed was just "naccha" with no distinct tradition. Whatever the maharis demonstrated later was just learnt from the gotipua (a rigorous, more folksy ritual dance) gurus' (2015a: n.p.). Venkataraman also paraphrases Priyambada Mohanty Hejmadi's claim that 'nobody actually had seen a Mahari perform, for she sang and danced whatever little she did, only for Jagannatha [. . .] The proscenium version of the Mahari's dance was a later develpment by gurus' (2015b: 56). Many of the Odissi specialists I interviewed also emphasized this same point: that maharis did not have a robust dance practice. However, Venkataraman does emphasize that 'Sashimoni without any of the systematic dance training was, according to all who saw her, a born dancer' (2015a: n.p.).

57 See, for instance, the footage of mahari performances *in Given to Dance* (1985); the lecture-demonstration by Sharmila Biswas in the 2003 SNA colloquium; Dinanath Pathy (2007: 50–1), quoting Dhiren Dash's Odia articles on mahari dance as his basis, explains the structural elements of mahari dance: (1) Dhupa Nata (2) Patuara Nrutya (3) Sabha Nrutya (4) Hera Nata (5) Chatau Taranga (6) Abhishekh (7) Bheta (pata shringara). These sources provide evidence of a wide-ranging dance repertoire belonging to the

than doing interpretive dances set to poems, it seems that the maharis drew upon a repository of rich compositions, combining body technique with expressive *abhinaya* traditions.[58]

For those of us who have not witnessed mahari rituals firsthand, we can only imagine what the dances must have been like in the atmosphere of the temple. The mahari service was qualitatively set apart from the other modes of worship. Its origination in the female body, its immersion in *rasa* and its affective dimension made it a spiritual offering unparalleled by any other kind of worship. Babaji, a *mahant* (spiritual leader) at a local *matha* (monastery), elaborates eloquently on the singularity of dance as puja:

> I believe that [. . .] among all the kinds of [temple] services performed [. . .] the devadasi's service [was] the most important. [It] is a soul service, an emotional service, a service from the inside; there is nothing superficial about it. The service that devadasi offers god, god recognizes and appreciates. Other things like food, flowers, jewellery, clothes, whatever we have given—we cannot know whether or not god receives them, though we bring them to him anyway. But whatever the devadasi offers—god fully takes

maharis. Sanjukta Panigrahi also noted that in her efforts to aid the construction of Odissi dance in the 1950s, she consulted a mahari as one of her sources (see Varley 264). Indrani Rahman did the same (see Chapter 6). Before the mid-twentieth century, other descriptions of devadasi performance are available in the *Chaitanya Charitamrita*, colonial travel accounts, Abananindranath Tagore's memoirs, and the *Record of Rights*, among others; see Chapters 5 and 6 and Appendices D and E.

58 The alleged lack of a 'real' mahari dance is often cited as the reason for the peripheralization of maharis from Odissi's revival process (see Lopez y Royo 2008). Many of the dancers and gurus who I informally spoke to in the course of my fieldwork said the maharis primarily performed *abhinayas*, rather than complex dances like the gotipuas; others even denied they were dancers, saying that they were 'just' singers who interpreted song lyrics using basic hand gestures and facial expressions. However, dancers like Rupashree Mohapatra, Sharmila Biswas, Ritha Devi, Ratna Roy, and those from the Pankaj Charan Das lineage have explored the legacy of mahari dance in their work.

this gift, and no one else can conjure it again. This is a great service (2008; my translation).

Dance here is envisioned as an ineffable gift—a pure act of giving, mingling devotion with pleasure. In Babaji's view, mahari dance was a form of private, sensuous exchange with the deity, contingent upon the presence of the body. Further, dance was a renewable gift, something which could be offered again and again, precisely because it was inalienable from the body of the person producing it.

The idea of devadasi performance as a consecrated gift to the deity was historically reinforced by its correlation to the times of puja (worship) and *bhog* (food offerings) in the Jagannath temple. Jasobanta Dhar believes that, based on her research, performers used *upasana mudras* (postures and gestures) and that 'different hymns and stor[i]es were rendered before Lord [Jagannath] at different times' (2008: 18). The Nachuni presented her *nritta* during Sakaladhupa, a morning ritual performed while food is prepared for distribution to devotees at the temple whereas the Bhitara Gauni sang during Sandhyadhupa/Badasingara, as the deities were prepared for sleep with the last puja of the day (Acharya and Devi 331–2). At Sakaladhupa, the Nachuni performed a purely non-narrative dance set to percussion, which highlighted her rhythmic dexterity and skill. According to Marglin, the devadasi did not face the deity—the dance was intended for the devotees gathering for *bhog* on the temple premises although her body was positioned in such a way that the deity could still have a glimpse of the performance if he wished (1990).

Although the Nachuni did not directly serve the deity with her dance in this instance, its close connection to *bhog* ensured its status as a central feature of puja. What Lawrence Babb writes of puja in Chhatisgarh[59] rings true in Puri's Jagannath temple as well:

[W]ithout a food offering of some kind the ritual would simply not be puja in the conventional sense of the term.

---

59 At the time of Babb's writing in 1975, Chhatisgarh was part of the central Indian state of Madhya Pradesh. On 1 November 2000, it acquired official statehood. Chhatisgarh's eastern boundary borders Odisha.

[. . . A]lways, in puja, some kind of food is given, and however the act may be elaborated under particular circumstances, the mode of giving seems always to be the same: food is given to the deity, it is taken back, and it is distributed to the worshippers as *prasad*. The food offering is as essential a part of the ritual sequence as the preliminary purifications, and [. . .] it is some ways the central and indispensable act, the core around which all else is elaboration and overlay (1975: 54).

This applies to devadasi performance, which can be seen as an 'elaboration and overlay' of the broader puja event centering food offerings. The Sakaladhupa dance used to take place simultaneously with the preparation of the daily *bhog*, preceding its public distribution, while the Sandhyadhupa performance would take place immediately after the deity's evening *bhog*, conducted as a private ritual in the innermost chambers of the temple. The correlations and overlaps between food and dance, the pleasure of the senses and the ecstasies of devotion, were invoked synaesthetically in the poetics of *rasa* (as flavour, as feeling).[60]

At the Jagannath temple, the devadasi dance resonated with layers of meaning, synthesizing Brahmanical, Tantric, Shakti and Vaishnav thought, with the abiding influence of Tantra visible in the performance of the *panchakarma* rituals. In a reverse valuation, *panchakarma* represents five elements forbidden to Brahman orthodoxy but fully embraced by disciples of Tantra: *matsya* (fish), *mamsa* (meat), *mudra* (money), *madya* (alcohol/intoxicants) and *maithuna* (sex). These *panchakarmas* are metaphorically integrated in the special puja, with *maithuna* symbolized by 'a peculiar kind of dancing by Devadasis (*uktachanritya*)' (K. C. Mishra 1984: 153). Ileana Citarasti elaborates on this practice, describing 'a time, when during the tantric Panchamakara puja preceding the singing of the *Geeta Govinda* song, the attending devadasi had to execute some *bhandas* or acrobatic poses corresponding to some of the 64

---

60 On this aspect of *rasa*, see Richard Schechner (2001) and Bharat Gupt (2006: 260–73).

bandhas of the *Kama Sutra*. Known as "Maithuna Nritya", this dance symbolized sexual union in the tantric puja' (1987: 52).

Marglin has delineated in detail this aspect of the dance, sharing the Rajguru's view that the Nachuni's dance represented *maithuna*, creating an atmosphere of *shringar rasa*, a state of erotic intensity and ecstasy that ultimately united the worshipper with her object of devotion. As an embodiment of *maithuna*, the dance symbolically generated sexual fluids on temple grounds. Whereas in orthodox worldviews, effluvia was seen as a contaminant and thus prohibited from the temple, with the devadasis it was elevated and deliberately transformed into a holy substance, keeping with the Tantric symbologies assimilated into the cult of Jagannath. In Tantric tradition, female secretions were regarded in sacred terms as *madhu* (honey), as nectar, as a sweet intoxicant (Shaw 1995: 157). The dance also imparted a *rasa* that complemented the Tantric meaning. Embracing these beliefs, devotees witnessing the performance would later roll on the ground where the mahari had danced, in the hope that her auspiciousness would accrue to them; this was also a direct and visceral way of absorbing the *rasa* created by her dance (Marglin 1990). It should be noted that this is an esoteric intepretation; in popular perception, taking dust from the mahari's feet is a show of respect, and yields an *ashirbad* or blessing (Mohanty Hejmadi and Hejmadi Patnaik 2007: 41–2).

As a ritual service, the dance symbolized the sexual and spiritual union of the mahari with her deity-consort while presenting a separate enactment of puja. The position of dance as a ritual service crystallized the non-reciprocal nature of the gift to the gods. Dance is both a highly material activity, located in the intimate milieu of the dancer's body, and highly intangible, in that it cannot be fully captured outside the boundaries of those bodies. Lose the dancers and you lose the dance, which is why performance—cast as a unilateral offering in the ritual setting—was a singular kind of gift to the gods. As Babaji and the maharis argue, the nature of the dance is such that it cannot be commodified in the same way as other material goods in the ritual context. As *puja*, it has a specific quality that demarcates it—dance is an offering of the body, of passions that lie in the body and all that transcends the body, at once. While presents of food, clothing, money and other items used for worship can travel among devotees, none—except those who actually embody it—can 'give' the ritual dance.

Because dance performance cannot be divided from the body, it is different in character from those commodities that circulate in the world as autonomous objects and which symbolically stand in place of the donors. While in the religious context these gifts acquire a holy aura, in an extra-religious context they simply serve as human forms of sustenance: rice and ghee are everyday nourishment, not *mahaprashad*; clothes and jewels cover the body for the sake of social modesty; money is used for worldly transactions. These ordinary things, in extraordinary settings, are transformed; they lack innate and fixed signifying powers. Mahari Naach, and the mahari identity, in contrast, were always already holy. Once consecrated to the temple, maharis achieved an eternally auspicious status. Unlike objects and practices that could change meaning outside of a religious context, the maharis retained their elevated position after entering a sanctified state, accomplished through their marriage to Jagannath. The mahari presence brought devotees into the realm of the spiritual while heightening the devotional ambience of the temple.

Dance served as a potent emblem of spiritualized eros at Jagannath-Puri. At Sakaladhupa, the Nachuni's dance was instrumental for intensifying the emotional experience of the devotees; and at Sandhyadhupa, the Bhitara Gauni's performance for the deity became an erotic encounter infused with *shringar rasa*. The devadasi's body became a site of sensual power, as she channelled religious sentiment and mediated encounters between the worlds of the mortal and the divine; her dance emblematized the intertwining of the sensual and the sacred. By day, her ritual was made public; by night, it was privatized, secluded to the inner chambers of the deity (Shashimoni Devi 2003 and 2008; Parashmoni Devi 2012).

Ritual Dance and the Distributed Body

In the social order of things, the devadasi institution was unusual, even exceptional. It was one of the only systems designed to integrate women into ritual service in the temple hierarchy, in a context where religious authority was usually considered the purview of caste-privileged men. Historically, the devadasi role existed as one in a range of social roles available to women in medieval and colonial India: as reproductive agent and moral guardian of the family (daughter, wife, mother); as peasant or labourer (usually women in the service class, from lower-caste and working-class groups); as artist (courtesans, poets, public entertainers); as ruler (queens, princesses), and spiritual agent (philosophers, ascetics, mystics), to name a few.

At first glance, while the repertoire was indeed limited, and women's public roles were severely diminished in comparison to men's, the interplay of gender and caste presented a more complex picture. Certain feminist readings of the devadasi practice often emphasize the dancer's position as part of a patriarchal order in which women's bodies are controlled by male agents—kings, priests and even the deity himself—and configured as the object of their gaze (see, for instance, Hanna 1998). However, looking at the devadasis in the context of their local social system and values demands a reorientation of such a reading. Compared to conventional gendered modes, the devadasi order functioned as an exceptional matrilineal enclave within a larger patriarchal system, giving women an avenue for accruing material and religious power. While maharis never enjoyed absolute freedom (given the constraints and rules that governed their lives), relative to other women, their position was undoubtedly a privileged one.

Devadasis, as the perpetually auspicious brides of Jagannath, enjoyed social authority predicated on their superior status: they had access to wealth, property, education and ritual praxis; they could never be widowed, and were thus never subject to the stigmatization and exclusion the status entailed. Simultaneously mortal and divine, their proximity to the deity endowed them with extra-ordinary eminence. Their position was unmatched by any other service group, since they were the deity's exclusive intimates, intermediaries between the celestial and terrestrial worlds, the very embodiment of goddess Laxmi.

Thus the devadasis inhabited an exotic milieu whose contours were altogether estranged from that of ordinary women. This was particularly palpable in the concept of women as reproductive agents. For devadasis, the idea of reproduction reiterated their special standing—they were expected to engage in sexual relations with an approved class of men, especially the king-as-Jagannath. But this ritual/sexual service had no procreative duty or significance attached to it.[61]

Yet the absence of a responsibility for bearing children in no way suggested the devadasis could shed responsibility for reproduction in a larger sense—the reproduction of a *body of ritual knowledge*. With the devadasis, reproduction was still a feminine act, yes, but instead of implying direct procreation (as it would under quotidian norms), it implied *cultural* reproduction through the *dancing* female body. That is, the devadasi's power lay in her creative capacities, not her procreative propensities, as was the case with ordinary women. Indeed, the transmission and reenactment of cultural capital became the devadasi's special assignment. In both the everyday (social) and exceptional (religious) instances of reproduction, the instrument was the same—the female body— but their labour and somatic significations were qualitatively different. In the context of the devadasi order, there was a move away from the domestic arena of family labour and social reproduction to the religious arena of ritual service and animation of cultural heritage.

Rituals are primarily embodied acts, endowed with social power and partitioned from normative routines and conventions, conducted by authorized agents (Hobsbawm 1983; Bell 1992

---

61 Indeed, procreation was discouraged, and there was no direct need for it to sustain the mahari system, since adoption perpetuated the order. Having children would in fact diminish the devadasi's status, blurring the line between her position and that of an ordinary woman. For maharis who did become biological mothers, the children's affiliation to the temple was an important way of keeping the rituals alive, and perhaps also a way of keeping the temple's property and wealth intact—girls generally became maharis, and boys were trained as musicians. The situation changed in the mid-twentieth century and the children of maharis gradually entered mainstream life. For more on this, see the interviews with surviving maharis in *Given to Dance* (1985); their perspectives are recorded as well in Marglin's ethnography (1985b).

and 1997). They are highly performative, relying on a repertoire of citational gestures, often framed as part of traditions with mystical beginnings, traditions cast as timeless and unalloyed. Most significantly, they create a world parallel to the quotidian—a world which, though temporary and transient, is nevertheless transformative and registers real effects.

As a ritual form that relies on mimesis and co-creation with the embodied forms of the deity and the temple, Mahari Naach produces a kinesthetic theory of the subject that, I argue, resonates with eminent anthropologist Alfred Gell's concept of 'distributed self'. In *Art and Agency*, Gell defines 'distributed personhood' as 'personhood distributed in the milieu, beyond the body boundary' (1998: 104). Discussing idol-worship, and the agentic qualities of iconic images of the divine, Gell theorizes the art object as a mediating force in cultural life, dwelling on the forms of social power it generates and the circuits it is embedded within, critiquing the semiotic approach in which the art object is positioned as a passive text to be 'read.' What Gell proposes, in short, is a theory of the art object as performance.

Analysing religious idols and their specific corporealities as 'not portraits, not depictions, but (artefactual) *bodies*,' (ibid.: 98; original emphasis), Gell speaks of representations and what he calls their original or authentic essences as virtually indivisible. He argues that the image *extends* rather than *substitutes* the entity in question, and 'forges a direct link between the image as an index of the prototype, and the index as a (detached) *part* of the prototype' (104). In other words, if the image is an index rather than a sign, its substance can be immediately conflated with it, as the index is a symptom rather than symbol of the thing represented. 'We are not accustomed to think of images [. . .] as parts of persons, *limbs*, as it were' (ibid.: 104; emphasis added). This indexical relationship repudiates a semiotic approach in which the signifier and the signified retain their separate coherences, and posits a relationship of synechdoche in its place:[62]

62 Gell, drawing on Charles Sanders Peirce's semiotic theory and his delineations of the icon, index and sign, uses the well-known example of smoke and fire to illustrate his point about framing the index as part of the entity in

[I]f the 'appearances' of things are material parts of things, then the kind of leverage which one obtains over a person or a thing by having access to their image is comparable, or really identical, to the leverage which can be obtained by having access to some physical part of them; especially if we introduce the notion that persons may be 'distributed,' i.e. all their 'parts' are not physically attached, but are distributed around their ambience (ibid.: 105–06).

This indexical relation allows Gell to speak of an object's emanations as its material ambassadors, as 'flying simulacras' and 'limbs' that elongate the presence of the thing, expanding its reach into other spaces and times (ibid.: 105).

Gell's idea of the art object as anaphoric embodiment—as performance—is a particularly productive insight that relates to dance and other bodily practices as interventions in the world.[63] Substitute 'dance' for 'art object' and imagine the mahari's moving body as 'flying simulacra' that touches with its 'limbs' the space of the temple and the icon of the deity, vivifying both—and receiving, in turn, their consecrating force. Then picture the body of the deity, his vibrant stillness engendering space and transforming it, returning the gaze of the dancer and empowering her through the indexical experience of *darshan*, of sight-as-touch. And conjure the body of the temple, activated and anthropomorphized through its relation to the rejuvenating relations with dancer and deity. In this continual cycle, the three elements—the body of the temple, deity and dancer—disperse among themselves, mutually incorporate each other, reenact each other, co-constituted in a triangle of corporeal power.

In speaking of a distributed body as it related to devadasi performance at the Jagannath temple, I am arguing that dance had a diffuse property—dispensed across bodies, spaces and

---

question (1998: 104). Likewise, Gell refuses the distinctions made between iconic and aniconic idols (1998: 97–8).

63 In my view, the traditional idea of the sign in the semiotic framework too has value. Instead of abandoning either one, then, we can arrive at a more textured approach to dance theory by embracing both sign and index, meaning *and* mediation, as modes of analysis.

objects—even as it coalesced in the mahari's body, granting its bearer a complex intersubjectivity. Further, ritual dance mobilized the concept of the distributed body in perpetuating itself as tradition. For ritualization created a principle of embodiment that is neither just singular nor plural, neither just one nor many, neither partible nor complete—it was one constructed liminally in between these states as a transindividual force.[64] The distributed body was no fragmented body, however; there was a wholeness and auspiciousness ascribed to it, and its sacredness derives precisely from its distributed capacity—its ability to enact, translate and propagate customs associated with religiosity. In the mahari context, the singular dancing body became porous and fractal, regarded as auspicious, infused with spiritual properties; through the ritual activity, the body became sanctified, part of a sacred lineage with complex religious and ideological attachments. In thinking of the distributed body, we can think of an intangible heritage made tangible; the materialization of the abstract in a multiplicity of forms; the corporeal conjuring the ethereal.

Through ritualization, the distributed body was collapsed not only into other bodies but also into the space surrounding it. The temple acted reciprocally as an archive of corporeal relations. Architecturally conceived as a body and containing manifestations of that body, it was itself a distributed body that housed other bodies, both still (in the form of sculpture), animated (in the form of the deity) and moving (in the form of pilgrims, pandits and performers). The aura of auspiciousness was magnified through

---

64 These are insights borrowed from Marilyn Strathern (1988) and Roy Wagner (1991) in their theorizations of 'dividual personhood' and 'fractal persons' respectively. Strathern argues, based on her fieldwork in Melanesia, that '[f]ar from being regarded as unique entities, Melanesian persons are as dividually as individually conceived. They contain a generalized sociality within' and are cultivated through 'the plural and composite site of the relationships that produce them. The singular person can be imagined as a social microcosm' (1988: 13). Wagner pursues the related idea that 'a *fractal person* is never a unit standing in relation to an aggregate, or an aggregate standing in relation to a unit, but always an entity with relationship integrally implied' (1991: 163; emphasis added).

mimesis. As it carried out its ritual functions, the dancing body affirmed the sacred status of the temple and the deity through its intense exaltation in performance. Dance became a form of divining the body—of the dancer, the deity and the temple.

The distributed body was one expression of the subject that lives among a range of other conceptions in Hindu thought. It distributed spiritual properties into the live dancing body, and animated the still body of the deity and temple, allowing the spiritual presence to materialize in the world: and it distributed itself across different bodies through the 'restored behaviour' of transmitting and replicating movement and gesture (Schechner 2004; Schneider 2011). As Vatsyayan underscores, the notion of 'one form trasnmitted through different physical bodies' is the key idea 'which sums up [an] Indian world view and its concepts and its strategies of concretisation' (1982: 15).[65]

The construct of the distributed body offers a strong counterpoint to the trope, often promulgated in Western dance and performance theory, of the dancing subject as eternally vanishing. Supposedly elusive and ephemeral, dance signals the 'disappearing' ontology of performance, ungraspable, elusive and ephemeral, as it moves fleetingly at the edges of the 'vanishing point' (Siegel 1973; Phelan 1993). Yet, this fallible discourse of dance's impermanence conceals the actual evidence dance *does* leave behind, evidence of its substantive qualities, its resonance, its effects—the 'inscriptions of gesture' it leaves in sculpture and scripture, in scaffolds of flesh, and memorializes in muscle and bone (Connerton 1989; Ness 2008). These indexical traces allow for the continual reenactment of a given dance performance.

The notion of the disappearing subject of dance is a potent myth, governing much of the discourse in which the temporal presence of dance is twinned ineluctably with its purported and palpable absence (Foster 1995; Lepecki 2004). But that idea is predicated upon the privileging of the *individual* body, and holds weight principally in discourses in which the singular self acts as imprimatur. In systems like Mahari Naach, where the self was

---

65 See also Zarrilli (1984 and 1998) on this point.

decentred in place of distributed personhood, the question of 'vanishing' was elided. While the impermanence of the singular body was acknowledged, it did not hold absolute import. This is not to suggest that mahari ritual practice promoted the notion of the interchangeability of dancing bodies. Far from it. Rather, the idea of a transindividual subject surfaces powerfully in such ritual thought. Sacrificing the pure agency and temporality of the 'one' allowed for the possibility of producing 'many' dancing bodies through acts of transmission in the ritual concatenation, leading to the continuity of dance *in* time rather than its constant interruption *by* time. Strikingly, the reenactments of the dancers mirrored that of the deities to whom they were dedicated—even those divine bodies were not considered singular but plural and continually reproducible in the cycle of rebirth, as witnessed in the Nabakalebar ceremony.

The distributed body, simultaneously a sign and index of the dance, became larger than the solo self; in its transindividual framing, it suggested a practice of renewal, a constant re-emergence through multiplication and re-embodiment, through what Diana Taylor calls 'acts of transfer' (2004). For in the ritual dynamic, 'the place of residue is arguably *flesh* in a network of body-to-body transmission of affect and enactment—evidence, across generations, of impact' (Schneider 2011: 100). Mahari Naach refused the cult of the individual *and* the cult of the collective, mediating between these two tendencies. The distributed body transmitted dance across multiple subjects—subjects who receive their knowledge of dance through direct transmission from another, as gift— offering an alternative for imagining the implicit fragility of danced knowledge, and posing a new opening: dance as an abiding material act, translated from body to body. These successive bodies indexed each other, embedded in a diffuse set of relations, revealing the continuity and the permanence of the dance in all its migrations, resonating beyond the corporeal boundary of a single subject, beyond the finite limits of flesh and bone. And in moving to intersubjectivity, the dancing body reverberated in the performative bodies of the deity and the temple, connecting the three entities in a dispersed, distributed corporeality.

The idea of the distributed self in Mahari Naach stands as something of an intervention into, and interruption of, normative models of personhood. One of the popular (if reductive) truisms about Indian identity in the standard scholarship centres on the absence of an individualist theory—the notion being that the individual is subsumed by the group.[66] Indian personhood in this schema is posited as relational and hierarchical and appears to be coercively determined by superseding institutions and powers. This dichotomized and Orientalized idea of the subject subtends much of the discourse on Indian cultural practices, especially ritual. But these neat categorizations fall apart when we test these claims against actual performed repertoires. What these dominant and totalizing narratives fail to consider are contesting notions of the subject, which, though marginal and misapprehended, still radiate a powerful presence. As Richard G. Fox reminds us, 'even if the [dominant] Indian cultural conception of the person is based on the effacement of individuality, it is not wholly constitutive of all self-identities' (in Dissanayake 1996: 106).

The importance of the distributed body as a concept goes well beyond the interrogation of abstract theories of subjectivity. Additionally, it challenges the tenets and tenor of contemporary Odissi performance. As argued, Mahari Naach vitalized, and was in turn vitalized by, its surrounds; the dance, temple and deity were interdependent and mutually constituting corporeal agents. By appropriating Mahari Naach in its fold, Odissi dancers today often claim to propagate what they posit as the devotional essence of the mahari performance. Yet, as developed for the proscenium stage, Odissi presents an acontextual, dehistoricized and atemporal version of mahari ritual. Aesthetic strategies such as using ancient temples as a performance backdrop for public Odissi performances, placing images of Jagannath on stage and rhetorically identifying Odissi as a devotional dance because of its partial

---

66 See, for instance, Louis Dumont (1986). For a countering view of the complexities of Indian notions of 'self', see Avanthi Meduri (1992); Thomas P. Kasulis et al. (1993); Wimal Dissanayake (1996); and Phillip Zarrilli (1998); for a broader discussion of religious selfhood and performances of agency, see Talal Asad (2003) and Saba Mahmood (2005).

alliance with mahari tradition, are all gestures designed to bring the atmosphere and interiors of ritual space outside the physical parameters of the temple. These are attempts to recreate Mahari Naach, or at least approximate its feel. Such Odissi performances gesture towards a complex history that it both invokes and erases in the same moment.

What cannot be replicated today is the tradition or philosophy that produced Mahari Naach, even if its elements are now preserved in Odissi's repertoire. Under the rubric of Odissi, mahari ritual was excised from the ritual process and exhibited as its analeptic relic. The content was partitioned from its past context. Dance, of course, involves much more than simply importing a set of movements and transposing them onto new bodies; habitus matters as much as technique. Odissi is ideologically committed to promulgating Mahari Naach but fails in the appropriative manoeuvre precisely because what it seeks is ungraspable. In the absence of the spatial and iconographic relationships that shaped Mahari Naach, Odissi in its concert form loses the potential of producing and mobilizing the distributed body, installing a fully modern subject in its place.

I do not mean to lament the loss of mahari ritual in the present and, concomitantly, its discursive and aesthetic knowledge; for Odissi produces its own spatial and spectatorial relations. Rather, my aim here has been to recognize the different paradigm in which mahari ritual operated and acknowledge its conceptual significance while deconstructing a narrative in Odissi that suggests a total identification between the two. The crux of the difference, I have argued, lies in the concept of the distributed body. The potential of Mahari Naach to posit an alternative subject is, however, diminished by postcolonial movements that deny the importance of ritual dance, either by stigmatizing or sanitizing it. The attempt to replicate the aura of Mahari Naach in Odissi represents both futility and impossibility: a failed reenactment. And so perhaps the potential of the distributed body lies not in the present or future, but only in disparate gestures of history, in the recesses of the past.

Chapter 3

DOMINANT HISTORIOGRAPHIES
DANCE AND THE MUSLIM THESIS

On a cool Delhi evening, wandering around the courtyard of the Crafts Museum with a friend, we ran into a troupe of young Odissi dancers, brightly robed in silk saris woven in the elaborate Ikat designs for which Odisha is renowned.[1] An array of intricate silver ornaments adorned their tiny frames. Delicate white *shola* flowers embellished their tightly bound tresses, while a *shikhara*, shaped like a miniature temple spire, rose up from the chignon.[2] Filigreed *thiya* dangled from strands of their hair. Each child's face was decorated with drops of *chandan* along the arc of the brows, then around a large red bindi in the centre of their foreheads—the pale colours contrasting with the dark *kajal* painted around the eyes in a thick line, like the silhouette of a fish. Like the eyes of the goddess Durga (fig. 3.1).

---

1 Ikat is a pattern of geometric motifs created through a special technique of weaving and tie-dyeing silk or cotton cloth. Odishan craftspeople are known for their artistry in this realm. See Kokyo Hatanaka (1996); G. K. Ghosh and Shukla Ghosh (2000); Rosemary Crill (1998); and Chelna Desai (1988) for histories, analyses and visual examples of this fabric art.

2 *Shola* refers to pith, a type of dried reed used to make crafts and jewellery in Odisha, West Bengal and Assam, and to make religious images—especially icons of goddesses—and decorations for dancers. The *shikhara* is a type of head-decoration worn by Odissi performers. *Thiya* are small, silver hair ornaments usually worn in the centre of the chignon; they are supposed to resemble Krishna's flute. *Chandan* is sandalwood paste. *Kajal* is black kohl. Many of these dancerly adornments are prescribed in texts detailing the aesthetics of Odissi, like the *Natyashastra* and *Abhinaya Chandrika*, as beautifying oneself is considered auspicious. See D. N. Patnaik (2006: 94–8).

FIGURE 3.1. A gotipua from Dasabhuja Gotipua Odissi Nrutya Parisad, the troupe started by legendary guru Maguni Das and based in Raghurajpur, near Puri, Odisha. Photograph courtesy of Maguni Das.

Shyly, the dancers exchanged smiles and greetings with us upon our encounter in the open space, then gracefully hurried away to ready themselves for the twilight performance. Wrapped around their ankles were the *ghungur*, strings of small bells that softly chimed each time they took a step. We were charmed by the appearance of this gaggle of giggling girls. Except—they were boys.

A surprise, or an anomaly? Neither. These were the famous gotipua dancers—young boys who dress up as girls for public

Odissi recitals—uniting masculine and feminine expressions in a single body. Seemingly unusual, their presence and their performances of gender are neither startling nor strange within the contours of the Odishan cultural imagination.

The tradition of gotipua (literally, 'single boy') is one of the cultural practices which contributed to the formation of Odissi.[3] Several gurus responsible for the dance's regeneration in the twentieth century—including Kelucharan Mahapatra, Deba Prasad Das and Mayadhar Raut—were trained as gotipuas in their youth, and consequently brought with them the techniques, vocabularies and styles of spectacular presentation infused in the genre's past to the present body of Odissi. Patrons, teachers and practitioners who sustained gotipua dance as an autonomous art form in the twentieth century into the present include Chandrashekhar Patnaik, Birabar Sahoo, Gangadhar Pradhan and Maguni Das. The visibility of the gotipua practice, anchored deeply in the cultural life of Odisha, has achieved further recognition beyond the region, in tandem with the rise of Odissi dance.

Formations of the Gotipua Tradition

As with other antecedents of present-day Odissi, the stories of the gotipua tradition's beginnings cannot be confidently narrated as they lean more towards conjecture than verifiable facts. What the threads of these narratives illuminate, however, are certain discourses about the gotipua past—some layered in legend, others in history and yet others amalgamating both. The line separating myth and reality is difficult to draw in a cultural context where the two are so deeply intertwined that they appear interchangeable. Myriad narratives coexist.

A common figure in many of the stories is Sri Chaitanya Mahaprabhu (1486–1533 CE), a Bengali mystic and founder of

3 Gotipua performances are the subject of several films such as Santosh Gour's 1999 film *Sakhi Pila* (Boy Odissi Dancers); the documentaries *Bandha Dance (Gotipua Dancers, Orissa)* by Aloka Kanungo (Center for Cultural Resources and Training 2004); and Gulbahar Singh's *Gotipua* (n.d.).

FIGURE 3.2. A popular-art style of representing Sri Chaitanya. He is reaching for a food offering to give to a youthful Krishna. From a mural on the exterior wall of Sri Sri Gour Gobinda Ashram, Puri, Odisha, 2 December 2012. Photograph by the author.

Gaudiya Vaishnavism,[4] claimed as the gotipua tradition's keen progenitor (Das 2008). Sri Chaitanya is so revered that he is variously honoured as an avatar of Krishna, the dual personification of both Radha and Krishna, or Krishna/Jagannath's most passionate devotee (fig. 3.2).[5]

---

4 Gaudiya Vaishnavism represented an eastern branch of Bhakti, a popular religious movement identified with poet-saints across India. The name translates literally as 'Bengali Vishnu-worship', one of the ancient names of Bengal being Gauda. Because of its unique philosophy and practice, which I will discuss, Gaudiya Vaishnavism is distinct from other styles of Bhakti in North and South India.

5 In some narratives, Chaitanya is even identified with the Buddha. This telling emerged from Bauddha Vaishnavism, an Odishan religious tradition merging Buddhism and Vaishnavism, in which Buddha is identified as one of the ten incarnations of Vishnu. As an avatar, Buddha is then linked to Jagannath and Krishna, forms of Vishnu themselves. For a discussion of Bauddha Vaishnavite philosophy, see Tandra Patnaik (2005).

According to the first tale, when Chaitanya arrived in Odisha as an incarnation of Krishna, he anticipated a ceremonial welcome by the devadasis. However, they were performing dance services for other deities and failed to recognize Chaitanya's divine essence. Spurned, Chaitanya asked the young boys in the vicinity to dress up as female dancers, catalysing a new custom (Belgaumkar 2007).

The second tale: Enchanted by the Chandan Yatra festivities, Chaitanya wanted to include the dance service in the full 21-day cycle during which the ceremonies took place as a way of continually propitiating the gods (Ratnakar 2009). Depending on the narrator, either the orthodox Brahmans refused to allow devadasi performance for the entire time or Chaitanya himself recognized the impossibility of including women for such a long duration, given religious norms. In orthodox Brahmanical thought, women's bodies harboured both power and danger; these qualities multiplied during their menstrual cycles, presenting a threat that had to be contained. Blood also transformed the female body into a contaminating presence—blood in a Hindu religious space being a polluting substance.[6] Chaitanya came up with the ingenious idea of having boys dress up as girls to perform during the festival, thus avoiding the taboo while still ensuring the presence of auspicious feminine energies and feminized bodies at the puja.[7]

The third tale involves an opposite ideology of Gaudiya Vaishnavism. Gotipua performance, it is said, came about as a result of Chaitanya's proscription of women's dances based on

---

6 Rules of blood pollution, for example, prohibited maharis from entering temple grounds on the days of their menses. However, ritual rules differed for devadasis across India. Andhra Pradesh's *kalavanthulus*, for instance, state they did not have to observe the rules of blood pollution; see Davesh Soneji's ethnography (2004).

7 The rationale for replacing the devadasis with gotipuas during Chandan Yatra seems spurious, since devadasis had routinely performed at the festival before the gotipuas entered the scene. And as discussed in the previous chapter, different groups of devadasis were able to rotate their performance duties, thereby abiding by the blood prohibitions.

their alleged immorality.[8] Krishnadas Kaviraj Goswami, in his hagiography *Chaitanya Charitamrita*, recounts that the saint disapproved of the sexes mingling freely (1975). Under Gaudiya Vaishnavite logic, women were cast—in bizarrely diverse modes— as temptation, distraction, competition and as superior spiritual models, impossible to emulate.[9] In any case, Chaitanya went to great extremes in admonishing his followers to repudiate contact with women (Mukherjee 1979: 9). On the other hand, a contradictory Gaudiya Vaishnavite belief in Sakhi Bhava[10] encouraged men to feminize themselves as a way of expressing their boundless love for Krishna, who they saw as the ultimate manifestation of *purusha*, the supreme male principle (Schweig 2002). Ramananda Ray, a trusted minister of the Odishan king Prataparudradeva (*r.*1497– 1540), intrigued by Chaitanya's preachings, went on to become his disciple and helped to popularize Bhakti in Odisha, eventually leaving the court to follow a spiritual path (Goswami 1975; *Chaitanya Charitamrita, Madhya* 8.302).[11] The sovereign himself, equally mesmerized by Bhakti, initiated the gotipua style as a

---

8 See R. Sathyanarayana in Pandarika Vitthala (1998: 273) and Priyambada Hejmadi Mohanty (2017: n.p.).

9 It should be stressed that this was not the case with other Bhakti movements, in which women are preeminent—Mirabai, Andal and Avvaiyar, among others. Madhu Kishwar suggests that for these female mystics, Bhakti created an escape from the 'life legislated for most women' (1989: 3), while allowing them to pursue their creative and spiritual impulses. For more on women and Bhakti, see Kishwar and Vanita (1989).

10 Sakhi Bhava is the assumption of the emotional state (*bhava*) of Krishna and Radha's female attendants (*sakhi*)—an internalized feeling as well as an outward expression of devotion through the act of offering one's self to Krishna.

11 There is a temple commemorating Chaitanya's close friendship with Ramananda Ray, off the Bada Danda (main road) near Puri Jagannath. Profound thanks are due to Devadutta Samantasinghar, a cultural researcher who, on 12 December 2010, kindly gave me a tour of this place, the Jagannath Bhallav *maath* and other sites in Puri related to important aspects of devadasi and gotipua history.

tribute to his new religious orientation (D. N. Patnaik 2006: 64; Kothari 2001: 94).

There is a fourth tale, in which the incipient gotipua tradition is linked to the decline of the devadasi system—a direct consequence of sixteenth-century Muslim rule in Odisha. In this telling, the region's 'golden age' abruptly ended when Afghan rulers in neighbouring Bengal usurped the Ganga dynasty and began pillaging the state. Motivated by religious zealotry, combined with the usual interest in increasing their own exchequers, the Afghans repeatedly plundered the Jagannath temple. During these times, it is said that the temple priests fled with the idols. These repeated assaults naturally disrupted temple life. Protecting the devadasi system, especially, was a problem in this turbulent political environment. Moreover, the purdah system instituted by Muslims made it necessary for boys to dance in place of women, either because the new patrons forbade it or because the devadasis themselves wanted to eschew contact with *mlecchas* (foreigners), in accordance with orthodox thought (Kanungo 2006–07: 81; D. N. Patnaik 2006: 64).[12]

It took more than a century, but the Odishan kingship was finally reinstated as a result of an alliance with the Mughal emperor Akbar, whose armies crushed their Afghan rivals in the struggle to annex Odisha. The state became part of the Mughalbandhi in 1592. Akbar restored the Khurda raja, Ramachandradeva, to the throne; the king brought the images of Jagannath, Subhadra and Balabhadra back to Puri from Kujang, where Bisan Mahanti had hidden them; he reinstalled them in a special Nabakalebar ritual— a story recorded in the *Madala Panji* (Kulke 2010: 404). The raja also established *akhadas*, or gyms, and granted the public a street, 'Akhada Chapa Pali', where young boys trained in both martial arts and dance (R. Sathyanarayana in Pandarika Vitthala 1996: 3.273).[13]

---

12 This explanation fails to make sense if we consider that women danced in Mughal courts. There are records proving this in the *Ain-i-Akbari* (Fazl 1873) and François Bernier's travelogue (1916), both of which mention of *kanchenis*, or dancing girls, in Akbar's court.

13 According to Aloka Kanungo, gotipua is a twentieth-century term that started circulating in 1946 (2006–07: 80). Before that, *akhada pila* (gymnasium boys)

The gotipua order grew out of this new system designed to pro-mote both self-defence and corporeal discipline. Given the changed circumstance of governance under the Mughals, and aware of the history of threats to the devadasi order, the king promoted public gotipua performances on religious occasions. Gradually, gotipuas took over the functions of female artists on ceremonial occasions. Their presence enabled the perpetuation of ritual dance; they replaced and eventually displaced devadasi service.

In the Odishan imaginary, this is the most common and com-pelling explanation of the gotipua tradition's genesis. According to D. N. Patnaik:

> due to the successive [M]uslim invasion[s] and weak political authority there must have been moral degenera-tion on the part of the maharis. Because, it is from this period that Maharis, who were originally intended for temples and Gods alone, came to be employed in royal courts as well. From now on, the Maharis ceased to be respected as *dasis* of the Lord and came to be associated with concubinage (2006: 60–1).

Indeed, this is the story I heard over and over again from several sources—from gurus, dancers, critics, historians and dance scholars.[14]

The empirical evidence and present-day gotipua practice, however, suggests that these narratives need to be radically revised. Broadly speaking, the role of Bhakti in shaping the gotipua tradition has been minimized while the supposedly adverse Muslim role has been magnified. My view dovetails with dance historian Sunil Kothari's, who suggests that 'the main reason for the rise of the

---

was the accepted name. Shyam Sundar Rath has mined further back to argue that a variation, 'akheda' appeared during the reign of the Ganga dynasty in the twelfth-century CE (2005: 239). To avoid confusion, I refer primarily to the term gotipua rather than *akhada pila*, as it is more commonly used in the literature.

14 Based on interviews with Leela Venkataraman (2007) and Shanta Serbjeet Singh (2007). See also Sharmila Biswas (2003–04).

gotipuas was embedded in the cult of *sakhibhava*'—he is speaking of Gaudiya Vaishnavism—'a religious movement in which devotees consider themselves the consorts of the Lord' (2001: 94).

The gotipua tradition was very much a product of the historical turbulence of the sixteenth century, a time 'of turmoil and transformation [that] ushered in a struggle between the Afghans and the Mughals, in which the kings of Odisha also became involved' (Ray 1997: 225). The devadasi institution was shifting due to changes in political rule and religious ideology. Ganga rule had ended and, with it, a system of stable patronage dissipated. The continual raids on Jagannath-Puri, among others, periodically interrupted ritual service and the strength of the temple order. On the cultural front, the Bhakti movement spread out to Odisha.

It is likely that gotipua practice began as a combination of all these factors. While what I will call the 'Muslim thesis' is usually spotlighted as the reason for its emergence, my intention is to focus on the influence of Bhakti, specifically the import of Chaitanya and the philosophy of Gaudiya Vaishnavism, on the development of gotipua performance.

My argument is that the gotipua system developed in Odisha primarily as part of a pattern of bringing Hindu religious practices into the public sphere. Gotipua performance was one instantiation of a new category of gender practice in the ritual realm, initiated and popularized by the Bhakti movement. However, before exploring these close connections with Bhakti in the following chapter, I will address the 'Muslim thesis' and how it functions among those who adhere to its claims.

The Muslim Thesis

The correlation between the 'decline' of the devadasi institution and the rise of the gotipuas cannot be explicitly cast in causal terms. Rather, during the period in question, myriad changes took place under the new cultural and political orders altering the Odishan landscape. The prevailing view is that the devadasi system changed overnight with the Muslim rulers' incursions into Odisha.

But this view affirms a problematic historiographic framing which divides the Indian past into discrete periods of 'Hindu' and 'Muslim' dominance. It fails to take into account the nuances and patterns of religious relations in the area while it also effaces the general changes affecting the devadasi system and temple order over the long term.[15]

As an example of the representative view, K. C. Panigrahi bluntly states that after the Muslims arrived, Odisha 'became a benighted country' and plunged into a 'dark age' (2008: 245). In a double move, he blames Islam both for encouraging sexual licentiousness *and* for oppressing women. He even holds the Muslims responsible for the rise of a 'voluptuously lewd' literature, which he alleges had a ruinous effect on Odisha's cultural life (ibid.: 246). In a similar though more subjunctive vein, Kali Charan Patnaik spoke about Odissi's moral and aesthetic tarnishment at the 1958 Sangeet Natak Akademi seminar on dance, musing that

> due to lack of proper patronage and culture Odissi dance could not preserve its sanctity and true techniques. Perhaps from the days of Mohamedan conquest of Orissa, Odissi dance ceased to enjoy a place of esteem in respectable families; its culture became neglected and it was practised by people who had no true devotion for the art, nor proper knowledge of the Shastras. It is only very recently that that people have begun evincing interest in the culture of dance (2013[1958a]: 213).

---

15 When I interviewed her in 2007, dance scholar Urmimala Sarkar Munsi pointed out that the myth of the devadasi's descent suggests a rather abrupt change in the system, brought on by Muslim rule. This view neglects the internal changes in the system, as the role of the devadasi expanded and redefined itself, and ignores the prior history of sexualization attached to it. The main change instigated by certain periods of temple desecration are yet to be investigated, but some commentators suggest the loss of support from the temple (due to its diminishing resources) forced some devadasis to find new sources of income through secular patronage and prostitution. I discuss this later.

In his chronicle, which also mentions incursions by other rulers, the impact of Hindu intrusion is glossed over while the negative effect of the Muslim presence is overemphasized (ibid.: 206).

The idea of a cultural decline dramatically ushered in by Muslim rule—as expressed by D. N. Patnaik, K. C. Patnaik, K. C. Panigrahi and others—aligns with and rehearses a common trope of conservative Hindu historiographies of India.[16] It supports the sectarian view that Muslims were, and are, ultimately foreign agents, bent on destroying India, drawing a clear line from the conqueror Mahmud of Ghazni to the contemporary Muslim community as intrinsically inimical to (Hindu) Indian interests. The uncomfortable truth is that there is a strong Hindu bias in Indian dance scholarship, which reflects and retierates a broader trend of conservative narrativization.[17]

Vinayak Damodar Savarkar's *Hindutva: Who Is a Hindu?* (1969[1923]) is the classic articulation of a communalist perspective: 'Hindustan must be looked upon both as a fatherland (*pitribhu*) and a holyland (*punyabhu*),' he wrote. 'Muslims and Christians cannot be incorporated into Hindutva because their holy land is in far off Arabia or Palestine. Their names and outlook smack of a foreign origin. Their love is divided.' Arguing that India is a 'Hindu Rashtra' (Hindu nation), Savarkar's vision of 'Akhand Bharata' (united India, or literally, 'unbroken' India) influenced conservative historians and cultural analysts who claim Hinduism as authentic to India and Islam as essentially alien.

The idea is pervasive in right-wing popular culture and politics as well, with the rise of Hindu nationalist parties in recent years who have taken power and made it their mandate to rewrite the national curriculum through the prisms of their ideologies, allying their projects with 'the early ideologues of communalism,' like Savarkar, for whom 'the religious interpretation of history was the

---

16 For more examples of this tendency, see R. D. Banerji (1931) and Krishnan Ramaswamy et al. (2007).

17 See Daud Ali (1999) and Sumit Sarkar (2002) on this.

necessary ideological groundwork for recovering the Hindu nation'
(Panikkar 2001).[18]

This contentious situation reflects the ongoing contest over the
idea of India itself, a contest over who may legitimately claim the
right to belonging and representation in the past and the present
and thus, the future (Inden 1990; Habib 2009). For many conser-
vatives, 'Hindustan' is for Hindus—all the rest are interlopers,
especially the Muslims because they wrested power from the
'rightful' rulers. 'In many instances of popular remembrance,
Musalmans figure as defilers of various sorts,' observes Shahid
Amin (2005: 20). This 'communally-oriented construction of the
past,' Sudhir Chandra notes, attributes the degradation of cultural
values in the subcontinent to the advent of Muslim rule, with the
bodies of women metonymically serving as objects of violation
and subjugation (1992: 129). Chandra describes the illustrative
case of Sati (widow self-immolation), which, 'in keeping with the
ascription of nearly every social evil to Muslim rule, was explained
as a consequence of [its] lecherous nature' (1992: 129). The same
could be said of the decline of the devadasis. The attitude of antipathy is evinced in the following commentary by Projesh Banerji:

> The invaders from the North-West were mostly uncivilised
> people whose religion also forbade participation in pas-
> times having the touch of idolatry and the consequence
> was that the decline was very rapid and the art became
> confined to a much lower class of people who had no idea
> of aesthetics. Thus we find, during the Muhammedan
> period the aesthetic and spiritual elements of the Hindu
> dance declined with the introduction of Nicha or Kulata

18 The issue became a flashpoint of controversy at the turn of the millenium,
when the ruling Bharatiya Janata Party sought to rewrite history textbooks by
purging them of left-wing and/or secular perspectives. Progressive academics
from the Indian Historical Research Council opposed the measure and sought
to defend their scholarship on the grounds of academic freedom. See Partha
S. Ghosh (1998) and K. N. Panikkar (2001), writing in *Hindu* and *Frontline*
respectively. Attacks on progressive scholars continue today, amplified by
social media.

Nritya. There is no authentic book of this period and in
the Muslim age on account of the observation of Purdah
dancing by society women was altogether lost in oblivion
(1942: 47–8).

The devadasis' dispersal from the temple into the decidedly non-
sacred world of mass entertainment is associated with a
picture of moral degeneracy inaugurated by the arrival of the
menacing Muslims, intent on desecrating both the Hindu temple
and the devadasis themselves.

In this discourse, the reality and fluidity of dance practices in
Odisha is expediently erased. Prior to the inauguration of the
devadasi institution in Odisha, dance had been a public art. With
the political shifts towards a temple-ordered society, dance also
shifted context, often embracing its pre-institutionalized forms.
Even with the formalization of the devadasi order in the twelfth
century at Jagannath-Puri, the system continued to gradually transform. Female servitors outside the temple may have coexisted with
ritual specialists inside the temple, and this was reflected in the
categories of female attendants instituted by the king, including
the *raj angila* or *rajdasis* (royal courtesans) and the *rudra-ganika*
(prostitutes). While these women were also considered maharis at
one time, they eventually stopped performing ritual functions and
were later excluded from mahari groups (Acharya 2002; Lowen
2007). Frédérique Apffel Marglin also describes the *deis*, another
group that held lower status than maharis (1985: 26). With disturbances in temple service and changes in the patronage system,
these groups needed to tap into new sources of support. To earn a
living, some devadasis may have become courtesans for affluent
patrons; some may have entered prostitution; some may have
taken to dancing professionally in public venues (the *Chaitanya
Charitamrita*, for instance, describes devadasis dancing in Jagannath
Bhallav plays, as I describe in Chapter 4). And so the dance perhaps
reverted to its pre-temple roots as it oscillated between the temple
and sites outside of it, especially the court (Biswas 2003–04). The
precise choreographic changes are difficult to identify, but the
shifts in sites appear to be historically verified. Although no records

tell us so definitively, it stands to reason that the function of the maharis' dance changed and emphasized entertainment to accommodate their new artistic and economic circumstances; that when the maharis were recalled to the temple, they resumed their ritual practice. These changes occurred gradually, sealed in the aftermath of Prataparudradeva's rule.

Importantly, although the scale and scope of these dynamics were extensive, the social relations surrounding and, to a large degree, defining the dance were neither new nor transformative; they expanded out of pre-existing dance categories. The shift lay in the ideology accompanying the sexualization of dance outside of the temple. It is true that a line of separation was always delineated between devadasis and prostitutes, but it didn't separate sex workers from 'asexual' ritual specialists; rather, it separated ordinary women from extraordinary women. The label 'devadasi' determined a woman's sacred status and sexual accessibility in relation to privileged or ordinary bodies; it did not entail a suppression of sexuality itself. Indeed, the maharis integrated *shringara* into the temple context through their worship practices; and they often engaged in sexual relationships with high-caste males.

Marglin's groundbreaking research revealed that maharis and *deis* both had sexual relations with men attached to the temple and the court (1985: 26, 39, 75). 'Dancing and prostitution were synonymous until the 1920s when dance was removed from its traditional association and became an art accessible to properly married women of high caste,' she notes. Observing the 'association between dance and sex is very strong,' she states that dance held a symbolic value as *maithuna* (sexual union) in the ritual life of the Jagannath temple (ibid.: 95). Sexuality is embedded in the devadasis' own language; they called themselves *swarg-beshyas* and *apsaras* (heavenly courtesans and dancers; ibid.: 98).[19]

Although devadasi identity was once simultaneously 'sacred' and 'sexual,' it is possible that greater contact with non-Hindus

---

19 *Beshya* is the Odia version of *veshya*, one of the words used to describe prostitutes, traceable to ancient India. See Monika Saxena (2006).

and various caste groups, in settings apart from the temple and palace, reconfigured the image of the dancer as impure and inauspicious. There is no evidence, however, that this was the situation at the time. Until the arrival of Gaudiya Vaishnavism, and within their own religious communities, the vision of the devadasi in Odisha appears to have stayed much the same. The mahari system persisted despite shifts in circumstance, and despite threats of outside stigma and violence—albeit jaggedly, discontinuously, uncertainly.

In the standard narratives, it is often presumed that Odissi's origins lay in Mahari Naach, and that this history accounts for its traditional and sacred status. The story of Odissi's trajectory is usually narrated as a movement from inside the precincts of the Hindu temple to the secular proscenium stage; whether this movement from the sacred interior to the areligious exterior is framed as progressive or problematic depends on the perspectives of the narrator. The consensus seems to be that as classical dance comes to inhabit a wider spatial and ideological field, its ritual meanings are diminished, even extinguished, and the fragments of the meanings that do remain become more and more ambivalent. In these characterizations, the spatialization of Odissi and its dispersion into diverse social fields coincides with allegations of its degeneration and its transformation into an object of scandal. When dance exists outside the temple—or even the atmosphere of the temple—and moves into the public sphere, some essence is allegedly lost and degraded. Its spatialization mitigates its sacredness. Its distance from religious contexts signals a decline in its moral value. And the role of sexuality is central to these claims of desacralization.

Thus it seems that modern, conservative judgements are being telegraphed into the past to attach an immoral dimension to Odissi, its overt sexualization and movement into public spaces, when no such evidence exists of these associations at the historical period in question. At least in the devadasis' own contexts and communities, there was no sense of moral degradation. Rather, self-proclaimed foreigners from Central Asia, Afghanistan and Persia cast aspersions on devadasi practice, ostracizing the dancers as prostitutes.[20] The Persian scholar Alberuni, for example, writing as early as 1030 CE, spoke indignantly of temple dance:

> People think with regard to harlotry that it is allowed with [Hindus] . . . In reality, the matter is not as people think, but it is rather this, that the Hindus are not very severe in punishing whoredom. *The fault, however, lies with the kings, not with the nation. But for this, no Brahman or priest would suffer in their idol-temples the women who sing, dance, and play.* The kings make them an attraction for their cities, a bait of pleasure for their subjects, for no other but financial reasons. By the revenues which they derive from the business both as fines and taxes, they want to recover the expenses which their treasury has to spend on the army (1964: 2.157; emphasis added).

In Alberuni's world, then, the temple dancers seduced their pious patrons on behalf of the royal ruler, intent on recovering monies spent on military expeditions. He underscored the economic benefits brought about by the devadasis apparently through the duplicitous use of religion. Alberuni, like many after him, equated the devadasis with common prostitution or 'play' and so denounced their rituals on moral grounds.

The questions that linger for me are: Why do conservative historians accept the negative values ascribed to danced displays of female sexuality, but vindicate the authorizing discourse of Hinduism to which it is attached? Why do they binarize sexuality and spirituality, when historically these were complementary in important strands of Hindu thought? Why have they adopted a view that mirrors that of self-proclaimed outsiders and arbiters of Indian culture, who saw dance and sexuality as corrupting influences on religion? And why do they characterize the proliferation of dance outside the temple in terms of decline, when the discourse of the day does not support such an interpretation?

---

20 The trend of denouncing 'temple prostitution' continued into colonial times, a topic explored in Chapter 5.

This idea of the devadasi's 'fall from grace' seems to be rooted in a conservative Hindu nationalist standpoint which demonizes Islam and holds on to a narrative of Hindus victimized by barbaric Muslim hordes. It is an interpretation which coincides directly with the larger discourse of Hindutva, in which the age of Muslim reign ushers in a period of general cultural ignominy (Basham 1967; Thapar et al. 1970; Athar Ali 2009). In this discourse, the degradation of Hindu culture—symbolized by the transformation of the devadasi from an object of grace to disgrace—is inevitably linked to the 'Muslim period' in Indian history.

Patterns of Muslim Rule

The designation of a 'Muslim period' is itself evidence of a specific bias in dominant Indian historiographies. We have the Vedic age, which precedes, coincides or overlaps with the Indus Valley civilization (depending on the historian, this can range anywhere from 5000/3000/1500 BCE to 1000/500 CE), with the Buddhist and Jain periods in-between (from the sixth century BCE to the tenth century CE), followed by the Muslim period (approximately 1000 CE to 1750 CE, depending on the region in question), also known as the late medieval period in Indian history.

Although descriptive at one level, these labels function performatively and ideologically, implying a unified, harmonious 'Hindu' age, in which a subcontinental civilization flourished, followed by an equally unified era of 'Muslim' authority which brought about a fall into 'medieval' values and destroyed cultural achievements of the preceding times. Recall that the 'golden age' of India is conventionally identified with the Gupta era, and, from a local point of view, with the Ganga era in Odisha—both prior to encounters with Islam. Curiously, the 'Muslim age' is not followed by the 'Christian age' or the 'secular age'. Historical nomenclature changes instead to denote the style of government (colonial, democratic) and its geographic affiliation (British/Indian), a mood (modern, postmodern) or political condition (postcolonial, post-Partition, post-Independence).

The linguistic constructs marking the precolonial period set up a starkly confrontational view of historical change, driven by religious difference alone, or, more pertinently, in terms of religious hostility. The Hindu–Muslim binary suggests a 'clash of civilizations' in an Orientalist frame while naturalizing Hindu hegemonies through nativist logic. As Finbarr B. Flood argues, 'in a retrojection of the values of the nation-state, the denizens of premodern South Asia have been figured as the noble citizens of "Hindu India" valiantly resisting the Muslim onslaught' (2009: 3). To maintain this fiction, Hinduism's history of violence and assimilation is erased, and variations in expressions of Hinduism de-emphasized.

Importantly, sects defined as 'Hindu' today did not label themselves as such—because the composite category later named 'Hindu' did not exist at least until the eighth century (see Arvind Sharma 2002). The retrospective classification disregards the complex history of tensions and negotiations between followers of Vedic Brahmanism, Bhakti, Shaivism, Shakti, Tantra—and other groups that together would later come into Hinduism—along with the non-Hindu influences of Buddhism, Jainism, Sikhism, Zoroastranism, Judaism and Christianity, among others. It is well known that Islam influenced Hinduism directly—as witnessed, for example, in the philosophy of Kabir and other mystics. Some of these sects could have been loosely assembled together under the label Sanatana Dharma ('the eternal way'); others were Brahmanic and Shramanic; and still others, like the lineage-based groups, insisted on the specificity of naming their own practices. The term 'Hindu' was first used by Arabs and Persians as a sign distinguishing the non-Muslim inhabitants of India and aggregating these disparate traditions into a whole, although it was originally a *geographic* referent; it came into use as a primarily religious designation under British colonial rule.[21]

---

21 On this point, see Athar Ali (1997: 217–20 and 2009:109–118); Romila Thapar (2000b: 77–82) and Jyotirmaya Sharma (2003). See also Pralay Kanungo's (2003) and Mohammed Yamin's (2009) discussions of the historical particularities of Hindu–Muslim relations in Odisha.

To state the obvious, Muslim practices were equally heterogeneous. Different intra-religious groups competed for legitimacy among constituents and converts, and held opposing views on matters of theological doctrine and devotional practice. Romila Thapar points out that '[w]hat we today call the Muslim community was equally differentiated between the Sunnis, Shia'hs, Ismai'lis, Sufis, and Bohras, not to mention the Navayats and Mappilas of south India' (2002: 439). More importantly, 'people of India curiously do not seem to have perceived the new arrivals as a unified body of Muslims' (Thapar 2000b: 78). This picture of diversity contrasts with the picture of Muslims as a single mass, bound by common interests and ideals, and uniformly hostile to other religious sects. In fact, history shows how many of these groups experienced intracultural conflicts, illustrating that there was no natural affiliation between them simply because they shared the same broad religious banner. Of course, this is similar to what was happening among the Hindus, who were also divided into various sects which had no organic affinities and were sometimes political allies, but often not.

The myth that the Hindus, Buddhists and Jains formed one religious strand and opposed themselves to the Muslims as a united front is also a faulty historical premise, since there is much evidence to show that all these groups engaged in conflict and contestation with one another over time throughout the subcontinent. Moreover, this picture disregards the reality of both intrareligious conflict and cross-religious alliance. Historical records show that the Hindu kings frequently fought among themselves; the Mughals and Afghans struggled to wrest power from each other; for strategic reasons, sometimes they fought together in a single army (Panigrahi 169–70). Principally this is because 'Hindu' and 'Muslim' were not recognized as totally distinct communities; the heterogeneity within their contours reflected their heterogeneous geopolitical locations and interests. 'People were more frequently identified by caste, occupation, language, region, and religious sect, than by the religious labels we use today' (Thapar 2002: 438), and interacted in a complex cultural crucible.

Politically speaking, there was no singular pattern of Indian Muslim rule. The Delhi Sultanate, the Afghan kingdoms of Bengal and the Mughal empire each generated different visions of the state in theory and practice, as did individual rulers. To suppose that because they were 'Muslim,' they were committed to the same political approach, the same ideological agenda and the same religious views, is pure fallacy: 'Like most teleologies, these scenarios operate through a collapse of all possible identities into a single monolithic identification, producing as singular, static, and undifferentiated what was often multiple, protean, and highly contested' (Flood 2009: 3).

The specification of a 'Muslim period' ascribes a seamless temporality compartmentalizing the beginning and end of a specific historical phase. This partitioning of the past also fails to take regional variations into account; from the local Odishan perspective, the 'Muslim period' began in the sixteenth century: Husain Shah's invasion attempt in 1510 was followed by Sher Shah's in 1538; Kalapahad's infamous attack on Jagannath-Puri took place in 1558; and the ensuing struggles culminated in Odisha's 1592 annexation by Akbar's forces, led by Raja Man Singh. In comparison, from a North Indian perspective, the Muslim period had commenced at least 500 years earlier; and as for the South Indian experience, there were intermittent pockets of rule without a hegemonic Muslim regime. Thus the discourse of historiography is regionally distinctive and disjunctive—the only common element being the fabrication of an essentialized Muslim 'Other' opposed to cohesive Hindu interests.

In the medieval and early modern period, the subcontinent was divided into kingdoms and principalities whose rulers vied with each other to build empires and expand their territory, influence and wealth. So interreligious relationships were not necessary confrontational—they were contingent on the particular politics of the region in question and on understanding which groups were in a dominant or subordinate position. Where common political interests could be identified, different religious parties entered into alliance—until the next political upheaval or opportunity announced itself.

There were three major patterns of Muslim rule relative to Odisha's history. The first involved regional rule, with Muslim authority scattered over parts of the subcontinent, largely concentrated in north India. The Delhi Sultanate was one such example, its area of control sometimes extending as far as Bengal but never quite including Odisha. And although the Sultanate may have had the goal of conquering India, it never managed to do so; by 1526, it had partially dissolved and partially integrated into the Mughal empire.

The Ganga dynasty successfully staved off attempts at annexation, and the Sultanate lost power before it could fulfil its territorial ambitions (K. C. Panigrahi 2008). Beyond these conflicts, the sultanate and the Ganga regime had little interaction, cultural, economic or otherwise, and seem to have coexisted as autonomous political entities.[22] Because of its geographic position, Odisha was never the first target of conquerors coming from the West nor from central Asia and Arabia; as a result, their impact on Odisha at this juncture was virtually nonexistent. This is attested by the fact that northern India came under the Sultanate (1206–1526 CE) when Kalinga was consolidating its kingdom and experiencing its golden age (1078–1434 CE). It was a time when Kalingan borders expanded along the coast; when architectural splendours such as Konark, Lingaraj and Mukteshwar were built; when a temple-ordered society was thriving; when devadasi service commenced at Jagannath-Puri; and when new religious forms came into prominence, especially Bhakti, along with syncretic practices combining Devi worship, Shaivism, Buddhism and Vaishnavism (K. C. Mishra 1984).

The second pattern of Muslim rule, which *did* adversely affect Odisha, were the raids motivated largely by the desire to establish religious domination. Idols were smashed, coffers looted, images defaced. From the raider's perspective, these actions had the double advantage of desecrating the sacred space of the 'infidels' and

---

22 The Deccan Sultanate emerged as more of a threat, but, thanks to a series of alliances and its superior army, Kalinga retained its independence well into the sixteenth century (Prabhat Mukherjee 1979: 22).

destroying their morale while evacuating the economic resources that sustained the temple order. Interestingly, unlike the later Mughals and earlier sultans, most of these raiders maintained their identity as outsiders and had no interest in settling in India nor in building bridges across difference; this is starkly evident in the trail of destruction they left in their wake (K. C. Panigrahi 2008). Their main aims were to humiliate and terrorize the non-Muslim populace, and declare the supremacy of their interpretation of Islam.

These raids began in India's northwestern frontiers with Mahmud of Ghazni (in Afghanistan), whose obsession with stamping out idol worship resulted in repeated incursions between 1000 and 1026 CE. His exploits are minutely detailed by his Persian chronicler, Alberuni, a witness to the events of the time.[23] There is no specific mention of eastern India in Alberuni's writings, but Mahmud established the raids as a precedent for others. Bengal-based Afghan and Turkic conquerors were largely responsible for attacking Odisha's temples, the most notorious among them being the sixteenth-century Sultan Sulaiman Karran and his general Kalapahad who killed the Odisha raja and made it their mission to destroy every Hindu edifice they came across, including the temples at Konark and Puri. The *Madala Panji* records the destruction of Jagannath-Puri in 1568, an event retold by the *pandas* of Shri-Kshetra today. This catastrophic event instigated a break in Odisha's history.

In the tumultuous time between 1434 and 1592, the devastation of temples resulted in the suspension of ritual services. The *Sirot-i-Firuz Sahi*, a fourteenth-century Persian chronicle of Sultan Firuz Saha, for instance, disparages the devadasis as 'female devil Sannyasis' (trans. N. B. Roy, cited in D. N. Patnaik 2006: 58–9), a characterization that draws on a familiar set of tropes, like Alberuni's earlier account.

---

23 The book, *Alheruni's India* (1964), is a self-described foreigner's view of India, but also reveals a sceptic who was not altogether convinced about Mahmud's aims.

Given the biases of a history written by the victor and not the vanquished, the truth of accounts such as Alberuni's and Saha's can be convincingly interrogated. For example, D. N Patnaik acknowledges that, in the post-Ganga period, 'there must have been certain degeneration and irregularities in the temple services but not to the extent it is described' in these reports which often exaggerated the conqueror's feats (2006: 58). K. C. Panigrahi concurs that these texts are full of hyperbole—because they 'want to magnify the exploits of the invaders', they 'do not appear to be credible' and are 'neither clear nor unimpeachable' (2008: 142, 139, 174). Nevertheless, the raids ended only when the Mughals emerged victorious against the Afghans in their struggle for control of the region, although some sectarian rulers instigated attacks even under new frameworks of governance (Mubayi 2005: 40–4).

Regardless, the extreme violence of these raids may explain why there is a selective focus on assaults by Muslim rulers in Odisha's history; the memory of these events is ingrained deep in the cultural imaginary.[24] But consider the contrast to Emperor Ashoka who also killed thousands in Odisha by his own account, and yet is a lauded figure nationally. The Hindu kings who warred among themselves, and who slaughtered Buddhists and Jains are no less admired today for these acts (Thapar 2000b: 73–5; K. C. Panigrahi 2008: 39–42, 137–42, 169–71). Apart from the bloodshed, the problem conservative historians seem to have is that adherents of Islam threatened what they perceive as the sanctity of a Hindu Indian order.

The Mughal empire constituted the third pattern of rule which, from the perspectives of art and religious freedom, left a legacy of mixed consequences. Some potentates were directly motivated by religious ideology. However, during the reign of emperors with liberal outlooks, such as Akbar (*r.*1556–1605), Jehangir (*r.*1605–27) and Shah Jahan (*r.*1627–58)—all of whom promoted religious

---

24 In March 2008, the *pandas* of Jagannath-Puri told me this history of desecration by Muslims was one of the reasons the temple was not open to any non-Hindus.

pluralism in their individual ways, even the intermingling of different faiths—interculturalism flourished and the arts attained high levels of excellence in the context of the renewal of temple and court cultures (see on this especially Das 1994 and Ernst 2016).

Among the Mughals, Akbar stands out for his support of the arts and for his commitment to interfaith dialogue. Under his supervision, the model and apparatus of the state fundamentally changed (Mubayi 2005). Sixteenth-century India was essentially a loose assemblage of autonomous kingdoms and principalities, with no unified body of law and governance. Imperial rule transformed the structure of the state, both in terms of its conceptualization and organization. Again, the parallel with Ashokan rule is striking: the Mughals inaugurated another empire, as the Mauryas had done centuries before. This for only the second time in South Asian history.

Historian M. Athar Ali poses a key question: 'What was new—or if not new, then, at any rate, exotic—in the polity of the Mughal empire?' And given Akbar's extraordinary success in establishing a far-reaching empire, Athar Ali asks: What were 'the new elements of political chemistry out of which Akbar compounded such a large, stable, long-lasting political structure?' (2009: 60) Answering his own question, Athar Ali suggests a combination of factors, including 'an extreme systematization of administration, a new theoretical basis for sovereignty and a balanced and stable composition of the ruling class' (ibid.: 61). To this can be added three other factors: a wide-reaching network of political capital; a secular outlook; and cultural patronage.

The scale and scope of Mughal rule was unprecedented, covering the widest swathes of Indian territory up until that time, extending from Rajasthan to Bengal and into the Deccan. The strength of the Mughal army and artillery was another asset that helped to sustain a strong imperial presence (Spear 1990: 44). The most impressive feature of Mughal governance was its central system of administration. Akbar reimagined the state as a sophisticated network of alliances interweaving local rulers all over the subcontinent. This model of empire drew from and expanded on the Delhi Sultanate, but with the difference of maintaining the strategic appearance of integrating and bolstering local authorities to accomplish the goal of political conquest (Ahsan Raza Khan 1997). 'The regime was essentially a military occupation out of whom the local inhabitants could make their living if they were lucky and obedient,' explains Percival Spear. 'Akbar's method was to make a deal with the Hindus and to do this through their militant representatives, the Rajputs. [. . .] Thus in effect the Rajputs became partners in the empire and through them the whole Hindu community came to accept the Mughal government as in some sense their own' (1990: 34).

The concentration of power remained in the centre, with authority for regional rule dispensed to local officials. The empire was divided into 12 subahs (provinces), each subdivided into sarkars (districts) and parganas (sub-districts) (ibid.: 42). Each division was jointly managed by a pair of officers, responsible for tax revenues and legal supervision, respectively. Importantly, despite taking control of taxes and criminal matters, 'the Mughal Empire was not a legislating state, that is creating its own law independent of and suspending customary and religious laws' (Athar Ali 2009: 90). Thus regional cultural autonomy was preserved to a significant degree.[25]

A nascent 'social contract theory', presaging the early modern state, lay at the heart of Akbar's philosophy of government (ibid.: 125). Two significant accomplishments emerged from this model.

25 Percival Spear further clarifies that '[t]here was no elaborate system of judicial courts' and points out:

[E]ach community had its own personal law which it administered through its own agents. These were the *qazis* for the Muslims and the pandits and caste or village *panchayats* for the Hindu. [. . .] Order was maintained in the villages largely by the village elders themselves, whose arrangements were fascinating and intricate, or else by agents of a local landholder. Thus the villager saw the government mainly in the guise of a revenue-collecting agent, who fleeced him occasionally, as a judge in a dispute, or as any army which plundered him. It did not matter much who ruled in Delhi—Mughal, Maratha, or Englishman (1990: 43).

First, outside of wartime, ordinary people did not experience the imperial order as a purely intrusive force, since it operated as a fairly remote entity and 'appeared to the people in the countryside mainly as a revenue-collecting agency' (Spear 1990: 42). Second, local rule and customary practices appeared to be undisturbed in exchange for full allegiance to the emperor on by regional sovereigns, like the raja of Khurda. M. Athar Ali states of the Mughal empire under Akbar:

> If it had some rudiments of an unwritten constitution, it yet did not claim for itself the legislative power and functions that are the hallmarks of the modern state. It was essentially the perfection of a medieval polity, made possible by certain early modern developments. Though this gave it the stability and power denied to its predecessors, [there was a] contrast between the sense of unity infused in the imperial ruling class, in spite of its heterogeneity, and the absence of the consciousness of such unity among the mass of imperial subjects. In other words, the subcontinent of India had a centralized quasi-modern state without any developing sense of nationhood (2009: 71)

The prevalence of a unified 'Hindustan' in state discourse and popular imaginaries was based on attachments to a landscape where mythological events had transpired and where Hindu 'places of pilgrimage lay scattered' in the form *of* the *char dham* which demarcated a mythopoetic but politically imaginable India (ibid.: 81; see also Chapter 2). Yet this proto-national consciousness could not be forged through political persuasion—it was burgeoning in the cultural sphere, as I discuss later.

Under Akbar's system of rule, the Odishan kings retained control over their social affairs by establishing agreements with the Mughal emperor. The kings benefitted from Akbar's doctrine of interfaith harmony, known as Sulh-i Kul, variously translated as 'peace among all' or 'absolute peace' (Iqtidar Alam Khan 1997: 79). In this, Akbar's views were profoundly influenced by Sufi saints and philosophers such as Moinuddin Chishti and Abu'l Fazl—the latter also being the emperor's biographer and author of

Ain-i-Akbari and *Akbarnama* (1590 CE).[26] It might be argued that Akbar propounded a vision of pluralism loosely resembling that of Ashoka's, two millenia earlier (Amartya Sen 2005).[27]

Akbar had gradually moved away from Sunni orthodoxy, and, as his faith became more universal and his practice more pluralist, he embraced those religious ideals which veered more and more away from the monumental and towards the mystical. Later in life, he denounced religious conversion and practised an ecumenical approach—not only in his personal affairs but at the political level as well. His encouragement of religious tolerance is well documented in his *firman* (royal proclamations/decrees) supporting religious minorities at important political junctures (Husain 1997; Prasad 1997); in his establishment of forums for interfaith exchange or Ibadatkhana; in his initiation of a new religious order, Din-i-ilahi, an amalgam of Hindu and Muslim thought; in his marriages to Hindu, Muslim and Christian brides; and his abolishment of the poll tax on non-believers (*jizya*) and pilgrimage tax on worshippers travelling to non-Muslim shrines (Iqtidar Khan 1997: 83, 85). Oddly, by 1601, his aversion to orthodox Islam was so great that that he had taken the unusual step of 'withdraw[ing] all support to maintenance of mosques, and even ordered the destruction of some' (ibid.: 95).[28] Spear succinctly summarizes the range of Akbar's achievements: 'He provided India with the first Muslim dynasty to receive the free allegiance of Hindus as well as Muslims and whose claim to rule was accepted for reasons other than the possession of superior force. The obverse side of the medal was that he deeply offended the orthodox Muslims in the process' (1990: 37). Despite such idiosyncracies, he was sympathetic to variegations of religious belief.

---

26 The *Ain-i-Akbari* (literally, Akbar's 'laws' or 'rules') is the third part of the *Akbarnama* (*The Book of Akbar*) and describes Akbar's system of governance. Abu'l Fazl was Akbar's official chronicler.

27 A doctrine of religious harmony was instilled as a legal measure of sorts in Ashoka's time, communicated in his rock edicts (see Chapter 1).

28 According to Iqtidar Alam Khan, this is affirmed in firmans issued by Prince Salim, Akbar's son (1997: 93–4).

Akbar's secular sensibilities explain the reasoning behind his decision to return the title of Jagannath temple superintendent to the Khurda raja Ramachandradeva in 1592. The king immediately reinstated the trinity of deities at Puri and recommenced ritual services (Mohan Khokar 1998; Mohanty 1960 [*Madala Panji*]). B. C. Ray has argued that '[n]on-interference of the Mughal officials in the worship of Jagannath and other deities, and the celebration of the festivals in the usual way, encouraged the influx of pilgrims in good number. From [a] religious point of view, there ushered a new era which restored confidence' to the people of Odisha (1981: 28).

It seems safe to speculate that if the rituals returned to 'the usual way', Mahari Naach in Odisha most likely met with no direct opposition in Akbar's time. This is likely because earlier writers like Alberuni and later ones like François Bernier brought up devadasis in their accounts—implying a basic continuity of the ritual dance service—and they would have hardly escaped negative scrutiny by Mughal authorities if suppression was their intent. The English trader Thomas Bowrey, writing a century later during Emperor Aurangzeb's reign, also relayed his impressions of the 'dancing women' of Jagannath-Puri at the Rath Yatra, indicating the mahari system was still intact (see Chapter 5).

It is well established that many Mughal emperors and other Muslim rulers supported music, dance, painting and other forms of expressive culture—not only because they were aesthetes but also because such patronage increased their political power and individual prestige (Fazl 1873: 210).[29] Pala, a syncretic performance tradition of Odisha, flowered during Akbar's reign (see Appendix A). Classical Kathak, as it is well known, enjoyed sponsorship from Muslim nawabs as well as Hindu rajas, and reached the peak of artistic excellence in the royal courts. Wajid Ali Shah (1822–87), the ruler of Oudh and a dancer himself, contributed immeasurably

---

29 See also the discussions by Françoise 'Nalini' Delvoye (1997); Som Prakash Verma (1997); and Irfan Habib (2009).

to the development of Kathak's Lucknow and Kolkata *gharanas*.[30] Bhagavatham Melam, one of the forms folded into what would later become classical Kuchipudi, benefitted from the support of the Golconda Nawab Abul Hasan Tana Shah, who, legend has it, was so awed after a performance, that he provided a land grant to the hereditary families practising the tradition; the village survives to the present day.[31] This support of new cultural forms serves as proof of Thapar's claim that 'far from being dark,' the medieval period 'was a period of illumination as it was germane to so many later institutions,' artistic institutions among them (2002: 448).

Dance also flourished in Akbar's court, as he was a connoisseur of the fine arts.[32] In *Ain-Akbari*, Abu'l Fazl, in an amused tone, praises the emperor's interest in Indian aesthetic philosophy: 'His majesty has a considerable knowledge of the principles explained in the *Sangita* and other works, and what serves as an occasion to induce a lethargic sleep in other mortals, becomes to him a source of exceeding vigilance' (1893: 258).[33] Among the entertainers, Abu'l Fazl mentions the *natwas*, who 'exhibit some

---

30 See Shovana Narayan (1998); Sushil Kumar Saxena (2006); Pallabi Chakravorty (2008); and Margaret Walker (2016) on the development of Kathak as a syncretic style.

31 I visited Kuchipudi village in 2012, where the local inhabitants and dancers repeated this story; it is also etched in dance history. See, for instance, Mohan Khokar (1984: 56–7); Swapnasundari (2005: 32); and Rumya S. Putcha (2013, 2015).

32 Among other examples, Akbar supported works of scholarship on Indian performance. As R. Sathyanarayana writes, the *Nartana-Nirnaya*, a major treatise on music and dance, was written by the Pandarika Vitthala 'under the patronage of the Mughal emperor Akbar.' Mandakranta Bose verifies that the Jaipur version of the manuscript contains a part in praise of Akbar, further lending credence to this claim (1991: 84). A versatile and erudite scholar, Pandarika Vitthala 'was uniquely authoritative in several cognate art disciplines such as Karnataka music, Hindustani music, Persian music, classical and folk idioms of dancing, poetics, lexicography, etc. He is much esteemed, respected and borrowed by later authorities on music and dancing in both South India and North India' (R. Sathyanarayana in Pandarika Vitthala 1996: 2. *vii*).

33 For a fascinating discussion of the development of the arts during Akbar's reign, see Bonnie C. Wade (1998).

graceful dancing,' and female singers and dancers—'His Majesty calls them kanchanis' (ibid.: 257).[34] The *kanchanis* surface again in François Bernier's account of his travels, where he describes the reign of Shah Jahan and the fairs held in the women's palace quarters with the emperor's approval:

> He certainly transgressed the bounds of decency in admitting at those times into the seraglio singing and dancing girls called *Kenchens* (the gilded, the blooming), and in keeping them there for that purpose the whole night; they were not indeed prostitutes in bazaars, but those of a more private and respectable class, who attend the grand weddings of *Omrahs* and *Mansebdars*, for the purpose of singing and dancing. Most of these *Kenchens* are handsome and well dressed, and sing to perfection; and their limbs being extremely supple, they dance with wonderful agility, and are always correct in regard to time; after all, however, they were but common women (1916: 273–4).

Of Shah Jahan's son and successor, Aurangzeb, who was filled with religious zeal and followed the most orthodox and conservative precepts of Islam, Bernier says that he 'is more serious than his father; he forbids the *Kenchens* to enter the seraglio'—but even he permitted the dancers to go 'every Wednesday to the *Am-Kas*, where they

---

34 Even more intriguingly, Abu'l Fazl mentions another type of performance called *Akhara*, described as:

> an entertainment held at—night by the nobles of this country, some of whose (female) domestic servants are taught to sing and play. Four pretty women lead off a dance, and some graceful movements are executed. Four others are employed to sing [. . .] Besides the usual lamps of the entertainment, two women holding lamps stand near the circle of performers. Some employ more. It is more common for a band of these *natwas* to be retained in service who teach the young slave-girls to perform. Occasionally they instruct their own girls and take them to the nobles and profit largely by the commerce (1873: 258).

I speculate that this style of entertainment could have been a precursor for the *nautch* (dance) parties later held by the British as a mark of their power (see Chapter 5).

make the *salam* from a certain distance, and then immediately retire' (ibid.: 274). Bernier also notes that in a fairly generous gesture, Aurangzeb—who had imprisoned his own father—still allowed Shah Jahan to watch 'the singing and dancing women' (ibid.: 166). Yet Aurangzeb had issued orders for the demolition of the Jagannath temple in a 1692 firman, but apparently a judicious bribe to Mughal officials in his administration precluded this disaster (Dash 2011).

In another vein, Abu'l Fazl speaks of indulgence in dance leading to the 'downfall' of the powerful. Equating dance with abandon and the loss of self-possession, he notes that his father resisted its intoxicating power, and 'did not approve of the ecstasies of music and dance affected by the Sufis. He spoke against the followers of this practice' (1873: 440). Dance was a sign of refinement, luxury, and power, and simultaneously of danger and profligacy; nevertheless, despite these ambiguities, it held a privileged place in Mughal life.

It appears the emerging gotipua system did not meet with any direct opposition either; though conspicuously absent in the literature of the time, this very absence indicates either tolerance, ignorance or indifference on the part of the emperor. The only fleeting reference I could find is an intriguing description of a group of cross-dressing religious performers in the *Ain-i-Akbari*: 'The *Kirtaniya* are Brahmans, whose instruments are such as were in use among the ancients. They dress up smooth-faced boys as women and make them perform, singing the praises of Krishna and reciting his acts' (ibid.: 257). Kirtans are religious songs, and the *kirtaniya*s sound remarkably like Gaudiya Vaishnavites or even gotipuas, though the evidence is admittedly thin, and the early date suggests a pre-existing tradition of Bhakti performance—perhaps an ancillary style from Bengal or north India which may have influenced the gotipuas. Or it may signal the nascent development of a gotipua-type form, before its institutionalization in the *akhadas*.[35]

---

35 In the *Chaitanya Charitamrita*, the term *kirtaniya* is used to refer to Gaudiya Vaishnav celebrants singing and dancing at the Rath Yatra festivals (Goswami 1975). See for instance *Chaitanya Charitamrita*, *Madhya* 13.32–54 (Dimock and Stewart 2000: 520).

Allowing the development of arts based on Bhakti ideals would have been commensurate with Akbar's beliefs, for Akbar is known to have admired the principles of Gaudiya Vaishnavism. In 1570, he met with a disciple of Chaitanya, Jiva Goswami, in Vrindavan, and contributed towards the construction of a Radha temple there (Iqtidar Alam Khan 1997: 85; Mahanidhi Swami 2003). His Sufi-influenced outlook dovetailed to some degree with that of Bhakti saints. The acceptance of cross-dressing boys was also nothing new for Mughal emperors, who employed eunuchs in their courts to serve in a range of roles—as political advisers, occasional lovers, royal attendants, and guardians of the seraglio.

While the imperial state did not directly support devadasi service and gotipuas, it did create the cultural atmosphere for the resurrection of these practices when Ramachandradeva entered an alliance with the Mughals. (That the raja willingly did so is no surprise, for, according to M. Athar Ali, 'Mughal emperors [shone] in contrast with their despotic contemporaries,' the Bengal-based Afghan rulers [2009: 65]—although we cannot overlook the violence of any expansionist project.) Indeed, it could be argued that the devadasi system was able to survive, and the gotipua system able to emerge, because of Akbar's specific intervention—a novel instance of the Mughal state choreographing the resurgence of Hindu ritual performance, although not an anomalous one.

In briefly rehearsing these patterns of rule, my intention is obviously not to minimize or dismiss the genuine devastation caused in Odisha by figures like Kalapahad and others; rather, it is to interrogate the picture of uniformity presented by the 'Muslim thesis' of history painted by conservative scholars; to critique the negative readings of Muslim rule by highlighting the contributions of figures like Akbar; and to question a historical paradigm which alleges, as its founding premise, the unity and uniformity of a theological-political agenda advanced by a homogenized religious group. The sheer diversity among Indian Muslims indexed differences in styles of governance. In ideology, strategy and spiritual expression, the Muslim rulers, like their Hindu counterparts, radically diverged.

The simplistic notion that for Muslims, religious motivations exclusively guided their politics, is frequently perpetuated by conservative historiography and historians. However, some like K. C. Panigrahi do acknowledge that 'Hindu sentiment or Muslim sentiment was not the guiding factor in wars; it was the self-interest' (2008: 171). As some of the examples demonstrate, and as any banal and obvious reading of history reveals, the aims of conquest among Muslims and non-Muslims were rather similar: the creation of wealth; the extraction of economic resources; the generation of new labour sources; expansions of territory; an elevation in status for the sovereign; exercises of military might; complete submission of the 'enemy'; and, in several instances, the desire to establish religious dominance (Mirza Nathan 1936; Eaton 2000 and 2001). For both Muslims and non-Muslims alike, the common project was generally power and empire.

Even if one were to accept its spurious premises, the 'Muslim thesis' does not do one crucial thing—it does not explain the aesthetics and ethics of the gotipua genre itself. Despite desecrations of the Jagannath temple, the devadasi tradition continued in the post-Ganga, pre-Mughal era. If its features had substantially changed, then why, in this context, weren't the devadasis simply replaced by male performers who would take up their functions as temple servitors? How did transgender performance come to be integrated as an act of surrogation in public ritual? And what influenced the *formal* aspects/dimensions of the gotipua tradition? To answer these questions, in the next chapter I will explore how the gotipua tradition finds its principles and inspirations in Bhakti ideations. I argue that just as Bhakti brought religion into the public sphere, the gotipuas brought their ritual performance into public space as a proselytizing technique.

Chapter 4

ECSTASY AND MADNESS
GOTIPUAS, GENDER PERFORMANCE AND THE BODY OF BHAKTI

I hear everyone chanting the holy name of Kṛishṇa. Everyone's body is thrilled with ecstasy, and there are tears in
everyone's eyes.

— Sri Chaitanya Mahaprabhu,
Chaitanya Charitamrita, Madhya, 8.42[1]

To exist is to be in ecstasy.
— Victor Turner, *The Ritual Process* (1969), p. 138.

Your form is a veil of attributes. Your attribute is a block
to your true essence.

Anything that is a form of knowledge and gnosis,
know that it is infidelity to the world of attributes.

Striving comes from the body; attraction arises from
the soul. Movement arises from abandoning both.

— Mir Ali[2]

---

1 See Goswami 1975. Citations from the *Chaitanya Charitamrita* are referred
to according to part, section and verse or line. *Chaitanya Charitamrita Madhya*
8.42 refers to the middle part of the biography, section 8, line 42. *Adi* indicates
the beginning, *Madhya* the middle and *Anta* the final part, each corresponding
to a phase in Chaitanya's life. In some translations, the sections are replaced
by the numbers 1, 2 and 3, as in the Dimock and Stewart (2000) edition.

2 These lines, originally in Persian, are from a calligraphy by Mir Ali (c.1505–
45, Iran or Bukhara). For a visual of the calligraphy, see Elaine Wright (2008:
209, Plate 38B). The English translation of the text is on p. 301.

The Bhakti movement began in South India around the sixth century CE, soon spreading throughout the subcontinent and remaining prominent into the sixteenth. In eastern India, Bhakti was preceded by a brand of Vaishnavism—evinced in the cult of Jagannath—which slowly supplanted the previously reigning Shaivite orders in the region. Increasingly centred on Krishna, Bhakti accentuated this shift.[3] The rise of Bhakti posed a challenge to orthodox Brahmanism and gained popularity among diverse classes and castes who enthusiastically accepted it. Bhakti interrogated the dictates of caste and ritual rules set out in high Hinduism, much as Jainism and Buddhism had done centuries ago. While authorities in the dominant religio-political aristocracies frequently castigated its proponents, Bhakti found a strong a following among ordinary people all across the subcontinent. Its message of egalitarianism, and love as the foundation of an authentic relationship with the divine, resonated deeply with the masses.

Bhakti aimed at the democratization of religion by bringing it into public space. Sacred knowledge was no longer specialized, esoteric or closely guarded by a single privileged group like the Brahmans. Bhakti philosophy was expressed and disseminated in vernacular languages (Tamil, Bengali, Brajbhasha and so on), making it accessible to a wide cross-section of people from

---

3 Bhakti also marked a divide from the religious orders supported by the upper castes, since the power of these groups was amplified by the adoption of classical Hindu philosophy and its social systems. The dominant Brahmanical order represented a mutually reinforcing system of power between royalty and religious authorities, with selective and occasional support from lower-caste groups, depending on their need for political capital. However, they never quite succeeded in their hegemonic project—their power was always challenged or amended, and they were required to make concessions to maintain their power over groups that gradually came into the 'Hindu' fold through complex negotiations and coercions. There was a strong correlation between Brahmanical ideology and social privilege, then, which was continually contested by the other members of society who wished to gain power for themselves or democratize social relations. For more on historical caste relations in India, see M. N. Srinivas (1952, 1989); Romila Thapar (1990, 2002); and Nicholas Dirks (2001).

diverging backgrounds, especially those who did not enjoy literacy in Sanskrit. Bhakti allowed the people to participate in religiosity without requiring the sanction of temple officials and priests, regulations of caste or any other form of authority standing between devotee and deity.

Bhakti also powerfully illustrated the centrality of religion in the formation of a putative 'Indian' consciousness. Madhu Kishwar writes that Bhakti 'is known to have played a crucial role in shaping the social life of people of all religions in the subcontinent. [. . .] The religious establishments continued a dialogue with the *bhaktas* and the many streams of thought and practice frequently coexisted, and at times merged with one another' (1989: 3–4).[4] Even the Mughal empire, with its expansive powers, could not instigate such pan-Indian feeling; if there was an emerging 'national' consciousness, it was *felt* in cultural, rather than political, terms.

I use the word 'felt' deliberately, as attuned awareness of sentiment and embodiment were central to Bhakti praxis.[5] Spiritual knowing (as set against religious knowledge), far from being unattainable, could be experienced within the precincts of the body. Bhakti's dual rejection of rationality and embrace of emotionality appealed to a wide constituency who could now allow religiosity to enter their everyday lives without relying on the priestly class to mediate their encounter with the divine. Bhakti, then, represented both the democratization of devotion and the democratization of

---

4 Kishwar also describes the interface between Bhakti and Sufi movements, and their joint production of a syncretic mystic mode (1989: 4). Romila Thapar, who has also written of Bhakti's resonances with Sufi philosophy, remarks on how 'Sufi ideas attracted interest in India, particularly among those inclined to mystic teachings and asceticism, since much of the symbolism was similar. Their dialogue with the *bhakti* movement was to the advantage of both, as they questioned orthodoxy in their explorations of the meaning of religion and of the human condition' (2002: 488). On the Sufi-Bhakti nexus in the cultural field, see also Ainslee Embree (1988: 447–89); Jayant Lele (1981); David Lorenzen (1995); J. J. Roy Burman (1996); Scott Kugle (2007); and Pallabi Chakravorty and Scott Kugle (2009).

5 For a discussion of Bhakti and its embodied expressions, see A. K. Ramanujan (1989) and Karen Pechilis Prentiss (1999).

the devout. In the Bhakti paradigm, religious affect trumped the laws of the social.

Gaudiya Vaishnavism in Odisha

An influential form of Bhakti from Bengal, Gaudiya Vaishnavism, entered Odisha through the charismatic figure of Chaitanya in the sixteenth century CE. His arrival heralded profound alterations in the region's religious discourse. Vaishnavism, and the worship of Nilmadhava and his cognate Jagannath, had been well established by this juncture, becoming pervasive in Odisha's cultural land-scape. The meanings and magnitude of the Puri temple, too, had multiplied. As great philosophers like Shankaracharya (*c.*788–820 CE), Ramanuja (*c.*1077–1137 CE), and other eminent saints had graced the city with their presence, with *mathas* established to propagate their teachings, Puri's reputation as a centre of learning and auspiciousness increased. Chaitanya's arrival heightened Puri's position of prominence. And with Gaudiya Vaishnavism, the cult of Jagannath converged with the cult of Krishna, drawing on pre-existing traditions of Vaishnav worship in Odisha (Mukherjee 1981).

Krishna, the dark and luminous beloved of Radha in Hindu iconography, is widely adored in Odisha. He is one of the only deities in the Hindu pantheon who shares the same world as his devotees, a figure whose biographical arc is mythologized from birth to death. The synchronicity of his status as both mortal and immortal, worldly and heavenly, intensely human and sublimely divine, makes him a special figure of worship. In the *Bhagavata Purana* (*c.*ninth/tenth century CE), Krishna assumes diverse forms as Yashoda's mischievous child, the killer of demons, and revealer of the cosmos. He is the embodiment of eros in poet Jayadev's twelfth-century CE masterpiece, *Geeta Govinda,* the playful lover consorting with Radha and the gopis. He expresses universal wis-dom in the *Bhagavad Gita* (*c.*first century BCE). Krishna's traditional 108 poetic names illuminate his multiple traits—Shyamsundara, the beautiful one, dark and lustrous as night. Madhava, who ushers in the spring. Sakshi Gopal, the witness. Jagdish, the protector.

Govinda, pleasing to all. Vishwarupa, reflection of the world. Madan, god of love. Mohan, the enchanter.

Krishna worship was widespread in Odisha, popularized by Vaishnav poets like Jayadeva, but it only reached its zenith with Chaitanya's arrival on the scene.[6] Krishnadas Kaviraj Goswami, a disciple of Chaitanya as well as his biographer, relates in the *Chaitanya Charitamrita* the saint's fervour for union with Krishna, recalling his words: 'My Lord Govinda, because of separation from You, I consider even a moment a great millennium. Tears flow from My eyes like torrents of rain, and I see the entire world as void. [. . .] Krishna is My life and soul. Krishna is the treasure of My life. Indeed, Krishna is the very life of My life' (Goswami 1975: *Antya,* 20.39, 20.58).[7] When Chaitanya came to Puri in 1509, he sought *darshan* at the Jagannath temple, weeping and fainting in bliss: 'Staying near the Garudha-stambha [pillar], the Lord would look upon Lord Jagannath. What can be said about the strength of that love? On the ground beneath the column [. . .] was a deep ditch, and that ditch was filled with the water of His tears' (ibid.: *Madhya,* 2.54). To this day, devotees flock to the Garuda pillar, where they say Chaitanya's body made an impression in his endless visits to Jagannath-Puri.

Gaudiya Vaishnavism influenced a panoply of religious and cultural practices in Odisha. Its paratopic religiosity generated the gotipua tradition, where Gaudiya Vaishnavite values of embodiment and sentiment found their ideal translations in dance. Parallels between the Bhakti worldview and gotipua performance are transparently evoked and witnessed in current-day Odissi practices. The

6 On the special place of Krishna iconography in the Indian arts, see Edward C. Dimock Jr and Denise Levertov (1967); P. Banerjee (1984); John Stratton Hawley (1988); Edward C. Dimock Jr (1989, 1991); Lalit Kala Akademi (1991); John Stratton Hawley and Mark Juergensmayer (1992); Alka Pande (2005); Caron Smith (2005); Walter Spink (2005); Shovana Narayan (2007); and Harsha V. Dehejia (2008). On the *Geeta Govinda* especially, see Lee Siegel (1978 and 2009) and Barbara Stoler Miller (2004).

7 *Chaitanya Charitamrita* literally means 'the essence' or 'nectar' of Chaitanya's character, in Bengali, the language of the book.

adoration of Krishna, the use of vernacular languages, the transgression of conventional masculine norms—accompanied by the exclusion of women from ritual practice—are all features of Gotipua style which may be traced to Gaudiya Vaishnavism. Perhaps the most striking themes connecting the mystical movement to the gotipuas are the mutual commitments to Sakhi Bhava, transgender performance, and the configuration of dance as a mode of public worship, subversion and ecstasy.

Transgender Performance

The gotipua tradition is one of several styles of transgender performance in Odisha. My use of 'transgender' in this context refers to a cross-gender identification assumed for the duration of a ritual event. This provisional definition requires recasting the idea of transgenderism, which typically denotes an identity rather than a *bhakti bhava*, or a state assumed for a religious purpose and sanctioned for spiritual ends.

My qualification of 'transgender performance' is a departure from what the term 'transgender' generally stands for in Western queer theory, where it acts as a referent for persons 'who move away from the gender they were assigned at birth, people who cross over (*trans-*) the boundaries constructed by their culture to define and contain that gender,' as Susan Stryker explains while emphasizing that, in the English-speaking communities of the West, 'because transgender is a word that has come into widespread use only in the past couple of decades, its meanings are still under construction' (2008: 1).

While a segment of Indian society endorses the circulation and adoption of Western notions of the queer in contemporary India, the label does not translate smoothly into local Indian contexts where multifarious indigenous categories cannot be easily bound or unified under this homogenizing banner. Indeed, there are several practices and identity formations that may look 'queer' to the Western gaze but have wildly different contexts and nuanced histories which cannot be easily reconciled with it.[8] The historical association of 'queerness' with notions of shame, strange and bizarre sexual proclivities and social stigma in Western societies, for instance, are incommensurable with cultural frameworks that have traditionally held attitudes towards minoritarian gender expressions that ranged from respecting such identifications to ambivalence, rejection and complete indifference. In the case of the gotipuas, they were celebrated for their artistic virtuosity and religious devotion.

This is perhaps the conundrum of postcolonial politics, when it confronts the Western delineation of the 'queer': What name can we give to a category of gender which was traditionally minoritarian but still recognized as part of the social spectrum, which was not marginalized but venerated, which was not shamed but existed as a legitimate space of difference and honour within dominant cultural logics? I have chosen the notion of the 'extraordinary' to evoke such a sense, and to account for the ways in which such practices were not ordinary (as in majoritarian) gender expressions, but framed as 'special' in terms of their difference, and integrated into both religious and non-religious spheres.

Secondly, I do not wish to confuse the idea of 'transgender performance' developed here with any notions of 'third gender' or 'transgender' as categories that refer to one's identity or construction of self in everyday Indian life.[9] These third-gender/transgender categories are ontological (and may include hijra, aravani and jogappa communities within their contours, for instance) while 'transgender performance' is based on the intentional assumption

---

8 On this point, see Inderpal Grewal and Caren Kaplan (2001); Ruth Vanita (2002b); and Gayatri Gopinath (2005).

9 On 15 April 2014, India's Supreme Court handed down a landmark decision granting the right of transgender communities to officially identify as a third gender beyond male and female, citing the historical recognition of transgender subjects in India. See *National Legal Services Authority v. Union of India and Others*; the full text of the judgement is available at https://goo.gl/2zfQ6G (last accessed on 25 June 2018).

of a temporary identification and practice. I propose transgender performance here as an act, not as an identity.

Finally, I do not want to collapse 'transgender performance' into 'queer' as a rubric for lesbian, gay, bisexual, pansexual or other non-heterosexual orientations (biological, political or otherwise). Indeed, transgender performance is not about the display of the subject's sexual identification, I argue; this is because there is no necessary correspondence between gender presentation and sexual desire or practice. From the standpoint of critical theory, too, these are discrete arenas of power (Rubin 1992). In the case of Odisha's gotipua tradition, the separation of these spheres is particularly relevant.

While traditions of transgender performance existed in Odisha before the sixteenth century, it appears that none had been formalized prior to this time (Khokar 1998; Kanungo 2006–07). Transgender forms intensified and proliferated, I argue, in the context of Akbar's empire and the association with the Khurda raja, Ramachandradeva. The gotipua tradition then spread throughout Odisha thanks to the patronage of zamindars, nobles and other wealthy elites who could afford to sponsor performance troupes (Napoleon Patnaik 2012).

Sakhi Pila, Chhau and adivasi ritual dances dedicated to the cult of the mother goddess in Odisha all exalted transgender bodies in their repertoires. Despite striking differences in doxa, these practices point to a shared spiritual orientation in which embodying the feminine, in specific, was and is regarded as an auspicious act.[10] The individual performances are tethered to multiple and oppositional doctrines of the feminine, ranging from the Shakti cult's belief that the goddess represents a divine but deadly force whose dangerous aspects can be quelled through acts of appeasement such as trance dances, to the Bhakti perception that a spiritual union with the supreme deity Krishna is possible only

---

10 See Francesco Brighenti (2001) and D. K. Tripathy (2007) for discussions of Odishan rituals conducted by a diverse communities, which incorporate transgender performance.

when the devotee is transformed—in body and affect—into Radha, his female consort. Thus, regardless of whether the feminine principle is conceived as dangerous or benign, embodying the feminine becomes a shared mode of honouring the divine.

Priyambada Mohanty Hejmadi, D. N. Patnaik and other Odissi scholars have argued that gotipua performance is a Vaishnav tradition but did not exist in Chaitanya's lifetime. Considering the extant (but limited) historical sources, I agree with this view. The *Chaitanya Charitamrita*—a supremely important text for understanding the discourse of performance in sixteenth-century eastern India—contains several passages that offer meditations upon various enactments of dance, drama and *rasa,* but makes no reference at all to gotipuas. The work does highlight the contribution of Ramananda Ray—minister of Raja Prataparudradeva, devout Vaishnav, a shudra by caste and close spiritual companion of Chaitanya —in teaching two devadasis of the Puri temple to dance in his play, *Jagannath Bhallav Natak,* in 1509, which may represent the first public performance by the devadasis outside sanctioned temple rituals and festivals (Goswami 1975: *Antya* 5.11– 49, 13.77–87); or, it may be more accurate to say, the first recorded instance that is available to us.[11] Some scholars speculate that Ray may have spearheaded the gotipua custom as well—K. C. Panigrahi, for instance, suggests that 'the gotipua dance appears to have originated in the reign of Prataparudradeva (1497–1540 CE) and gained popularity in the subsequent Muslim period on account of the rigidity of the purdha system which led to the seclusion of women and made their presence scarce on festive occasions'—repeating the familiar xenophobic trope of the Muslim threat to Odisha's cultural integrity and ignoring descriptions in *Chaitanya Charitamrita* which suggest that devadasi performance took place in public even in Prataparudradeva's time. No known proof exists of either the king's or Ray's involvement in the gotipua tradition's inception.

---

11 See Mohanty Hejmadi and Hejmadi Patnaik (2007: 48–9) for more on this. See Goswami 2000[1581]: *Antya* 5.11–24, 31–41, and 13.77–87; also notes to lines 11,12 and 18 on p. 842. See Tarini Charan Rath (1920: 448–53) for a discussion of the excerpt.

There is no doubt among students of history, though, that gotipua performance emerged in the late sixteenth century, in the post-Chaitanya period, and that its aesthetic was shaped by Chaitanyite practices and beliefs. D. N. Patnaik asserts that Gaudiya Vaishnavas 'preached and practiced the cult of *Sakhi Bhava* and introduced boy dancers *in place of women*' (2006: 65; emphasis added). While they occasionally danced at the temple, he states '[f]or the first time, the temple dance came out of its home and began to be performed by these Gotipuas in public. [. . .] Vaishnavas chose this dance of Gotipuas as a medium of publicity of their cult and philosophy' (ibid.).[12] Similarly in Ragini Devi's view, with the advent of Mughal rule in Odisha, the maharis, 'who were exclusively dedicated to temple service, were henceforth employed to dance at the royal court of Khurda, and from that time they lost their religious status. In order to maintain the religious festivals of Jagannath, the raja of Khurda appointed Gotipuas [. . .] as dancers' (2002: 142). A handful of others like Mohan Khokar held the minority opinion that the gotipuas 'were *not a substitute for the maharis*, for they had no link at all with the temple' (1998: n.p.; emphasis added). Another possible genealogy with a scandalous hue: analysing two modern documents, Gopal Chandra Praharaj's *Kabisurya Granthabali* and *Jibanacharita* (both 1928), Mohanty Hejmadi and Hejmadi Patnaik mention Praharaj's speculation that the gotipuas emerged as a respectable counterpart to the 'vulgar' performances by Andhra prostitutes who lived in the neighbouring region and deeply influenced the arts of southern Odisha (2007: 42–3).[13]

---

12 Priyambada Mohanty Hejmadi and Ahalya Hejmadi Patnaik (2007) and Sunil Kothari (1990), among others, have noted the same.

13 For an explanation of how these Oriya-language texts, along with Praharaj's comprehensive lexicon, *Purnachandra Oriya Bhashakosha*, Part II (1932) and Part IV (1934), detail the musical and movement repertoires of the gotipuas in the early twentieth century, see Hejmadi Mohanty and Hejmadi Patnaik (2007: 42–3). *Purnachandra Oriya Bhashakosha* is available online at: http://dsal.uchicago.edu/dictionaries/praharaj/ or https://goo.gl/M7hdDe (last accessed on 25 June 2018).

After contemplating the differences—current and historical—between Bhakti performance and the rituals practised at the Puri temple, I share Khokar's conclusion. Gotipua and mahari styles had different religious inspirations, aeshetics and goals. This is one of the reasons I believe that the gotipuas did not 'replace' devadasis; rather, they each served distinct ritual purposes and fulfilled different ideals appropriate to the particular performative circumstance. We can conclude that the gotipua and mahari systems coexisted as institutionalized forms. For instance, the Odia poet Bhupati Pandit, in his literary work praising Krishna, *Prema Panchamrita*, dated 29 January 1694, wrote of devadasi dances: '*Sri Jayadeva kavikrita Gayani gaile basanta. Bina mridanga tala nade Nachuni nachanti anande. E rupe sanamana kari Ta pachhe karana pachari*': The dancers (*Nachuni*) performed joyfully (*nachanti anande*) to the musical accompaniment of the *bina* (stringed instrument), *mridanga* (drum) and *Geeta Govinda* songs (quoted in Tripathy 2009: 27). And European travelogues, too, corroborate that 'temple dancing' continued to thrive in Odisha well after the gotipua system came into place.

The divides between the temple-centric and Bhakti ideologies can be discerned in the modes of devadasi and gotipua performance. The mahari system was sustained by royal authorities and linked directly to the temple context; the gotipua troupes were sponsored by royalty as well as wealthy zamindars and prominent community leaders. Mahari rituals were designed to honour the deities primarily inside the shrine whereas the role of the gotipuas was to spread the message of Bhakti outside, without regard for caste or class. In one instance, the devotee came inside a tangible sacred *place* to witness the dance; in the other, the dancer travelled to the devotee and created a temporal sacred *space* with their bodies, for the duration of the choreographic event.

Devadasi dance was confined to the Jagannath temple and witnessed only by co-religionists who were able to legitimately enter the temple premises—except on limited occasions when devadasis were permitted to perform in public during festivals like Rath Yatra and Chandan Yatra. Therefore, their audience was self-selected, their position elite. Elaborate regulations circum-scribed their entire lifestyle giving them ritual power and privilege but also restricting their social and spatial mobility. The *Madala Panji* and the *Record of Rights* (1956) specify the maharis' service obligations, rules of initiation and the benefits to which they were entitled; their performances were highly circumscribed by these customary laws.[14]

The gotipuas, in contrast, could negotiate their relation to both sacred and secular time and space more freely. This diminished their auspiciousness relative to devadasis and other temple servi-tors, but the relationship between their everyday life and ritual performance was much more fluid, and they could traverse these lines with greater ease than other ritual specialists. The major difference was, of course, that the gotipua identitfication was an ephemeral one, lasting only until adolescence, whereas inhabiting the devadasi identity signalled a permanent elevation into the ritual world and conferred lifelong propitiousness.

The gotipuas trained in dance as well as allied movement prac-tices at *akhadas,* and so at one time were also called *akhada pila* (boys of the *akhada*). They were taught these physical disciplines to acquire cultural knowledge and train for combat. Traces of these local martial arts—employing a mix of meditation, yoga, gymnastics and stylized deployment of weaponry—were assimilated into vari-eties of Chhau performance; in Phari-khanda-khela (sword-and-shield play); and in the Paik (soldiers') dances, developed primarily in the villages of coastal Odisha, among an array of forms.[15] Ileana

14 For fine-grained analyses of mahari service, see Frédérique Apffel Marglin (1985); Rahul Acharya and Parama Karuna Devi (2008); Priyambada Mohanty Hejmadi and Ahalya Hejmadi Patnaik (2007: 22–42); Ratna Roy (2009); and Purna Chandra Mishra (2013).

15 See Shyam Sundar Rath (2005) and Ileana Citarasti (2011, 2012) for nuanced discussions of Odisha's martial traditions, their histories and techniques. *Paik* is a contraction of the Sanskrit *padatika*, or foot soldier. The term may have originated under the Ganga dynasty, when a *paik* force noted for its valour and designated to receive superior miltary training was first developed under its supervision (Rath 2005: 21, 238).

FIGURE 4.1. A famous present-day *akhadha-ghara* (gymasium, but more a combination of physical training and cultural centre) in the neighbouhood of Balia Sahi, Puri, Odisha, 24 December 2014. Photograph by the author.

Citarasti reminds us that in the story of the classical dances, 'their ritualistic and religious origins have generally been more emphasised then their martial derivation' and underscores how 'the *akhada* in the villages of Orissa acting as centres of cultural confluence' enable us to picture 'an important link towards a more complete and comprehensive conception of body culture' in the region (2011: n.p).

The paradigm of performance here encompassed two opposing activities: martial performance as a regimented rehearsal for self- or community-defence, and ritual performance as sacred and creative art. Bodily discipline was the foundational idea connecting combat training with the dancing, with masculine power cultivated in the former and feminine *shakti* in the latter. Choreography was thus deployed as a mode of refining and strengthening the body

in service of both war and worship (Chandralekha 1980).[16] Consequently, gotipua practice engendered multiple effects: religious,
aesthetic and political.

Gotipua and Devadasi Choreographies

According to the prevailing Odissi literature, a division of labour
historically existed between maharis and gotipuas in terms of the
movement styles and gestural vocabularies embraced by each.
The devadasis partitioned their labours according to the specific
category they occupied—as Gauni (singer), Nachuni (dancer) or
Pathuari (procession participant)—but importantly, they rarely
mixed their functions. The Nachuni specialized in pure rhythmic
dances—resembling Pallavis and Sthayee (or Batu)—but she did
not sing. The Bhitara and Bahara Gaunis sang, but did not dance.
At most, the night-singer, lulling the deity to sleep, accompanied
her lyrics with gestures and facial expressions in what was perhaps
a raw form of *abhinaya*. The movement was graceful, subtle, the
lines of the body languid and soft—the very embodiment of *lasya*.[17]
Except in ceremonial occasions, they performed solo.

In contrast, gotipua movements were defined and expansive,
partly because there were few spatial restrictions, and partly
because they were aware of the importance of formal elements

---

16 I focus on the danced aspect rather than the martial dimension in this
chapter for three reasons: one, documentation on gotipua dance is fairly accessible; two, the connection to dance continues to be prevail, as the martial training declined with the organization of formal armies in modernity; and three,
there is a paucity of historical research on the *akhadas* as centres of martial
training. More investigation is required on this topic on the whole.

17 I am inferring this based on the mahari style of Odissi I have seen performed live by Ritha Devi (2003a); Shashimoni Devadasi (2008); and
Rupashree Mohapatra (2012); film footage in Ron Hess' *Given to Dance* (1985);
video documentation of dances by Guru Pankaj Charan Das, who introduced
the mahari style into modern Odissi's repertoire; and Sharmila Biswas' reconstructed mahari choreographies for the concert stage (see SNA 2003); archival
photographs; from descriptions gathered in historical and contemporary texts;
and from interviews conducted as part of my formal fieldwork (2007–14).

FIGURE 4.2. *Bandha-chitra*, also called *kandarpa ratha* (chariot of love), composed of female figures forming the image of a horse as a vehicle for Krishna and Radha. From author's private collection.

in the display of dance as religious articulation on the public stage. The *Abhinaya Chandrika, Abhinaya Darpanam Prakash*[18] and *Natyashastra* contain descriptions of the vigorous performance

18 This seventeenth-century CE text by Jadunath Singh exists as a palm-leaf manuscript and contains valuable information on Odissi dance (Pathy 2007: 59–61; Citarasti 2001: 100). While it makes no direct mention of the *Natyashastra*, it does include the term 'Odra-Magadhi' and thus can be linked to Odissi history.

techniques constituting gotipua practice, and recommend a set of demanding acrobatic contortions, called Bandha Nrutya[19] or simply *bandha*, for particularly agile dancers.[20] Temple sculptures and palm-leaf illustrations, too, present a glimpse of this practice.

Maheshwar Mahapatra's *Abhinaya Chandrika* is especially valuable since it presents 'the earliest textual reference to *bandha*' and contains 'probably the first historical reference to the *udra* [odhra] style of dancing' (R. Sathyanarayana in Pandalika Vitthala 1998: 3.274, 277). It catalogues the features of Bandha Nrutya as:

> very venerable (*mahaghora*: awesome? terrible?), difficult for the danseuse (*natikastapradayini*), feasible only to the limbs of a teenager (*kisora-anga sapeksa*), but difficult after youth (*visamam yauvanatare*). It demands the placing of feet in odd and intricate positions, awkward and complex bending of hands as well as tortuous combinations of hands and feet. It is impossible to learn and succeed without a (proper) guru. It is totally bereft of word text, *bhava* or *rasa*; it consists only of profuse, sinuous body movement and disposition of limbs. The movements are standardised (established?) in respect of *nada* (i.e. *pata* phrases or *bols*). But all bandha affords pleasure to everyone. [. . .] At the end of the bandha the dancer offers mental obeisance to the guru and assumes a fixed pose while engaged in gentle footwork (*Abhinaya Chandrika* 1.165, 166, 1.197 and 3.126–9, in Pandarika Vitthala 1998: 3.277; original emphasis).

Additionally, the *Nartana-Nirnaya* provides intricate *bandha* 'scores'. Interestingly, the very title of the text frames as its subject the male dancer, *nartaka*, indicating that dance was a shared

---

19 *Nrutya* is the term used for performances by male dancers dressed as female characters.

20 R. Sathyanarayana comments that the term bandha refers to the metaphor of knots, since the dances required dancers to contort their bodies into challenging acrobatic positions (in Pandarika Vitthala 1998: 3.277), and includes a list of positions used by gotipuas: Angavatarana, Lalatatilaka, Latavrischika, Sakatasya, Chakramandala, Atikranta and Mayulalita (273).

FIGURE 4.3. Maguni Das' gotipua troupe in a practice session at their *akhada* in Raghurajpur, Odisha. They are in a *bandhya-nrutya* formation, reminiscent of *bandha-chitra* paintings, depicting the supreme power of Krishna. Photograph by the author, March 2008.

activity rather than an exclusively masculine or feminine enterprise at the time of its writing. This is further borne out by Jadunath Singh's *Abhinaya Darpanam Prakasha*, which states that men and women both train and participate in *bandha* as *tandava*, though later it would become the province of male dancers [ibid: 3.274]). The gotipua repertoire developed from the period of *Abhinaya Chandrika* to include *nritya* and song (thus no longer 'bereft of word text, *bhava*, or *rasa*') in its later manifestations. Modern gotipuas have largely continued to adhere to *bandha* specifications laid out in the aforementioned works.

For maharis, nuances of expression, intimated to the deity alone, held greater significance than the spectacular elements present in gotipua choreographies. Their audiences differed: maharis performed principally for the gods, the gotipuas for the people ('bandha affords pleasure to everyone'). Their language differed: gotipuas relayed their songs in the vernacular Odia while the maharis were asked to follow a legal decree to sing verses exclusively from the Sanskrit *Geeta Govinda*.[21] Their movement aesthetics differed as well: the same inscription asked the maharis to align their choreographies with Shastric principles. Gotipuas, on the other hand, had greater freedom of movement—*abhinaya* and pure dance, *lasya* and *tandava* fused in their repertoire. Unlike the maharis, gotipua roles were usually interchangeable; they performed solo or in duets or ensembles, alternately singing and dancing, using expansive movements, formations that required bodily contact, and extended spatial pathways. As emissaries of Bhakti, they necessarily had to integrate a deeper sense of theatricality to appeal to an eclectic audience. [22]

This narrative of difference depends on highlighting the 'lyrical feminization' of the devadasi body and the 'muscularity' of the masculine body (often cast as a distinction between *lasya* and *tandava*). But how much of this is true? We know that devadasis once undertook the demanding labours of Bandha Nritya, and that their movements were just as elaborate and intricate as those of the gotipuas, even if practice quickly faded.[23] It appears, then,

---

21 There is no precise information available as to whether devadasis actually followed this decree into the nineteeenth century CE, but in Ron Hess' *Given to Dance* (1985), two of the devadasis clearly sing Odia-language songs in an apparent violation of the dictum. It seems that by the twentieth century or even earlier, the tradition had become flexible enough to include vernacular poetry and song.

22 R. Sathyanarayana notes that the *Abhinaya Chandrika* frames the bandha as a rural (*gramya*) dance, though it is also 'fit to be performed before the king and his retinue' (2.314–19 and 3.80, cited in Pandarika Vitthala 1998: *Nartana-Nirnaya*, 3.277).

23 Moreover, some scholars have proposed that the gotipuas seem to have initially modelled and mirrored devadasi movement patterns, with the difference being that they did so for public display. Mohan Khokar speculates: '[W]hat

that given some similar techniques, the public context of gotipua performance and its cross-gender dimension acquire salience in terms of situating the significance of this distinctive practice.

Images created by the assemblage of gotipua bodies, reminiscent of *bandha chitra* representations, tend to depict the manifold stories of Krishna in complex group formations. In Vritanga, the dancers arch their bodies, feet touching head, and roll along on the ground like the wheels of Jagannath's chariot at Rath Yatra.[24] They create pyramid-like structures, standing on each other's shoulders, with Krishna playing his flute at the pinnacle, replicating depictions of the *kandarpa ratha* (chariot of love) in elaborate Patachitra and Chitropathi. In *abhinaya* compositions, gotipua metamorphose into a miniature Radha and her *sakhis*, performing praise songs composed by a host of Odia poets—Banamali, Kabisurya, Jayadeva.[25] Their expressive dances evoke the mythology of Krishna-lila, when the god manifests as lover and beloved of the enchanted gopis, indulging in divine play and dalliance. The lila, says Geeti Sen, 'is a moment of ineffable purity and effulgence, revisited time and again through centuries in word and song, performance and painting, and remains the core of aesthetics and theology of Vaishnavism' (2005: 209).[26] These performances of extraordinary gender, of Sakhi Bhava, are drawn from a Chaitanyite devotional ethic, marked by the twin traits of 'humility and passion' (Schweig 2002).

they danced had a strong affinity with what the maharis offered. The dance styles co-existed, each independently, but with palpably common roots' (1998: n.p). This would align with the gotipua ideal of simulating feminine personae and gestures. Yet there is no definitive proof of this perceived commonality or fusion.

24 Aloka Kanungo details the practices associated with Bandha Nrutya in her excellent 2006–07 overview.

25 For a full discussion of gotipua repertoire, see D. N. Patnaik (2006); Priyambada Mohanty Hejmadi and Ahalya Hejmadi Patnaik (2007); Ratna Roy (2009); and Chitta Ranjan Mallia (2013).

26 On the much-discussed concept of lila, see also Edward C. Dimock Jr (1963, 1966, 1989 and 1991); Rochelle Kessler (2005); and Graham M. Schweig (2007).

Characteristics of Gotipua Dance

Much more than simply adopting 'feminized' bodily adornments and gestures, gotipua performance involves the enactment of a total affective attitude. The depth of the disciple's devotion and adoration is measured in terms of its full display, a display amply highlighted in the performance event. Yet the gotipua's devotional expression is by no means restricted to the boundaries of the ritual event. While the dance is set apart from everyday life as an extraordinary act—made all the more extraordinary for its performances of (trans)gender—the gotipua must otherwise display an adherence to religious tenets that qualify him to participate in and propagate the tradition. Compared to the devadasis, the regimes imposed on gotipuas were lesser in terms of both degree and decree, but this does not mean they were entirely absent. Unlike devadasis, though, gotipuas could blur the boundaries between public and private, inside and outside, performing in temple and non-temple spaces.[27] Yet their presence did not index a synthesis of secular and sacred; rather, through their paratopic performance, their bodies sculpted a new sacralized space. Gotipua dancers extended the contours of ritual performance by taking it outside the temple and into the public sphere. Their position as prepubescent males (in everyday life) and ritual performers embodying the feminine (in religious life) allowed them to traverse the boundaries of both gender and space in such fluid ways.

Critically, being a gotipua is an evanescent identification that takes place only within the bounds of ritual performance. Like actors, gotipuas performed a role for the duration of the ritual event alone. However, unlike actors, gotipuas had a limited ability to cultivate an individual self on a volitional basis. They belonged to a community of ritual specialists and were expected to conform to everyday social roles as soon as they exited the space of the stage. Since most gotipuas did not assume wholly feminized personae in

---

27 Gotipuas participated in temple festivals like Chandan Yatra and Jhulan Yatra and were involved in celebrations of other events during the ritual calendar (Raja Panda 2012; Mallia 2013: 59).

terms of their offstage social identities, they were expected to reabsorb the local norms of masculinity outside the ritual context.

In its own cultural frame, this abrupt metamorphosis between masculine and feminine performance was normalized and so was not perceived as posing a crisis to the actor's gender identity, partly because the boundaries between the realm of dance and the quotidian were very clearly drawn; partly because of the versatilities of gender coding within Bhakti discourses; and partly because the religious rules that enabled this transformation rarely situated masculinity and femininity as purely oppositional. Androgyny, sexual diversity and magical incarnations of gender were common dimensions of all kinds of Hindu mythology, obviating the moral problematic of shifting genders for religious performance. Gender bending is a common theme in Hindu epics and legends. The androgynous Ardhanareeshwara is half-Shiva, half-Shakti, while Prajapati is an intersex Vedic deity. The Mahabharata recounts how Vishnu transformed into Mohini, the enchantress, to seduce the demons and preserve the *amrita*, nectar of immortality, for the gods; and how Krishna turned into a woman, Aravani, to become the lover, for one night, of a protagonist who was sacrificing himself in the great war. The deity Ayappan is born of the coupling of Vishnu (as Mohini) and Shiva, and, in the *Padma Purana*, King Bhagirath was born from two mothers (Vanita 2005). In other images, Krishna is one with Kali. And Chaitanya himself is said to dually embody Radha and Krishna. These mythologies emphasize gender as fundamentally *maya*, a problem of form rather than essence.

Transgender performance by the gotipuas was aligned with and authorized by its sacred aura. In the context of Bhakti and Sakhi Bhava, gotipua performance also revealed gender as an illusion, as a construction and an aspiration all at once.

The Efficacy of Effeminacy

The efficacy of gotipua performance is measured in terms of the dexterous display of 'effeminacy', translated as the ability to transcend the crude body and engage the potent *shakti* residing within but locked away in everyday life, opened and released in the context of ritual performance. Thus, the performer's ability to authentically embody the feminine stereotype became an index of virtuosity. Crucially, in gotipua discourse, performing the feminine is regarded less as a revelation of a sexual essence or truth and more as the exhibition of complete religious devotion. Seen in this light, gotipua performance was hardly a display of normative masculinity in crisis; rather, it was a potent staging of spiritual fervour and aesthetic talent. Because of the demarcations between categories of everyday life and ritual, there was absolutely no contradiction between the performer's perfect enactment of the feminine figure on stage, and his deployment of dominant codes of masculinity in quotidian contexts. The practice did present a space for subjects who identified as homosexual, effeminate, trans-gender or ambiguous about their gender presentation to express themselves through the aesthetic frame. However, this alignment would be regarded as coincidental—and then camouflaged—rather than constructed as a performance ideal; becoming feminine required a certain labour, a discipline one had to acquire. In terms of sexuality or gender, there was no equivalence posited between the body on the street and the body on stage.

In pubescence and adolescence, the biological changes that transformed boys into men made the camouflage of gender impossible, as the performers' sexed attributes and sexualities became prominent. There seems to be a specific narrative at play which is embodied by the actors in gotipua performance, one that involves the discourse of childhood and its ambiguities of gender. Childhood is posited as a malleable state in which social difference is not yet fully manifest, allowing for complex negotiations—and representations—of masculine and feminine which are rarely conceptualized, in any case, as dichotomies in Hindu thought. The child's body is an extraordinary expression of gender, representing a condition prior to the body being biologized and socialized into male and female corporealities. Under the auspices of the religious tradition underpinning it, the transgender body proposed in

gotipua practice is a symbol both of the child's ambiguous body—
its pliability signifying the truth about *human* essence and the
illusions of gender which enchain it—as well as femininity as an
intangible essence that can migrate from one form to another. That
is, there was no immediate collapse between femininity and the
female body or masculinity and the male body. Rather, femininity
is conceived as a travelling property which can be incorporated,
possessed, and performed by *any* body.[28]

Sakhi Bhava and Sexual Ambiguity

Speaking of Gaudiya Vaishnavites, Gayatri Chakravarty Spivak
suggests that the 'most striking characteristic of this group is the
near-institutionalization of sexual indeterminacy. But the chief
appearance of this phenomenon was men affecting the feminine.
The most superior *bhava* was the *sakhi bhava* toward Krishna [. . .]
Many of the male *bhaktas* were also called by female names' (2001:
127). This expression of transgender sentiment is intriguing. At
one level the Gaudiya Vaishnava discourse was anti-patriarchal, as
it symbolically rejected male domination; yet, at another, it was
hyperpatriarchal in enforcing the segregation of women and men
and propagating the idea of an essential difference between the
two sexes. The need to shield male bodies from the power of the
female is mentioned repeatedly in stories tied to the sect. For example, in an episode in *Chaitanya Charitamrita*, Chota Haridassa, a
disciple of the saint, is excommunicated for accepting food from
the hands of a female *bhakta*, Madhava-devi: 'I cannot tolerate
seeing the face of a person who has accepted the renounced order
of life but who still talks intimately with a woman,' Chaitanya says,
disgusted. Unable to bear this condemnation, Chota Haridassa
commits suicide. Hearing the news, Chaitanya 'smiled in a pleased

---

28 Uttara Asha Coorlawala (1996) looks at the ways in which the gotipua practice enables a critical mode of viewing classical dance and argues that Keluchа-
ran Mahapatra's performance of multiple characters and identities on stage,
influenced by his adoption of gotipua technique, disrupts scopophilic notions
tied to the male gaze and disallows the objectification of the feminized body.

FIGURE 4.4. An image of Shi Chaitanya dancing ecstatically at Rath Yatra. From a mural at Sri Sri Gour Gobinda Ashram, Puri, Odisha, 2 December 2012. Photograph by the author.

mood and said, "If with sensual intentions one looks at women, this is the only process of atonement."' (Goswami 1975: *Antya*, 2.117, 2.165).

Yet this extreme patriarchal perspective appears to have had less to do with asserting power over women alone and more with the desire to appropriate the power of feminization. In a seemingly contradictory mode, Gaudiya Vaishnavas considered Radha the supreme deity, and followers of the sect longed to become her mortal surrogates, thereby transforming themselves into the eternal lovers of Krishna. Chaitanya's yearning to become the feminine is poignantly revealed when he exclaims, 'I have now converted My body and mind into the ecstasy of Srimati Radharani; thus I am tasting My own personal sweetness in that form (Goswami 1975: *Madhya* 8.288), leading Krishnadas Kaviraj to remark, '[s]uch is

the state of transcendental madness. Why is it difficult to understand? When one is highly elevated in love of Krishna, he becomes
transcendentally mad and talks like a madman' (ibid.: *Antya*, 14.14,
14.15)—but he also seeks divine sanction, assuring us that Krishna
himself 'accepted the position of Srimati Radharani in the form of
Sri Chaitanya Mahaprabhu' (ibid.: *Madhya*, 2.80).

In the logic of Chaitanya and his followers, 'being male like
other kinds of privilege, is an obstacle in spiritual experience, in
attaining true inwardness. [. . .] The male saints wish to become
women; they wish to drop their very maleness, their machismo.
Saints then become a kind of third gender. The lines between male
and female are crossed and recrossed in their lives' (Ramanujan
1989: 10–11). This traversal, again, is not at all unusual, as
androgyny and transgenderism were governing tropes in the scene
of religious performance and myth.

Gender Is Performance, Performance Is Gender

The relationship between gender and performance complicates
the ideas posited by Judith Butler in her elegant theorizations of
Western gender construction.[29] While in her argument, gender is
about performance, the gotipuas invert this formulation to show
how performance is about gender.

For Butler, gender is 'an identity instituted through a *stylized
repetition of acts*' (1988: 519; original emphasis) and 'a performative
accomplishment compelled by social sanction and taboo. In its very
character as performative resides the possibility of contesting its
reified status' (ibid.: 520). Looking at modern quotidian life, she
observes how 'gender is constructed through specific corporeal
acts, and what possibilities exist for the cultural transformation of
gender through such acts' (ibid.: 520); that '[g]ender reality is performative which means, quite simply, that it is real only to the
extent that it is performed'; and that 'the performance renders

---

29 Here I focus on Butler's arguments in three texts: 'Performative Acts and
Gender Constitution' (1988); *Gender Trouble* (1990); and *Bodies that Matter*
(1993).

social laws explicit' (ibid.: 527, 526). Butler specifically produces this definition '[i]n opposition to theatrical or phenomenological models which take the gendered self to be prior to its acts' (ibid.: 520), and suggests that these performances are unthreatening precisely because of the gap between the real and the fantastical that they presume. This gap provides a locus for the restoration of gendered norms, promising the possibility of return to what is held to be natural, authentic and true in the body, from the vantage point of a theory committed to biological essentialism (ibid.: 527).

Thus, in Butler's view, gender is always already a performance in its quotidian expressions, prior to the body's conscious and volitional entry into ritual, aesthetic and liminal fields. Thus, performance alludes to a whole spectrum of embodied expressions and is not limited to the spheres of 'intentional cultural production' alone. Although naturalized in the nexus of habitus and hegemony, everyday gender is consciously constructed and cultivated as much as any practice of extraordinary gender. There is no 'natural' body to be identified in the social field, contrasted with the deliberately 'unnatural' body aligned with artistic and ritual practice. Both everyday and extraordinary genders are manufactured.

The gotipua performance, in contrast, is about confounding prevailing logics of gender. What was unique about the gotipua is that rather than assuming the 'gendered self to be prior to its acts', as Butler asserts, s/he actively effaces the social body and reassigns a newly gendered body, temporally produced *through* ritual acts and significations. Gotipua performances illustrated the confines of the gender system,but instrumentally in service of sacred contemplation rather than spectacle alone. Gotipua practice indexed an extraordinary embodiment, illuminating the illusions of gender and the body itself for spiritual ends. Yet, the revelation of gender as a 'construction' was designed to demonstrate the difference between secular and sacred while preserving the sanctity of each realm; the recognition of gender as both a limit and something to be transcended was meant to coax the devotee into a spiritual path, outside of *samsara,* worldly life. As A. K. Ramanujan observes: 'Anatomy doesn't bind the spirit of either male or female. Only culture constructs gender roles, makes male and female into masculine and feminine, restricts attainments in art, society, knowledge, or things of the spirit' (1989: 11). Unlike the project of revealing gender as a performance to advance social transformation, the gotipuas' was a project of revealing performance as a ground to enact spiritual transfiguration. Escaping the strictures of gender through religious performance, however, left their social expressions intact. As Kelucharan Mahapatra elaborates about his gotipua training, 'it was the highest praise to hear people say: "How lovely, he dances just like a pretty little girl." We even wanted to dance better than the girls, to look more feminine than the girls. We have a different ideal than the Europeans. Our [art is] concerned with the concept of absolutely beauty. We attempt to translate this concept into dance; perhaps only in dance can we achieve it for a few moments' (1983: 50). Gotipua performance thus simultaneously supported and subverted gender norms. Abandoning the constructs of gender would be akin to abandoning everyday codes of comportment; the process would not lead to egalitarian male–female relations in the social milieu but, instead, represent a temporary *freedom* from that milieu, an emblem of embracing the path of piety.

The subtext here, however, is that it is precisely this power of performance to unsettle dominant norms, since it transpires in a liminal space and time and challenges the socius, without being appropriated by it. Bhakti practices 'have to be constantly renewed, reinterpreted, and rescued from the domestication they suffer. But they do offer alternatives, humane and creative ways of being and acting'—in other words, *performing*—'to both men and women' (Ramanujan 1989: 14).

Ramanujan issues a potent reminder about how practices immersed in Bhakti, like the gotipua system, are redolent with possibility. The very exceptionalism of performance—its life as a specific event, or set of repeated events, outside the bounds of the everyday—also highlights the mundane as a site of fabrication. When the gotipuas transformed themselves into feminized subjects, they displayed the gestures and attitudes of gender as 'acts', as social constructions, as malleable and protean practices—

despite the truth-claims advanced on behalf of normative, natural-ized bodies (Butler 1988: 528).

It is equally true, however, that such depictions of difference were not readily accepted outside the space of ritual performance; at least the reception was highly ambivalent. 'As a corporeal field of cultural play, gender is basically an innovative affair,' Butler observes, 'although it is quite clear that there are strict punish-ments for contesting the script by performing out of turn or through unwarranted improvisations' (ibid.: 531).

The 'girling' of the male body in gotipua performance deliberately blurs gender codes, rather than sharply demarcating them. The gotipua performed the union of the martial, masculine body with the feminine dancing body. The gotipua could thus shift social positions, in one moment embodying the robust fighter, and in the next instant, becoming the devout gopi in Radha Bhava. A single body was able to take on plural positions, summoned into a different set of corporeal arguments and comportments.

In the paradigm of Sakhi Bhava, (biological) boys could achieve lasting intimacy with Krishna but they had to persuasively perform femininity in order to do so. In strange opposition to the terms of patriarchal discourse, the gotipua attains power by transcending his gender while effacing the biological female body from his spiritual and social space. Thus, his ability to appropriate the 'feminine' depends on the paradoxical removal of the 'female'.[30] Rooted in the extraordinary performance of Sakhi Bhava, then, gotipuas represent a phenomenon of 'femininity without women'.

Gotipua significations are thus filled with ambiguity, contra-diction and paradox. The simultaneous incorporation of female *shakti*, and denial of quotidian female materiality, allowed for a new expression of feminine power in masculine form, reflecting the

---

30 Peggy Phelan offers a similar reflection, that the gotipua tradition 'reminds the spectator of the absence of the female (the lack) rather than of her pres-ence'. She continues by analysing gotipua dance from a queer psychoanalytic perspective—acknowledging that she is looking at it as an isolated practice rather than 'reading' it through its own cultural logics (1996: 160, 162).

Gaudiya Vaishnava ethos. This transgender enactment aligned uneasily with elements of Hindu belief that suggested gender was essentially a fantasy, a 'performance' of a role that was ultimately inauthentic, for one's true essence lies beyond appearance and gender. The real self is animated by a divine force that bestows the life-sustaining powers of *prana* (breath, energy), *atma* (spirit) and *bhakti* (devotion).[31] Yet this discourse of gender-as-illusion in Gaudiya Vaishnavism transparently benefitted men in the movement and doubled their patriarchal power while epistemically banishing women's bodies to the periphery.

Religion, Gender and Dissent

An antagonistic relationship between religion and sexual freedom is often posited in critical social theory. Yet the gotipua performance tradition highlights this binary as historically false. Religion here becomes the ground for a practice of freedom for male agents, as a space for recognizing the illusory nature of gender.

Madhu Kishwar makes an important point about the power of dissent attached to Bhakti. She rejects the anti-religious assumption, often espoused by secular scholars, that

> since [bhaktas] operated within a religious framework, and used a religious idiom, they can only become useful symbols for reactionaries. This criticism ignores the fact that for most of history, protest the world over has been couched in a religious idiom. The development, on any significant scale, of a non-religious idiom of protest is a relatively recent phenomenon. Religious protest always had social as well as religious dimensions (1989: 6–7).[32]

---

31 The genderless nature of the soul is a theme endlessly reiterated in strands of Buddhist, Jain and Hindu thought—although the question of whether this theme is effectively translated into the practice of everyday life remains contested.

32 Although Kishwar is speaking of women bhaktas in specific, her insights are relevant to Bhakti as a whole.

Rather than harbouring a 'truth' about bodies as sacrosanct, gotipua performance shows the potential of recognizing that gender ideologies are tied to the crude problem of *formal appearance* in the everyday world. To truly surpass earthly impediments and enter the realm of the ethereal, ideologies of pure gender difference have to be cast aside. Indeed, abandoning the attachment to the mirage of gender and the material body is the highest mark of spiritual freedom in Bhakti; instead, the body is used as an instrument of transcending itself.

'Dancing with Fanatics': The Saint's Delirium

In addition to deploying and institutionalizing Sakhi Bhava in ritual performance, the gotipuas drew on the Chaitanyite belief in dance as a form of ecstatic worship and a display of devotion in the public commons.[33] Besides making visible performances of extraordinary gender, the open exhibition of dance fulfilled three aims: it reinforced Bhakti's message of mysticism, of refusing the authority of the temple; it positioned love as a disruptive social force; and it constructed a devotional body which obeyed no limit, no restraint, no social law. It specifically equated dancing with freedom from dominant norms, the absence of social control, as the expression of pure joy for those lost in the search for Krishna. While devadasi dance immersed itself in the discourse of religious discipline, rhetorically, the Bhakti ideal was to *undiscipline* the body, to release it from the delusions of daily life into spiritual delirium. The signs of pure faith manifested themselves in emotional expressions—intelligible, articulated by the body, somatically felt. Bhakti then constructed the dancing, devotional body as a container of transgressive affect. Together these effects valorized the potential of dance as a subversive site.

An episode in the *Chaitanya Charitamrita* illustrates the radical role of dance in Gaudiya Vaishnavism and the challenge it

33 On the Vaishnavite movement and Krishna and Radha bhakti, see Harsha V. Dehejia (2005) and Steven J. Rosen (2005).

posed to the Advaitist acolytes of Shankaracharya—known as Mayavadis—who valued text-based knowledge and the study of philosophy. The episode relates how Chaitanya succeeded in converting everyone he encountered into becoming his follower, 'even the *mlecchas* [foreigners] and *yavanas* [non-believers]'—all, of course, except the Mayavadis (Goswami 1975: *Adi-Lila* 7.39). Clearly threatened by his power and charisma, they spread contemptuous rumours about him, disdainfully declaring, 'Although a sannyasi, He does not take interest in the study of Vedanta but instead always engages in chanting and dancing [. . .] This Chaitanya Mahaprabhu is an illiterate and therefore does not know His real function. Guided only by His sentiments, He wanders about in the company of other sentimentalists' (7.41, 7.42). As they continued to insult him, Chaitanya decided to reveal his divine nature, overwhelming them with his effulgence. Mystified, the Mayavadis kept asking: 'Meditation and the study of Vedanta are the sole duties of a sannyasi. Why do You abandon these to dance with fanatics?' (7.69). In response, Chaitanya spoke of his deep faith, relating his experience of reciting Krishna's name as *mahamantra* (great mantra):

> While chanting the holy name of the Lord in pure ecstasy, I lose myself, and thus I laugh, cry, dance and sing just like a madman. [. . .] Perspiration, trembling, standing on end of one's bodily hairs, tears, faltering voice, fading complexion, madness, melancholy, patience, pride, joy and humility—these are various natural symptoms of ecstatic love of Godhead, which causes a devotee to dance and float in an ocean of transcendental bliss while chanting the Hare Krishna mantra (*Adi-Lila*, 7.78, 7.89–90).

The physical effects of the devotional trance described by Chaitanya are exceptional, and the contrast with the orthodox sects could not be more vivid—the Mayavadi emphasis on objective, rationalist philosophy, for instance, contrasted with the Gaudiya Vaishnavite's emphasis on subjective sentiment. The dynamism and vibrancy of Chaitanya's expression of bhakti exposed the sterility of Mayavadi learning. Chaitanya's dance also signalled in important difference from high Hinduism, where ritual dance was contained in the temple, representing a sanctioned bodily discipline, performed by a preauthorized group of performers and directed towards honouring the deity. In Bhakti, dance was an expression of ecstasy and delirium, representing a pure celebration of the spiritual. Instead of being an act of self-discipline and self-possession—as it was with the devadasis—dance displayed the wild jubilation of the devotee, lost in prayer and chanting, lost in dance, possessed by a supernal force. The idea of losing oneself in a trance was a significant trope in Bhakti which glorified the values of total submission and surrender. By opposing prevailing religious tenets, Chaitanya demonstrated how Bhakti became 'a parabasis or inter-ruptive irony of rule-bound high Hinduism as well as the *advaita* [non-dualist] mind-set' (Spivak 2001: 126).

Chaitanya's *bhakti* was not, however, uniformly praised in Odisha. Sarala Das, author of the Odia Mahabharata, is said to have severely rebuked Chaitanya for his alleged immorality in romanti-cizing *madhurya-rasa* (sweetness of conjugal love) and *mahabhava* (transcendental ecstasy). Apparently he objected to the affective position demanded of the followers of Gaudiya Vaishnavism which stressed an exultant passion rather than reflective, restrained devo-tion. Others praised Chaitanya's fervour. As Krishnadas Kaviraj says admiringly: 'Ecstatic love for Krishna is wonderfully deep. By personally tasting the sweetness of that love, Sri Chaitanya Mahaprabhu showed us its extreme limit' (Goswami 1975: *Antya*, 17.67).

The exuberance of the *bhaktas* proved threatening to the proponents of social laws and systems, since the *parodharma* preached by Chaitanya transcended worldly dharma. Though efforts were made to marginalize Bhakti, it was always a powerful movement that was by no means confined to the periphery; instead, orthodox Hinduism was ultimately forced to accommodate in its fold Bhakti and the Puranic cults on which it was based, as it was the most popular movement in terms of adherents, affective pull and sheer longevity in the cultural sphere. It also seems to have answered, in practice, the promise of radical egalitarianism rhetorically called for in Islam, Buddhism and Jainism. While some of these communities genuinely preached caste equality, they had either enjoyed their heyday in the past and were now distant and scattered; or retained imprints of caste relations; or were relatively institutionalized, with intermediary authorities standing between deity and devotee. Indeed, the intimacy and immediacy of the divine in Bhakti was an important reason for its appeal. Through *parodharma* and parabasis, then, the Gaudiya Vaishnavite tradition produced a paratopia, subscribing to spiritual and gender expressions that formed another universe of meanings, parallel to dominant religious cultures. This paratopic ideal was manifested in gotipua performance.

The gotipua practice allowed an alternative form of Hinduism to assert itself, and became a paratopic form in its own right, by offering another enactment of gender that defied the norm. It became a form of masculinizing the dance while perpetuating highly feminized representations of the devotional body.

Extraordinary Genders and the State

As I have argued, several cultural encounters and historical changes in the sixteenth century coincided to produce the gotipua system: the arrival of Mughal rule in the region and the attendant restoration of the raja of Khurda; changes in the Jagannath temple and the mahari system; the growth of *akhadas* in urban centres; and the influence of pre-existing traditions of transgender performance in Odisha and elsewhere. I have rejected the 'Muslim thesis' as the reason for the nascence of gotipua performance—a thesis which suggests the position of the gotipua rose as the mahari's declined, an event brought on by the aggressive politics of Muslim rule. While they did come into prominence at a time when the old orders of governance in Odisha were changing as a result of Afghan and Mughal rule, the emergence of the gotipuas cannot be attributed purely to these political interventions. I have sought to understand the ways in which Bhakti exerted considerable influence in constructing the tradition. Arguably, the proliferation of the gotipua system could not have been accomplished without the active support of the state and its resources.

If the formal elements of gotipua performance were influenced by Bhakti, it derived its power as a cultural apparatus from royal authority. Just as Chodagangadeva had formalized the devadasi system, making it an essential part of ritual service at the Jagannath temple, Ramachandradeva institutionalized gotipua practice by establishing the *akhada*s during an era of political and cultural transitions.[34] As before, the state had intervened to cultivate a new category of performance. And arrestingly, once more, this extraordinary aesthetic site served as a domain for the expression of extraordinary genders—an act sanctioned by discourses of religiosity and sealed by royal authority. But what was the purpose of supporting practices so far outside the norm?

I have argued that Odissi dance as performed by these extraordinary figures reified the extraordinary position of the king as divinity and head of state. The art he supported became a sign of his own belief as well as proof that his doctrine was being disseminated for the benefit of the larger populace. Gaudiya Vaishnavite dancing became an emblem of a new religious discourse which challenged the tenets of Hindu orthodoxy and democratized spiritual experience. The body was displayed as the site and instrument of spiritual salvation, a vehicle of transcending the illusions of gender, and, concomitantly, the illusions of worldly difference. Gotipua dance became a metaphor for realizing the impermanence of the corporeal form, an argument for abandoning the body as a temporary shell and embarking on a quest for spiritual freedom.

What was striking about both devadasi and gotipua performance was the way in which extraordinary gender was treated in social discourse. As minoritarian practices, they were constructed as elite and auspicious acts instead of being stigmatized for their otherness. In each space, the conversion of feminine difference,

---

34 Both of these processes, of the state's implementation of devadasi service and *akhadas*, are mentioned in the *Madala Panji*. While *akhadas* may have existed prior to Ramachandradeva's rule, it appears that the network of these centres was strengthened and supported under his supervision.

from overpowering and ominous threat into a mark of of privilege, drew on integrated discourses of both Shakti and Bhakti.

These performances were privileged because they were sanctioned by royal and religious forces. Their endorsement ensured the positive reception of gotipua and devadasi performances as exceptional enactments. The stamp of approval from these social authorities amplified their auspicious standing among ordinary subjects. At the same time, the association of devadasi and gotipua dance with the monarchy and religion required them to submit to a prescribed set of social and physical regulations. The power of the king allowed these dancing subjects to engage in a practice of freedom from quotidian models of gender, but in a highly circumscribed mode which rendered them subject to intense discipline and surveillance within their ritual worlds. In Foucauldian terms, their 'means of correct training' involved a religious ascesis that produced 'docile bodies' which nevertheless promulgated paratopic expressions of gender—illustrating the dual deployments of power as limiting *and* liberating (1979).

Thus we have an unusual model for treating minoritarian identities and acts. Unlike discourses in which extraordinary gender expressions are negatively framed, the histories of the devadasi and gotipua illustrate another possibility—a paratopic possibility—in which alterity is exalted instead. Gendered difference thus loses its automatic link to deviance, and simply becomes one manifestation among many, coexisting with the dominant and normative, albeit within a highly defined field. Of course, this association of gendered difference with auspiciousness depends on a strongly religious hermeneutic—and one which often stands apart, like Bhakti and Shakti, from the tenets of Hindu orthodoxy. Devadasi and gotipua praxis thus reveal the potency of paratopic ideals of gender and corporeality embedded in Odisha's regional performance—transgression transfigured as transcendence.

Chapter 5

'OH, THE HORROR OF IT!'
THE SCANDAL OF TEMPLE DANCE IN COLONIAL ODISHA

> In many of the sacred cities dancing girls abound—all women of evil life: they are closely connected with the temples—and it is in this that vice in India differs from that in the West—obtaining their living even within the temples. They are spoken of as 'temple girls', or, officially, as devadasis—'servants of the gods;' their initiation ceremony takes the form of marriage to the gods. Vice sheltering itself under the cloak of religion—oh, the horror of it!
>
> —English missionary Frank Deaville Walker,
> *India and Her Peoples* (2006), p. 104.

> The categories used by state agents are not merely means to make their environment legible; they are an authoritative tune to which *most of the population must dance.*
>
> —James Scott,
> *Seeing Like a State* (1998), p. 83 (emphasis added).

An image of the Rath Yatra, Puri, 1857 (fig. 5.1):

An elaborately carved chariot is being pulled by a group of devotees. Designed to look like a miniature mandir, the chariot with Jagannath ensconced inside is festooned with flags fluttering in the wind. A pair of sculpted horses decorates the façade. The king is perched above them in a surprisingly casual pose and greeting his subjects. To the side, a member of the royal family views the events from his seat atop an elephant while other nobles and soldiers gather to take in the festivities. A motley

FIGURE 5.1. 'The Ruth Jatthra, a Hindoo Festival Held at Juggernath, in Orissa, from a Native Drawing'. From the *Illustrated London News*, 28 November 1857, p. 540. From the author's private collection.

group of mendicants, priests, monks, courtiers and families surrounds the chariot. Distinctions between social groups are irrelevant during this festival, for Jagannath is the god of all people and has come to meet all the faithful. The crowd stretches far back into the distance, and some pilgrims stand near the silhouette of a temple tower, probably Jagannath-Puri, faintly visible in the background.

Besides being an important religious event, the Rath Yatra is also a good place for business—hawkers and merchants, oblivious to the action around them, are busy selling their wares and haggling with keen customers. It must be a hot day, since some celebrants are shielding themselves from the heat of the sun with parasols. A pandal, where refreshments are being served, provides a restful oasis for some while others welcome the shelter of trees.

FIGURE 5.2. Close-up of the female dancers in the drawing from *Illustrated London News*, 28 November 1857, p. 540. From the author's private collection.

A host of ritual performances take place in the foreground: jubilant Vaishnav bhakts dance, enraptured, as they accompany Jagannath on his procession through the streets; some of their compatriots appear to be singing and chanting on the sidelines; musicians play the pakhawaj. And right beside them are the maharis, dancing. I imagine their hands painting lyrical gestures in the air, their flowing white saris enhancing the impression of supple grace. Their movements seem delicate and precise, restrained in comparison to the exuberant Vaishnav bhakts with their outstretched arms and vigorous leaps but no less dynamic or euphoric.

This 1857 drawing, from the 28 November edition of the *Illustrated London News* is perhaps one of the last images of maharis dancing during Rath Yatra. Soon they would almost disappear from the scene, driven underground and prohibited from ritual performance by colonial and Indian elites.

From Divination to Deviation

With the advent of the colonial era in Odisha, the discourse of the devadasi underwent a major transformation, from symbolizing the positive expression of extraordinary gender to signifying deviance. This new discourse, generated by missionaries, travellers, colonial officials and Indian social activists invested in the politics of moral reform, reconfigured the social position of the devadasi and led to the regulation, criminalization and, eventually, abolition of 'temple dancing'. Colonialism produced new patterns of signification, inventing the social and legal category of the devadasi as 'prostitute', a figure embodying the decadent dispositions and stigmatized sexuality of the Orient.

There is by now a large body of scholarship on this history of the devadasi's metamorphosis into the prostitute, predominantly focusing on South India. In Tamil Nadu, Andhra Pradesh, Karnataka and Maharashtra, female ritual specialists known colloquially as *devar adigalar, kalavuntulu, jogathis* and *basavis* generated regional genres of dance performance such as Sadir Kacheri and Dasi Attam—the antecedents of Bharatanatyam, Kuchipudi and a host of other classical forms. Many of these forms developed in courts, salons and other spaces in the public sphere (Soneji 2012). Yet, because of a homogenized Western picture of 'temple dance' and the 'devadasi'—which subsumed the particularity of local practices into a single capacious container—there is comparatively little scholarship on the specific status of maharis in Odisha during the colonial period. Given the import and fetishization of Mahari Naach in Odissi dance, this seems to be a critical absence in dance literature. And so my intent in this chapter is to trace the modern genealogy of a discourse of 'temple dancing' in Odisha. I look closely at representations of maharis in travel literature; texts generated in service of social reform campaigns; media reports; and the legal domain, for the perception of dance inflected by the politics of gender, religion and culture under the colonial gaze.

In looking at colonial writings, it is striking to see the fundamental role the *idea* of Odisha and its ritual dancers played in the Western imaginary. What stands out is the association of the Odishan body with degraded sexualities, the disapprobation of religious practices tied to Jagannath and Krishna, and the status of the temple dancer as both enchanting and debased. Unlike in previous eras, where the performance of extraordinary gender for religious ends was regarded as auspicious, the entry of colonial modernity brought about the repression of what its agents perceived as overt performances of sexuality, and, consequently, the imposition of normative European regimes of morality on the dancing body. As Lauren Benton and John Muth write, '[t]he threat posed by indigenous authorities and performance urged a sharper definition of separate cultural identities' in the colonial context (2000: 1). In Odisha, the discourse of the deviant dancer began as a general condemnation of Hindu ritual and Oriental excess, and, by resignifying the sexuality of the dancer, ended up conflating the devadasi with the common performer and the prostitute.

Odisha under Colonial Rule

The colonial period, far from being a homogenized time, went through three distinct phases, each of which influenced political conditions in Odisha. The Company era (1803–57) refers to the reign of the East India Company, established in England by royal decree in 1600. Starting with a mandate of establishing trade relations with the Mughal empire, the Company gradually wrested control over the entire subcontinent.[1] Crucially, this period of rule

---

1 The East India Company received a royal charter legitimizing its business affairs on behalf of the British Crown. Soon after, in 1608, the Company landed in India, ostensibly for trade purposes; however, it gradually used its military prowess to gain control over local administrative and economic

was instigated by a *diwani* forcibly extracted by the Company to operate in Bengal, Bihar and Odisha, making Odisha a key gateway territory for the inception of British empire.[2] Crown rule (1857–1919) came about after the dissolution of the Company,

---

affairs. The Company received permission from the Mughal emperors, as well as regional leaders, to establish trade endeavours viewed as mutually beneficial at the time. Its victory at the Battle of Palashi (misrendered as 'Plassey') in 1757 against Siraj-ud-Daulah, Nawab of Bengal, and its obtaining the *diwani* (rights to tax collection and legal supervision) for Bengal, Bihar and Odisha in 1765 from Mughal Emperor Shah Alam II—whom it defeated at the Battle of Buxar along his allies, the Nawab of Awadh and Mir Kasam—helped significantly strengthen its position. However, Odisha was controlled by Maratha forces at the time, so the *diwani* transferred power to the Company over an entity that the Mughals technically had no major jurisdiction over. The Company governed India until the Mutiny of 1857, after which power was transferred to the Crown—an era marking the commencement of the 'British Raj' which lasted from 1858 to 1947. See Secretary of State for India in Council (1909: 5) and K. M. Patra (1971) for more.

2 This firman (imperial order) was issued by Shah Alam II on 12 August 1765 to Lord Clive as part of the Treaty of Allahabad, following the battle of Buxar. A copy is located in the British Library (item no. IOR IOR/A/2/20):

> Firmaun from the Mogul for the Northern Sircars. In these happy times, our Firman, full of splendour and worthy of obedience, is descended [. . . we have] given [the English Company] the aforementioned Sircars [Bengal, Bihar and Orissa] by way of Iniam or free gift [. . .] it is incumbent therefore on you our sons, Omrahs, Viziers, Governors, Muttasseddees, for the affairs of our Dewanship, Mootecophils, for those of our kindgom, Jaghiredars and Karorees, both now and hereafter, for ever and ever, to use your endeavours in the strengthening and carrying into execution this our most high command, and to cede and give up to the above-mentioned English Company, their heirs and descendants, for ever and ever, the aforesaid Sircars, and esteeming them likewise free, exempt, and safe from all displacing or removal, by no means whatever, either molest or trouble them, on account of the demands of the Dewan's office, or those of our Imperial Court. Looking upon this high Firmaun as an absolute and positive order, obey it implicitly. Dated the 24 of the moon Sophar, in the sixth year of our reign, equal to the 12th of August, 1765 (Shah Alam II 1765: 25–6. See also A. Berridale Keith 1922: 20–1).

imposed after the Indian Mutiny in which the sepoys, Indian soldiers, instigated a revolt against the British rulers. The framework of rule changed again in 1919 with the introduction of a dyarchy—a system accommodating elements of democracy within the colonial structure—under the Government of India Act (Curtis 1920). For the first time since the colonial intrusions, elected representatives of each Indian province participated in co-managing affairs of the nascent nation-state. This dyarchic system also served as the prequel to India's political independence in 1947.

However, relations between Odisha and the West went beyond these formal and asymmetric political relations. In the years preceding the colonial encounter, travellers, merchants and missionaries frequently visited the region to pursue pleasure, profit and proselytization, respectively. What interests me is the sheer uniformity that characterizes Western accounts of Odisha from the precolonial into the colonial period. Images of Odisha figure prominently in Orientalist symbologies, metonymically deployed to characterize the extreme savagery and primitivism of Indian culture itself, setting the stage for its moral recuperation through Western rule and missionary intervention.[3] Perhaps because of Odisha's remote geographical location, its difficult terrain, the preponderance of tribal groups in the area and its unique religious practices, it attained a reputation as the extreme fringe and was used to illustrate India's absolute difference from Western civilization. Within Indian boundaries, Odisha served as a contrast to other parts of the country that were deemed comparatively receptive to education in Western manners and mores—Bengal being a shining example. Thus Odisha was marked by the trope of double savagery.

Images of Jagannath and Krishna, the Rath Yatra, temple dancing, Hindu pantheism, erotic art, the obscenity of mother-goddess cults, heathen rituals, caste oppression, Sati, tribal savagery, thuggery and dacoitry, infanticide and human sacrifice—in these recurring motifs tied to Odisha, the dangerous, the scandalous and

---

3 On this, see Bernard Cohn (1996); Manjusri Dhall (1997); Nicholas Dirks (2001 and 2008); and Otis R. Bacheler (2007).

the exotic converge, and, in the colonial imagination, this cultural chaos could only be tamed by the edifying power of Western imperialism.[4]

The existence of a common discourse in travel literature about the unusual rituals attached to the Jagannath cult, even before the entry and establishment of the official colonial apparatus in India, suggests an early fascination with difference—sometimes alluring, sometimes terrifying—that bolstered the Manichean allegory contrasting the civilized West and the primitive and wild Orient (Jan Mohamed 1985; Bhabha 1994), an Orient that was 'Strange', 'lascivious', 'wicked and detestable' and 'full of depraved desires'.[5]

Colonial Images of the Jagannath Cult

The iconography of Jagannath was integral in the imaginaries of, and about, Odisha: '[A]ll those who ruled Orissa [. . .] sought

---

4 See, for instance, *Selections from the Records of the Government of India* (*Home Department*), *No. V: A History of the Rise and Progress of the Operations for the Suppression of Human Sacrifice and Female Infanticide in the Hill Tracts of Orissa* (Government of India Home Department 1854).

The Russell Report of 11 May 1837 condemns Meriah, a tribal tradition of human sacrifice, and recommends how to suppress it: 'Our aim should be to improve to the utmost, our intercourse with the tribes nearest to us with the view to civilize and enlighten them, and so reclaim from them the savage practice, using our moral influence rather than our power' (Government of India Home Department 1854: 8). Later, a court dispatch of 14 June 1854 mentions the need to arrest the practice among the 'rude inhabitants of the country' immediately. It commends the officials in charge of the meriah operations:

> They have maintained an attitude of firmness without unnecessary resort to forcible measures. They have calmed angry feelings by conciliation, and have opposed rational persuasion to popular prejudice and error. [. . .] It is obvious that the germs of an ultimate civilization have been planted in the country, and we may entertain a confident hope that the advance of the population towards a higher social condition will be in an accelerated ratio of progress (ibid: 134).

5 These are characterizations repeated across travelogues by Sir Richard Carnac Temple (1903); Abbé J. A. Dubois (1906); and François Bernier (1916), all of whom I discuss later in this chapter.

legitimacy and hegemonic control by acknowledging the supra-temporal authority of Jagannath, at least notionally. [. . .] Jagannath remained a potent rallying symbol, reinforcing the collective regional and ethnic identity of the territorially fragmented Oriyas. Consequently, an identity incorporating Jagannath as a crucial unifying element took shape' (Kanungo 2003: 3294).

The Rath Yatra in particular intrigued colonizers and missionaries for centuries. One of the great myths that circulated about the festival was the supposed practice of worshippers throwing themselves under the wheels of the great chariot, to be crushed to death in a final and dramatic act of devotion. Yet there was no such custom. It is true that thousands flocked to Puri for Rath Yatra, and that there may have been sporadic accidents (perhaps unavoidable in such large crowds), or even occasional suicides, but there was no religious sanction for devotees taking their own lives at the festival. The myth of the Rath Yatra seems to have been conjured by foreigners intrigued by the Jagannath cult which they found both abject and mesmerizing, the ultimate display of Indian degeneracy and the dangers of Hindu idolatry (Guernsey 1878; Banerjee-Dube 2001). 'Did [God] enjoin us to suffer ourselves to be crushed to death under Chariot Wheels, as some of the Heathens of Indostan do, out of respect to their idol Jagannath?' asked the seventeenth-century German evangelist, Thomas Horneck (1704: 283–4). A corrupted version of the word Jagannath even entered the English language on the basis of this myth—'juggernaut', referring to a monolithic force that tramples anything in its path.

It appears that many foreigners were simply overwhelmed by this 'performance of great magnitude,' to use Richard Schechner's phrase, and sought to assert their control through techniques of the archive, principally through acts of narrative and visual representation. So they wrote extensively about the temple and the festival, the unstoppable power of the great chariot, the frightening iconography of Jagannath, the strange abandon of the devotees and their trance-like states. These fantasies were directed at Europeans, of course—those in the metropole and those governing the colony. Indeed, accounts of the Jagannath temple became a staple in discourses about Indian religious life and later were even deployed to justify exertions of colonial authority. Without understanding the particular cultural logics of worship, European travellers and colonizers took to denouncing idolatry and what they perceived as the atrocities perpetrated in its name. And as a consequence, rituals associated with the Jagannath cult, including devadasi practices, were immediately tainted. Thus Mahari Naach assumed political importance in European and Indian cultural lexicons as a sign of region and religion, sexuality and gender.

Precolonial European Discourse

A large crowd is gathered around a group of entertainers displaying their assorted skills and talents. An edifice protrudes into the picture from the right side of the frame, presumably the temple of Jagannath; its tiered roof and decorative elements are visible. A cluster of musicians surrounds the performance space. Three play their drums while the rest play impressive-looking wind instruments. All eyes are directed to the centre of the action where a group of dancing women entertains the rapt crowd. One juggles multiple balls in the air while another bears long spikes on her body. In-between, a third does an impossible-looking head-stand on a pyramid-shaped object set on the ground. Another balances two children on each of her hands, with a third standing on top her head. Beside her, a woman with her hands at her waist confidently carries two tiny figures on her shoulders and a third on her head; the latter holds a spear in one hand, a pair of large rings in the other, and precariously holds out one leg out while remaining balanced on the other.

The dancing women wear full skirts with tops that leave most of their upper bodies bare—much like the male musicians—while the female instrumentalists and onlookers are amply covered in pleated dirndl skirts and long-sleeved tops. In contrast to the audience of women, whose hair is shown covered and tied back into buns, the dancers wear their tresses long and loose; the juggler's hair alone is styled into waves around her face. Each dancer's body is lightly adorned with jewels— necklaces, nose-rings, bangles, anklets; one even wears a tiara. Palm trees, heavy with fruit, stand imperiously in the background, and, hidden among the leaves, a tightrope-walker teeters on a rope suspended above the performers, taking in the scene from a bird's-eye view. The organization of perspective in the image makes it seem as if the dancing women are looking directly at the viewer outside the frame, as if they are performing their spectacular feats for us.

This is the first known illustration of 'dancing women' at the Jagannath temple in *India Orientalis* by a European traveller (fig. 5.3; Carnac Temple 1903: 14,2),[6] and appears in *A Geographical Account of Countries Round the Bay of Bengal, 1669–1679*, a seventeenth-century travelogue by Thomas Bowrey, an English merchant and sailor.[7] Bowrey was writing at a time when Mughal emperor Aurangzeb was in power, when the East India Company was simply a trading entity and had not yet established its rule over Odisha.[8]

Credit for the drawing goes to Bowrey himself; he illustrated his writings to conjure the Indian cultural landscape for his readers. Bowrey's is quite an exaggerated depiction and cannot necessarily be taken as an accurate report, even as he insists that he was an eyewitness at the scene and beheld the maharis at the temple, 'their activities of body, danceinge before the front of the Pagod as I my Selfe have often Seene with admiration much rarer then Ever I beheld amongst us Europians, or indeed any Other people in Asia' (ibid.: 14). Certainly the movement vocabulary in his illustration

---

6 It should be mentioned that Domingo Paes, a Portuguese traveller, referred to female temple dancers in his writings as early as 1510. However, he wrote about devadasis in South India and never visited Odisha. See Domingo Paes and Fernao Nunes (1900).

7 The travelogue, originally published in 1688, was edited by Sir Richard Carnac Temple (an anthropologist, military official and colonial functionary) in the early twentieth century. Here, I reference the 1903 edition. Bowrey wrote a chronological account of his trip. Upon arriving in India, he first set foot in Odisha and Bengal, and, judging from his text, it must have been early in in his journey, at least in 1669–70.

8 In the introduction to Bowrey's narrative, editor Richard Carnac Temple suggests that, most likely, Bowrey started writing about his Indian travels in 1688, after touring other countries and returning to Britain.

FIGURE 5.3. 'Dancinge women at the Great Pagod Jno. Gernaet', Puri, Odisha. Dancers, jugglers, musicians, acrobatics and other performers in front of the Jagannath temple, as illustrated by Thomas Bowrey, c.1688. From Richard Carnac Temple, *A Geographical Account of Countries Round the Bay of Bengal, 1669–1679*, by Thomas Bowrey, 1903, p. 14. Image from the public domain.

departs from the ritual aspects of dance historically emphasized in mahari performance. Given what we partially know or surmise about the performance style traditionally attributed to them, which excluded the contortions and stunts depicted here, and given that the image does not show a festival context where they would usually make a public appearance (unless Bowrey was unaware or ignorant of such a context), it does not seem likely that the drawing relates exclusively to maharis. Interestingly, the acrobatics of the dancing women depicted here are similar to the agile and acrobatic choreographies of the gotipuas engaged in Bandha Nrutya, as well as other professional artists.

234 ● ANURIMA BANERJI

The embellished portrait suggests the author conflated maharis with performers working outside the sphere of the temple. At best, perhaps he saw the dances during the Rath Yatra procession and embroidered the images to highlight the marvels he witnessed at the event (ibid.: 17). Regardless of whether the image is a deliberate fabrication, a product of Bowrey's confusion, or a clumsy but genuine rendering of what he saw, it does suggest his focus on and fascination with the dancers; his narrative confirms that his aim is to depict the maharis in particular as opposed to secular entertainers. The accompanying text also shows Bowrey's ambivalence about the mahari system, how he admired and disapproved of it in equal measure.

Early on in his peripatetic travels, Bowrey went to 'Orixa' and described its peoples, the 'Fackeers', 'Gentues' and 'Brachmans' and their 'Pagods' venerating strange gods like 'Jno. Gernaet' (Jagannath). Speaking of the Jagannath cult, Bowrey remarks that the 'Native Inhabitants' are 'a Sort of harmlesse Idolatrous people; they Worship many Gods of Sundry Shapes [. . .] but theire Chief God of all is in form of a man Somethinge deformed, and is Set up in their great Pagods, or temples' (ibid.: 6). Of the Rath Yatra and the fervour of Jagannath's devotees, he writes:

> The maine Spectacle and purpose is to behold their graven God Jno. Gernaet, which at Such times is carried in a Chariot (richly adorned and of curious and costly Workmanship) round the Pagod and through the broadest Streets of the towne in great triumph and with great Solemnitie. [. . .] And which is both Stranger and more incredible, many of them come a great many miles to End their days here, Under the wheels of this ponderous but [. . .] holy Arke. They Voluntarily and with great Couradge castinge themselves Under the wheels thereof, as it is drawne alonge, and are there crushed to death, the which is accompted by all of this Sect a most Noble, Heroick, and Zealous death (ibid.: 17–18).

This is a soon-to-be familiar trope in colonial discourse, used to affirm the savagery and ignorance fostered by Hinduism and to portray it as a site where faith, fatalism and the fatal are inseparably intertwined. And by invoking this trope, Bowrey draws the boundaries of racial and cultural difference.

Discourses of gender and sexuality are essential in projects of racialization, as is evinced in Bowrey's account of the dance rituals related to the Puri temple:

> The Brachmans are theire Priests, but I am Sure, and without all controversie, very Diabolicall Ones. Many hundreds of Women are here maintained to dance on theire festivals and days of Sacrifice and Offerings, with all Varieties of musick that Asia affordeth, to play before theire Gods, vzt. pipes, drums, trumpets, with Varieties of Stringed instruments, with multitudes of Voices very delicate to heare and behold were it acted in a better Sence, and not onely soe in this theire Cathedral Pagod, but in all Others, as many as theire Abilities will Extend to the maintainance of, and for their activities of body are much admired by all Spectators. They are for the most part very Streight handsome featured and a welll limbed people. These Dancinge Women have a priviledge above all Others in these Easterne parts, which causeth such multitudes to Endeavour to attaine to Such Employs, where they may Enjoy Earthly pleasure Enough, without any Scandall to themselves or relations. They are wholly at theire entire own choice whether they will marry or noe, or live Subject to any one man, and have the liberty to be made use of by whom they please; therefore I think Seldom or never that they leave this life to retire to theire homes and leade a Chast life, or to marry, whereby theire pleasure is very Uncertaine, not onely through the means of a jealous Husband, but for that Diabolicall Custome of this Sect in Generall, that by theire longe practiced Evil ways, cause the Wifes to be burnt to ashes in the fire at the Death of the Husbands (ibid.: 13–14).

Bowrey's remarkable commentary refers precisely to the maharis who dance in public on ceremonial occasions (the Pathuaris); he also mentions the category of singers (Gaunis) among the many women employed as ritual specialists. He observes that the maharis are held in high esteem, that they are praised for their beauty and their adeptness in the 'activities of the body'. Taken aback at the dancing women's ability to pursue a degree of sexual autonomy—unapologetically, and without penalty, 'wholly at theire entire own choice' and 'without any Scandall'—he notes that they enjoy a space of comparative freedom from norms governing ordinary women, and thus escape the violence of the Indian patriarchal order. Interestingly, then, he stops short of calling the dancers prostitutes; though he observes they 'Enjoy Earthly pleasure Enough', he makes no mention of their trading sex for money, and reports that the women could basically do as they pleased in their sexual affairs as long as they abided by the codes of temple life. And he is surprisingly critical of a heteronormative system in which women suffer under male domination, as he contrasts the mahari favourably against women forced to submit to controlling husbands and the 'Diabolicall Custome' of Sati.[9]

Yet Bowrey is full of equivocations about temple dancing, and writes graphically of the exploitation of young girls brought to the site, characterizing the priests as sexual predators with holy pretensions who deflower their virgin-victims with full religious sanction (ibid.: 23). Again, although not empirically 'true' (or at least, not an entirely provable assertion), the claim highlights the general motif of sexual debasement connected to temple dancing in European eyes—irrespective of whether it was the dancers or the priests who instigated such purportedly immoral behaviours. Bowrey's own drawing of heavily ornamented women, their bodies exposed, holding the viewers in thrall, underscores the link between dance and decadence even as it attests to the author's own enchantment with the scene. The corrupt culture of the temple at large, Bowrey argues, amplified the aura of danger and vice associated

---

9 The question of Sati, its meanings and its status in Hindu ritual life are all topics of contentious debate in the scholarship on South Asia. For an illuminating critique of the colonial discourse on Sati, see Lata Mani (1998).

with the mahari system. This theme was not new, of course; nor did Bowrey's account represent the end of the refrain.

François Bernier expressed sentiments similar to Bowrey's as he wrote about his time in India from 1656 to 1668. Bernier served as Emperor Aurangzeb's doctor and completed his Indian travels just before Bowrey set out on his sojourn. Bernier calls Odisha 'Jagannat' eponymously, after both the god and the temple. The myth of violence at Rath Yatra, where devotees allegedly came to die spectacular deaths, is also relayed in this work.[10] And after describing the chariot festival, Bernier turns his attention to the temple dancers, as he castigates the 'wicked' and 'detestable' Brahmin priests and their strange affinity for ritual:

> These knaves select a beautiful maiden to become (as they say, and as they induce these silly, ignorant people to believe) the bride of Jagannat, who accompanies the god to the temple with all the pomp and ceremony which I have noticed, where she remains the whole night, having been made to believe that Jagannat will come and lie with her. [. . .] In the night one of these impostors enters the temple through a small back door, enjoys the unsuspecting damsel, makes her believe whatever may be deemed necessary, and the following morning when on her way to another temple, whither she is carried in that Triumphal Chariot, by the side of Jagannat her Spouse, she is desired by the Brahmins to state aloud to the people all she has heard from the lustful priest as if every word had

---

10 Bernier memorably writes:

> And while the chariot of hellish triumph pursues its solemn march, persons are found [. . .] so blindly credulous and so full of wild notions as to throw themselves upon the ground in the way of its ponderous wheels, which pass over and crush to atoms the bodies of the wretched fanatics without exciting the horror and surprise of the spectators. No deed, according to their estimation, is so heroic or meritorious as this self-devotion; the victims believe that Jagannat will receive them as children, and recall them to life in a state of happiness and dignity (1916: 305).

proceeded from the mouth of Jagannat. [. . .] In front of
the Chariot, and even in the *Deuras* or *Idol Temples*, public
women during festival days dance and throw their bodies
into a variety of indecent and preposterous attitudes,
which the *Brahmens* deem quite consistent with the religion
of the country. I have known females celebrated for beauty,
and who were remarkably reserved in their general
deportment, refuse valuable presents from *Mahometans*,
Christians, and even *Gentile* foreigners, because they considered themselves dedicated to the ministry and to the minis-
ters of the Deura, to the Brahmens, and to those Fakires
who are commonly seated in ashes all around the temples,
some quite naked with hideous hair (1916: 305–6).[11]

Bernier repeats the idea of Hindu degeneracy while describing the
devadasis with a mixture of pity and admiration. In his eyes, they
are both gorgeous seductresses and naive victims—'unsuspecting
damsels' preyed on by priests but also 'indecent and
preposterous' in their danced displays. Stupefied by faith, the
dancers submit themselves to the perverse demands of religious
freaks and charlatans.

   Combining Bernier and Bowrey's narratives, we can see the
familiar trope of the devadasi take shape. While there are some
differences of tone in their travel memoirs, both are unquestionably united in their stance of denying agency to religious female
subjects, perpetuating the divide between masculine and feminine,
mind and body, reason and religion—common dichotomies in
Western modern thought. Already there was astonishment that
the devadasis, as sexual libertines, could command social respect
and authority. Already there was a sense that these women, considered extraordinarily auspicious in their own contexts, somehow

---

11 Fakir is a Hindi, Urdu, Bengali and Persian word, with etymological roots
in Arabic and refers to wandering ascetics, holy men or mendicants with
special powers who seek alms for a living. It originally referred to Sufi
dervishes but is now used as a general term to acknowledge Hindu and
Muslim spiritual seekers, and those with indeterminate or ambiguous religious ties.

embodied immorality. Already the marriage of the sacred and the sensual in Hindu ritual performance invited condemnation.

This Eurocentric attitude of wonder mixed with outrage took hold immediately when travelers first encountered Odisha, as seen in the travel literature and eyewitness reports discussed here. What is even more remarkable is that the discourse about Jagannath cult and the temple dancers had crystallized well *before* Europeans contemplated colonial designs on India—confirming the claim that the purpose of accentuating these purportedly 'bizarre' customs was simply to reiterate the gap between the European subject and the Indian one, and justify the former's acts of economic appropriation, moral intervention, and political conquest. In foreign eyes, the dancing bodies tied to the Jagannath cult enacted this absolute cultural difference.

Bernier's and Bowrey's accounts offer proof of how sexualized discourses of Indian dance (and Odishan dance in particular) prevailed in the Western imaginary. While colonial authorities constructed the official paradigm of the devadasi-as-prostitute, these Orientalist depictions of native dancing bodies, proliferating in travel literature, served as their precedents. And so, although these early travellers may have had a different aim and agenda than those of later, direct colonizers, they nevertheless provided the discursive prelude and pretext for the projects of European empire.

Colonial Narratives of Scandal

The arrival of the East India Company on Odisha's shores ushered in a new set of discourses about the temple dancers of Puri, thanks to shifts in the cultural and political environment. It was in the Company era that a centralized corpus of laws designed to govern the Indian populace was put in place, along with an administrative apparatus for regulating religious activities. The position of the maharis ineluctably changed in this radically new context, a shift instigating fierce debate.[12]

---

12 Ruchika Sharma (2016) makes a related argument.

As noted, the Company began economic relations with India within the first decade of its inception, drawn by the promise of profit (Hoernle et al. 1906: 137). In 1615, Thomas Roe, a Company representative and emissary of the British monarch, went to Delhi on a diplomatic mission to meet with Mughal emperor Jehangir in the hope of setting up trading posts in India (ibid.: 138). Gradually, the Company usurped the Mughals and Marathas and took over the reigns of power, colonizing India region by region.

In the incipient years of the Company, however, there was apparently no clear consensus or plan to establish political rule over Indian principalities. Pankaj Mishra speculates that these early arrivals to India 'had little awareness of being part of a great civilizing venture' (2005: 443)—they had certainly arrived to extract wealth, labour and resources, but the imperial strategy had yet to be fully mapped out. Later apologists of empire suggested that the 'duty' and 'burden' of rule had been thrust upon the British, and that they had simply taken on the 'responsibility' out of a resigned sense of *noblesse oblige*. The English historian John Beames, for instance, writing of the Company's intentions in Odisha, noted that '[t]he Court of Directors in 1764 express[ed] their great pleasure at learning that the proposed expedition against the Marathas in Balsore and Cuttack had been given up as "conquests are not our aim." *They little foresaw what an amount of conquests would soon be forced on them by circumstance!*' (1883: 245; emphasis added). In his contemporary defense of British imperialism, Niall Ferguson even argues that Indians 'allowed themselves to be divided—and ultimately, ruled,' citing Indian writer Gholam Hussein Khan's 1789 opinion that there was 'nothing strange in those merchants having found the means of becoming masters of this country' as 'they had simply availed themselves of the imbecility of some Hindostany sovereigns, equally proud and ignorant' (2004: 34, 36).

The Company first established a presence in Odisha in the early part of the seventeenth century, and Odisha had 'the honour of containing the first settlement made by our countrymen in any part of the Bengal Presidency. By a firman, dated February 2nd, 1634, the Emperor Shah Jahan granted them permission to establish a factory at Pipli on the Subanrekha [sic]' (Beames 1883: 248).[13] The people of Odisha saw this as a dubious 'honour' at best. Due to hostilities with local rulers, the English left the region but managed to return in 1691 'when a firman was granted by Aurangzeb for the re-establishment of the factories in Bengal' (251). And finally 'Orissa was acquired by the East India Company in 1765, by virtue of the firman of Shah Alum, emperor of Delhi, granting the dewanny of Bengal, Bihar, and Orissa' (Thornton 1857: 735). In 1803, after ousting Mughal and Maratha rulers in the region, the Company took over administration of the province.

Once they had occupied Odisha, Company authorities immediately preoccupied themselves with asserting their dominance by scrutinizing, analysing, measuring, counting and categorizing local cultural practices. Through minute attention to detail, through tabulation and calculation, they believed they could consolidate their power and increase their efficiencies of rule. Thus they developed financial reports, gazetteers, population figures, land surveys and a census. *Numbering*, clearly, played a central role in colonial praxis and imagination, and data collection allowed the British mastery over their territory and populace—it not only gave the regime a nuanced idea of the intimate practices of their subjects but also allowed for a 'scientific' approach to regulation, surveillance and management of native bodies (Appadurai 1996: 114–36). Confronted with the kaleidoscopic multitudes of India, quantification enabled colonial officials to convert the shambolic 'zoo of difference' into ordered, intelligible, 'enumerated communities' (ibid: 134).

The reports on Jagannath-Puri illustrate this belief in the power of colonial calculus and classification. Almost immediately after it took over, the Company sent officials to study the affairs of the temple even while rhetorically espousing a position of deference to local sentiment, with Governor-General Lord Wellesley

---

13 At this moment in history, the Bengal region included northern Odisha. The town of Pipli, famous for its appliqué crafts and artists, is located between Bhubaneshwar and Puri. The Subarnarekha is a famous river that cuts across coastal Odisha and runs through West Bengal and Jharkand as well.

declaring that they would 'employ every possible precaution to preserve the respect due to the Pagoda, and to the religious prejudices of the brahmins and the pilgrims' (in Swaro 1990: 92).

The ensuing reports, most notably by Charles Grome and George Webb, can be interpreted as attempts to taxonomize the qualitative dimensions of native religion, and to impose order through the deployment of the list as pure fetishization of a quantitative ideology. The reports detail and record almost *everything*: daily rituals and seasonal festivals; classes of temple functionaries, and the numbers of each, their associated wages and land grants; sales of *mahaprasad* (food sacraments); the price of rice, lentils, salt, molasses and ghee; the maintenance costs of the stable of horses and elephants; purchases of camphor, sandalwood, saffron and oil; expenses for silk thread and ivory dice; and proceeds from the pilgrim tax.[14] One of Grome's lists even reveals the intriguing and incongruous contents of the storehouse alone: broken gold ornaments; decorative fringe; pistols inlaid with silver; nose rings; 'jewels with false stone'; tongue scrapers; chintz handkerchiefs; bows and arrows; saddles and bridles; 'very small' rubies and emeralds; swords; petticoats; a small cot; 'silver chains for the waist of Jugernauth,' and so on (2002: 127–39).

And it is in this curious archive of numbers that we also find evidence of the maharis' footprints. Grome's document of 10 June 1805 includes 'Bheetur Moohory' (*moohory* being a corruption of *mahari*) and 'Bheeter Gouneah [Bhitara Gayeni]' (or Bhitara Gauni, one class of maharis; original parentheses) among the listing of temple servitors, cryptically described as women '[w]ho sing devotional songs in the temple prior to application of sandal paste' (113, 164).[15] Other groups include 'Sumpeordah Nejoog'

---

14 The tax maintained by the British in the aftermath of Mughal rule; see Governor General in Council (1806) and Nancy Cassels (1988).

15 In List No. 13, Establishments of the Temple (2002: 104), Grome also records Bhetur Mahoorey Sebuck (*bhitur mahari sevak*, no. 191) and Bhetur Gayaney (*bhitur gauni*, no. 203). Under the records of Servants Wages [sic] on p. 114, he lists them as 'Bheetur Gawooney'.

(Sapradanijoga) and 'Nettokey Sebuck' (Nartaki Sevak).[16] Webb's report of 19 December 1807 similarly mentions the 'Beter Gownees' (also Bhitara Gaunis), a group of 'temple musicians, exclusively women, who used to sing and dance in the Jagamohan [audience hall], near the Jaya Vijaya [Victory] door . . . both daily and on various festive occasions' (200). According to the documents, the Bhitara Gaunis received a salary of 45 Khawans, and the bhitur moohorys, 50 Khawans (Grome 2002: 113, 114; Webb 2003: 67).[17] Grome states the maharis 'do not receive any fees' for conducting the daily ceremonies, 'but merely [receive] their respective allowances and *Khetee* (*Khei*) or allowance of *Mahapershad*' (2002: 44).

We may infer from these records that the idea of the devadasi as a prostitute had not yet taken hold at the turn of the century; earlier chronicles had hinted at the alleged obscenity of the system, but stopped short of labelling the women as courtesans or harlots. Grome's report, for instance, mentions that *kusbees,* defined as prostitutes, were prohibited from entering the precincts of Jagannath temple, chiefly on the grounds of their low-caste status (ibid.). And in the local context, there was a clean line demarcating prostitutes and devadasis, a distinction at least nominally acknowledged by European officials when they first occupied Odisha. Any associations or overlaps between the two may have been implicitly addressed, but the idea remained inchoate, in a mild and latent form. A new discursive shift became palpable just half a decade later when Western narratives about the devadasis started to proliferate, drawing explicit links between temple dance and prostitution.

William Ward, a Bengal-based English missionary writing about the customs of 'Hindoos' in 1811,[18] paints this picture of the 'Temple of Juggernaut' and the Rath Yatra:

---

16 See Grome (2002: 104) for List No. 13, Establishments of the Temple, nos 201 and 202.

17 The Khawan was a unit of currency used in India at the time, equivalent to 1280 cowries (see Grome 1805: 168).

18 While Ward published the original version of his text on Hindu manners and customs in 1811, I have relied on the abridged and updated editions of the same, dated 1815 and 1823.

The Idol is a carved block of wood, with a frightful visage painted black, and a distended mouth of a bloody colour. [. . .P]riests and satellites of the Idol, surrounding his throne [. . .] occasionally address the worshippers in libidinous songs and gestures. Both the walls of the temple and the sides of the car are covered with the most indecent emblems, in large and durable sculpture. Obscenity and blood are the characteristics of the Idol's worship. [. . .] *A body of prostitutes are maintained in the temple* for the use of the worshippers; and various other systematic indecencies, which will not admit of description, form a part of the service (1823: 2.53)

Despite his protestations to the contrary, Ward goes on to 'admit a description' of devadasi service at sites of Hindu worship: 'A religion more shameful or indecent has never existed among a civilized people. [. . .] Besides the ordinary daily worship paid at the temples, a company of females are connected with these temples, who morning and evening perform their religious service of singing and dancing' (ibid.: 2.59). He is, of course, alluding to the Sakhaladhup and Sandhyadhup ceremonies at the Jagannath temple (see Chapter 2). Then:

After the worship of the day, many rich men engage of a number of prostitutes, richly dressed and almost covered with ornaments, to dance and sing before the idol. The songs are exceedingly obscene; the dances highly indecent; and the dress of the dancing women no less so; *their clothing so fine as scarcely to deserve the name of a covering.* The tresses of some are thrown loose, hanging down to the waist. During the dances, the doors are shut to keep out the crowd, as well as the Europeans, who are carefully excluded. Six, seven, or eight women thus dance together, assisted by music, for about four hours. Rich spectators, when remarkably pleased with part of the song, throw to the singer as much as four, eight, or sixteen roopees; besides which, those who engage these women make them presents of garments, and of considerable sums of money. The

sons of the rich natives are highly pleased with these
dances (2.73; emphasis added)

Cautioning his readers on the effects of these sensual displays,
Ward writes: 'It will excite no astonishment that a superstition
thus appealing to the senses, administered by a priesthood receiving divine honours, connected with splendid and fascinating
ceremonies, including music and dancing, and gratifying every
voluptuous passion, should captivate the heart, and overpower the
judgment of youth' (ibid.: *iv*).

In a similar vein, American evangelist Amos Sutton recounted
his views on the culture of the 'Jugurnaut' temple in his *Narrative
of a Mission to Orissa* (1833):

> Here is the 'Lord of the World,' impiously so called, has
> for successive ages established his destructive sway [. . .]
> The walls of these temples, and especially of the great tem-
> ple, are covered with the most filthy representations in
> durable and massive sculpture [. . .] These obscene figures
> and emblems are a very common appendage to the
> temples in Orissa. [. . .] *Among the servants of the idol in this
> temple are* [. . .] *120 dancing girls, prostitutes of course, to dance
> before the gods* (60–1; emphasis added).

This charge of illicit sexuality levelled against the maharis reap-
pears in William Ferguson Beatson Laurie's *The Idol-Shrine* (1852),
where the author lists among Puri ritualists '*Bhittur Gaonees*,
prostitutes, who sing the songs in the temple which precede the
anointing of Jagannath with sandal-wood' and the mardala
[percussion] instrumentalists, who play 'during the dance of *Dauree*
(or prostitute)' along with '*Tullee Sawucks*, or *Daurees*' who 'dance
on the spot called *Jugmohun*, and on the holy boat, occupied by
Mudun Mohun [Krishna], in the festival of Chundun jattra; also
under the canopies built on the Burdand, or great street, at that
festival' (p. 28, nos 68, 69 and 70).

Finally, here is Abbé J. A. Dubois, a French missionary who
also wrote an (in)famous account about the rites at Hindu temples
in 1816:

To the sects both of Siva and Vishnu priestesses are attached, that is to say, women specially set apart, under the names of *wives of the gods,* for the service of one or other of these deities. They are quite a distinct class from the dancing-girls of the temples, but are equally depraved. [. . .] Though these women are known to be the mistresses of the priests and other dignitaries, still, for all that, they are treated with a certain amount of consideration and respect among their own sect. [. . .] The courtesans or danc- ing-girls attached to each temple [. . .] are called *devadasis* (servants or slaves of the gods), *but the public call them by the more vulgar name of prostitutes.* [. . .] And these lewd women, who make a public traffic of their charms, are con- secrated in a special manner to the worship of the divini- ties of India. Every temple of any importance has in its service a band of eight, twelve, or more. Their official duties consist in dancing and singing within the temple twice a day, morning and evening, and also at all public ceremonies. The first they execute with sufficient grace, although their attitudes are lascivious and their gestures indecorous. As regards their singing, it is almost always confined to obscene verses describing some licentious episode in the history of their gods. [. . .] The courtesans are the only women in India who enjoy the privilege of learning to read, to dance, and to sing. A well-bred and respectable woman would for this reason blush to acquire any one of these accomplishments. [. . .] Of all the women in India it is the courtesans, and especially those attached to the temples, who are the most decently clothed. Indeed they are particularly careful not to expose any part of the body. I do not deny, however, that this is merely a refine- ment of seduction. Experience has no doubt taught them that for a woman to display her charms damps sensual ardour instead of exciting it, and that the imagination is more easily captivated than they eye.

God forbid, however, that any one should believe me to wish to say a word in defence of the comparative modesty and reserve of the dancing-girls of India! (1906: 133, 584–7; emphasis added)

What is the total picture of the temple dance in Odisha that emerges in these accounts? A dance that is sensual, lascivious, lewd, obscene, indecent, vulgar, graceful, libidinous, charming, filled with indecorous gestures. Dubois hints at the element of *abhinaya* when he speaks of the songs depicting 'some licentious episode in the history of their gods;' and Ward is likely speaking of the influence of the *Geeta Govinda* on Indian performance as he describes how Krishna's 'intrigues with the milk maids, and especially with Radha, his favourite mistress, are familiar to any Hindoo, being incorporated into their popular songs' (1815: 52). The trope of the seductive and scandalous temple dancer brought together Orientalist ideas of forbidden, exotic sexuality, evoking the East as a site of excess. It also signalled a new move of conflating the 'devadasi' and the 'prostitute' within the colonial worldview.

It was not the first time, of course, that devadasis were represented as 'temple prostitutes' on a pan-Indian basis—this was a prevailing characterization as far back as the tenth century CE, in Alberuni's time. What was different about the colonial era was the appearance of a centralizing discourse on the devadasi-as-prostitute among Western officials, and the consolidation of that discourse through the instruments of policy and law (Benton 2000). As discussed in Chapter 3, the Muslim discourse on dance was much more fragmentary and manifested differently under Turkish, Afghan and Mughal rule. The absence of a *totalizing* discourse demonizing dance had ensured the continuity of ritual performance in the temple, however jaggedly, as attested by the persistence of devadasi practices across India into colonial times.

Prior to the era of British rule, a largely decentralized political system prevailed, where communities lived by highly localized norms, even under the panoptic gaze and machinery of the supervising state—during the Mughal empire, for instance. This produced a range of laws, formal and informal, varying from region to region, capably of flexibly addressing the shifting and specific needs of the community in question—though such ideals and processes varied in application, depending on the rigidity or openness of the authorities. Yet the legal apparatus remained as a general mix of customary and written codes. Confronted with the heterogeneity of Indian practices, British colonial officials sought to simplify the matter of governance by homogenizing them as much as possible, and implemented a single legal system, comprising a universal criminal code and personal laws stipulated by religion (Mukherjee 2010).

Romila Thapar (2000b), Arvind Sharma (2002) and Pralay Kanungo (2003) have all discussed how the category 'Hindu' began to index a specific religious identity in the colonial period, while previously it had been a more ambiguous label, referring eclectically to inhabitants of India, or all non-Muslims and non-tribals, or adherents of Brahmanical philosophies in particular. Pratap Bhanu Mehta points out that 'congeries of movements over the years have sought to explain and create a unified Hindu identity. In the modern period, most critically, a single Hindu identification began to emerge as a product of state formation (first colonial and then sovereign) in the nineteenth and twentieth centuries' (2004: 109). However, colonial authorities 'started to consolidate Hindus into a single *legal* community' in the eighteenth century (ibid.: 112).

The venture of imposing a streamlined system of law on Hindus in the subcontinent unfolded in the late 1700s, culminating in the publication of two influential works—William Jones' and Chamney Haugton's translation of *Institutes of Hindu Law, or the Ordinances of Manu* (see Manu 1869), and Henry Colebrooke's translation of *A Digest of Hindu Law* (see Jagannatha Tercapanchanana 1874). Both were translations and interpretations of ancient Shastras, produced with the help of native religious specialists. Not surprisingly, these texts reflected and reified conservative Brahman values. The new codes also introduced logocentrism as a commanding discourse; the 'performance' or 'repertoire' of regional law would be inferior to its centralized 'archive' (Taylor 2003). This ensured that regional systems would be annulled and replaced by so-called traditional sources which lacked inherent elasticity. The new approach was completely alien to the Indian context; as Mehta points out, 'Hinduism has mostly known only local forms of authority' rather than a universal kind, especially in terms of juridical logic where customary law reigned rather than standardized doctrine (2004: 109). By appealing to the ancient past as a resource and repository for (re)constructions of 'authentic' Hinduism, and positioning classical Sanskrit texts, authorities and ideals as the essence of its religious philosophy, colonial officials deployed an incipient mode of Sanskritization while constructing these new frameworks in law.[19] Through the adoption of Sanskritizing strategies, and centralization—which reified legal relations and processes that had been far more flexible and fluid—'the 'natives' were given back their own history, of which they had been previously ignorant' (Nair 1996: 20).

The distillation of disparate practices into the single category of 'Hindu' enabled the British to manage the majority while supporting their 'divide-and-rule' strategy of stratifying the social order along religious lines. For it is under colonial reign that Muslim and Hindu nationalisms began to emerge as antagonistic forces. As Janaki Nair (1994 and 1996), Nivedita Menon (2004) and Ratna Kapur (2005) have argued, the new structure of jurisprudence

---

19 Sanskritization has two interconnected meanings. As articulated by the pioneering sociologist M. N. Srinivas in his 1952 classic *Religion and Society Among the Coorgs of South India*, Sanskritization is commonly thought of as a process of cultural gentrification by lower-caste groups who selectively embrace the ideals of upper castes as a mode of enhancing their own social privilege and power (1952). More literally, Sanskritization can also refer to the legitimation or elevation of cultural forms by reshaping them according to the values and mores of the Hindu Shastras. This is accomplished through the appropriation and reinterpretation of antique Sanskrit texts, which are said to evoke the ideals of an 'eternal' Indian civilization in an originalist mode. Some scholars might argue this was an invocation of Sanskritic principles, rather than an instance of Sanskritization; however, drawing from J. F. Staal, I believe the concept is broad enough to define it as I have here. See Staal (1963) for a discussion of the flexibility of Sanskritization as it pertains to both anthropology and classical Indology.

reflected the British concern with defining and dominating the Indian body politic.

The materialization of this legal complex ushered in an intensified form of governmentality, representing the state's 'consciousness of itself' (Foucault 2008: 2). Nowhere is this more apparent than in the colonial era, when a racialized split was imposed between governor and governed. Later in postcolonial India, the racial division would be replaced by class schisms, creating an elite–subordinate relation in place of the discourse of race. The self-consciousness attached to governmentality thus remained, salvaged by the postcolonial state order.

The colonial system additionally contributed to what we might call the formal 'judicialization of performance': using colonial juridical instruments to generate and assign new legal categories of identity; criminalize, punish or permit designated activities; and resolve 'core moral predicaments, public policy questions, and political controversies' in the cultural space (Hirschl 2008),[20] eventually displacing the authority of customary and regional practices, with deleterious consequences for the maharis and other sexualized subjects. By invoking 'judicialization', I want to draw attention to the ways in which dance and other aesthetic acts took on heightened meaning when they were subject to moral scrutiny under an integrated imperial legal system. Culture thus became an object of law when it was once a space of social contest and negotiation, regulated by adjunct political institutions.

---

20 My phrase is based on and adapted from Ran Hirschl's concept of the 'judicialization of politics' which he defines as the modern phenomenon by which power adverts to the courts instead of other state bodies, establishing a 'juristocracy' in the process (2008: 119). Extending far beyond the normative procedures of legal decision-making, it involves instead 'the wholesale transfer to the courts of some of the most pertinent and polemical political controversies a democratic polity can contemplate' (120). While Hirschl sees judicialization as a late-twentieth-century trend continuing in the present, I would argue that it is possible to consider a longer history for its operations if we analyse how the law worked as a primary institution in the colonial context, mobilized to consolidate and expand the reach of imperial authority.

This corpus of colonial laws functioned to fix the image of the devadasi as prostitute under native rule, which worked to undermine arguments for Indian cultural sovereignty—an image that circulated in the social domain and was brought into the legal sphere. The advent of the Indian Penal Code (see Government of India 1861), the introduction of the Contagious Diseases Act (1868) and the Prevention of Dedication Acts (1934, 1947), along with the 'anti-nautch' campaigns launched in the 1880s, illustrate the abrupt transformation of the devadasi 'from sacred servant to profane prostitute', from auspicious artist to 'dangerous outcast', from extraordinary to degenerate, from divine to deviant.[21]

Law and the Body of the Dancer

The year 1857, when the image that opens this chapter also appears, was a critical historical juncture. The Great Sepoy Mutiny, the Indian soldiers' revolt against their British conquerors, had started in March. Hindu and Muslim sumptuary laws forbade the consumption of beef and pork respectively, but the cartridges of the guns given to native soldiers were lined with animal fat, causing outrage among the ranks and instigating rebellion. The soldiers were joined by opponents of the regime from every social strata—from peasants and civilians to the Mughal emperor Bahadur Shah Zafar (he would be the last). The Mutiny thus became a popular uprising against imperialist injustice. It also catalysed the Indian nationalist movement and set the stage for achieving independence through protest less than a century later. The fight was intense and bloody: the rebels killed British military officers and in turn were imprisoned, maimed and slaughtered, their bodies hanged from the trees lining Delhi. Through a violent suppression, the British recaptured power in 1858, although they had not escaped unscathed. The Crown took over as the East India Company disintegrated and, in a pacifying gesture, declared a policy of non-interference in the private domain of Indian religious practice. This was more a

---

21 These evocative phrases are respectively taken from the titles of texts by Kay K. Jordan (2003) and Sumanta Banerjee (1998), respectively.

rhetorical move than political reality, however; the state continued to manage religion under the alibi of modernizing it. The successful legislative effort to regulate, criminalize, and eventually prohibit the devadasi system provides an illustrative case.

If we look at the particular genealogies of the legal discourse branding devadasis as prostitutes, we can locate them largely in narratives by Western traders, travellers and missionaries who were scandalized by the union of the sacred and the sensual in aspects of Hindu society broadly, and performance particularly. Crucially, while early chroniclers nominally preserved the distinction between common prostitutes and devadasis, nineteenth-century missionaries and reformers in Odisha engendered its collapse and caused the complete coalescence of the two identities by the time of the Crown's intervention. The implementation of the Indian Penal Code of 1860 and subsequent statutes cemented this change.

Under the new legal codes, distinctions between 'temple dancer', 'devadasi', 'nautch girl' and 'harlot' essentially disappeared, although each category referred to entirely different identifications and acts, histories and contexts. Rules governing devadasi behaviour varied from region to region. What they shared despite their varying provenance was a strong affiliation with the temple as ritual practitioners; elevated ritual status; matrilineal systems of adoption, land and wealth transfer; and freedom from everyday gender constraints while being subject to special religious norms. They possessed some element of choice in their romantic relationships and could enter into an alternate system of 'gandharva' marriages; but they did not have to trade money for sex, as professional prostitutes would, since the state generally provided for their economic support and guaranteed their exclusive social position. In other words, historically speaking, devadasis were neither economically dependent on men nor on the traditional family system to gain social status or cultural capital. In the nineteenth century, the line of delineation between devadasi and prostitute was perceptibly clear within Odisha's cultural frameworks. Ultimately, the inability of colonial authorities to comprehend native cultural values translated into the regulation, criminalization and eventual prohibition of devadasis by the state apparatus.

Under colonial eyes, the ambiguous category of 'temple dancers' ranged from professional artists commissioned to dance at special religious events on an occasional basis, to women who worked at the temple in non-dancing capacities, to the rajdasis (court dancers or royal courtesans) and the actual devadasis themselves. 'Nautch girl' could include any and all of these meanings but usually referred to the dancers who performed in royal courts, artistic salons, *kothas* (brothels), festivals, and private dance events.[22] 'Harlots' could have meant ordinary prostitutes who traded sex for money, or just 'loose' and 'fallen' women who had consensual sexual relations outside of marriage with one or many lovers (Parker 1998: 562). The liberal appearance of the 'temple harlot' in colonial writings underscored this tangled meaning, as many devadasis did have unconventional relationships—even though the temple was decidedly not the brothel.[23] The nexus between dance, sexuality, and Orientalized femininity ensured the grouping of these different classes of women into the single identity of the 'prostitute'.

Historian Philippa Levine notes that with this new shift, 'convictions for dedicating girl children to "temple harlotry" under sections 372 and 373 of the Indian Penal Code became increasingly common' (2003: 192). The 1860 law made it a crime to sell or buy minors for 'for the purpose of prostitution or illicit intercourse with any person or for any unlawful and immoral purpose' and could

---

22 'Nautch' is the Anglicized version of *naach*, a generic North Indian word for dance. Nautch parties were popular with the British and there are accounts as early as 1757 of these performance events. See Hasan Shah (1993) and William Dalrymple (2003).

23 See, for example, the Christian activist Mrs. Marcus B. Fuller's discussion of the nautch-girl, where she conflates dancers, prostitutes and devadasis (1900: 145–7). See also Charu Gupta (2002) and Ashwini Tambe (2009) on the broader issue of women's bodies treated as signs of religious and national communities in India by colonial rulers.

be interpreted broadly enough to cover the consecration ceremony; penalties included fines and incarceration up to 10 years.[24]

The 1868 Act for the Prevention of Contagious Diseases, known colloquially as the Contagious Diseases Act, was another law ostensibly designed to deter prostitution of all kinds.[25] There was an impression that soldiers in the British Indian army were particularly susceptible to the physical charms of native women and contracting sexually transmitted diseases as a result of their dalliances.

Aimed at containing such outbreaks, the Act set out provisions for a woman who is a 'common prostitute' to submit to 'periodical examination' (in Lyon 1873: 196). The Act also specified that women found 'disobeying any rule' could be imprisoned, fined, or forcibly examined (196–7) and that those who left the hospital without medical authorization could be 'taken into custody without warrant by any officer of police' (198). If it was discovered that she was infected with a sexually transmitted disease, she would undergo detention in a lock hospital, or *lal bazaar,* until the authorities decided to release her (197). The coercive procedure paternalistically disavowed the woman's consent in the process, and, worse, left her vulnerable to the whims and stratagems of colonial officials. There were also punishments for women practising sexwork without certificates proving they were disease-free—or, at least, for those who 'conducted' themselves, or performed under the eyes of the law, as prostitutes (198).[26]

---

24 The full text of the Indian Penal Code (Government of India 2000), which includes most of the laws discussed here, is available at *IndianKanoon.org* and *VakilNo1.com.* For an explanation of the laws in use at the time, see H. T. Rivaz (1889).

25 In *Race, Sex, and Class Under the Raj* (1980), Kenneth Ballhatchet discusses the debates around and repercussions of the Contagious Diseases Act, originally passed in Britain in 1864 and introduced in India in 1868.

26 Veena Talwar Oldenburg discusses the resistance to this law by the *tawaifs* (courtesans) of Lucknow, outlining the tactics they used to circumvent its intrusions (1990). See also Regula Burckhardt Qureshi (2006); Doris M. Srinivasan (2006); and Karen Leonard (2013).

The image of the beguiling dancer was central to this narrative of military men lured by sirens into sexual indulgence. An article published in the *New York Times* on 20 June 1892, for instance, makes insinuations about nautch girls seducing soldiers. 'Sepoys Entranced By Dancers', the headline proclaims:

> An enormous tent has been pitched in the lines, and at night time it is brilliantly lit up with countless oil buttees [lamps]. Inside it is packed with a dense crowd of sepoys, all sitting round in ranks and watching the dancing girls, who are gyrating to the sound of the beloved tom-tom in the middle. [. . .] After the Colonel and the rest of the British officers have gone, which is generally about 11 pm, the work of the evening commences in earnest. The sitting multitude swing themselves a little more forward so as to get a fuller view of the not very beautiful nor very young ladies who are dancing and singing with such vigor; the tom-tom men whack their instruments with redoubled energy; pan-supari is handed round to each sepoy, and every one prepares himself to make a night of it.
>
> And if any curious observer should pass by that tent at break of day next morning, he will still see the dancing girls—of whom, of course, there are relays—dancing away to the satisfaction of the sleepy but attentive audience, who have sat there the whole night admiring the performance. [. . .] Now, when it is remembered that the crowd in the tent is composed of rough fighting men who have placed their lives at the disposal of the State for the trifling remuneration of 7 rupees per month, it must be owned that their manners are uncommonly good, and that they are possessed of that inborn politeness which is the truest good breeding.

The report manages to be both coy and prurient about the nautch, and obfuscates perhaps the real reason behind Acts like the one dedicated to the Prevention of Contagious Diseases: to protect the virility of military men, quietly allowing them to seek out the sexual services of the native women who would inevitably bear the brunt of the law's effects. In any case, the attitude of the authorities cast prostitution as 'an unpleasant but real necessity' (cited in Levine 2003: 193). The figure of the prostitute stood out as a double-edged symbol of allure and peril, of pleasure and danger: she promised to fulfil the straight male soldiers' sexual needs but also threatened to contaminate them.[27]

Lock hospital reports dating to the proximate period are instructive here. Relative to Odisha, an 1878 document about the Hazareebagh cantonment in Chota Nagpur division broadcast how the medical centre, supervised by Surgeon Edward A. Birch, worked efficiently to register prostitutes (with the brothel-keepers paying the fees) and control the outbreak of sexually transmitted diseases there. The women were examined every Monday and 28 of them were treated over the course of the year; others refused to attend the exams and paid fines or 'absconded' (Birch 1878: 2). The number of registrants had decreased—probably, the doctor says, due to 'the old resident prostitutes, who had made Hazareebagh their home when a full regiment was here, dropping off one by one to seek better fortunes elsewhere' (2). Though syphilis poses no threat in the area, Birch laments that cases of gonorrhea among soldiers increased fourfold from the previous year to 19 cases in total, and 'it has been proved that the Contagious Disease Act can do little or nothing to check this minor and comparatively unimportant venereal affection' (1). In spite of this, Birch interestingly discloses 'no extraordinary means are adopted to prevent unlicensed prostitutes frequenting the regimental lines, nor are there are special measures taken for the control of prostitution' (2). Overall he agrees that the 'ordinary regulations are sufficient, and that the Act is well administered on the whole in the town' (2).

Still, the Act proved to be a controversial measure. To start with, it never precisely defined its terms. Ratnabali Chatterjee

---

27 In using the phrase 'pleasure and danger', I cite the title of the generative essay collection *Pleasure and Danger: Exploring Female Sexuality*, edited by Carole Vance (1992), which is rightly regarded as a landmark text in queer and feminist theory, and sparked a debate within feminist circles about the dual-edged nature of women's gendered and sexual expressions.

points out that the class of 'prostitute' in the Act was broad enough to include a range of women, and had no substantive meaning except that determined or assigned by colonial authorities (1992). Thus, one was a prostitute because she was named as one; the law mobilized its full performative power to transform the subject's identification. Yet, far from being precise, in legal parlance the concept of the 'prostitute' retained a chameleon quality, such that any woman *suspected* of illicit activity or relations could be subjected to surveillance by the authorities. This was significant, as the 'prostitute' was not always a prefigured subject but one who could be constructed by the law *post facto*.

In the starkest terms, a woman was not regulated because she was a prostitute—rather, she *became* a prostitute because the law identified her as an object of sexual regulation. The accusation itself served to seal a woman's identity, rather than any specific activity she had carried out, intentionally or unintentionally. Since the law served as the evidence rather than as the framework for the evaluation of proof, 'prostitution' tautologically became a self-fulfilling prophecy (R. Chatterjee 1992: 10–11; Levine 2003: 192).

The Contagious Diseases Act was the perfect symbol of the conjunction of a medico-juridical discourse that certified the deviance of unruly female bodies. But even this legislation, coupled with the laws protecting minors, failed to curb temple dance, and so the government continued to target the system, advancing the stigma of its association with prostitution. Levine reveals that in the 1870s, the surgeon-general of the Indian Medical Department called the devadasis 'a somewhat dangerous class of prostitutes' (2003: 192). Geetanjali Misra and Radhika Chandiramani confirm that devadasis even served as a subject of debate in Britain's House of Commons in 1885, cited again as symbols of India's general backwardness (2005: 229).

Kay K. Jordan discusses a fascinating 1872 inquiry set up to investigate the possibility of introducing tougher legislation that would effectively lead to a ban on the religious dedication of girls (2003). While officials in the Madras and Bombay presidencies concluded such a ban would be culturally disruptive, given the preponderance of the practice, officials in Bengal did not concur. Jordan writes, 'J.C. Geddes, the Magistrate of Puri, reported that forty adult women called "*maharies*" and "*debadasies*" resided in Puri. He indicated that they were succeeded by their own children or by upper caste children adopted, purchased, or kidnapped in infancy. He stated that they "prostitute themselves" with any one belonging to the upper grades of Hindu society.[28] He believed the custom of dedicating women to deities to be of recent origin and that these women posed no serious obstacle to the proposed legislation' (ibid.: 61–2). Thus, the investigation suggested that the Puri maharis were either open to the reform endeavour because their ritual practices were not yet well-entrenched—a surprising claim—or, more cynically, that the women were not powerful or consequential enough to resist the reform efforts.

However, this was contradicted by at least one source who claimed the dancers of Odisha represented themselves as 'greatly needed in pujas and the auspicious performances, and the entertainment of them is closely connected with the management of temples and shrines; from which it is evident that their existence is so related to the Hindu religion that its ceremonies cannot be fully performed without them' (according to the generically named 'Dr. Murdoch', cited in Fuller 1900: 119)—although this report cannot be verified, since the voices of the women are conspicuously absent. This absence itself is articulate, as it speaks to the women's marginalization in the whole 'debate'.

Regardless of what the devadasis wanted for themselves, the campaign to proscribe the dedication of girls to temples gained real momentum when interest arose among of a motley crew of nationalists, feminists, missionaries, the media and medical authorities in spearheading joint efforts at moral reform in the 1880s. This 'Anti-Nautch' campaign magnified the links between temple dance, entertainment and prostitution, increasing the dishonour associated with ritual performance.

---

28 The custom of maharis having relationships with high-caste men is also confirmed in Marglin's ethnography (1985b), where many of the women she interviewed speak about their long-term romantic relationships.

In his well-known account of Odisha, for instance, W. W. Hunter commented on the mahari tradition: 'The most deplorable corruption of Vishnu-worship at the present day, is that which has covered the temple walls with indecent sculptures, and filled their innermost sanctuaries with licentious rites. [. . .] In a religion of this sort great abuses are inevitable. [. . .] Faith and love were instruments of salvation, and voluptuous contemplation its approved spiritual state' (2005: 1.111–12). Further, his antipathy to Jagannath-Puri rituals can be evinced in subsequent writing: 'The baser features of a worship which aims at a sensuous realization of God, by endowing Him with human passions, appear in a band of prostitutes who sing before his image. [. . . I]ndecent ceremonies disgrace his ritual, and dancing-girls put the modest female worshippers to the blush by their demeanor' (446, 450).

The condition of the maharis also drew international interest, as can be seen in an 1878 *Harper's New Monthly Magazine* article on Odisha, which reports how 'the dancing-girls amuse [Jagannath] with voluptuous gyrations. [. . . V]arious obscenities have crept into the system, some of which rival the lascivious mysteries of ancient Babylon' (Guernsey 1878: 226).

Ironically, the devadasi body itself was suppressed while representations of the temple dancer abounded in Western aesthetic performance.[29] This obsession with Oriental mystique could be seen as part of the story of 'the Indian conquest of the European imagination', as William Dalrymple suggests in *The White Mughals* (2002). Yet the image of the sensual temple dancer only perpetuated the idea of Oriental excess and accentuated the construction of racialized bodies as spectacle for the Western gaze. The very politics of prohibition and marginalization that contributed to the criminalization of the devadasi in India incongruously served to elevate the image of the Oriental dancer as an exotic object of desire and appropriation in the Western art world. In classical ballets and

---

29 On nineteenth-century Orientalized performance and the image of the Indian dancer, see Amrit Srinivasan (1985); Jane Desmond (1991); Amy Koritz (1997); Emily Apter (1999); and Priya Srinivasan (2007, 2009, 2012).

operas like *La Bayadère, Lakmé, The Temple Dancer* and *The Nautch Girl;* at colonial exhibitions; and in modern dance choreographies by Ruth St Denis and La Meri, the romanticized Indian dancer proved to be a potent and provocative cultural motif.

One vocal proponent of the ban on devadasi dedication, Mrs Marcus B. Fuller, protested passionately against what she regarded as the fundamental oppression of temple dancers, including the Puri maharis. Linking the local devadasi practice to a general atmosphere of moral turpitude in Odisha, she dismissed the sculptural art on houses of worship as 'rude', 'exceedingly indecent' and 'disgustingly obscene' (1900: 115). Writing in 1900, Fuller's rhetoric is remarkably reminiscent of the missionary accounts although they preceded hers by almost a century:

> Whatever may, in the very beginning, have been the conception of thus devoting girls to gods and temple service, it is now, and has been for centuries, a most debasing custom. They are invariably courtesans sanctioned by religion and society. [. . .] These girls are the common property of the priests. Wicked men visit the temple, ostensibly to worship, but in reality to see these women. And what shall we say of the simple-minded, but well-to-do pilgrim, should he fall under their power? He will probably return a ruined man. [. . .T]hat Indian boys should grow up to manhood, accustomed to see immorality shielded in these temples with a divine cloak, makes our hearts grow sick and faint. [. . .] Some of [the devadasis] are in possession of landed property which has been given to them for their maintenance. [. . .U]nder whatever name they pass, and however much the details of the customs among them may differ, the principle is the same in all, immorality under the shelter of religion and custom (ibid.: 119–120, 125).

Religion, again, was posed as an oppressive force antagonistic to individual volition. *Indian* religion, that is. That agency and religiosity were fundamentally incongruent with each other, that the Indian subject had to be 'liberated' from the constraints of the

Hindu faith in order to embrace the promise of modernity—these were abiding colonial convictions.

The campaigns by moral reformers had spawned a network of 'Anti-Nautch and Purity Associations' across the country—their *raison d'etre* self-evidently embedded in the name. These groups held annual conferences, publicized their cause in newspapers like the *Indian Social Reformer*, lobbied governmental authorities and won the support of a broad cross-section of indigenous and Western elites in the name of ushering in progress and moral enlightenment (see Appendix E). The campaign continued to gain momentum into the 1920s, and finally succeeded in its aims of bringing about legislation to curtail temple dancing in the form of the Prohibition of Devadasi Dedication Acts in Bombay (1934) and Madras (1947).

As the issue grew to prominence on the public stage, a polarizing debate ensued between the self-proclaimed reformers and the self-appointed guardians of Hindu tradition. The complex attitudes towards the mahari institution are reflected in an article by an anonymous author, printed in the Odia newspaper *Star of Utkal* on 16 March 2012; it mounted a spirited defence of the mahari position, comparing it to the role of Christian nuns, while acknowledging the perception of its iniquity and arguing for its restructuring:

> In this much married age, if we may get a band of noble Hindu girls devoted to the   service of God and man, what harm? [. . .] If enrollment to nunship is not stopped, why should enrollment to Mairiship be? The Deva Dasis of Jagannath are not like the Dwarees of Southern India, that go through mock marriages to live a life of prostitution. To abolish the class of Deva Dasis would not only be interfering with Hindu religion, it would be ruining an institution that may be turned to very useful purposes. [. . .] No doubt many Mairis fall. In all countries, poverty leads to immorality. [. . .] If sufficient allowance may be provided from the temple and the Pariccha be compelled to exercise strict supervision and if proper arrangements

be made for education, the Mairees may be made into a very useful body of helpers. They cannot be turned out of the temple, but they may be considerably improved (in Mohanty Hejmadi and Hejmadi Patnaik 2007: 34–6, 49).

This opinion is notable for its emphasis on mahari practice as productive ('useful') economic and cultural labour for the society it serves, while accepting the verdict of its susceptibility to corruption. However, it offers solutions to reigning in the excesses of the system in the form of implementing greater vigilance over mahari activities on part of temple authorities; access to modern schooling; and importantly, increasing the salaries of the maharis to ensure their value is reflected in their remuneration. Thus, even as maharis would be subject to extra discipline, they would receive resources and compensation commensurate with the prestige of their service duties.

However positive its impact according to the author, the mahari system continued to be under duress socially and politically. By the time the issue came up in the 1923 Legislative Assembly Debates, a speaker documented as one Mr. Misra, representing Odisha, registered his support of the devadasis by noting, albeit anemically, that they 'have existed from time immemorial. [. . .] They are regarded as a necessity even for marriage and other parties, and for singing songs in invocation of God' (3.4.2826).

The celebrated Bengali painter Abanindranath Tagore circuitously became part of the debate through his stylized depictions of dance in Odisha. Tagore had journeyed to the Puri area in the first decade of the 1900s, as the city served both as a centre of pilgrimage and a coastal resort for Indian tourists. And since northern Odisha had long been part of Bengal Presidency (from 1765 to 1912) as determined by colonial authorities, the Bengali presence in Puri district was particularly robust. There, Tagore became fascinated by the local artistic traditions. Thus we have two rare and valuable pictorial interpretations of Mahari and Odia Naach of the early 1900s, in Tagore's *Devadasi* and *Kajari Dance*.

The sojourn to Odisha ushered a new phase in Tagore's aesthetic development. Already a famous Swadeshi artist, and a founder of the Bengal School of Art, '[t]he pictures he made after the Orissa visit—*Kajari, Devadasi, Nata-Nati* among them—with their wealth of suggestiveness, are in strong contrast with his work of the preceding period' (Mukherjee 1988: 36–7). Apart from dance, Tagore was equally awed by the sculptural heritage at Konark temple, and witnessing its beauty 'strengthened the realistic trend as may be seen from the work done after the Konark visit' (ibid: 37).[30]

Tagore idealized the image of a Puri mahari in his painting *Devadasi*, exhibited at Britain's Festival of Empire, Crystal Palace, in 1911 (Mitter 1994: 322). That Tagore took on this subject at a time of profound debate about the legitimacy of mahari praxis and emblematized the devadasi as an iconic figure of Indian femininity speaks to the reverence with which he regarded the custodians of the ritual tradition.

Tagore's painting was based on his experience of witnessing Mahari Naach, an event he chronicled in his memoir *Jorasankor Dhare* [Beside Jorasanko; in Bengali].[31] Gargi Gangopadhyay observes that the book contains 'a very poignant passage describing a performance by the devdasis inside the Jagannath temple' (personal correspondence, 2012). I quote it at length, since it is one of few firsthand accounts of Mahari Naach by an Indian subject, available from that historical period:

That time [in Puri] I had seen the dance of the devadasis in the temple. I had not seen the dance [before], and I could not leave without seeing it. I would see the dance first, and then sign the notebook. The *panda* [temple priest] would not budge, and said, 'it will take a lot of money.' I said, 'That will be arranged, don't impede me for that reason. I will see the dance that happens in front of the god.' Greedy for my signature, greedy for money; the *panda* agreed after much

30 For more on the Bengal School of painting, see Amita Ray (1990).
31 Based on his letters and other evidence, it seems most likely that Tagore visited Puri sometime between 1907 and 1911—the latter being the year his painting is dated.

FIGURE 5.4. *Kajari Dance*. Painting by Abanindranath Tagore. Based on a dance he saw in Odisha in 1913, it was reproduced in *Bharati* and *Prabasi* in 1917 (Mitter 1994: 364–5). From R. Siva Kumar, *Paintings of Abanindranath Tagore* (Calcutta: Pratikshan, 2008), p. 107. Reprinted courtesy of R. Siva Kumar.

cajoling. He said, 'Then tomorrow I will come to take you in the early hours of the dawn. Please be ready.'

At dawn I went alone with him. At that time there were no crowds at the temple, in the darkness I could see one or two people here and there, probably pandas. The panda seated me in the natmandir [dance hall]. On one side drums were playing, a flambeau was burning, a devadasi was dancing. The devadasi was turning and pirouetting in her dance, and the flambeau followed her turns, the light falling on her body, as if Jagannath was watching her, and

FIGURE 5.5. *Devadasi*. Painting by Abanindranath Tagore. From R. Siva Kumar, *Paintings of Abanindranath Tagore* (Calcutta: Pratikshan, 2008), p. 107. The image in the book is reproduced from a print, not the original. Reprinted courtesy of R. Siva Kumar.

sitting in the corner, I watched [the whole scene]. She was showing various *bhavas* [repertoire of emotional expressions] to the deity.

Imagine the *abhinaya* dancer's puja. I have really seen the devadasi's dance in the temple. It's wonderful! After coming back [to Kolkata], I drew a picture of the devadasi (Tagore 2003: 181; my translation).[32]

---

32 In his account, Tagore described the process of absorbing the dance and creating the image for the watercolour: 'In Puri I sat watching the ocean, and

Tagore's correspondence with Anand Coomaraswamy further provides us with a glimpse of attitudes towards mahari practitioners prevalent in the early 1900s. Alluding to the unfinished *Devadasi*, Tagore wrote in a 1907 letter:

> About the picture of the dancing girl, I don't think it will be wise to take it up just now when my head is full of Omar Khayy'am. I intend doing it in one of my quietest moments when my mind is quite free from all other influence. So far as I know the Devadasis are specially maintained for dancing before the idols. They are allowed to come out of the temple [as in Puri]. They came to our house, sang poems from 'Jayadeva' (*Gita Govinda*) but absolutely refused to dance (in Mitter 1994: 322).

It seems from Tagore's account that devadasis could move about freely without the same kinds of restrictions that bound them at earlier points in history—an ironic development, considering that the reform movements sought to restrict the devadasis' physical freedom to move in public space, along with their ritual choreographies. The devadasis even exercised their freedom of refusal, their decision *not* to dance on occasion.

Writing about the creation of *Kajari Dance*, Tagore mentioned again in *Jorasanko Dhare*: 'I saw [the dance] in the Puri commissioner's house also. A garden party, with cloudy skies, a few raindrops falling, some big flowering trees, beside them the Odia girls were dancing' (2003: 181; my translation).[33] There is very little

---

the dance; I did not do my drawings there. Much later, sitting in Kolkata, I drew all those pictures' (2003: 181; my translation).

33 Drawing from the same memoirs, Neelima Vashishtha summarizes Tagore's creativeprocess:

> As an artist he enriched his mental collection of images as he travelled to distant places like Mussoorie, Darjeeling, Puri and Konark (Bhubaneshwar). These travels had a great impact on his work and creativity. He was overjoyed to see the ocean and the *sikharas* of the temples of Puri and Konark [. . .] The painting of *kajari* dance was drawn after he saw some girls dancing near a tree at the Commissioner's garden party, to which he was invited during his

mention of the incident, yet Tagore was sufficiently moved to make it the subject of his artwork, circulated some years after *Devadasi*.

Both *Devadasi* and *Kajari Dance* might be seen as exemplars of what Christopher Pinney calls 'corpothetics—embodied, corporeal aesthetics' (2004: 8). Critiquing modern Western models of what he terms 'anaesthetic' or detached spectatorship, Pinney identifies 'corpothetics' as a historically situated, local Indian practice of visuality that is 'synaesthetic, mobilizing all the senses simultaneously' (ibid.: 19), and which specifically involves 'the sensory embrace of images, the bodily engagement that most people (except Kantians and modernists) have with artworks' (ibid,: 22). As Pinney argues, a shift from the idea of the image as textualized representation to one rooted in 'corpothetics' permits it to assume a performative as well as affective force: 'The relevant question then becomes not how images "look," but what they can "do"' (ibid.: 8).

This corpothetic perspective is richly evident in Tagore's paintings, not only pertinent as a manoeuvre of *reading* the images but also relevant for understanding the artist's process of *making* them. Tagore recounts his many feelings and sensations as he watched the devadasi choreography, and his paintings are anchored in the experience of 'bodily engagement' with the performances encountered during his Odisha tour. The dances served as the impetus for his artwork; unlike the paintings by Orientalists, for instance, they were not conjured solely in his imagination but materialized out of his lived experience.

From the corpothetic standpoint, Tagore's *Devadasi* and *Kajari Dance* idealize women's traditions routinely pilloried in this time and place as debased and heretical. In these two paintings we find visions of Odisha and its dances that run radically counter to colonial-elite discourse: if in real life the devadasi was framed as aesthetically crude and morally suspect, on Tagore's canvas she is a splendid and graceful figure, worthy of admiration for her ritual

---

stay in Puri. [. . .] The memories of the *kajari* dance and also of the *devadasis* seen at the temple stayed with him and were relived when he came back to Calcutta' (2004: 117–18).

role and talent; and if Odisha was ideologically synonymized with 'savagery', the lyrical and refined dances depicted here are morally redemptive, opposing this association.

The placement and positions of the bodies in each painting are unorthodox and telling, too: note the absence of any deities in *Devadasi*, implying that she is autonomous and exclusively deserving of the viewer's attention, that she is a subject in her own right rather than inherently in relation to the divine, her gaze deliberately directed away from the onlooker and refusing the viewer the thrill of acknowledgement or recognition; and note the differing orientations of the women in *Kajari Dance*—one decisively with her back to the viewer, the other in profile and yet another turned obliquely to the front, though her gaze is slightly averted, all seemingly resisting a scopophilic regime that would otherwise demand their total objectification.

Each of the scenes possesses a unique kinetic force. The solo devadasi is caught in a temporary moment of arrest during a taut and dynamic sequence, poised to resume her movement. And in *Kajari Dance*—a folk tradition, typically performed in Odisha with the arrival of the monsoon—all three women wear the same gold-bordered white sarees and move in a circular formation in close proximity, though the lack of correspondence between their movement patterns is striking: one gently suspends her arms, outstretched yet slightly bent; another exhibits a *mudra* that looks very much like Katakamukha with her left hand, perched at her shoulder, while her right (partially concealed) rests in a languid *mushti* at the hip; and the third's left arm hangs in the air in a gesture wholly reminiscent of Dola Hasta, with her right arm curving into what strongly resembles Hansasya. These unexpectedly different poses individuate the dancers even as other visual elements conceptually unite them, delivering the impression of a general complementarity.

These compelling but modest portrayals, in combination with the simple and subdued palettes, lend a sense of elegance and harmony to Odia dance, in contrast to the colonial picture of an untamed and uncivilized Odia people. Aesthetically, Tagore's paintings also present gossamer traces, or uncertain evidence, of a possible connection between Mahari Naach and Odia Naach, ritual dance and folk dance.

To create these images of dance at the height of the anti-nautch campaign and oppose the normative moral–political consensus of the moment was a great act of defiance by Tagore; and it was a move that invited controversy and condemnation from the colonial and native establishment. Coomaraswamy praised Tagore and his contemporaries for the 'revival of painting in Bengal', observing that 'the return of idealism has brought with it a renewed apprecia-tion of indigenous art and popular mythology, as has sought expres-sion in creative activity' (1918: 134). Tagore's detractors, however, accused him of indecency; the critic Suresh Samajpati, well-known editor of the journal *Sahitya,* fiercely condemned the artist and his subject matter of Kajari dance:

> [H]is painting seems to be a caricature of the dance. If he wishes to ridicule the sublime then he certainly has succeeded and we fail to keep up with the turns taken by 'Indian art.' How can I describe these three beautiful creatures with stick-like limbs? Do God's beautiful creation, women, really assume such a grotesque form in this dance? Abanindranath offers the past as an excuse, but in fact the inspiration is not so ancient. We Bengalis still experience these shameful burlesques at wedding pro-cessions. Our Indian Raphael has depicted the same crude shameless gestures in his work (quoted in Mitter 1994: 364).

Dance as a set of shameless gestures, dance as shameful burlesque, dance as the grotesque: in place of these conjurings, Tagore offers an aestheticized rendering that lifts traditional choreography out of the frame of the 'crude', even if his critics consider it a 'caricature'.34 What these unorthodox images of *Kajari Dance*

---

34 Partha Mitter notes that Samajpati's objections to Tagore's art, and modern art in general, stemmed from his bourgeois pretensions and ideological convictions: 'Underneath Samajpati's banter lay the bhadralok perception of

and *Devadasi* 'do' corpothetically, then, is to invert the anti-nautch politics espoused by Samajpati and others of Tagore's time—while the pictorial style simultaneously evokes timelessness—and stand as subtle indictments of stereotypes about a sybaritic Odishan culture.

Among other abolitionists who sought to suppress 'the shameful burlesque', the attitude that the colonial presence was a civilizing force became replete in the public discourse, leading up to the implementation of the Madras Act restricting devadasi rituals. *The Calcutta Gazette* of 28 February 1912 recorded the proceedings of the Bengal Legislative Council meeting of 12 February, during which assembly member Babu Bal Krishna Sahat raised the issue as it pertained to the Jagannath temple: Was the government aware of the open letters condemning devadasi practice, published in the local paper *Satya Sanatan Dharma* (14 November 1910 and 6 April 1911) and 'supported by nearly the entire Indian Press, not only by those in favour of reform, but also by such orthodox Hindu papers such as the [Bengali-language] *Hitobadi* and *Hita Varta* of Calcutta'? (Government of Bengal 1912: 19). The letters, he emphasized, '[bring] to light the custom of dedicating female children to the Temple of Jagannath in Puri who, when grown up, lead immoral lives as long as they live' (ibid.). Pointedly he asks those in charge to outlaw the practice. The Honorable Mr Stevenson-Moore, representing British officialdom in Bengal, responded that they were aware of the situation, and that the 'Government has ascertained that about 100 dancing girls are attached to Jagannath Temple at Puri and are dedicated to its service. The allogations [sic] referred to are believed not to be applicable to any other temple in the province'. He goes on to convey the Government's carefully crafted response:

> Government would view with favour and lend its support
> to any organized attempt made by Hindu society at large

---

oriental art as a threat to naturalism, the universal artistic canon. A conservative Hindu and a *swadeshi*, Samajpati accused the new-fangled art of destroying Hindu values, his case strengthened by the fact that many of its staunch advocates were Europeans' (1994: 365–6).

to eradicate the evils which have grown up round the system at Puri, but it considers that any such movement
should emanate from the people themselves, and it does
not propose to initiate reforms on its own motion in a matter so closely connected with religious observance. (ibid.)

Although the statement appears high-minded and respectful, this
posture of leaving religious matters in the hands of 'the people'
was decidedly disingenuous, as the British government never
hesitated to interfere in religious affairs when it was politically
expedient.[35] Instituting the pilgrim tax for devotees of Jagannath-
Puri, creating laws designed to restrict temple dancing and 'temple
harlotry' and enshrining personal laws for different religious
communities are all actions that may be swept under the rubric of
'religious observance.' In fact, the following year, the government
worked on legislation to limit devadasi dedication, an initiative
which failed at that moment but was resurrected in the late 1920s
(*Times of India* 1927: 11).

An insight into the colonial state's strategy is provided by the
contents of a letter addressing the devadasi issue, sent fromthe
Home Department to officials in Madras, Bombay, Bihar and
Odisha. Dated 8 March 1928, the letter reveals:

The Government of India trust that pending the consideration of legislation to suppress the evils of the devadasi
system, action will be consistently taken under the existing law in all cases in which the circumstances give a fair
prospect of success. If vigorous action is taken, a great
deal could, in the opinion of the Government of India, be
done to discourage the practice even under the law as it
stands; for even if prosecutions fail, they will notice of
Government's policy and intentions in the matter (Government of India Home Department 1928: 3).

An amended version of the circular was sent to local governments
to elicit their response to proposed curtailments of devadasi

---

35 On the negotiations between local and colonial systems of governance in
Odisha, see Nancy Gardner Cassels (1988) and Kartik Chandra Rout (1988).

activities, and shows that the Home Department authorities hoped
to wield an influence outside the legal domain to affect broader
social attitudes towards the ritual system. Documents appended to
the letter disclose the following:

> Bombay, B. and O. [Bihar and Odisha] and High Courts at
> Madras, Bombay and Patna support the proposed legisla-
> tion. B. and O. is, however, of opinion that the proposed
> amendment will not prevent a girl under 18, joining a tem-
> ple of her own accord; that it would be necessary even
> under the proposed amendment to prove that the girl has
> been adopted or given to a devadasi. If no such evidence is
> available and if no one can otherwise be brought within the
> purview of sections 372 and 373 for being in possession of
> the girl, the law will be frustrated (Enclosure no. 3, p. 5).

There is reason to believe that Odisha offered tepid support,
although another memo suggests 'the local Government approve
the principle of the proposed legislation' (Enclosure no. 6, p. 13).

Because parts of then-Odisha fell under the jurisdictions of the
Bengal and Madras Presidencies, it is important to consider these
state reactions too. While Bengal offered no opinion 'because the
custom does not prevail in the province', respondents hastened to
add they 'have no doubt the enlightened section of the people will
welcome the proposal' (Enclosure no. 3: 6, 13). Replies from
Madras were more complicated, registering both strong support
and spirited opposition:

> The Government of Madras are against the proposed
> legislation. [. . .] They are not convinced that Hindu social
> and religious opinion is sufficiently mobilized behind the
> Government to justify the proposed legislation and they
> cannot help feeling that, if the influence of those who
> demand this legislation over Hindu opinion generally in
> this matter were as great as their sincerity is undoubted, the
> fact would have been evidenced by organized opposition to
> the institution itself. They are also of opinion that in these
> matters the Hindu community possesses immense powers
> of internal regulation, and that extraordinary and premature

legislation, the efficacy of which is open to doubt, may
merely provoke a reaction against influences which might
in time end or reform this institution by the sheer force of
public opinion (Enclosure no. 3, p. 6).

Here we find intriguing arguments in support of letting Hindu
publics govern themselves on the basis of their ability to negotiate
their cultural affairs among invested constituents. For many Indian
subjects perceived the laws as attacks against their religious beliefs
as well as cultural and regional performance practices.

At the same time, there was room for nuanced views on the
controversy. In the 1929 edition of *Bihar and Orissa District
Gazetteer: Puri*, P. T. Mansfield refuted some of the more out-
rageous claims of colonial and reformist observers about dance at
Jagannath temple with an unprepossessing assessment—even if
slightly minimized or mischaracterized, perhaps to mitigate the
social panic surrounding the devadasi tradition:

> Another class about whose position there has been some
> misconception is that of the dancing girls. [. . .] It is
> reported that there is no indecency in any of the rites, and
> no dancing girl has part in the [Jagannath] ritual. One girl,
> it is true, performs an antiquated dance to the accompa-
> niment of a small drum during Jagannath's morning
> meal; but this is not regarded as an essential part of the
> ceremony, and her absence does not interfere with its per-
> formance. Again, at night [. . .] one of the dancing girls
> comes (after a bath whatever the hour may be) and sings
> a song in the presence of the deity. But, should any of the
> dancing girls enter the inner sanctuary, except on these
> two occasions, the whole shrine is considered defiled, and
> a ceremony of purification has to be performed before the
> rites can continue (121).

Other social activists, oblivious to the complexities of arguments
circulating within Indian communities directly affected by governmental acts, as well as reports by measured observers, freely sought
to change public opinion on the subject. Katherine Mayo, in *Mother
India* (1927), polemically took up the cause:

In some parts of the country, more particular in the Presidency of Madras and in Orissa, a custom obtains among the Hindus whereby the parents, to persuade some favor from the gods, may vow their next born child, it be a girl, to the gods. Or, a particularly lovely child, for one reason or another held superfluous in her natural surroundings, is presented to the temple. The little creature, accordingly, is delivered to the temple women, her predecessors along the route, for teaching in dancing and singing. *Often by the age of five, when she is considered most desirable, she becomes the priests' own prostitute.* If she survives to later years she serves as a dancer and singer before the shrine in the daily temple worship; and in the houses around the temple she is held always ready, at a price, for the use of men pilgrims during their devotional sojourns in the temple precincts. She now goes beautifully attired, often loaded with the jewels of the gods, and leads an active life until her charms fade. Then, stamped with the mark of the god under whose aegis she has lived, she is turned out in public, with a small allowance and with the acknowledged right to a beggar's livelihood. [. . .] *And she and her like form a sort of caste of their own, are called devadasis, or "prostitutes of the gods,"* and are a recognized essential of temple equipment (47–8; emphasis added).

Mayo's account, intended as propaganda, is a mix of exaggeration and fabrication. Like her abolitionist compatriots, Mayo seems to be mixing up the lives of common prositutes, dancers in *kothas* and (inauspicious) widows. At least in Odisha, girls were not usually dedicated until 9 years of age, not 5. This was not a system of standard sexwork—and so there was no financial exchange involved between the women and their partners, since the maharis controlled their own wealth and were otherwise supported by the temple and the monarch. Moreover, because they had land and property rights, they were not 'turned out in public' or forced to beg; it was only with the decline of the system and the prevention of dedication that the remaining devadasis were forced to fend for themselves (Hess 1985; Shashimoni Devadasi 2008).[36]

The anti-nautch campaign continued to have an effect well into the decades after the initial legislation passed. In the Friday, 3 December 1948 Constituent Assembly Debates, speakers aired a fascinating array of opinions on devadasis and the value of their ritual art in the context of a discussion on human trafficking. While the usual political polarization on the subject was on display, two arguments are notable. Bishwanath Das, representing Odisha, was the only one who brought up the urgent need to take measures against the sexual oppression of women while positively acknowledging 'the influence of dances before temples which preserve our national art and music from time immemorial'.[37] Another member, Giani Gurmukh Singh Musafir, supported the prohibition of devadasi service on the grounds of prostitution. But in a novel twist, he regarded sex work as the legacy of colonialism, rhetorically sanitizing Indian culture in opposition to a hypersexualized West. In his native Hindustani, Musafir declared: 'I would like to say that prostitution is not in accord with the Indian civilization. It was imported from the West and with the departure of Western rulers it must come to an end. [. . .T]he curse of prostitution should go from this country' (Government of India 1948: n.p.; translated in proceedings).

Whether native or colonial reformers, Musafir, Mayo and others brought up the issue of sexual relations between the men of the

---

36 See Appendix E and Government of Orissa (1956) for details on the status of maharis in the mid-twentieth century CE. See also Ron Hess (1985), Frédérique Appfel Marglin (1985b) and Davesh Soneji (2012) for perspectives from the devadasis themselves.

37 An amendment to Article 17 was put on the table, to prevent the trafficking of devadasi women in particular. G. Durgabai (Madras) pointed out that despite its good intentions, the text was moot, since a law against devadasi dedication had already passed by then in South India. Incidentally, Law Minister B. R. Ambedkar presided over this session and decided not to accept the narrowly drafted amendment (see the proceedings in Government of India 1948).

temple and the devadasis, which they saw as exploitative. And it very well may have been so, well into the twentieth century: given the young age at which girls were consecrated to temples, there is no doubt that they were vulnerable and subject to sexual abuse.[38] Unfortunately, it was not considered abuse at the time, or even seen as anomalous in the context of a set of discriminatory social norms where girls were sexualized and, from a modern vantage point, married off relatively early to their husbands or initiated into the temple order to wed the god-king. In the colonial period, both child-brides and devadasi girls fell within the assigned 'age of consent'.

The critical difference is that institutions like marriage were never singled out as a serious social problem whereas a whole matrilineal system in which women did hold relative privilege became an object of opprobrium. (In fact, marriage was quixotically posed as a form of 'rehabilitation' for the devadasis; see Shankar 1990). That is, as with the institution of marriage, the devadasi system could have been preserved while inaugurating efforts to eradicate the sexual violence that often accompanied it. Opponents of the system conflated prostitution with sexual relations outside heterosexual marriage, and justified ending the practice for this reason—not child protection in particular. What was really behind banning the system altogether, instead of implementing meaningful feminist reforms that respected the choices of devadasis?

Another issue that troubles the waters is the framing of sexuality in narratives about the devadasi women as opposed to girls pushed into child marriage: often, female sexual autonomy was translated as sexual oppression to bolster colonial and nationalist projects of moral reform, regulation and criminalization in relation to the dancing subject. The truth remains an enigma.

As the discourse of degradation proliferated, and assaults on their customs intensified, the women affected by the legislation began to vocalize their dissent. Yet, while the campaigners targeted Odisha's maharis, the strongest expressions of protest registered

38 See, for example, Mohanty Hejmadi and Hejmadi Patnaik (2007: 36–8); and interviews with Puri maharis in Apffel Marglin (1985b).

among women in the South. This was probably due to sheer numbers, as the system was far more widespread there; these were the
women whose livelihoods were truly in jeopardy. The 1881 Madras
Census records 11,573 devadasis within its borders of Tamil Nadu,
Karnataka and Andhra Pradesh, compared to 120 maharis at Puri
in 1900 (Fuller 1900: 118); this already small number had dwin-
dled to 22 by the mid-twentieth century, as listed in the *Record of
Rights*, and even further thereafter (Pati 2017; Government of
Orissa 1956; see Appendix E for details).

Importantly, unlike devadasi orders in South India, the mahari
system in Odisha was never officially outlawed—and in a testament
to the strength of the institution in Odisha, maharis continued
to be initiated into the temple into the 1950s. But the practice
slowly deteriorated, based on the universal stigma of prostitution
that came to haunt devadasis across India. The maharis, too,
experienced the repercussions of legislation in the South, and felt
the fallout of changing moral attitudes towards their profession;
eventually, the system died out. At the same time, the gotipuas
faced no such opposition, most likely because their performances
lacked the prestige and visibility of the maharis' service, and their
mobile tradition was not as intimately affiliated to the ritual life of
Jagannath mandir. Gotipuas, however, seem to have operated
uncontroversially and escaped the colonial radar, circumventing the
laws targeting dance—perhaps because their practices could have
been assimilated into the category Jatra, exempt from regulation
under the 1876 Dramatic Performances Act.[39]

The loss of their economic, social, and moral status was felt by
the remaining devadasis, who continued their poignant struggle
for respect, and a return to the days when they were considered
the eternally auspicious brides of Jagannath.[40]

---

39 The last provision of the Dramatic Performances Act (1876: no. 12) clearly
stipulates: 'Nothing in this Act applies to any Jatras or performances of a like
kind at religious festivals' (in Ghose 1921).
40 Ron Hess (1985); Frédérique Apffel Marglin (1985b); Shashimoni Devadasi
(2008); Parashmoni Devadasi (2012).

The images of the devadasi as prostitute in colonial discourse, and as auspicious bride in Hindu discourse, suggest a clash of choreographies, in which the paratopic performances of gender opposed the sexual norms imposed by the imperial state. The extraordinary body of the devadasi transformed into a site of scandal. Mahari Naach embodied this difference and deviance.

The institution of a centralized legal apparatus represented the entry of a Western biopolitical machine in India—a system designed to regulate native bodies as part of the civilizing project. The new legal machine presented a kind of teleological discourse of sexuality, with the primitive body demonstrating sexual indulgence and the ennobled body exhibiting sexual restraint, disciplined in service of colonial power. The performative valence of the law came into full force.

In the first period of Company rule, the figure of the temple dancer served to reify a generalized sense of Oriental depravity, in the eyes of the rulers; in the second period, under the Crown, the body of the temple dancer served as an object of regulation and criminalization; and under the dyarchic framework, the devadasi system was prohibited altogether, as the newly respectable 'classical dancer' emerged. With the end of Mahari Naach in the modern nationalist period, on the cusp of India's liberation from imperial rule, we have to ask: Who performed as the subject of sovereignty? And whose 'independence' was it?

PART III

MOKSHYA
CONCLUSIONS

Chapter 6

A MUSEUM OF MOVEMENT

THE POSTCOLONIAL STATE OF CLASSICAL ODISSI

In order to restore India to its pristine condition, we have to return to it. In our own civilization there will naturally be progress, retrogression, reforms, and reactions: but one effort is required, and that is to drive out Western civilization. All else will follow.

—Mohandas Karamchand Gandhi,
Hind Swaraj (1938), p. 82.

I consider the establishment of the three National Akademis—Sangeet Natak Akademi, Sahitya Akademi and Lalit Kala Akademi—soon after India attained the status of a Sovereign Republic, as a great Act of the State. It was a recognition of the important place that Literature and the Arts should occupy in the life of a Nation.

—Justice P. V. Rajamannar, SNA Chairman, Opening Speech, All-India Dance Seminar, 30 March 1958, p. 7

While all utopian worlds are built out of other worlds, only better, the museum literally takes the world apart at its joints, collects the pieces, and holds them in suspension. [. . .T]he museum puts people and things into a relationship quite unlike anything encountered in the world outside. The museum brings past, present, and future together in ways distinctly its own.

—Barbara Kirshenblatt-Gimblett, 'The Museum—A Refuge for Utopian Thought' (2004), p. 1.

FIGURE **6.1**. Three generations of dancers: Laxmipriya Mahapatra (seated, left) with daughter-in-law and Odissi doyenne Sujata Mohapatra (centre) and grand-daughter Pritisha Mohapatra, an upcoming artist (right). At home in Bhubaneshwar, Odisha, 4 December 2010. Photograph by author.

Annapurna Theatre B, Cuttack, 1947: *The legendary duo of Lakshmipriya and Kelucharan Mahapatra step on stage. Dancing in the trance of Dashavatar, they turn into captivating apparitions and magical figures: a fish plunging into the universal ocean; a tortoise, bearing the weight of the world; Narasimha, half-lion, half-man, tearing open the body of his adversary; calm and compassionate Buddha; Kalki, the destroyer, on his majestic white horse. Night after night, the two dancers perform the Dashavatar, the ten incarnations of Vishnu, and have the audience marveling at their transformations. They are performing in the style called Odia Naach, an early incarnation of Odissi.*

Calcutta, New Empire Theatre, 1953: *Dance prodigy Sanjukta Panigrahi, a 9-year-old disciple of Kelucharan Mahaptra, presents Odia Naach for the first time outside the state and wins First Prize at the Calcutta Children's Little Theatre Festival.*

The Inter-Youth Festival, New Delhi, 1954: *A celebrated performance by Priyambada Mohanty Hejmadi and D. N. Patnaik brings the new dance style from Odisha to the attention of influential national critics and connoisseurs. There is rumour and controversy: Did Rukmini Devi* *really call it the 'poor cousin of Bharatanatyam'? Others, like Charles Fabri, laud it as a landmark discovery.*

1955: *Kali Charan Patnaik names the dance Odissi. Chhau and Odissi are featured at the National Dance Festival in New Delhi.*

Cuttack, 1957–58: *Jayantika, a virtually all-male group of dancers, scholars and cultural connoisseurs comes together to reshape Odissi dance. For months, from night to dawn in the home of Loknath Mishra, they hold impassioned debates, constructing Odissi's contemporary look and technique, drawing on theatre, music, ritual, sculpture, Shastras and local traditions. Legend holds that they signed a vow in blood to abide by the new aesthetic. Later, gurus Pankaj Charan Das, Kelucharan Mahapatra, Mayadhar Raut and Deba Prasad Das will each go on to develop individual branches of Odissi.*

New Delhi, Sangeet Natak Akademi, 1958: *The status of Odissi as an Indian classical dance is debated at the All-India Dance Seminar, leading to its official recognition by the government in the early 1960s.*

In this chapter, I examine how Odissi escaped the trope of double savagery that haunted it during the British Raj and went on to become a 'classical dance' in post-Independence India. The official designation of 'classical' was ascribed to the whole group of dances appropriated into the national pantheon of art after Indian Independence in 1947: Bharatanatyam; Kathak; Manipuri; Kuchipudi and Kathakali; Satriya; Mohiniattam; and Odissi. Situating Odissi's revival, reconstruction and institutionalization, I discuss its ties to regionalism and the nationalist project, attending to the role of the state in both advancing and limiting Odissi's classical projections, and the ideological implications of this process.

The (unfinished) story of classical Odissi begins in the 1930s, with the rise of institutions, aesthetic projects and cultural advocates who set the stage for Odissi's appearance, and culminates in the 1960s, when it won official recognition by the SNA and the Indian government. The integration of Odissi into the classical taxonomy remains a major milestone in the history of postcolonial performance but it is an accomplishment that cannot be attributed to any single personality or moment, for it was a collective endeavour carried out by a spectrum of individuals and agencies, each garnering for Odissi validation and appreciation on the national platform. These figures stand out for their early efforts: Kali Charan Patnaik. Pankaj Charan Das. Mohan Mahapatra. Durllav Singh. Kelucharan and Laxmipriya Mahapatra. Sanjukta Panigrahi. Shyam Sundar Kar. Priyambada Mohanty Hejmadi. Minati Mishra. D. N. Patnaik. Deba Prasad Das. Indrani Rahman. Charles Fabri. Mayadhar Raut. Organizations like the Utkal Sangeet Samaj (Orissa Music Society, founded 1933); Annapurna Theatre (formed in 1936); Odissa Theatre (inaugurated 1939); National Music Association (established 1943), Kala Vikash Kendra (established 1952); Odissi Sangeet Natak Akademi (established 1955); and Jayantika (established 1957), all played a central role in the development of classical Odissi. The Jagannath temple maharis, the *akhadas* and even the Odia film industry contributed their part.

While the appellation Odissi had not yet been coined in the 1930s, a 'structure of feeling' for the dance emerged through a set of cultural infrastructures and artistic networks burgeoning in pre-Independence Odisha (Williams 1977). Indeed, a strong case can be made on behalf of the claim that modern Odissi dance formally developed out of the theatre, and that the Jatra, drama and music associations launched in the 1930s created the conditions of possibility for its consolidation.

The gotipua tradition and other theatrical genres were thriving.[1] As predominantly male-dominated practices, and practices woven intimately into the fabric of rural and urban life, they had escaped the moral scrutiny and state surveillance imposed on the mahari

---

1 Kali Charan Patnaik eulogized the gotipua teachers who protected their dance from colonial subjugation in the 1930s to the 1950s, naming Basudeba Mohapatra (Khura), Kartik Sahoo (Bringarpur, Puri), Somnatha Mohapatra (Cuttack) and the Bral and Praharaj parties for their persistence (2013[1958]: 207). Chandrashekhar Patnaik and Jagabandhu Mohanty were noted gotipua patrons early in the twentieth century, as I learnt from my interviews with Napoleon Patnaik (2012) and Priyambada Mohanty Hejmadi (2012). See also Mohanty Hejmadi and Hejmadi Patnaik (2007: 42–9).

tradition—but the ignominy attached to 'nautch' and women's dancing continued unabated, precluding its general flourishing in the region. National opinion towards devadasi and courtesan performance had dramatically shifted since the last century; the diffusion of these attitudes also shaped the cultural imaginary in Odisha. However, the salient point here is that despite dominant sentiments against it, there was great ambivalence about women's freedom to follow an artistic path and attitudes in Odisha proved to be complicated, neither fixed nor unanimous. As an example: in spite of the legal ban on dedicating women to temples in the Madras Presidency in 1947, and the judgements of prominent national leaders and lawmakers as well as the English-language media, injunctions against mahari service were never locally adopted in Odisha and the women continued to serve at the temple into the 1960s—honoured by some and disparaged by others. It does appear, however, that mahari dedication was restricted by then to the Puri area and was never as widespread as it was in the South, which may account for decreasing interest in mahari service as an object of national concern. Further, Kali Charan Patnaik noted that Odia dance 'failed to receive appreciation from the English-educated people of the country' in the colonial period, and, as a result, 'not a single girl from a respectable family came forward to learn Odissi dance' (2013[1958]: 207). Nevertheless, the values of Indian concert dance, and the talents of Uday Shankar and Rabindranath Tagore in this regard, were widely appreciated.[2] Some women from privileged and liberal families were able to pursue serious dance training. After the devadasi debacle, women gradually came to be accepted again as part of the artistic scene and started working with local theatres and troupes (Sehgal 1989: 77; Citarasti 2001; Venkataraman 2015b). Noted Odissi exponent

---

2 Shankar was a pioneer of modern Indian dance (then labelled 'creative dance'). Tagore invented a composite form, blending folk sources with Kathakali and Manipuri, taught at Santiniketan and which came to be known as Rabindra Nritya in Bengal; it still enjoys semi-classical status there. Both choreographers worked with a mixed group of male and female artists. For more on this subject, see Prarthana Purkayastha (2014).

Sonal Mansingh remembers learning dance in the 1940s and 1950s as a child, thanks to her parents' encouragement, since 'it was something all young girls of proper families were expected to learn'—yet later, when she wanted to pursue dance professionally, 'they didn't want me to take it up seriously. I did it anyway, but it was a real fight' (in Volkoff 1974: n.p.). This juxtaposition between the rhetoric practiced in public and the tactics of subversion practised behind the scenes, on the margins and in other spaces of implicit resistance, is most compelling. These debates about women's dancing bodies, these layered negotiations of gender, are revealed in the trajectory leading up to Odissi's eventual classicization.

Priyambada Mohanty Hejmadi's recollections of the period are of special interest here. Her father Bhagbat Charan Mohanty and mother Nisamoni Devi supported the Indian freedom movement and belonged to the Utkal Sangeet Samaj, part of the Utkal Sahitya Samaj (Odia Cultural Society), which gave Priyambada the opportunity to interact with the world of artists (2012). Quite unusually, while most Odia girls were discouraged from dancing due to its disrepute, Mohanty was encouraged by her family to take it up (see Sethi 2015: 37–8). In her book *Odissi*, she remembers:

> In the early 1940s, a Bengali dance teacher, Shri Banbehari Maity, from Midnapur arrived in Cuttack to make a living as a dance teacher. Little did he know that Oriya girls just did not learn dance. Of course, this was a time when love for music and specifically dance in Bengal, had been sparked by people like Uday Shankar and promoted by Gurudev Shri Rabindranath Tagore. Orissa being a neighboring state, he thought people must be interested in learning dance and therefore he came to Cuttack—the centre for cultural activities in those days. Of course, Utkal Sangeet Samaj had been started as early as 1933 and people were taking interest in teaching children music but nobody danced. My father and some of his contemporaries took pity on him and hired him as a dance teacher more to rehabilitate him than to teach their daughters dancing.

This is how dance entered the aristocratic families and
Maity gave lessons in about half a dozen of them (Mohanty
Hejmadi and Hejmadi Patnaik 2007: 54).

In terms of the specifics of the dances learnt at this stage, she
recalls participating in ensembles where 'the choreography was all
about circumambulating Radha and Krishna' as she played the
sakhi, Radha's confidant (in Sethi 2015: 38). The open and flexible
attitudes of Mohanty's parents allowed her to first explore dancing
as a hobby, and later to engage in its deep study.

Many of the artists who became professional performers and
teachers had experience in Jatra, gotipua and Rasleela as well as
music, and they imparted this knowledge to their pupils through
the proliferation of organizations that gave them the space to foster
their talents and create for dance a new identity. Kali Charan Patnaik's and Somnath Das' efforts in this area may be regarded as
foremost—the former created the Odissa Theatre in 1939 while
the latter formed Annapurna Theatre in 1936, initially a touring
ensemble but later, in the 1940s, acquiring long-term spaces in
Puri (A-group), Cuttack (B-group) and Brahmapur (C-group).
Dancing and acting merged in their stage productions, as they did
in many other traditions. Odissi music, too, held a prominent place
in the region's cultural life— after the Utkal Sangeet Samaj, the
National Music Association of Cuttack was established in 1943.
Odia Naach was born from the conjunction of these drama and
music movements. A capacious category, it incorporated an array
of techniques drawn from folk and popular styles along with
gotipua and Mahari Naach elements.[3] Odia Naach sequences were

---

3 Sources on gotipua performances of the early twentieth century CE reveal
great continuity with elements of older aesthetics. Mohanty Hejmadi and
Hejmadi Patnaik (2007) describes the features of gotipua dance, drawing
from Gopal Chandra Praharaj's *Kabisuriya Granthabali* and *Jibanacharita*
(1928) and *Purnachandra Oriya Bhashakosha*, Parts 2 and 4 (1932 and 1934),
both Odia-language texts. Gotipua troupes were expected to know Kishori
Champu, for it was popular (Mohanty Hejmadi and Hejmadi Patnaik 2007:
42). A single artist who sang, danced and showed his *bandha* skills was known
as 'gotipua' while groups of *abhinaya* exponents were called 'sakhi pila' (43).

interwoven into plays for stage presentations, but the dance itself had no identity outside this context.

The process of adapting Odia Naach into Odissi inadvertently began at the Annapurna Theatre B in 1947, when Kelucharan Mahapatra and his dance partner Laxmipriya worked with directors Pankaj Charan Das and Durllav Singh to originate the *Dashavatar*, marked by an arresting fusion of *nritta* and *abhinaya* elements set to a poem from Jayadev's *Geeta Govinda* (Citarasti 2001: 70). Now a standard part of the modern Odissi repertoire and one of its best-known and longest compositions, the piece narrates the myth of the god Vishnu's 10 incarnations. At the suggestion of Durllav Singh, who knew the poem from his days of acting in Kali Charan Patnaik's *Jayadeva Natak* (1943), the dance was featured as part of the play *Sadhava Jia* (The Merchant's Daughter). Ileana Citarasti meticulously relays the details of its choreography—generated before Odissi's codification and Sansktritization and before the nominative category of Odissi officially existed—in her biography of Kelucharan Mahapatra, *The Making of a Guru*:

> A decision was taken to retain the *tala* of 10 beats and the raga Shuddha Kalyan as in the earlier composition [in Patnaik's play]. [. . .] Specific *mudra* or hand gestures were required to distinguish one *avatar* from the other, and the people involved in the composition were not yet acquainted with texts, *Natya Shastra* or *Abhinaya Darpana*. [. . .] Durllav suggested that the book, *Dances of India*, by Projesh Bannerjee, containing descriptions and drawings of the different *mudras*, should be consulted. [. . . F]or the first time in Orissa a dance sequence was composed following the guidelines of a written text as far as hand gestures were concerned. The rhythmic score was set by Durllav Chandra [. . .] In an alternating sequence of *abhinaya* portions the ten *avatars* are introduced through hand grestures and facial expressions, and rhythmic interludes with appropriate dance steps to suit the character of each avatar (2001: 71–3).

Several points are of interest here. The passage reveals that although dance discourse had advanced nationally among a small group of specialists, there was little connection between those theorists and many regional practitioners. By the 1920s, the *Natyashastra* and *Abhinaya Darpanam* had been compiled, translated and analysed; in the 1930s, they were deployed as foundational texts for the invention of Bharatnatyam in places like Kalakshetra. That this knowledge had yet to be absorbed generally into Odia Naach suggests that, outside of a privileged cultural elite, there was little focus on these texts, that customary practice prevailed but also that there was growing interest in sources documenting dance vocabularies in an effort to enlarge the basic performance repertoire.

Contemporary interpretations of *Dashavatar* still use the same template and music as the original in the proto-Odissi style, bearing out Citarasti's observation that '[t]his dance composition has remained more or less the same today' (2001: 73). Thus the continuity of Odia Naach into Odissi is manifest in this singular item, still an essential piece for dancers to showcase their technical proficiency and often presented as a solo item or a major component of a full-length concert. For her part in popularizing *Dashavatar*, Laxmipriya Mahapatra is illustriously acknowledged as the first female Odissi exponent on stage (Mahapatra 1983: 50).

Although the *Dashavatar* structure is replicated in modern-day performance, and thus preserves a part of the past, the many technical changes introduced into Odissi over the last 40 years make it difficult to comprehend the nuances of Odia Naach in its own time. But a small glimpse of what it might have looked like in the 1940s comes by way of a rare filmic representation of Odia Naach, coinciding with the time of *Dashavatar*'s creation and presentation.

The 1949 black-and-white film *Lalita* directed by Kalyan Gupta—the 'first movie released after Independence' and 'the second Odia-language film ever made'[4]—features a short dance,

4 The clip, unearthed by Cassidy Minai (2013), can be found on the website *Cinemanrityagharana* along with Minai's excellent research and analysis of Odissi on screen.

FIGURES **6.2–6.5** (THIS AND FACING PAGE). Screen grabs from a sequence in the film *Lalita* (1949) depicting a dancer performing Odia Naach.

presumably intended as a loose approximation of Mahari and Odia Naach combined (Minai 2013). Remarkably, portions of this early aesthetic share a resemblance to what would be later termed Odissi. The Mahari connection is made clear by the film's narrative strategies, as an unseen male character announces with authority: 'Lalita will lead the rituals of the Lord. Sarala [and] Sabarimala will perform dances in front of the Lord.'[5] The dancers are called *seba dasi* or those who perform ritual service. The setting is a temple interior, with the idols of Jagannath, Balaram and Subhadra in the background, surrounded by lamps. The clip begins with a priest and a female devotee (Lalita?) venerating the deities while another servitor fans them. This scene fades into the next segment, a medium shot of a dancer bowing from her torso, arms extended forward in Anjali Samjukta Hasta with thumbs crossed, demonstrating the sophistication of the technique (fig. 6.2). She rises from the position calmly and, with a luminous expression, brings her folded hands in front of her chest in a Namaskar, a gesture of reverence (fig. 6.3). With slow and deliberate movements, she moves into a soft Chowk position, though her arms are not exactly in line with her shoulders, nor do we see the Pataka Hasta typically associated with it—her fingers stay apart, the thumbs extend outward, the hands are deeply curved and elongated from the wrist, somewhat reminiscent of Javanese or Cambodian court-dance gestures (fig. 6.4).

---

5 The original clip has English subtitles.

Her other *mudra*s are pellucid and precise. The dancer uses Hamsasya ('the swan gesture') to create a prominent arc with first her right, then left arm, curving slightly towards each side to create a harmonious line, ending in Alapadma ('lotus') with knees gently bent (fig. 6.5). She then transitions into two tiny jumps on each side, one hand in Mushti ('fist') resting at her waist, the other constructing a filigreed pattern while subtly rendering the Sundari Greeva Bheda (neck movement). Although her foot patterns cannot be seen in the frame, the familiar sound of ghunghru and sharp rhythms are audible with each stamp and step. Strikingly, the classical rule of symmetry is evidence in her phrases—what is done on the right side of the body is repeated on the left. The lilt of her body, too, resonates with Odissi.

The dance is obviously structured for the cinematic gaze as surprisingly, in an irreverent display, the dancer faces the camera rather than the deities, signalling the film's choice to break from ritual convention in favour of visualizing the dance and gods together in the same diagetic space. Also of interest is that the dancer performs to instrumental music here whereas vocal accompaniment was part of the mahari tradition and would become the Odissi norm; in another connection, the music was by Kali Charan Patnaik—the same personality credited with championing Odissi as a classical art, who later gave the dance its name and published the first known work on the subject.[6]

---

6 Patnaik also wrote about Odissi music in detail; see his paper in the *Journal of the Music Academy on Madras* (1958b). In it he indicates there was a discussion

FIGURE **6.6**. From left to right: The maharis Kokilaprabha, Suhasini (in full dance regalia), Haripriya and Sashiprabha. *Circa* 1960s, Puri, Odisha. Suhasini Mahari, one of the last to be dedicated to the Jagannath temple, is wearing the special attire for ceremonial performance. Photograph courtesy of Sangeet Natak Akademi, New Delhi.

The dancer's costume in *Lalita* consists of a shiny blouse, a dark-hued sari draped dhoti-style and an ornamental waist belt. She wears heavy silver jewellery on her upper body, though facial make-up is minimal. As noted by Cassidy Minai at *Cinemanrityagharana*, '[t]he film dancer's blouse is not velvet (as was customary for Maharis) but rather sateen, and her jewelry-lined ears and deco-rated side bun seem unusual'—indeed, the hairstyle is similar to the Mohiniattam convention instead. Minai also points out the waist belt looks much like those found in early Manipuri costumes. It's conceivable that elements of Manipuri—popularized by Tagore in Bengal—may have been borrowed by the Odia theatre, since 'the artistic design is similar to that worn by Kelucharan Mohapatra and Laxmipriya' in their 1947 *Dashavatar* performances as is appar-ent in visuals from that period (Minai 2013).[7]

about the musical tradition's classical identity at a seminar the prior year (91), a debate that is still ongoing.

7 See also Ileana Citarasti (2001) for photos of *Dashavatar* and other perform-ances in the 1940s.

It may be said that after the creation of *Dashavatar*, Priyambada Mohanty (later Mohanty Hejmadi) and D. N. Patnaik's perform-ances at the first Inter-University Youth Festival in 1954 were the next major events in the manufacture of Odissi. Mohanty Hejmadi made her first foray into Odissi under the tutelage of Shyam Sundar Kar, a versatile artist renowned for his knowledge of gotipua dance, music, Sahi Jatra and his association with a hered-itary tradition of performing services at the Jagannath temple.[8] He was Mohanty Hejmadi's music teacher, but decided to instruct her in an early form of Odissi dance for a recital organized by the Utkal Sangeet Samaj, with which he was affiliated. Mohanty Hejmadi recalled: 'Being a *mardala* maestro, he laid the foundation of mnemonics used in Odissi. Learning from him was a unique expe-rience. He would be seated indicating footwork and stance through hand movements. When he demonstrated, his dignity and feet, despite one leg being affected by filariasis, were amazing' (in Venkataraman 2005). The 15-minute repertoire he taught was fully *nritta*-based—no *abhinaya*. But this would soon change. Perhaps because she was already familiar with the basics of the nascent form, Kali Charan Patnaik invited her to represent Odisha at the Festival in Delhi, composing a piece adhering to *abhinaya* structure and integrating elements of Mangalacharan, Sthayee, Gumana Kahinki, plus Natangi (Sethi 2015: 40). Deba Prasad Das accompa-nied her on the pakhawaj. Mohanty Hejmadi remembers the two of them 'used to go to [Patnaik] every afternoon for over a month when my dance was polished over and over again' (2017: n.p.)

Fellow dancer Tripat recalls that Mohanty Hejmadi's entry 'was the controversy of the festival. Initially the organizers refused to accept it was a classical form and that it could even be considered for inclusion' (in Sethi 2015: 33). Mohanty Hejmadi speculates it was her tears upon hearing of this exclusion that eventually softened their stance, allowing her to perform (ibid.: 40). 'Clad in

8 I gleaned this from Leela Venkataraman (2005); Kumkum Mohanty (2010: 54–5); Arshiya Sethi (2015); and my interview with Priyambada Mohanty Hejmadi (2012).

a *dakhini* style costume with black velvet blouse and a white
Cuttack sari,' decked in gold and silver jewellery, 'a very unsure
Priyambada took the first step' (Venkataraman 2005; Mohanty
Hejmadi 2017: n.p.). At the competition held from 1 to 7 November
1954, Mohanty Hejmadi was ranked third among the female
dancers while her colleague Dhirendranath Patnaik won second
place among male artists for his rendition of *Dashavatar*.[9] Charles
Fabri wrote a favourable review of Mohanty Hejmadi's 'strikingly
original "Orissi" dance' for the *Statesman*, commenting that she
was 'obviously a born dancer. Though her style does not quite fit
in with any of the better known systems of dancing'—that is,
Bharatnatyam, Kathak, Manipuri or Kathakali[10]—it was 'expressive
and musical' (5 November 1954). Mohanty Hejmadi later went on
to secure first place at the same festival in 1956 for her interpretation of the Mangalacharan, Padanande Gananatha; Kalyan Pallavi;
and the *abhinaya Dekhiba para asare* (Citarasti 2001: 103; Sethi 2015:
43).[11] This time she wore a mahari-style costume (Sethi 2015: 41).

Tellingly, Mohanty Hejmadi's 1954 certificate only lists
her style generically as 'classical dance', a testament to Odissi's
negligible status at this juncture, although it represented an achieve-
ment of sorts, given its prior relegation to the fringe. Upgraded to
minor recognition later in 1956, Mohanty Hejmadi's award then
inscribes her tradition as 'classical dance (Oriya)' (Sethi 2015: 43,
44). This moment could be regarded as a victory for Odissi, for up
until then, it had a reputation as a regional dance of minimal aesthetic interest. Sita Poovaiah had reflected this position in her 1950
dissertation, the first comprehensive analysis of the major forms:

> Of the various schools the four that are commonly in
> vogue hail from Jaipur and Lucknow in the North [Kathak],

---

9 *Times of India*, 'Inter-University Youth Festival: Govt. Foresight Hailed' (9
November 1954: 8); and 'Inter University Youth Festival: Bombay Student
Wins Prize' (6 November 1954: 13). The latter article, however, incorrectly
reports that Patnaik won his trophy for Kathakali.

10 See Mohanty Hejmadi in Sethi (2015: 40).

11 See also Srjan.com, 'Milestones in Guru Kelucharan Mohapatra's Life'
(2016).

from Manipur in Assam [Manipuri], from Tamil Nad in the south [Bharatanatyam] and from Kerala in the far south [Kathakali]. Bengal, Bihar, and Orissa, Andharadesha, Mangalore, Gujerat, and other places have their own dance, but they do not come within the purview of the classical schools (576).

This distorted view about Odissi found an echo in the writings of Kay Ambrose, who described it as 'originally dance drama in the style of Bhavata Mela Nataka from the temples of Orissa', now 'redeveloped as a series of mostly solo dances for men and women' in *Classical Dances and Costumes of India* (Ambrose and Gopal 1983[1950]: 1), problematically framing it as a simple variation of an Andhra theatre form. In this context, it was vital for dancers to continue educating the public about Odissi and correct these misapprehensions.

Mohanty's and Patnaik's were not the first performances of Odissi outside the state; technically, this honour belongs to nine-year-old Sanjukta Mishra (later Panigrahi)—a student of Kelucharan Mahapatra since she was four—who received first prize at the Calcutta Children's Little Theatre Festival in May 1953 for her presentation of the 10-minute item 'Nahi ki koridela'.[12] Mohanty and Patnaik were, however, likely the first to expose audiences to the art in the national capital (Sethi 2015: 43).

From Odia Naach to Odissi

The inadvertent conversion of Odia Naach into Odissi dance occurred at a delicate time when a new Odia identity was being forged, following the formal establishment of Odisha as a state in 1936 and India as a sovereign nation in 1947.[13] Several artists

12 Srjan.com, 'Milestones in Guru Kelucharan Mohapatra's Life' (2016); Citarasti (2001: 90).

13 As discussed in the previous chapter, Odisha came under British colonial rule in 1803. Subsequently it was split up: while the northern and coastal areas were largely absorbed into the Bengal Presidency, the southern areas around Ganjam district were attached to Madras Presidency. In 1912, Odisha and

clearly felt that a strong cultural mandate needed to be generated in line with Odisha's and India's political birth. Further, as a result of the Shri Jagannath Temple Act of 1955, the state government took over administration of the institution due to the alleged ineptitude of the royal family (Shree Jagannath Temple Management Committee 1971). The decline of the Puri raja's influence, the transfer of power to the state and the decrease in sources of traditional patronage like the zamindari system—these were the converging factors that produced a situation where Odisha's cultural iconography had to be reimagined.

In this moment and milieu, the perceived absence of a cogent dance category took on new significance. An improvisational approach had guided the generation of Odia Naach material for the stage. While such an ethos enabled artists to demonstrate their resourcefulness and creativity, many believed that the lack of a codified dance system translated into a lack of aesthetic rigour. Rather than promoting customary practice, dance specialists sought out links to Shastric principles and texts in order to validate Odia Naach and burnish its image and credentials in the wider cultural field.

Kali Charan Patnaik is credited with an important intervention in this regard. In the mid-1950s, he gave the name Odissi to the dance adapted from 'Odia Naach' and further amplified its status by linking it to Shastric foundations. Odissi, like Odia Naach, meant 'the dance of Odisha,' and in that sense it intrinsically

---

Bihar were formally separated from Bengal, and Ganjam was returned to Odisha, drawing the basic contours of the state as it exists today. In 1936, Odisha achieved statehood on the basis of its linguistic and regional identity; its advocates argued it deserved recognition as a region autonomous from the hegemony of Bengali and South Indian cultures. Throughout this period, Cuttack retained its position as capital of Odisha, as it had been since the twelfth century CE; in 1948, Bhubaneshwar replaced Cuttack as the capital city. See Chakravarti (1897); Grierson (1903–28); and Indian Statutory Commission (1930) for reports on the Odia language and arguments for community recognition by Odia activists. Interestingly, despite the general spirit of unification, the Praja Mandal made vociferous demands for the separation of Sambhalpur from Odisha and an end to royal rule, although the movement was ultimately unsuccessful in its bid (Praja Mandal 1946–47).

represented the particularity of place. Patnaik had also chosen the name to complement the category of Odissi music which adhered to classical principles and already had a solid presence in the cultural life of the area. Through the Odissi designation, then, Patnaik simultaneously assigned to the dance firmly classical and regional roots.

Patnaik documented his contribution in a 36-page Odia-language text entitled *Odissi Dance* published by the National Music Association. He received substantial inputs from dance teachers Shyam Sunder Kar and Mahadev Raut in this endeavour. While the text's exact date is unknown, journalist Subhas Chandra Pattanayak believes it to be 1954 (2005: n.p.) whereas D. N. Patnaik (1990: *i*) and Leela Venkataraman (2015b: 60) suggest 1955.[14] Scholar Soubhagya Pathy, who translated the text into English for the journal *Angarag*, confirms its general provenance in the mid-1950s and describes its significance thus:[15]

> The monograph throws light on the Odissi dance before it was structured into the present form by the Jayantika group. [. . .] The repertoire followed in the then dance practice was completely different from the present one. It had predominantly *gotipua* flavour that was shaped into an Odissi dance structure, which the author calls *Amishra* Odissi. *Amishra* literally translated [as] unmixed, could also mean unadulterated, [implying] unstructured or raw form (K. C. Patnaik 2006a[1954–55?]: 67).

In his own writings, Kali Charan Patnaik declares that '[t]he custom and practice of dance in Odradesa or Orissa is called Odissi dance like we have Odissi cuisine, Odissi costume, and Odissi

---

14 In their book on Odissi, Priyambada Mohanty Hejmadi and Ahalya Hejmadi Patnaik reprinted the cover of Patnaik's text as published in 1954 by what they call Utkal Nrutya Natyakala Parishad (2007: Appendix 6, p. 122). It is not clear if this is the Utkal Nrutya Sangeeta Nrutyakala Parishad or a different entity.

15 Pathy states the original Odia monograph included 28 pages of text and 8 pages of illustrations.

jewllery', that it has been 'prevalent in Orissa since time immemorial' and offers it a solid theoretical foundation, delineating the links
between Odissi and authoritative treatises like the *Natyashastra,
Sangita Naryana, Abhinaya Darpanam Prakasa, Natyu Manorama*
and *Abhinaya Chandrika* (2006b [1954–55?]: 130, 133). The Odissi
nomenclature displaced other labels like Odra-Magadhi, Udranritya
and Odragandharva (Pathy 2007: 25). This is also the first instance
where the term 'Odissi' appears formally in dance literature,
although Ashish Khokar and Mohan Khokar suggest in 'the middle
of the forties the embryonic name Oriya Nacho was replaced with
Orissi' (2011: 227) and Ritha Devi tells us that Patnaik had chris-
tened the form as early as 1948 (2007–08: 27),[16] while Priyambada
Mohanty Hejmadi indicates a 1952 news item about her Kumar
Utsav performance 'named the dance type as "Orissi" and further
described it as *darshaniya* [impressive] and *ullekhajogya* [note-
worthy]' (in Sethi 2015: 40). Incredibly, K. C. Patnaik goes back even
earlier, taking credit for developing the first iteration of Odissi's
concert aesthetic, announcing in his 1958 Seminar talk: 'I took the
first initiative to present this dance form on the stage after effecting
certain refinements to it; the dancer was a girl. The popularity of
Odissi dance now is increasing from time to time' (2013[1958a]:
207).

The veracity of this particular claim notwithstanding, through
his creative and scholarly work Patnaik raised the profile of Odissi
in and beyond Odisha's border. He brought his research to the
attention of arts specialists and officials in important centres like
Madras and Delhi, prompting a national interest in the form
and opening an avenue for Odissi's inclusion in the 1958 Dance
Seminar, organized by the Sangeet Natak Akademi.

Two other key figures responsible for bringing Odissi into the
national consciousness were Indrani Rahman and Guru Deba
Prasad Das. Rahman, already a famous dancer, had learnt several

---

16 Kumkum Mohanty agrees the name 'Odissi' appeared in this year, stating
in a 2010 *Telegraph* article: 'The germination of the dance form began when
Mrs Laxmipriya Mohapatra performed a piece of *abhinaya* in Annapurna
theatre. This was announced as an Odissi dance item in 1948' (n.p.) No other
source is available, however, to support this notion.

classical forms thanks to the encouragement of her mother Ragini Devi, a key figure in the Indian dance world (see Mattson 2004). In a 1975 interview with Genevieve Oswald in New York, Rahman confessed that while she was at Kerala Kalamandalam learning Mohiniattam in 1957, 'what I was really looking for was the Orissi, dance of Orissa which I had heard a great deal about.' She gave a nuanced account of her efforts to learn what was a fledgling form that uncertainly veered on the edge the classical, dismissed as 'just' mahari ritual; her words are worth quoting at length for the insights they offer on perceptions of Odissi at the time:

> My mother [Ragini Devi] had told me years ago that 'in Orissa there is a temple dance, it is classical, I've heard about it, but never had in my career the chance, the time, to go and I'd like you to go and look for it.' [. . .T]o my mind some of the most beautiful temples in existence in India, and sculptures, are in Orissa. So I had written many, many letters to all sorts of people—artists and writers and government officials in Orissa—saying that I've heard of this style and please would you help me to contact performers and teachers and that I will come to Orissa and see them but I must make some contact first that I'm interested in this art. Everybody discouraged me from there saying, 'Oh, it's not classical; it's just a temple dance, prostitute art so to speak, of a very unimportant type and you won't like it and it's no use.' Discouraged me. But finally I was invited to see a little festival of this dance in Puri, in Orissa.
>
> [. . .T]he teachers and dancers were to perform. [. . .] I was living in Delhi and went especially.[17] After all, they had me come as a state guest and I saw the dancers and I *loved* it. I said, 'Oh, this is very exciting; I have to learn it and it's something very beautiful, very old, very classical, and I absolutely must help bring it out (1976: 34–5).

---

17 Sukanya Rahman, Indrani's daughter, mentions that Dr Mayadhar Mansingh and Charles Fabri arranged her visit (2009).

Rahman goes on to speak of the difficulties she faced as she sought
to learn dance directly from the maharis after witnessing their performances. As with the other early figures like Minati Mishra, Jayanti
Ghosh, Priyambada Mohanty Hejmadi and Ritha Devi, there were
considerable obstacles for her, given that dance was then a question-
able profession for 'respectable' women. Sanjukta Panigrahi once
told Sharon Lowen that, shockingly, 'people would express their
censure of a Brahmin girl dancing by spitting as they passed her
door' (Lowen 2014: n.p.). Yet Rahman's position was singular, as
she had been crowned Miss India in 1952, and this gave her a powerful platform and voice. Her revelatory account is an important
for what it says about the power she held as a dancer, the force of
her personality and her determination to learn the form despite
the social impediments that affected her ability to access precious
mahari knowledge. Of course, it is also a sober reminder of the
maharis' vexed and peripheral position in the time immediately
following 'Independence' and the continued conflations between
concert and ritual styles:[18]

> RAHMAN: Very few girls who were not temple dancers had
> managed to take dancing lessons with these teachers who
> are connected with the temples, the dance teachers. [. . .] I
> asked them that I would, however, like to see the temple
> dancers [. . .] That caste exists; it still continues. It's one of
> the few places in India where, in the temple, the dance is
> still retained and is performed by the traditional dancers.
> So I requested the people—'Oh! This is just what I was
> hoping it would be. It's very exciting and you're very wrong
> to discourage people and run your art down. You should
> be so proud of it. I want to immediately start training in
> this art and I want this teacher [. . .] But I want to see the

18 So great were the misconceptions about maharis that just about a decade
earlier in 1945, Santosh Kumar Chatterjee could wrongly but confidently
report: 'In the Oriya country the dancing girls are called *Gunis*, and they have
less connection with temples, not being even dedicated to the god' (64). As
noted earlier, the *Record of Rights* (1956; see Appendix E) provides details of
the mahari profession which survived into 1950s Odisha.

temple dancers dance.' And they said, 'Oh, you can't do that.' I said, 'Why?' 'They live in an area where a woman doesn't go and we couldn't have them come to our areas.' They were absolutely outcast at the time. And I said, 'Listen, I'm going. I don't care. I'm going alone. Give me a map but I'm definitely going and I must see this art and I'm not leaving Puri until I see this at any cost. Can't some man go with me? Can't someone take me?' And they said, 'No. It's out of question.' I said, "But can't you call one of them to come and dance for me here, in your homes?' They said, 'Oh never! Our wives and daughters are in the house.' So finally one lady who was sort of an older lady and a senior one amongst them came to discuss the matter. They didn't ask her to sit down; they made her stand in the doorway; they didn't ask her in the room. They told her what I wanted.

OSWALD: Was she a dancer, a teacher?

RAHMAN: She had been a dancer. She's a temple dancer and was older and so she came representing them. She looked at me and smiled and said I would be very welcome at her place if somebody could be arranged to bring me and if I had the courage to come. She would see that I saw the very best of what they had but she was afraid I may not like it because she heard I'm a Bharata Natyam dancer and my style is something very fantastic and highly developed and sophisticated. Maybe theirs would seem very humble in the face of that. I said, 'That's for me to judge.' [. . .] So I asked the teacher who I had selected [Guru Deba Prasad Das], 'Why don't you take me because it's out of love of your art that I am trying to do this and go.' And he said, 'Yes, I'll take you.'

OSWALD: Where was she living?

RAHMAN: She was in the red light district. [. . .] So I went the very next day and there they danced for me—a number of them had come, and the musicians. [. . .] And they're all solo dancers and they performed. They brought their costumes and wore them and they took great pains for me, to

FIGURE **6.7** (TOP). *Manini* in Odissi style by National Music Association, Cuttack, choreographer Deba Prasad Das. New Delhi, Sapru House, 10 March 1957. Photograph courtesy of the Sangeet Natak Akademi, New Delhi.

FIGURE **6.8** (BOTTOM). *Sakhi Gopal* in Odissi style by National Music Association, Cuttack, choreographer Deba Prasad Das. New Delhi, Sapru House, 10 March 1957. Photograph courtesy of the Sangeet Natak Akademi, New Delhi.

come and dance. It was so moving, I almost cried. It was *so* beautiful. They did these lovely songs in mime from the Gita Govinda, the love story of Radha Krishna, in such a moving manner—very spiritually. I mean, really, it thrilled me so that I almost wept. It was so elevating there was no question of anything being cheap and vulgar, or an art of low class or public women. [. . .] The art they had was something exquisite.

In the rest of the conversation, Rahman talks about her role as an advocate for Odissi, and how she used her influence with public officials to raise the profile of the dance in the national capital for the purpose of helping it attain classical status. She had witnessed Priyambada Mohanty Hejmadi's dance at the Inter-University Youth Festival and attended what seems to have been the very first symposium on Odissi in May 1957, organized by Utkal Nrutya Sangeet Nrutyakala Parishad in Puri (Nrutyayan.com 2012). On 1 December 1957, she and Guru Deba Prasad Das introduced Odissi to the Delhi elite in a demonstration at her Sujan Singh Park home, attended by luminaries of the dance world like Mohan Khokar, Kapila Vatsyayan, Usha Bhagat and Charles Fabri. [19] Indeed, she laboured to bring positive attention to the form.

The year 1957 was a watershed year for Odissi. In addition to Rahman's demonstration, Deba Prasad Das contributing to acquainting Delhi audiences with Odissi when he choreographed the dance dramas *Manini* and either *Sarat Rasa* or *Sakhi Gopal* for the National Music Association, Cuttack. [20] Das received an invitation from Bharatiya Kala Kendra to present his work, and the highly lauded event took place in Sapru House on 10 March 1957

---

19 See Sunil Kothari (2015); Nrutyayan.com (2012); and Ashish Khokar and Mohan Khokar (2011).

20 While the SNA lists the piece as *Sakhi Gopal* in its photo archives, Gayatri Chand's research for the biography, *Guru Debaprasad Das: Icon of Odissi,* indicates it was *Sarat Rasa* (2012: 47). Ashish Khokar and Mohan Khokar, authors of *The Dance Orissi,* also include the title *Sarat Raas* in their description of the National Music Association's productions in their book, giving credence to the idea that this may have been the actual name of the item performed in Delhi (2011: 212–14). I have not yet found enough information to verify either claim.

(SNA 2014; G. Chand 2012: 47). According to Maya Rao, a renowned Kathak dancer and one of the attendees at that performance, this marked the moment that Odissi truly came to be appreciated as a sophisticated aesthetic in the capital city (2012).

Jayantika also came into being in 1957, working into 1960.[21] The group held meetings at the home of chairman Loknath Mishra in Cuttack to standardize Odissi's dance codes, lay down its theoretical foundations, structure its concert repertoire and delineate its presentation style in accordance with regional norms and Shastric prescriptions (Mayadhar Raut 2007; D. N. Patnaik 2008). Associates included Kali Charan Patnaik, Pankaj Charan Das, Kelucharan Mahapatra, Deba Prasad Das, Mayadhar Raut, Buda Chowdhury, Dayanidhi Das, D. N. Patnaik, and Raghunath Dutta.[22] Sanjukta Panigrahi and Raut's experiences of studying Bharatanatyam and Kathakali, respectively, at Kalakshetra, and their knowledge of the classical curriculum developed there by Rukmini Devi, greatly assisted Jayantika's project of codifying the dance. As Kelucharan Mahapatra explained, 'There were several loose strands which had to be woven together. These strands had to be presented in a systematic manner. Every dance has a basic grammar. Our job was to devise the common *shabds* [words], after which it was easy to put the *aksharas* [letters] together' (in Sehgal 1989: 77; original italics). By using the analogy of writing, Mahapatra delineates how the group formulated the essential components of Odissi's vocabulary and syntax.

An announcement for the first official meeting, dated 21 June 1958, set out Jayantika's mandate:[23]

---

21 Ashish Khokar states that the group was originally called Nikhala Utkala Nritya Shilpi Sangha, but Mishra condensed the name to Jayantika (2010: n.p.).

22 This information is gathered from Ileana Citarasti (2001: 97–100); Citarasti (2014); and my interviews with Mayadhar Raut, D. N. Patnaik and Sunil Kothari.

23 The Jayantika documents are published in the October–December 2014 edition of *Nartanam* in a valuable article by Ileana Citarasti. For more details on Jayantika, see Ileana Citarasti (2001: 97–8), Dinanath Pathy (2007) and Sharon Lowen (2014).

> There was a time when our place Odisha was known for
> its artistic excellence. It's a matter of happiness that the
> art of dancing has now been rejuvenated and is getting
> accolades in national and international arena, thanks to
> the tireless efforts by few dance exponents. Despite its
> growth and spread we do not have a united forum of
> artists. There are troubles and crisis in the field which hin-
> ders the actual growth of Odissi. If we form a permanent
> body to address all these troubles and crisis, it may help
> us to overcome all the hurdles that we face (in Citarasti
> 2014: 18 [Odia]–19 [English]).

Association members clearly felt that only a collaborative approach
would enable Odissi artists to thrive and surmount the problem of
fragmentation in the dance world, while promoting a common
vision of their dance to a global audience. To bolster their project,
they premiered the Jayantika style at a dance concert on 14 September 1959, held at Cuttack's Nari Sangha Sadhan, an event feted
by the local press outlet *Prajatantra* and the state government:
'[F]or the first time in Orissa, Orissi dance had been presented and
demonstrated [. . .] The Chief Minister expressed the view that
this type of research and performance would be of utmost importance in future as well to prove the classicality of Orissi dance'
(cited in Khokar and Khokar 2011: 253).

It appears that activities oriented towards acquiring classical
status for Odissi reached their zenith in 1958. While the SNA's
All-India Dance Seminar in Delhi is typically situated as the main
event where Odissi was recognized by dance specialists as 'classical',
other important presentations preceded it. In January of that year,
Kali Charan Patnaik, Sanjukta Panigrahi and Kelucharan Mahapatra
showcased Odissi at the Madras Music Academy's annual conference (*The Hindu*, 3 January 1958). Panigrahi performed a *Geeta
Govinda abhinaya*, 'Lalita Labanga Lata'; Patnaik gave a paper on
Odissi's history and technique (Citarasti 2001: 101–02). Kala Vikash
Kendra released a souvenir publication the same year contextu-
alizing the 'Dance and Music of Orissa' with special reference to
'Orissi Dance'.

Indrani Rahman then gave a full evening-length Odissi concert on 19 and 20 February 1958. Her daughter Sukanya distinctly recalls the opening night and its aftermath in her memoir, *Dancing in the Family*:

> I was watching from the wings when the curtain went up before a packed audience at the All India Fine Arts and Crafts Theatre. The air crackled with electricity as my mother, looking like a Konarak statue miraculously come to life, opened the performance with a Ganesh sloka, describing the beauty and attributes of the beloved elephant-headed god. 'Last night was an important milestone in the history of Indian dancing,' wrote Dr. Charles Fabri, 'for this was the first time that a professional ballerina has presented true Orissi classical dances on the stage. He commented on 'the seductive charm of rounded liquid movements marked by exquisite grace and sinuous flowing lines,' comparing Indrani's dance to the charming dancers on the walls of the Rajarani temple of Bhuvaneshwar and the heavenly apsaras on the Sun temple at Konarak. 'When the history of Indian classical dance is written,' Fabri later stated, 'it will have to mention that it was Indrani Rahman who first brought together four great classical styles in one programme' (2004: 119–20).

Rahman's auspicious Delhi debut was followed by other performances the same year at Talkatora Gardens on 7 April, the Regal Cinema in Bombay on 23 September and the British channel ATV on 27 November.[24] She also wrote about Odissi for the *Illustrated Weekly of India*'s June 1958 issue. Unquestionably, the level of fame and respect she brought to the art heightened Odissi's domestic and international profile.

The collective labours of these and other Odissi artists led to a significant moment on the path to awarding it classical status, when the SNA invited Kali Charan Patnaik and his collaborators to give a

---

24 Rahman's 7 April performance followed the SNA Dance Seminar but was not technically part of that event. For more details of her contributions, see Charles Fabri (1958b: 5); Indrani Rahman (1958); and Sunil Kothari (2015).

presentation on Odissi at the All-India Dance Seminar in 1958. However, the Seminar was not the only place where India-wide discussions on classical dance took place; other prominent organizations convened colloquia inquiring into dance at the national level, although their importance was predictably eclipsed by the overriding prestige attached to the 'official' central government-sponsored event. When then-SNA secretary Nirmala Joshi framed the 1958 Seminar as the first forum to bring together 'scholars, experts, and exponents of all dance styles to exchange views' on a national basis (*Times of India* 1958: 7), P. S. Sangapani Ayyangar wrote a letter to The *Times of India* correcting the record, indicating '[t]he first attempt of this kind was by the Indian Institute of Fine Arts, Madras, on 13 February 1948, when the first Natyakala conference was held' (1958: 6). In fact, that event predated the creation of the SNA. The Sur Singar Samsad's festivals in Bombay also preceded the Seminar. In the opening months of 1955, the society organized the third annual Swami Haridas Sangeet Sammelan,[25] with the *Times of India* calling it 'an unprecedented event' featuring 'a series of lectures on the various aspects of Indian music and dance by recognised specialists' (Pollux 1955a: 10). One of the speakers was Ragini Devi, who gave a lecture-demonstration on 'Indian classical dance-drama' at Jehangir Art Gallery on 17 February (*Times of India* 1955: 3; Pollux 1955b: 10). Regrettably, it is unknown if anyone spoke about Odissi at either conference.

The SNA-sponsored National Dance Festival of 1955 had included 'Odissi dance' along with Chhau on its roster, complicating the narrative here, as it suggests that although Odissi had already been recognized by state bodies in the capital, it was definitively assigned to the pedestrian category of 'traditional' despite its classical ambitions.[26] The Bharatiya Kala Kendra coordinated the Festival, comprising a six-week-long programme of evening recitals, on behalf of the SNA. Purnima Shah points out that this was the first major dance event where the 'regional became represented as

---

25 Sur Singar Samsad had organized the very first Swami Haridas Sammelan in 1949 (Pollux 1959: 8).

26 SNA (1959[1953–58]: 44); SNA (1956, Bulletin 4: 4).

FIGURE **6.9**. Prime Minister Jawaharlal Nehru and Kali Charan Patnaik at a reception for the All-India Dance Seminar, April 1958. Photograph courtesy of the Sangeet Natak Akademi, New Delhi.

national culture' and that the state is continually invested in creating such platforms 'where desired fragments of an imagined or mythic past are institutionalized, museumized, and exhibited as object symbols of timelessness' (2002: 130, 138). The National Music Association of Cuttack and Mayurbahanj Chau dancers were listed as participants from the Odisha contingent.[27] This was likely the nascent iteration of the Odissi concert form hailed at the previous year's Inter-Youth University Festival, even if it was then called 'Oriya dance'—relegated for the time being to a lesser place in the dance hierarchy, later to be promoted to the classical canon. This appearance on a major platform in Delhi still failed to spark the kind of interest that Das' more intimate 1957 performance generated. The subject of Odissi's iconic status would then be taken up energetically at the SNA seminar.

---

27 SNA (1959[1953–58]: 44); see also SNA (1956, Bulletin 4 pictorial spread).

FIGURE **6.10**. *Geeta Govinda* at the All-India Dance Seminar in Odissi style. Vigyan Bhavan, New Delhi, 7 April 1958. Photograph courtesy of the Sangeet Natak Akademi, New Delhi.

The All-India Dance Seminar

Organized by a committee made up of the eminent scholars and artists V. Raghavan, Rukmini Devi, Hari Uppal and Uday Shankar, the All-India Dance Seminar took place at Vigyan Bhavan in New Delhi from 30 March to 7 April 1958 (SNA 1959[1953–58]: 40). In recognition of the milestone event, Prime Minister Jawaharlal Nehru hosted a reception honouring the Seminar attendees. The photo capturing the meeting between Kali Charan Patnaik and Nehru is a key artefact, reflecting the profound symbolism of the moment when the Odishan cultural advocate's path intersected with the national leader's through the dance connection, signalling the value assigned to performance in the reconstruction of Indian nationhood in the colonial aftermath.

The Odissi contingent at the Seminar included Babulal Doshi and Jayanti Ghosh of Kala Vikash Kendra, Deba Prasad Das and

FIGURE **6.11**. Odissi Dancers Group at All-India Dance Seminar, Vigyan Bhavan, New Delhi, April 1958. Photograph courtesy of the Sangeet Natak Akademi, New Delhi.

Patnaik (Khokar and Khokar 2011: 254; Kothari 2015). On 4 April, the meeting featured a paper on 'Odissi Dance' by Patnaik in the 3–5 p.m. slot[28] followed by a recital of *Radhika*, listed as '*Geet-Govind* (Dance-Drama in Odissi style)' by the National Music Association, Cuttack, during the 5 April evening concert, commencing at 9 p.m. in Talkatora Gardens Theatre.[29] Patnaik's paper covered the history of cultural production in Odisha, the technique of Odissi dance and its moorings in sculpture and Shastric tradition, its debt to mahari and gotipua traditions, its special traits compared to other

28 The same year, Patnaik was active in disseminating his research on Odissi nationally. He also published a paper on 'Odissi Nritya' in the *Journal of the Music Academy, Madras* (see Patnaik 1958c).

29 For details, see SNA (2014: 117 and 120) and SNA (1959[1953–58]: 42).

classical forms, and culminated with a series of prescriptions to ensure its future flourishing.[30] The momentous occasion was covered by the *Hindu* in a report entitled 'Dance Patterns of Orissa':

> The main subject of discussion in the Dance Seminar held in New Delhi recently was 'Odissi,' classical dance form prevalent in Orissa. [. . .] Mr. Kali Charan Patnaik, an authority on the subject, traced the history of the development of this style and said that unfortunately due to lack of proper patronage and culture Odissi dance could not preserve its sanctity and true techniques as in olden days. He added that recently people in Orissa had begun evincing interest in this dance and many schools devoted to the teaching of this dance were functioning in the State. 'I am, however, convinced,' Mr. Patnaik said, 'that there is no future for Odissi dance until students come forward to take up the art as their profession with true devotion and sincerity[.]' Mr. Patnaik suggested the establishment of a training centre to train teachers of 'Odissi' in proper lines and preparation of a guide book on 'Odissi' dance for the use of teachers. He also wanted a thorough survey of the literature and other sources of 'Odissi' to be taken up immediately (*The Hindu Weekly Review*, 1958: 15).

Charles Fabri in the *Statesman* also commended Patnaik for his 'outstanding' presentation and commented on the 'excellent' performance by 'Guru Devaprasad Das of Orissa' (1958a: 5). At a separate event on 7 April, Indrani Rahman danced at the Talkatora Gardens for an evening programme organized by the Youth Hostel Association, prompting Fabri to deliver an encomium to her and the Odissi form: 'Mrs Indrani Rehman danced four items, each marked by the exquisite grace and sinuous, flowing lines that distinguish Orissi from Bharata Natya. The abhinaya portions were delivered with Indrani's well-known expressiveness, but even more

---

30 The full text of Patnaik's paper on Odissi is published in the 2013 Sangeet Natak special issue on the Dance Seminar (Patnaik 2013[1958a]). See SNA (2013) and SNA (2014) for transcripts of all Seminar proceedings.

enchanting were the pure dance sequences in which Orissi excels' (Fabri 1958b: 5).

Despite the offerings of praise by the media and dance critics, a controversy erupted at the Seminar as the attendees fervently debated Odissi's aesthetic qualifications and deliberated a resolution requesting its inclusion in the classical dance canon. The transcript of the exchanges are reproduced in Mohan Khokar and Ashish Khokar's *The Dance Orissi* and a review of the discussion among dance specialists assembled at thee event yields some fascinating insights (2011: 254–6). U. S. Krishna Rao, K. Vasudev Shastri, Shivaram Karanth and Maheswar Neog favoured its recognition while Kamaladevi Chattopadhyay, Mohan Khokar, G. Venkatachalam and Nityanand Kanungo took a conservative approach, preferring to extend discussions on its status.[31]

Perhaps this unevenness among the respondents reflects the plural interpretations of the "classical" idea among officials in state institutions. Yet the conspicuous absence of a clear definition of the 'classical' is confounding.[32] The SNA kept the criteria for recognition deliberately nebulous and vague, perhaps to retain an elasticity for the 'classical' domain and permit flexibility and openness in the agency's evaluation process, or perhaps to reserve for the SNA final authority in determining what forms would be supported by state bodies, without committing to a set of parameters and positions that might open it up to critique, or coerce it into acknowledging a plethora of claims based on identifiable technical measures. However, G. Venkatachalam's words from the SNA Seminar offer some crucial clues about the criteria for establishing classical status:

> A classical dance must have certain distinct characteristics. One, it must have its roots in the past. Two, it must have an evolved technique. Three, it must have certain authoritative sources as *shastras*. And four, it must have certain perfected forms of expression and communication. Such

---

31 According to the transcript, Chattopadhyay referred to Odissi as a 'regional variation' of Bharatanatyam.

32 See also Anita Cherian's insightful discussion of this point (2009: 40–1).

a dance may be classical and not a dance that came up
40 years ago. Tradition and age are the foundations. An
individual cannot create a classical dance. What is created
may even be wonderful, but you cannot give it the label
classical (in Khokar and Khokar 2011: 255).

The importance of establishing the dance's identity in antiquity,
the principle of developing a movement vocabulary based on
ancient texts, the exhibition of aesthetic virtuosity, and the need
for a collective consensus in shaping the practice are cited here as
hallmarks of the classical. What is excluded is also revealing: religiosity is occluded as part of this definition, a striking omission
given its importance in contemporary notions of classical dance,
either because it is implicit, or served as marginal consideration.

In the 1959 SNA Report, mention is made of an Expert
Committee charged with evaluating Odissi's classical merits and
considering its addition to the list of 'approved' categories (SNA
1959: 12). Even so, the classical remained a basically undefined
category, to be appraised by this Committee, who were presumably
well-versed on the subject—although that knowledge remained
inexplicably implicit, guarded from the public. The imposition of
opaque bureaucratic norms and elite expertise only served to reify
the classical as a rarefied realm—a field so complex, so sophisticated, so mystifying, that it required specialists working behind the
scenes to decipher it. Did Odissi then deserve inclusion in the
classical canon, on the subjective basis delineated by the SNA? This
key question would not be officially answered until well after the
Seminar, into the 1960s.

The proceedings also make one wonder what Odissi looked
like at this juncture. The footage of Indrani Rahman's ATV performance on 27 November 1958 during her UK tour is illuminating, as
it gives us a sense of the emerging Odissi aesthetic at the moment
it sought validation as classical in the national and transnational
spheres. Rahman presents what appears to be a rapidly executed
Shiva Stuti, immediately followed by parts of an early version of
Mokshya.[33] Even if Rahman's flowing movements and Bhumi

33 Guru Deba Prasad Das is seen as part of the musical entourage.

Pranam are recognizable to contemporary students of the form, the Chowk and Tribhangi are not held as deeply as they are in today's interpretations; her movements are slightly more angular, the torso is less pronounced, the hips comparatively less constrained. The focus is largely on the upper body and foot patterns. Compared to the Odia Naach sequence in *Lalita*, Rahman's Odissi performance is far more formal and austere— perhaps as a consequence of the new principles and techniques introduced into the repertoire. The costume and music, too, bear the imprints of the aesthetic set by Jayantika, although Deba Prasad Das had innovated his own style, ably showcased by Rahman.

In the interview with Philip Garston-Jones afterwards, Rahman unambiguously states that Odissi is a classical dance. Recall that this was only a few months after the SNA Dance Seminar, where Odissi's classical position was the subject of conjecture. It may also be remembered that even though the Seminar apparently endorsed Odissi as classical on aesthetic grounds, official recognition would not be forthcoming until later, and there was still great uncertainty in this period about its intrinsic merit.

Even as sections of the media enthusiastically reported that Odissi had achieved classical recognition, the SNA and the government were working behind the scenes to evaluate its eligibility as such and delayed official recognition into 1960 (SNA 1959[1953–58]; Government of India 1959b). The *Statesman* suggested that Odissi's attainment of classical status was a fait accompli—Charles Fabri, writing on Rahman's 7 April 1958 performance at Talkatora Gardens, stated that '[i]t was a fit occasion for Mrs. Indrani Rehman to dance on the very day on which the Sangeet Natak Akademi officially Orissi dancing as a classical system equal with Bharata Natya and Kathakali' (1958b). However, Odissi's precarious status was confirmed by a 1958 *Times of India* report, in which the critic Nisshank offered this disparaging commentary in August—months after the Seminar had taken place and seemingly sealed Odissi's classical position:

> Orissa's *Odissi* dance, which is a conglomeration of the ill-sorted techniques of *Bharat Natyam, Bharat Nritya*

(*Natwari*) and *Ras*, has recently come into the news for securing recognition as a classical dance. [. . .] *Chou* dance-drama of Orissa a mask-dance for men alone, who also appear in the women's roles. There are more of visual aids (aiming at producing the effects of realism) than symbolic. It has bold localised dance-movements. This art is growing weaker with the insistence of Oriyans on the *Odissi* (Nisshank 1958: 18–19).

Thus the investments here lie in 'realism' and, tacitly, male performance, coded as 'bold' Chhau technique; why emphasize Odissi at its expense, and 'weaken' it? The writer laments the 'insistence' on the 'ill-sorted' Odissi, which has no real identity, mixing as it does an esteemed South Indian classical dance with folk forms centred on Krishna worship (i.e. the idioms of Natwari and Ras).

These pejorative popular opinions lingered precisely because official agencies like the SNA continued to equivocate on the question of Odissi's classical identity. In the organization's April 1958 bulletin, the secretary hailed the SNA and the 1955 National Dance Festival for presenting 'some of our less-known classical dance styles such as Odissi'—apparently acknowledging its obscure though august position—'for the first time on a national platform' (SNA 1958a, Bulletin 8: 6). Further, the SNA seemingly registered its support for Odissi by sponsoring the All-Orissa Dance Festival in May 1958; coming a month after the Dance Seminar, it appeared to be an encouraging gesture. Yet the language of the SNA document recording this event subtly indicates ambivalence about the dance's status, noting that the 'function was highlighted by the masterly recital of Odissi and South Indian classical dances' (SNA 1958b, Bulletin 9: 33) With this sentence construction, it is not clear if Odissi is truly included in the 'classical' category or not. This evasiveness reflected the approach of the Expert Committee, which a year after the seminar was still in the process of resolving if Odissi 'should be treated as distinct category apart from' the recognized styles of Kathak, Manipuri, Kathakali and Bharatnatyam, or if it 'should be subclassified' under one of them (SNA 1959[1953–58]: 12).

A behind-the-scenes account of attempts to undermine Odissi at the Dance Seminar came up during the 2 April 1959 Lok Sabha debate (Government of India 1959a). A representative from Bhubaneshwar, identified as Dr Samantsinhar, forthrightly complained the SNA had 'shabbily treated' the Odissi group, and said he had been alerted of cultural officials trying to scuttle their presentation which only went ahead after the intervention of other participants. While attendees 'decided that Odissi should be recognised as a classical dance', the statement was suddenly withdrawn two days later and delegated to the Expert Committee. Samantsinhar decried the 'little-mindedness and provincialism which influences' the SNA (ibid.: 9312). Another speaker, Shri Panigrahi of Puri, commented on the situation as 'something strange', wryly noting the Expert Committee in charge of determining Odissi's status was anything but: 'we find that only one person from Orissa has been included, and he is the Minister Shri Kanungo. I can say that he is may be artistic in his appearance, but he has nothing to do with the Oris[s]i dance itself, because he has never studied it, and he has no knowledge about it' (ibid.: 9303). Was he worried that the bureaucrat would sabotage efforts to catapult the dance into the space of the classical?

Panigrahi then spoke of their ongoing advocacy over the past two years to have Minister for Scientific Research and Cultural Affairs, Humayun Kabir, 'acknowledge Oris[s]i dance as a classical dance' (ibid.). Shri P. K Deo agreed Odissi 'is a classical dance with beautiful fluidity of movements of body [. . .] I think the footwork and the dance technique are quite different and original and it is a clear departure from the conventional types of classical dances we have got in this country' (ibid.: 9339–40). B. C. Mullick of Kendrapara concurred, appealing to the international stature enjoyed by Odissi:

> It has become very popular not only in India but also in foreign countries. Very recently one of the eminent artistes, Shrimati Indrani Rahman, performed some beautiful dances in London and Moscow. I am told that those poses were very much appreciated by them. I do not

understand why its recognition as one of the classical dances in the country has been delayed (ibid.: 9321).

Kabir gave an evasive response, citing procedural grounds, and entreated the House to wait for the Expert Committee's judicious determination (ibid.: 9348).

The SNA Report indicates the Committee decided not to immediately expand the approved 'classical' list, but they did arrive at a compromise by agreeing to provide funds to support Odissi training in the interim. On 17 December 1959, Panigrahi asked Kabir 'whether the Sangeet Natak Akademi has advanced financial grants during the 1958–59 and 1959–60 for encouraging Odissi dance', and if so, what amount has been allocated for this purpose (ibid.: 5543). Kabir replied that Rs 12,800 had been set aside towards the development of Odissi 'dance-drama' with funds granted to the Orissa Sangeet Natak Academy in Bhubaneshwar; Rs 3,000 to the National Music Association, Cuttack; and Rs 1,800 to Orissa Sangeet Parishad, Puri for encouraging *pakhawaj* study (Government of India 1959b: 5543–4).[34]

Given that progress on the classical issue was exceedingly slow, Odisha's representatives continued to press the case for central state endorsement. During the 28 March 1960 Lok Sabha session, Shri Mahanty, a speaker from Odisha, rebuked the SNA for its lackadaisical approach to managing cultural affairs and demanded to know what had been done to ensure Odissi would graduate to the classical locus (Government of India 1960: 8849–532). 'Orissi dancing has come into its own by its own merit and not on account of government patronage,' he argued, noting the state's support was still essential, that it had the duty to sanction the practice. 'There should be no reason why Orissi dancing should not be considered as classical, even though the experts who had gone into this question had given their view on the subject' (ibid.: 8464). Kabir deflected the criticism and deferred to the SNA's authority as an autonomous body, citing the Expert Committee's work,

---

34 This is further corroborated by the transcripts of the Lok Sabha debate proceedings for 2 April 1959 and 28 March 1960 (Government of India 1959a and 1960, respectively).

confirming it would have the final word 'as to whether Odissi dances can be regarded as classical or traditional form. It is already a traditional form' (ibid.: 8532). Since the report had not yet been submitted, the question of Odissi's inclusion into the classical cultural tapestry of the nation was suspended in limbo.

It was also in 1960 that the influential journal *Marg* released a special issue on Orissi Dance with commentaries by Mulk Raj Anand, Mohan Khokar, Mayadhar Mansinh, D. N. Patnaik, and others asserting its 'classical' identity. It seems that after this year, as a result of the pressures placed on the government by Odisha's Lok Sabha representatives, by the media, and with the progressive consolidation of its style and aesthetic, Odissi gradually became part of the classical world and gained support from the SNA in this regard.[35]

Styles of Odissi

Odissi is both exceptional and emblematic in the canon of classical dance—exceptional for its techniques of the body and unique cultural genealogies, and emblematic because it shares the universal tropes characterizing the corpus of classical choreographies.

While there are as many kinds of Odissi as there are dancers, four major styles predominate, each affiliated with a founding choreographer integral to the story of the dance's classicization through the Jayantika project.[36] Although they express different

---

35 The SNA appears to have acknowledged Odissi's new status in 1961, by mentioning the 'revival of Odissi classical dance' in its Bulletin 18 (April 1961: 58). Purnima Shah suggests 'Odissi was finally approved by the National Academy [i.e. SNA] as a "classical" dance of India in the mid-1960s' (2002: 135). According to Sanjukta Panigrahi, Odissi actually received classical recognition as late as 1966, when Kelucharan Mahapatra's art was honoured by the SNA (S. Panigrahi 1993: 8).

36 For a detailed discussion of Odissi's revival by gurus associated with the Jayantika project, see Priyambada Mohanty Hejmadi (1990); D. N. Patnaik (2006); Dinanath Pathy (2007); Aastha Gandhi (2009); and Ileana Citarasti (2014).

aspects of Odissi, these branches are united by a basic grammatical framework.

Pankaj Charan Das, who came from a mahari family, is distinguished as *adi guru* (first teacher), as he acquainted the other three with the temple-based style and originated Odissi's first concert choreographies. His technique, filled with *lasya*, is visually distinct in terms of its liquid lines and elegant gestural vocabulary, and marked by a subtle and sophisticated quality in the *abhinaya* (Roy 2006). The other trio of gurus trained in their youth as gotipuas, Jatra actors and Rasleela performers, infusing their dance with a different set of aesthetic sensibilities.

Kelucharan Mahapatra initiated what is now the dominant style—highlighting a refined body vocabulary, conforming to high classical codes. His signature technique and innovations include the division of the body into upper and lower halves; a deep control over the spine and hips; emphasizing linearity in the movements; and the Ardha-Chowk, which concentrates the energy of the body and allows the dancer greater control and mobility (Mahapatra 2008). He is also the author of intricate Pallavi compositions—Saveri, Kirwani, Mukhari, Arabhi, Shankarabharanam. And as a performer, he is best known for virtuosic performances of *abhinaya*, especially the *ashtapadis* of the *Geeta Govinda* in which he effortlessly radiates Radha Bhava. His artistic partnership with Sanjukta Panigrahi brought Odissi international acclaim.[37]

Mayadhar Raut's style, similar to Mahapatra's, is noted for its soft lines, its supple and ornamental gestures and refined Sanchari Bhava (nuances of expression). Deba Prasad Das departed from Jayantika norms, integrating tribal, Shakti and Tantric elements into his repertoire. Of special note, he is known for integrating Sabda Swara Patha into his pieces (Kothari 1970; Ranbir 2015; also see Appendix A). The sphere in which the body moves is expanded, compared to the Jayantika technique; the Chowk is lower, deeper,

---

37 On Panigrahi's immense contributions to Odissi and her efforts to expose global audiences to the form, see LACMA (1984?); S. Panigrahi (1988); Richard Schechner et al. (1988); Julia Varley 1988); Ron Jenkins and Ian Watson (2002); and Soubhagya Pathy (2006).

resembling the mandala, the movements percussive and vigorous. The thematic range of his *abhinayas* also move beyond the *Geeta Govinda*.

Although he is not part of the 'official' pantheon, I follow Alessandra Lopez y Royo (2008) in considering Surendranath Jena the auteur of a fifth style marked by incorporations of Shakti influences, quotidian movements, and distinctive imagery drawn directly from Odishan architecture. Jena's technique is noted for the use of straight leg lines, and the change in vertical planes between transitions in foot movements and body positions, as opposed to the characteristic bend in the knees and even height maintained during the execution of a *karana* by the dancers in other schools. His choreographies address imagery and themes marginalized in dominant Odissi discourses.

A sixth type which deserves mention is the Mahari Naach tradition established by the devadasis in the aftermath of the decline of ritual service by women in the Jagannath temple. The *Times of India* records that Haripriya Devadasi, for instance, 'had opened a school to teach young girls what was called the aesthetics of the system, besides singing and dancing' (1995a: 1). The direct teachings by maharis to their disciples like Rupashree Mohapatra produced a technique that may be distinguished in approach and content from the Pankaj Charan Das *gharana*.

And I would add a seventh style to this list: the new lineage established by Nrityagram (literally, 'dance village'), an institution inaugurated by the late Protima Bedi (see Bedi 1999). Her collaborators, Surupa Sen and Bijayini Patnaik, have carried on her legacy, initiating choreographic lexicons marked by great athleticism and agility, complex formations and a focus on designing patterns in space as well as time, expanding the boundaries of Odissi's vocabularies and themes.[38]

Many other dancers deserve credit for extending Odissi's aesthetic borders—Rahul Acharya, Sharmila Biswas, Ramli Ibrahim, Sharon Lowen, Ratikant Mahapatra, Sonal Mansingh, Aruna Mohanty, Madhavi Mudgal, Ileana Citarasti, Gangadhar Pradhan,

---

38 See Anurima Banerji (2017b) for an analysis of Nrityagram's aesthetic.

Durga Charan Ranbir, Kiran Segal, and Bichitrananda Swain are among the roster of justly celebrated artists.

Odissi's Repertoire

Odissi is thematically united with other dances in the 'classical' group to a large extent because its form and content is, like theirs, putatively traced to the ancient period and tinged with the codes of religiosity. The repertoire, fusing elements of *nritta* (pure movement) and *natya* (representational dance) overwhelmingly showcases Hindu myths and narratives, especially in the Shaivite and Vaishnavite traditions: episodes from the Ramayana, Mahabharata and Puranas abound, along with local myths. This Hindu orientation is changing through token inclusions of non-Hindu themes, as they appear in occasional choreographies.[39] Even beyond the literal theme or content, the structures of the dances themselves emphasize ancient Hindu philosophies around the use of music, rhythm and space, bodily figurations, as well as the ritual elements of performance ([Lopez y Royo] Iyer 1993).

Odissi modelled itself after Bharatanatyam and gotipua presentations for both the organization of its repertoire and its concert format. Partly because Bharatanatyam, as the first Indian classical dance—that is, the first to be organized according to modern precepts for the stage, and the first to be configured as classical by its inventors and state authorities—provided inspiration to other forms that sought a classical position among the arts. Additionally, several figures who spearheaded Odissi—including Mayadhar Raut, Minati Mishra and Sanjukta Panigrahi—trained extensively at Kalakshetra before dedicating themselves to the development of their regional art. Raut and Panigrahi especially 'were instrumental in applying shastric texts to Odissi dance' (Lowen 2014: n.p.). D. N. Pattanaik noted that when Raut 'came from the South after his training in Bharata Natyam and Kathakali, he gave them clues

---

39 For engaging discussions of the dilemmas of negotiating the history of devotional dance with a secular politics, see Ananya Chatterjea (2004c) and Urmimala Sarkar Munsi and Bishnupriya Dutt (2010).

[about] how to compose dances. The sanchara bhava were not there at the time. He introduced it' (in ibid.). Panigrahi reflected on her contributions, recalling that she returned to Odisha every summer during her residency in Chennai to share newfound knowledge of the aesthetic philosophies with her guru (in Varley 1998: 263). Initially, Rukmini Devi considered rejecting her bid to join Kalakshetra (ibid.: 257). Panigrahi's former teacher, N. S. Jaya-lakshmi, recalls that she was the first Odia student there, training in Bharatnatyam from the age of 8 to 16. For her admissions inter-view, Panigrahi had performed *Dashavatar* in Odia style, yet no one had yet heard of Odissi, and even her own family wondered why she chose to pursue Odissi instead of Bharatnatyam at which she excelled (Jayalakshmi 2012). Eventually, the format of the training structure at Kalakshetra helped her develop a systematic model for classical pedagogy (Varley 1998: 263–4). Panigrahi emphasized that she and her collaborators 'wanted to resurrect the style and transform it into a classical dance. We choreographed various dances. We worked day and night. [. . .] I thought obsessively that I had to make Odissi dance known' (in ibid.). Raut's and Panigrahi's studies led to the adoption of elements drawn from the *Natyashastra* and *Abhinaya Darpanam* and the corollary use of San-skrit vocabulary in the dance reconstruction process. It is evident in Odissi's organization of 'major and minor limbs' in *nritta*, the hand, head, eye, neck, foot movements and body positions— *mudras*, *sirabheda*, *dristabedha*, *grivadebedha*, *padabheda*, *charis*, *karana* and *bhangi*—as well as the subtleties of affective perform-ance, *rasa abhinaya* (Sehgal 1989; Lowen 2014).

The interlacing of Shastric injunctions with Odia and Mahari Naach, folk forms and the region's visual and sculptural heritage consolidated the Odissi technique.[40] And given their familiarity with dance drama and the gotipua tradition, the gurus' theatrical sensibilities came through as they crafted movement for the stage. The first Odissi presentations in the 1950s totalled barely 15 minutes; after Jayantika set the new repertoire, it came to constitute

---

40 See Minati Mishra in Pathy (2007: 51–4) for a detailed view of the technical matters related to the remaking of Odissi dance.

a full evening-length performance (D. N. Patnaik 2008).

Far from harbouring parochial concerns, the gurus involved in remaking Odissi drew their influences from a range of trans-regional sources. The impact of Bharatanatyam is well known; additionally, the concert forms developed by modern Indian dancers also affected their aesthetic sensibilities. Kelucharan Mahapatra, for instance, sought out training from Dayal Sharan, a dancer who had trained with Uday Shankar and later formed his own company. Mahapatra credits Sharan for investing him with a deep corporeal consciousness:

> Dayal Sharana showed me the way; he made me conscious of what my body was doing and what more could be achieved through exercises. [. . .] He made me understand that although there are classified mudras in the written texts, many more could be created deriving them from the observations of everyday life. He taught me how to compose small sequences of dance by putting together different steps; he opened in front of me the door of 'creativity' and once I went beyond its threshold I never looked back (in Citarasti 2001: 75–6).

In adapting Odissi for the stage, its architects emphasized Odissi's spectacular qualities while expressing an affinity with Shastric ideals. This interest in theatricality had precedents in gotipua dance and Jatra, and the impetus to highlight spectacle can be further traced to the *Natyashastra* which framed dance/theatre as *drishya kavya*, fundamentally visual genres designed to capture the audience's gaze. Panigrahi debuted the new two-hour concert format in 1958 in at the Annapurna Theatre (Lowen 2014). Kali Charan Patnaik detailed the components of the concert sequence in his 1958 Dance Seminar address:

1. Bhumi Pranam
2. Bighnaraj Puja
3. Batu Nritya
    (a) on Swara
    (b) on Badya-Ukuta

4. Ishta Deva Bandana

5. Swara Pallabi Nritta

6. Sabhinaya Nritya (Song, Bhava, and Abhinaya)

7. Tarijham or Shula, Pahapata Nritya

(2013: 209)

Today, the series of compositions has changed, assimilating elements of the original structure.[41] In Mangalacharan, Odissi's inaugural item, the dancer seeks the blessings of Ganesh and other divinities in the hopes of conducting an auspicious performance. Elements of choreography include the Ranga Pravesh (formal entrance), Bhumi Pranam (prayers to the earth-goddess), Pushpanjali (offering of flowers), a *sloka* in praise of a chosen deity and salutations to the guru and audience. The equivalent of this item in the Bharatanatyam *margam* would be a combination of elements from Ganapati Vandana and Alarippu. Jagannath is central in Odissi performance, and the stage is often adorned with his image—just as Bharatanatyam features the figure of Nataraj.

Batu, inspired by Odisha's Shaivite tradition, honours Shiva in his wild Batuka Bhairava form. This is not an *abhinaya* piece, however; the choreography depicts the sculptural images from temples in Bhubaneshwar and Konark and only abstractly connects these images of dance to the god. There is an *anibandha* named *batu* in the *Nartana-Nirnaya* (verses 875–98) that forms part of the gotipua tradition, revealing its long duration in Odisha's dance heritage (Bose 1991: 86, 213–14).[42] In Deba Prasad Das' style, Batu is replaced

---

41 Kay Ambrose catalogued eight items in the Odissi repertoire, which roughly aligned with K. C. Patnaik's list: Patra Prabesh (invocation/votive offering), Bhumi Pranam, Vignaraja Puja (these three now form part of Mangalacharan); Batu Nritya; Swara Pallavi Nritya (now Pallavi); Ishta Deva Bandana and Abhinaya Nritya (now *abhinaya* in general); and Tari Jhamo (now possibly Mokshya). See Ambrose and Gopal ([1950] 1983: 88–9). For more on the Odissi structure and format, see K. C. Patnaik (2006b[1954-55?]), Mohan Khokar (1985) and Leela Venkataraman (2015b).

42 There is a sequence in Batu that correlates exactly to a score written in the *Nartana Nirnaya*. Mandakranta Bose includes the description in *Movement and Mimesis* (1991: 214). The verse is printed in Sanskrit, from the manuscript

by Sthayee, a technically demanding display of *nritta*. Both share elements of Alarippu or Angikam in the Bharatanatyam context.

Pallavi (similar to Bharatanatyam's Jatiswaram) is the danced equivalent of a musical raga which moves from the slow and meditative opening notes (*alaap*) to textured elaborations of rhythm (*jor*) and culminates in a dramatic display of virtuosity before an exhilarating crescendo (*jhala*). Sinuous poses, sophisticated footwork and complex patterning are all emblematic of this item. Named after the ragas on which they are based—Basant, Kalyan, Arabhi, Deshakhya, Hamsadhwani, Mukhari and so on—Pallavis are often set to classical Odishan music, interweaving northern Hindustani and southern Carnatic influences into an indigenous style. Pallavis beautifully portray explorations of form, interplays with rhythm and melody, and the filigreed artistry of Odissi. Pallavi alludes to the flowering of a tree, and the dance captures and conjures that poetic meaning.

Odissi's *abhinayas* pay homage to the rich tapestry of Odisha's literature and draw from the *Geeta Govinda*, vernacular poetry and Hindu mythology (K. C. Patnaik 1967; Dhar 2008). Odissi is best known for its *ashtapadis*, depicting the dalliances of Radha, Krishna and the gopis, and describing their passions and melancholies. Other *abhinayas* are based on the epics, such as Pankaj Charan Das' *Panchakanya*, stories of five female characters from the Mahabharata, and Protima Bedi's *Jatayu*, relating an episode from the Ramayana. *Abhinayas* are equivalent to the narrative items like *shabdam, varnam, padam, javali* or *stuti* in Bharatanatyam. An interesting point is that while Bharatanatyam distinguishes between

---

in the Asiatic Society Library, Calcutta; the English translation is by Bose and the English transliteration is mine:

> Jaanubhyam bhumilagnaabhyam padabhyam va mandalakriti / namraprishtam latahastau paatram bhramanamacharet / tadasau baturityukta suryamandalavad gati (53a).

Translation: When the performer revolves touching the ground either with the knees or with the legs describing a circle [while her] back is bent [backwards] with her hands in *lata* then it is known as Batu [and its] movement is like [moving] in the orbit of the sun.

these *nritya* types, Odissi created the single category of *abhinaya* for all of these narrative forms, with a special focus on the subdivision of *ashtapadis*.

Stutis, venerations of specific deities, are folded into the broader *abhinayas* of Odissi. Although not identified as a distinct part of the standard repertoire, I believe *stutis* belong in a class of their own. Admittedly this is an arguable point. In my perspective, *abhinayas* excel at evoking *shringara rasa* and are perfect for exhibiting aspects of the *nayikas* (female archetypes) through Sanchari Bhava (kaleidoscopic displays of emotion). *Stutis*, on the other hand, are designed to evoke *adbhuta* (a mood of awe and wonder), *shanti* (peace and contentment) and *bhakti* (devotion) in their representations of religious iconography, creating a meditative atmosphere. Outstanding choreographies include Durga Charan Ranbir's paeans to the sun god Surya, and to the Dasamahavidya, the ten aspects of Devi; Kelucharan Mahapatra's composition of episodes from the *Bhagavata Purana*, depicting the life of Krishna; his collaboration with Sanjukta Panigrahi on *Ardhanareeshwara*, showing the union of Parvati and Shiva in a single androgynous body; and Bichitrananda Swain's homage to the great goddess, *Mahakali Stuti*. I would further place the *Dashavatar*, which formed part of Odissi's earliest *abhinaya* repertoire, in this class.

The final item of an Odissi performance is Mokshya, a rigorous *nritta*-based piece which is meant to symbolize the dancer's spiritual liberation and surrender. A closing *shloka* or *mantra* recited for a particular deity, such as Narayani, punctuates this theme of dissolving the self.

The entire trajectory of an Odissi performance is devoted to conjuring *rasa bhava*—the multilayered experiences of the dance, co-created by the performer and the perceiver. Debates are ongoing as to whether the aim of *rasa* is to evoke devotional feeling, or to display the dancer's command over the affective and corporeal techniques governing the form.[43] *Rasa* is subtly embedded in the *nritta* and is most palpable in *abhinaya*, which uses the body as

---

43 For two separate views, see, for instance, Alessandra Lopez y Royo (2008) and Cornelia Schnepel (2009).

medium to relay a narrative or elaborate a poem, translating the literary idea into gesture, as the dancer combines prescribed codes for conveying emotion with in-the-moment improvization, ideally offering the body of the dancer as an object of spiritual contemplation in service of the audience's elevation (Coorlawala 1996, 2004). The Hindu bias, however, reveals a major problem in dance history and politics. Classical dance conveys a set of religious codes, concepts and content that work in service of a conservative nationalism that images the Hindu subject at its ideological centre. Interestingly, this framing of 'Indian' classical dance as (mainly) 'Hindu' remains largely unquestioned in the literature while other religious and cultural influences are routinely minimized, cast as insignificant or inauthentic in the formation of the dance.[44]

Choreography and Composition in Odissi

It is relevant here to consider the concepts of 'choreography' and 'composition' in the world of Indian classical dance, distinctions which Odissi exponents generally embrace. In the prevailing model, 'choreography' is reserved as the term for addressing the dynamic of two or more dancers performing together in a given space, and to innovative or experimental works within classical idioms that depart from established repertoire. The governing conception of 'choreography 'is one that refers to duets and group compositions, and the conscious attention directed to space and formations in planning the exhibition or interaction of multiple dancers in the performance precinct. Thus, 'choreography' is not necessarily thought of as the invention, design or syntax of a dance piece; rather, a fixed dance sequence or arrangement is usually

---

44 This has happened, I believe, because many scholars and ideologues perform the strategic manoeuvre of gathering Jain, Buddhist, Sikh and tribal groups into the Hindu fold; many historians associate the general decay and decline of Indian dance with the rise of Muslim rule especially during the Mughal period, despite the interactions between Persian and Indian art that occurred in that very time; and influences of religious minorities on classical dance remain severely under-analysed.

called an 'item' or 'composition', what the *Natyashastra* terms
angahar, rechika and *pindi-bandha*[45] and what *Nartana-Nirnaya*
refers to as Bandha Nritta.[46]

Accordingly, in this view, the solo performance tradition
(*ekaharya lasya* in the vocabulary of the *Natyashastra*) is not concerned with 'choreography' per se, if we understand it as the decision-making procedures involved when thinking about harmonizing
multiple bodies and formations in the performance space. Instead,
it is focused on presenting items and compositions in an orderly
concert format. The underlying premise here is that the solo dancer
should command the audience with the spectacle of her virtuosic
ability, and that spatial awareness is of little or no concern, because
the dancer will improvise by using as as much of her surrounds as
required for her work; and because creating shapes, rhythms, and
affect take priority in classical dance over occupations of space.

Another layer to consider here is that a tacit idea of choreography is already at work in conventional Indian classical dance
presentations, residing in the idea of the mandala—a yantra
(sacred diagram) of square shape that is imagined as the ground
of performance, a normalized principle which organizes the
dancer's orientations on stage (Vatsyayana 1983). The mandala
principle may be the reason why Indian classical dancers typically
don't see the need to consciously attend to questions of spatial

---

45 In the *Natyashastra*, Bharatmuni describes a logical progression of movement sequences, based on an additive approach, that builds on the unit of the
karana (full-body movement). There are 108 *karanas* in total (Bharatmuni
1996: 24–31). Two *karanas* make a *matrika*. A group of *matris* create one *angahar*—two equal a Kalapaka, four make Sandaka and five a Sanghataka. An
angahar is described as *samayoga*, or the conjoining of multiple *karanas*
(23–4, 31–5, 39n4). Of *pindi-bandha*, there are four styles: Pindi (circular),
Srinkhalika (chain-like), Lata Bandha (interwoven like vines) and Bhedyaka
(divided into parts). As Adya Rangacharya explains, *pindi-bandha* means 'a
group formation of dancers' who create these images on stage (37) but also
generally '[g]iving shape and form to something indefinite' (35). In my experience, *pindi-bandha* is usually used among dancemakers in this latter sense,
as a type of compositional pattern.

46 See Bharatmuni (1996: 37) and Pandarika Vitthala (1998: 3.423–6, p. 117).
See also Chapter 6 in Mandakranta Bose (1991: 194–215).

design, since it exists in this predetermined and monolithic form. The mandala is often visibly marked out, but even in its apparent absence it acts as a kind of mobile and invisible architecture, anchoring the dancer's movements. With the mandala, which can be both material and metaphorical, the dancer typically works with preset choreographic axioms—such as constant returns to the centre of the real or implied yantra; moving in linear and circular patterns, forward and back, side to side, and diagonally within its bounds; making symmetrical movements to create equilibrium; producing physical shapes and geometries in space; and working with groundedness (Vatsyayan 1967). Kelucharan Mahapatra fortifes this theory by isolating grounded movement as the feature differentiating Odissi from Western ballet and folk dance: 'In the West, the dancers attempt to fly like birds, they want to travel through the air. Our art is different. We seek to be completely here and now, to remain on solid ground' (1983: 50). Therefore the topological concern is tacitly always already in operation, applied to solo or collaborative dancemaking.

These tendencies and terminologies regarding choreography in Indian dance are now changing, but I mention these registers since they are so culturally specific and germane to Odissi in particular. Indeed, there is a new effort to find a sustainable, unified language for 'choreography' as mapped out in Indian aesthetic philosophies and practices; so while it doesn't exist in any given treatise, *sama-rachana*—which embeds, in its meaning, both 'structure' and 'creation'—is one word potentially applied for this purpose.[47]

These ideas simultaneously contrast, complicate and share commonalities with the Western iterations of 'choreography' that dominate much of the current dance discourse worldwide. As Susan Leigh Foster has shown , the term 'choreography' encompasses two principal meanings in Western history: as 'dance writing' or a system of notation for representing dance on the page; and as 'the

---

47 Many of these ideas were explored in the Samarachana choreography festival, convened in Bhubaneshwar, Odisha, from 2 to 7 March 2012. During the dance seminar, I had the privilege of listening to leading artists and critics such as Sharmila Biswas, Sunil Kothari, Aruna Mohanty, Madhavi Mudgal, Leela Samson, and Leela Venkataraman expound on this topic.

staged presentation of movement resulting from the creative process of originating a dance' (2009: 100, 106), a notion which privileges the idea of the individual author and expression. In the Odissi community, the *Natyashastra* and other related aesthetic treatises are almost never referred to as 'choreographic' in the first sense, even as they participate in 'writing' dance. They belong firmly to the category of the Shastras. Expository and instructional, they identify and classify the principles, grammar, lexicon, purpose and rules of performance. Open to interpretation, the Shastras apply to a wide range of dance, music and dramatic genres that demonstrate their codes in multifaceted and idiosyncratic ways. But 'choreography' and 'Shastra' are not at all comparable categories, as Shastras on performance enjoy a privileged position in Hindu thought for their generalized value as disquisitions on aesthetics, technique, corporeality, and the like, and are treated seriously as philosophical discourses.

The second sense, of choreography as inventive artwork bearing the signature of its author, is sometimes cited in Odissi to frame non-standard (solo or group) compositions that circumvent the accepted templates or customary concert repertoire of a given *gharana*. This usage partially corresponds to and is borrowed from the Western—or, more precisely, English-language—locution. The aforementioned *samarachana* might serve as a translation of this choreographic mode. Further, *anibandha* (free movement) as defined in the *Nartana-Nirnaya*, equates perfectly with this practice of experimental or unconventional dancemaking (Bose 1992). However, the classical format continues to enjoy unparalleled authority in the world of Odissi.

Transformations of the Classical

There is no single moment in which 'Odissi classical dance' arrived; its naturalization occurred over time, through a cultural process generated in the grassroots movements of the 1930s and then managed by the apparatus of the state in the postcolonial period of the 50s and 60s (Sangeet Natak Akademi 2007; Vatsyayan 1972). This manifested as the symbolic renewal of the past through the 'restoration of behavior' in the dancing body (Schechner 2004). In Odissi, as with the other classical forms, the dance underwent a metamorphosis, from its status as regional practice to becoming a nationalized spectacle. For several of the styles, what might be called the classical sensibility emerged prior to actual Independence; however, the canonization and consolidation of 'classical dance' as a recognizable taxonomy only occurred after this event (Williams 1977: 128–35; Shah 2002).[48]

Purnima Shah argues the impetus behind the promotion of regional genres 'to the status of the "classical" reflected the institutionalized desire for the regional communities to rebuild and take pride" in their identity' (2002: 138). Beyond respect, classical Odissi dance importantly afforded political, economic, and cultural capital to the state of Odisha, a place that had historically been seen, and often seen itself, as a peripheralized place within the confines of the nation-state—geographically, materially and ideologically.[49]

In the process of making Odissi classical, a number of major shifts took place. With the rise of cultural organizations like the Sangeet Natak Akademi, the Bharatiya Kala Kendra, national dance festivals, university departments, public performance halls and research institutes—to give just a few examples of bodies that represent the continued centralizing impulses of the state—the practice of the dance moved to urban centres, to the proscenium stage, and, through mass media (such as Doordarshan television),

---

48 Take the situation of Kathakali and Bharatanatyam: the institutions devoted to the conservation of these arts, Kalamandalam and Kalakshetra, were established before 1947 (in 1930 and 1936, respectively), but the limits of their patronage and prestige were initially restricted to the regional level.

49 For example, Lal Mohan Patnaik, writing in *Resurrected Orissa*, dramatically bemoaned the loss of Odisha's magnificent cultural legacies and how its people 'were looked down upon by all and sundry', and issued a call in 1941 for the state to 'come into her own', proclaiming the 'need to muster strong and march into victory filling the air with the glorious song of resurrection' (1941: 356). See also testimonials in Indian Statutory Commission (1930).

into the public sphere.[50] The rhetoric of 'salvage' was important in ensuring bureaucratic benefactorship. 'Saving' the classical dance as a 'legitimation of survival' of Odisha's culture meant democratizing and popularizing it while retaining its mythological status as a sacred and sophisticated high art, so it became at once material and spiritual, embodied and empyreal (Hamera 2002: 82).

Richard Schechner offers a succinct summary of the shifts brought about by nationalism and the changes engendered in the postcolonial period as a result of making the dance a classical concert practice: 'standardization of the form, development of a [central] "vocabulary" of gestures, recognition by persons outside the area of greatest local concentration of the form ("export" even within India), concern about the continuity of the art: all of these are major evidences of modernization' (1977: 1). However, 'modernization' was not limited to stylistic elements alone; there was also an accompanying modernization of gender discourses associated with classical dance.

The Politics of Sanitization, Gender and Class

While in the precolonial and colonial eras, Odissi embraced performances of extraordinary gender, this shifted in the postcolonial period, as a relaxation of gender orthodoxies within each form

---

50 Inaugurated in 1952 in the capital, Sangeet Natak Akademi is arguably the most important of these government bodies. It acts 'as the apex body of the performing arts in the country, preserving and promoting the vast intangible heritage of India's diverse culture expressed in the forms of music, dance and drama. In furtherance of its objectives the Akademi coordinates and collaborates with the governments and art academies of different States and Territories of the Union of India as also with major cultural institutions in the country. The Akademi establishes and looks after institutions and projects of national importance in the field of the performing arts' (Sangeet Natak Akademi website, 2007). For more details on the mandates of the various arts bodies in India, see their websites, in Works Cited. The Sangeet Natak Akademi's 'Constitution', outlining the objectives of the state in protecting its performing arts heritage, is especially informative.

occurred.[51] However now, while anyone who could dedicate the requisite time and money for training could gain access to classical dances, the ascription of gender roles became conventional and binarized—for instance, women performing as female characters, men acting as male characters. Transgender performances, though still considered a mark of virtuosity for established artists, are depreciating in mainstream dance circles—proving that the democratization of bodies in dance has also had conservative political consequences, reigning in the progressive possibilities of gender expression and reinforcing highly gendered norms in performance instead. The idea of the gotipua body as the synthesis of male form and feminine comportment is rapidly diminishing in legitimacy as modern narratives of gender, bound to dichotomized ideas of masculine and feminine, prevail. And with the loss of Mahari Naach, the actualized conception of extraordinary gender as tied to the female ritual specialist has completely disappeared, even as its hauntings persist in the regional consciousness. Thus the domain of gender is another site where the regional concept is increasingly displaced by the national even as it is selectively appropriated. While the performance zone had been an arena that enabled a departure from everyday norms in terms of gendered practice, in the post-Independence period, because the sexual politics of classical dance were partly subject to state discipline, it became a sphere where modern ideals of gender and sexual difference asserted themselves.

The alleged democratization of dance also camouflaged complex politics of class. The chaste bourgeois woman became the ideal exponent of classical form, so the dance could experience 'its rebirth in a more "proper' class", as Amrit Srinivasan argues, becoming 'the exclusive entertainment of the respectable—the elite and middle class' (1988: 198).

The desire to purify and sanitize classical dance was further revealed as concert repertoires were delinked from the maharis, purged of overt erotic connotations and content, and recodified to naturalize their status as honorific and desexualized art (Ritha Devi

51 Kathakali and Kuchipudi, once all-male practices, could now be taken up by all genders, for example.

2003).[52] Classical compositions, framed as bearers of ritual mean-ing, emphasize mimesis, repetition and replication, apotheosizing an *aesthetic of imitation* rather than an *aesthetic of innovation*. Ideally, an intact form is to be handed down and embodied by multiple dancers over generations. For classical dance forms like Odissi, then, the ideal is a faithful act of transmission, accomplished through corporeal exchange within the *guru–shishya parampara*. The dance's ethos of timeless permanence is tied to its formal reproducibility, and even though the genre may change within established boundaries, the conferral of classical status and credi-bility is predicated on its maintenance of specific thematic and structural continuities. As such, a departure from codified aims and conventions is interpreted as contamination, degradation and violation of the classical nomos.[53]

---

52 This mirrors the ideological dynamic of classicization in Bharatanatyam, as Janet O'Shea (2007) indicates. She shows how modern dance specialists aimed to make it respectable by distinguishing its present form from what they saw as its morally corrupt past, attached to alleged depradations by devadasis and professional dancers.

53 Yet, such departures and interrogations are necessary components for producing aesthetics of innovation in contemporary dance. The work of radical choreographer Chandralekha, who broke away from Bharatnatyam, perhaps best dramatizes the conflictual status of the classical, as her provoca-tive interventions have totally reconfigured its very meaning—a theme which Rustom Bharucha engages in his book about her (1997). Through a synthesis of yoga, martial arts, and the basic Bharatanatyam grammar, she developed her own breed of movement, using indigenous resources to expand and redefine the accepted boundaries of her dance. A phenomenological interest in the body is centred in her work; consequently, a marked concern with the politics of sexuality, secularism, and explorations of the body's sensuality surface in her compositions, distinguishing it from orthodox interpretations. As she did away both with its routinized repertoire and its obsession with Hindu iconography, Chandralekha disturbed the mythical narrative to which Bharatanatyam is tethered. She was controversial for the perceived transgres-sion of making the dance overtly political by injecting current social concerns into its frame and rejecting a choreographic impulse based on dominant Hindu religiosities. See Chandralekha (2003) and also the important mono-graph on her work by Ananya Chatterjea (2004a).

The convergence between sanitized 'laws of movement' in the aesthetic and political domains is illustrated in the figure of the maligned devadasi. In the 1920s and 1930s, moral reformers succeeded in pushing through a number of legal initiatives instituted to ban the consecration of girls in South Indian temples, a situation that eventually affected Odisha's mahari system. Acts such as these served as the blueprint for postcolonial legislation.[54]

The referendum on the devadasi system went beyond artistic and activist circles; national leaders like Gandhi felt the issue was important enough to address it in a broader public forum. In *Hind Swaraj*, Gandhi voices his opposition to the devadasi practices. One of his interlocutors catalogues a whole host of practices attached to gendered violence in India—among them, the devadasi order, 'where, in the name of religion, girls dedicate themselves to prostitution' (1938: 56). Gandhi then defends the idea of Indian civilization while agreeing that child marriage, polyandry and devadasi systems are tarnishments that should be expunged on moral grounds: 'The defects that you have shown are defects. Nobody mistakes them for civilization. They remain in spite of it. Attempts have always been made and will be made to remove them. We may utilize the new spirit that is born in us for purging ourselves of these evils' (ibid.).[55]

---

54 The various acts legislated to restrict or abolish devadasi practices include: the 1861 Indian Penal Code (IPC) which targeted devadasis by criminalizing them as prostitutes; the Contagious Diseases Act of 1868; the 1924 amendments to IPC Sections 372 and 373 which made the consecration of girls to temples illegal; the Bombay Devdasi Act 1934; the Madras Act of 1929, limiting their land privileges; Devdasi (Prevention of Dedication) Madras Act 1947; Karnataka (Prohibition of Dedication) Act 1982; and the Andhra Pradesh Devdasi (Prohibition of Dedication) 1988. For more details about the effects of these laws, see Frédérique Apffel Marglin (1985b); Avanthi Meduri (1988 and 1996); Kunal Parker (1998); Kay K. Jordan (2003); and Lucinda Ramberg (2014).

55 Gandhi made this statement even as he made the contradictory claim that 'it behooves every lover of India to cling to the old Indian civilization even as a child clings to the mother's breast' (*Hind Swaraj* 1938: 57).

Gandhi's firm stance may have been shaped by an earlier encounter he had with a group of devadasis in South India, which convinced him of the need for widespread reform of ritual practices. About this incident, a writer in the *Calcutta Review* observed:[56]

> He does not care, if he upsets settled forms and disturbs complacent ease. The terrific words which he uttered at Neollore, where he met a set of women fallen from virtue cannot easily be forgotten. When he was told who they were, he was overcome by feelings of sorrow and sympathetic shame. He felt that honour was vital to the soul of womanhood and dishonour was a desecration of the holiness of love. What pained him most was the state of our society which could suffer such a system with conscience, the brazen hardness of men, the legality of temple ritual which knew not any mercy or justice, pity or shame. He made his hearers sensitive to a new delicacy in the law of chivalry that it is not he who does not go out of his way to tempt a woman that is virtuous but it is he who when tempted by her enables her to preserve her honour (C.S.R. 1921: 27).

Gandhi here was outraged just as much with the devadasi system as he was with the idea of cultural deterioration as emblematized by the figure of woman whom he perceived and pedestalized as the moral standard-bearer of Indian society (Kishwar 1985). The sexualized image of the devadasi naturally disrupted his projected image of feminine purity. While his views on gender were complex, his rejection of the devadasi institution as a house of 'fallen women' affected the attitudes of the publics who revered him as the principled leader of the independence movement.[57]

---

56 The student writer of this piece, cryptically credited as C.S.R., was revealed to be Sarvepalli Radhakrishnan, who later became a philosopher, professor and president of India.

57 As a testament to his vocal opposition, Moovalur Ramamirtham Ammaiyar, an activist working to abolish the dedication system, once received a letter from Gandhi in support of her efforts. She had been forced to follow the tradition and later abandoned it, despite fierce familial resistance. She had also met Gandhi in 1921—the same year the *Calcutta Review* write-up appeared—and felt encouraged by him to continue her crusade against what

The eventual dissolution of the mahari system due to wide-spread sexual exploitation is a matter that requires urgent address. Prepubescent girls initiated into temple service were often expected to submit to sexual abuse by men of age. Indeed, this is not a point of debate but a historical fact (see, for example, the accounts of maharis in Marglin 1985b). According to dominant social mores, this situation of sexual violence was framed as an acceptable sexual relationship, until dissenting voices transformed the discourse. In this, the status of maharis was historically similar to that of ordinary marriageable girls, until the standard age of consent changed.[58]

However, I would argue that sexual exploitation was not inherently a feature of the devadasi system, and the mahari order could have been preserved through simple reforms strengthening women's power—like raising the age of consent, formalizing rights to property and wealth, establishing a fair-wage scheme and preserving the role as a choice for women who freely wished to enter a life of ritual service and make dance and music their vocations. Consider the parallel example of marriage, which, in historical terms, and arguably in most regions of the subcontinent, was deeply oppressive to women. However, through feminist efforts, the role of the institution was maintained while enhancing women's rights within it. A similar project could have been initiated on behalf of the maharis. Yet, in their case, the allegation of prostitution shadowed all debate. Moreover, many devadasis wanted to continue their profession which afforded them considerable material and social capital. Listening to the women's life stories, considering the potential of the system as a matrilineal enclave that offered women relative power within a patriarchal structure, and considering the parallel transformation of institutions that historically exploited women, there are robust arguments to be made on behalf of retaining and ameliorating the devadasi system.

---

she saw as a system promoting women's slavery. For details, see S. Anandhi (2008: 397).

58 In 1892, the age of consent for girls changed from 10 years of age to 12; in 1949, it changed to 16; and in 2014, it changed to 18.

Interestingly, there was no legal resolution in Odisha banning the devadasi system, but the aftereffects of legislation in the South and the impact of changing mores were deeply felt, leading to the gradual disintegration of Mahari Naach.[59] The devadasis continued to be held in esteem, even into the present day; the cultural researcher Devadutta Samantasinghar argues that 'devadasis of Puri are highly respected in society here and not looked down upon by people of other places' (in Avinash Sharma 2015). Indeed, even into the 1930s, as their profession was declining due to anti-nautch agitations, the Orissa Hindu Religions Endowments Act continued to protect the devadasis' customary right to property (Government of Orissa 1939: Clause 19). Yet their ritual performance suffered because, as D. N. Patnaik has underscored, '[the] educated and cultured class didn't look at it as a sophisticated or cultured form of art' (2008). Crucially, however, the dance itself was not outlawed. Consequently, a strange situation of a 'dance without the dancers' emerged. As new aesthetic practices were being invented and authorized, the prior traditions that created their conditions of possibility were being effaced.

---

59 Sanjukta Panigrahi did try to revive devadasi service at the Jagannath Temple, but was unsuccessful in her attempt; see S. Panigrahi (1997) and Julia Varley (1998: 268). Five other women—Banalata Acharya, Snehalata Pati, Kajal Jena, Haripriya Jena and Jyotsnarani Swain—had also applied to serve as devadasis at the Puri temple, seeking Parashmoni Devi and Shashimoni Devadasi's mentorship; their bid was also denied by temple authorities (*Times of India* 1995b: 9). The two maharis, who said they hadn't been consulted in the process, further refused to take on apprentices as they said it would condemn their charges to a life of penury: 'We are not getting food to survive. Why should we adopt others?' (*Times of India* 1995c: 9). Consider this in relation to L. Panda's report that devadasis once received support in the form of 18 units of land as well as 9.50 rupees monthly allowance for food expenses, though the tradition abruptly stopped by the 1950s (see Appendix E; also see Mohanty Hejmadi and Hejmadi Patnaik [2007: 32]). While Panda does not clearly state the reason, this was likely due to the adverse effects of anti-nautch policies.

Democratizing Dance

The reformation of Odissi can be seen as part of the larger movement to assert a modern Odia identity, a phenomenon which
began in the 1930s. In 'A Memorandum on Behalf of the People
of Orissa', a testimonial submitted to the colonial government in
the quest for regional statehood, the authors wrote:

> In the great Indian body politic, the Oriyas emerge as a
> distinct factor. They have a history of their own and are
> distinguished from others psychologically and socially,
> ethnologically and linguistically, educationally and eco-
> nomically. [. . .] Is not the demand of the Oriyas for union
> a popular demand? (Indian Statutory Commission 1930:
> 390)

As early as 1920, in fact, Sachidananda Sinha, in the Indian Legislative Council, had spoken of the need to form a state, as
Odishans 'are foundling children; alien from the more favoured,
because better recognized Dravidian races; alien even in the origin
to which their ancestry has been traced' (ibid.: 394). Thus the Odishan agitators appealed for cultural autonomy on the grounds of
their deep historical marginalization.[60]

The Odisha movement had started as part of the nationalist
struggle, but sought to retain its own regional identity in the postcolonial period through the resurrection of precolonial traditions
and inventions of neoclassical forms. Political claims around its
cultural distinctiveness rested on invocations of an ancient past,
symbolized by living traditions such as theatre, dance, storytelling,
and other modes of performance which embodied the memory and
history of a region long subject to domination by self-proclaimed

---

60 See Pritish Acharya's (2008) discussion of regional and nationalist politics
in Odisha in the 1920s. Acharya argues that despite the agitations that took
place in this period, the primary nationalist groups did recognize regional
claims put forward by a range of cultural constituencies, and that due to this
development, the goals of nationalist and regional movements harmonized
rather than developing antagonistically. See also Nivedita Mohanty (1982)
and Chandi Prasad Nanda (2008) for vital discussions of Odisha's political
struggles.

outsiders. Performance embodied the memory and history of a region which had long been subject to domination by self-proclaimed foreigners. Dance then served as a mode of indigenous reclamation.

In postcolonial India, the instruments of the state helped to convert Odissi into a truly national figuration, assigning it with a new value and import. This political dimension of dance is illustrated in President Dr Rajendra Prasad's inaugural address at the third National Dance Festival in New Delhi on 2 November 1955, where he expounded on the profound role of the art in the Indian imaginary:

> It is, indeed, a happy augury that since Independence we have been going ahead not only in the field of economic and material development but also in the sphere of fine arts.
>
> Music and dancing have been an essential part of the life of the people of this country. [. . .] How the art of dancing developed in course of time, how it took different forms in different regions, how it became a household affair under State patronage and how it came to be looked upon as a source of entertainment and of achieving physical and mental health—of all these things, I am sure, you are already aware. The vicissitudes of time and foreign invasions in the middle ages led the dance away from the generality of the people, particularly in the North where a social stigma came to be attached to dancing and respectable classes kept away from its so-called evil influences. How far this attitude was correct or proper is a matter of opinion, which does not interest us here. Our duty in the changed circumstances of today should be to re-establish the time-honoured arts of music and dancing in their proper places so that they may be looked upon once again as a means of integral development of human personality. Let not the fount of these arts, conceived in an atmosphere of meditation, manifested in the traditional fervour of devotion and later patronised by kings, nobility

and religious institutions, dry up in secular India, where religion is an individual's affair and the basis of society is egalitarian. [. . .] Far from being a means of entertainment for any particular class, these are a source of recreation and healthy growth of the people of all classes. We could verily describe the present times as the golden age for the development of the arts (1992: 17.459–60).

This remarkable speech, delivered at a festival where Odissi and Chhau featured in the programme, gives us insight into the state's position vis-a-vis the complex relationship between the dance and the body politic.[61] Indeed, the link to spirituality is not at all subtle; Prasad is overtly linking dance to the project of self-actualization through piety, and giving it an ancient halo; dance is also linked to a model of national kinship, an affiliation nurtured by the state ('household affair under State patronage'); further, it has hygienic, purifying qualities ('achieving physical and mental health', a route to 'healthy growth'). Prasad naturalizes the Hindu nation-state, and the reference to 'foreign invaders in the middle ages' repeats the myth of dance-as-degenerate in the period of Muslim rule. Yet, the purported injury delivered to dance in the past is quickly dismissed (it 'does not interest us here'). Instead, dance is to be redressed by the redemptive powers of the postcolonial state, and restored to its true place of nobility and glory ('Our duty [. . .] should be to re-establish the time-honoured arts of music and dancing' in this 'golden age'), though he makes a swipe against secular ideals ('Let not the fount of these arts [. . .] dry up in secular India'). Nevertheless, dance is now configured as public good rather than private property; since it belongs to 'people of all classes', it is the responsibility of 'the Indian masses' to propagate it. In this speech, we thus confront the valorized narrative of dance and directly encounter its framing as pedagogy and patrimony as configured by state forces.

---

61 See also SNA (1959: 43–4).

The State as Actor

In post-Independence India, the state became an important actor in the field of cultural affairs, intervening to manage heritage at the national and regional levels.[62] As a consequence, Delhi has become a flourishing cultural centre for all forms of Indian classical dance. Odissi's presence can be felt in organizations like the Sangeet Natak Akademi, India's national arts institute, inaugurated in 1952; Shriram Bharatiya Kala Kendra, started in the same year and dedicated to the 'preservation of the country's cultural heritage and the promotion of performing arts'; and Indira Gandhi National Centre for the Arts, founded in 1985 with the aim of nurturing 'the performing arts of music, dance and theatre in their broadest connotation'.[63]

One state project directly pertains to the formation of Odissi. In 1955, the central government's Department of Culture sought out scholars from all corners of India to take up research in the arts. D. N. Patnaik was awarded a grant for Odissi. His pioneering research was integral to Jayantika's reformation of Odissi dance; he brought with him a deep knowledge of the Shastras, the temples and the living traditions which shaped the dance, making him a key architect of contemporary Odissi. Patnaik's contributions to the dance aesthetic, encouraging the assimilation of Shastric codes, was one of the reasons that eventually led to the Odissi's recognition as a classical form by the SNA (Patnaik 2008).

Besides offering training and support, the state sponsors tourist productions where artists can demonstrate their craft to an increasingly international audience. Two of the best-known performance venues, which accentuate the association of classical dance with antiquity and religiosity, are the annual dance festivals at Khajuraho (held every March since 1978) and Konark (held every December since 1989). Both festivals draw tourists by conjuring

---

62 For detailed studies of this point, see Bina Agarwal (1990); Sudipta Kaviraj (1991, 2010b); Partha Chatterjee (1993, 2013, 1997); Rajeshwari Sunder Rajan (2003); and Nivedita Menon (2004).

63 From the websites of these organizations.

an exotic landscape, where 'the essence of various classical dance forms' are showcased 'against the spectacular backdrop of the magnificently lit temples', promising an unforgettable experience, for '[t]he classical extravaganza is a journey through eternal ecstasy' (Festivals of India website). These functions are funded jointly by the Government of India, the Departments of Tourism in Madhya Pradesh and Odisha, respectively, and local agencies. 'The novelty of bringing classical performing arts to the stage for urban audiences has been replaced by annual cycles of concert seasons and dance festivals in which "stars" perform,' Joan Erdman observes (1983: 264). Aside from these national platforms, the government made the arts accessible to the public via mass media by televizing performances, producing documentaries, sponsoring publications, and arranging free symposiums and concerts. The Indian Council for Cultural Relations (ICCR) organizes international tours to promote classical dance in a global field.

The central government provides grants to the regional institutes responsible for promoting culture, such as the Kala Vikash Kendra, Odisha's central arts institute, founded in 1952 by cultural activist Babulal Doshi, and the Guru Kelu Charan Mahapatra Odissi Research Centre. The Kendra is notable for nurturing Odissi in its early days, and has seen the likes of Kelucharan Mahapatra, Mayadhar Raut, Balakrishna Das, Kumkum Mohanty, and Sanjukta Panigrahi grace its halls. 'The first Basanta Pallavi was composed at Kala Vikash Kendra and other ones followed. The dance-dramas in Odissi [were] first conceived by Kala Vikash Kendra [. . .] Right from the All-India Dance festival at Puri in 1957 and thereafter at Chennai, Hyderabad, [and] Delhi, Kala Vikash Kendra presented lecture demonstrations and followed up till Odissi was recognized as a classical style' (KVK website). The Kendra works closely with Odisha Sangeet Natak Akademi, a regional branch of the national institute started in 1957 by the state's Culture Department. The Odissi Research Centre, established in 1986, encourages scholarship, maintains a performance archive, and imparts formal dance training.

The state has further institutionalized the study of Odissi at Utkal University of Culture and Utkal Sangeet Mahavidhyala in

Bhubaneshwar. National and regional dance scholarship schemes are in place to fund young professionals, while the Naveen Kalakar project showcases emerging artists. With the support of state agencies and corporate sponsors, Odisha hosts a gaggle of festivals: the stages at Konark, Mukteshwar, Devadasi Nrutya Mandir, Dhauli Mahotsav and Konark Natya Mandap, among others, host annual dance programmes.

Besides providing economic support, the state opens up opportunities to access performance venues, training programmes, platforms for artistic exchange and networking, and, of course, promises exposure to a range of audiences. In these ways, the state has taken over functions of patronage once held by royals, zamindars and other social elites. Like them, the state invests in cultural promotion schemes for political purposes rather than altruistic activism. Erdman recalls that 'patron-princes' once appreciated the arts 'as accomplishments that adorned their states' (1983: 263), and the same is true of the Indian government today, which deploys culture to project decorative, seemingly 'depoliticized' images of national harmony and patrimony, reveling in the triumphant pluralism of India's 'unity in diversity' (Subramaniam 1972; Tharoor 1997). This instrumentalization of Odissi as well as other classical forms augurs a return to the explicit reassertion of dance as a mode of spatializing the state, realigning its appointment to the realm of the national from the regional, and constituting dance as an accomplice to power. Such a manoeuvre further indicates how dance contributes to the construction of the 'imagined community' of India, through mobilizing performance and the articulation of a shared corporeal consciousness—extending Benedict Anderson's argument, which privileges the role of print literature in fulfilling this ideological function of nation-building (1991).

The heavy involvement by the state in the arts can be traced to the principles enshrined in the Indian Constitution and policy directives enacted under Prime Minister Jawaharlal Nehru in postcolonial India. The Indian Constitution adopted on 6 November 1949 proclaimed India a 'sovereign socialist secular democratic republic', stating that two of the government's fundamental duties are 'to value and preserve the rich heritage of our composite culture' and 'to promote harmony and the spirit of common brotherhood [*sic*] amongst all the people of India transcending religious, linguistic and regional or sectional diversities' (Article 51A, [f] and [e]). To reiterate a striking point, these are *fundamental duties*.

Nehruvian socialism promoted a belief in the state as the prime actor in the advance toward social progress (Sunder Rajan 2000: 62). Nehru's vision was an expansive one. A. K. Singh reports that '[a]s the chief architect of modern India Nehru left an indelible mark in all spheres—be it science and technology, be it arts and culture, be it the creation of democratic institutions, be it the creation of economic infrastructure or be it the strategy of development' (1993: 93). With his belief in democratic socialism, he subscribed to the thinking that 'the means of production should be socially owned and controlled for the benefit of society as a whole' (Tarlok Singh 1993: 32). As a result, planning schemes served as a cornerstone of the Nehruvian model, and aligned with the aims of cultural activists like Mulk Raj Anand, who had presciently urged the public in 1946—prior to but just at the edge of Indian independence—that 'we have literally, and metaphorically, to build a new India' (5). Planning by the postcolonial state, in this context, became a paradoxical gesture of practical utopianism: inverting its associations with a 'mechanised, regimented life', Anand suggested planning instead involved 'dreaming of a new world' as well as taking concrete steps towards realizing it (1946: 4; see also P. C. Joshi 1983).

This was certainly true on the cultural front. Local arts, including dance, became a common property, and expressions of regional particularity transformed into symbols of a pan-Indian heritage. 'The art of a people is a true mirror of their minds,' Nehru once said. Creative production thus was central to the government's national reconstruction project.

As part of this agenda, the state summoned dance to perform domestic diplomacy on its behalf, and it was the role of the Sangeet Natak Akademi to actualize this aim. Its supervisory function was articulated aptly by Justice P. V. Rajamannar at the 1958 Dance

Seminar: 'For the first time, one Central Body had to first ascertain the varieties of art forms and to correlate them, to bring out the essential cultural unity in what may appear to be a perplexing diversity' (2013: 7). The project further evinced the workings of 'Indian federalism as a method of accommodation of regionalism in India' (Bhattacharya 2005: 3) and showcased the official system's attempt to moderate the powers between 'the nation and its fragments' (Partha Chatterjee 1993).[64]

A speech delivered by Maulana Abdul Kalam Azad, Minister of Education, at the 28 January 1953 inauguration of the Sangeet Natak Akademi highlighted the importance of performing arts in the public sphere, and decisively annointed the government as the ideal managing agent for the country's cultural affairs:

> India's precious heritage of music, drama and dance is one which we must cherish and develop . . . Nowhere is it truer than in the field of art that to sustain means to create. Traditions cannot be preserved but can only be created afresh. It will be the aim of this Akademi to preserve our traditions by offering them an institutional form[.] In a democratic regime, the arts can derive their sustenance only from the people, and the state, as the organized manifestation of the people's will, must, therefore, undertake [. . .] maintenance and development [of the arts] as one of [its] first responsibilities (SNA website).

Looking at cultural policies in context of the nation-building endeavour, it seems that state programs implemented since the early days of Independence have crystallized these sentiments and priorities (Vatsyayan 1972; Narayan 2003).

In this scenario, it is no accident that the aims of classical dancers and the ideals of the state often coincide. Both state actor

---

64 On this point of the contest over power between regional and national entities, as well as various players among dominant elites in the postcolonial period, see Sudipta Kaviraj (1988, 1991, and 2010b) and Partha Chatterjee (2008, 2013). In the cultural sector, the dominant-subordinate class relationship has been well analysed by Rustom Bharucha (1993 and 2000). See also Bernard Cohn (1967).

and performing artist engage in a delicate dance: one to maintain hegemony, a goal camouflaged in the rhetoric of harmony; and one to enter a system of benefits and privileges while maintaining artistic independence. For dancemakers, the possibility for enacting a vision opposed to the state's is naturally circumscribed. As Erdman argues, 'artists' dependence on state patronage limits protest just as the state's dependence on artists for the creation and performance of works of art accounts for its recognitions of artists' demands' (1983: 261).

Many of the dance specialists I interviewed expressed the view that government involvement productively enabled the expansion of the arts in post-Independence India. Its cultural initiatives serve as an important source of mobility for them, in terms of facilitating both geographical mobility (such that they are able to train, perform, or teach across the country and abroad) and social mobility (so they can ascend through the ranks of class hierarchy and attain recognition for their talent in metropolitan centres).

Critically, however, cultural petrification has also become one of the enduring effects of the state's involvement in the arts sector. Erdman argues that '[c]entral government cultural patronage has proved to be a conservative force, endorsing continuity in traditions and affirming past accomplishments, rather than encouraging experimentation' (1983: 262–3). Nevertheless, as my interviews with dancers and choreographers confirmed, by performing its *fundamental duties*, the state has become fundamental in the scene of classical dance.

The Consequences of the Classical

The cultural resonances of this relationship between dance and the state are thus complex. Classical dance was born in the nexus of colonial and postcolonial modernities, and this position meant that it performed a nationalist aspiration in a circumstance where Indian culture was once castigated as 'primitive' by colonial agents and their Westernized Indian doppelgangers. The production and deployment of the 'classical' by the Indian state signifies a mode of asserting the depth and dignity of Indic culture in the face of

colonial onslaught . This seems to be why, despite its critical prob-
lematics, the idea of the 'classical' survives and continues to exert
its hold on the Indian public imagination (Chakravorty 2000).

The other side of the classical legacy, however, is the stultifying
effect of its impositions. D. N. Patnaik once lamented to me that
while Odissi has grown into a virtual industry, cultivating artists
of high caliber is a problem in the current cultural environment,
with the unrelenting focus on commercial entertainment and
spectacle, and the pursuit of dance by amateurs rather than
professionals (2008). Another reason it is difficult for artists to
enter the field, however, is the perception of a conservative impulse
in classical dance (D. Pathy 2007). Odissi is, by all standards, a
remarkable aesthetic creation; however, the obsession with purity
and tradition has arguably hindered its artistic flowering. Take the
Kala Vikash Kendra as an illustrative example. Its mandate
proclaims that it 'was established with a mission and focused its
attention to revive, restructure and propagate the enchanting
features of Odissi dance and music as well as to *reject current trends
of modernization*', attesting that Jayantika or 'Guru Kelu Charan's
style of Odissi with *purity and perfection* are the prime focus' (see
its website; emphasis added). Countless such examples abound
where such values attached to preservation are endlessly extolled.

One symptom of this desire for formal codification is the emergence of a textual orientation in the dance community. Despite an
innate heterogeneity of styles, standardization has become an
important dimension of contemporary Odissi. This tendency is by
no means isolated to one classical dance: as early as 1958, the
Sangeet Natak Akademi formally recommended the study and
adoption of the Western Laban system, 'so as to evolve an Indian
system of dance notation to enable us to preserve our tradition for
future generations' (SNA 1958a, Bulletin 8: 71). Along with the
authority accorded to the *Natyashastra*, multiple publications and
videos have been developed after consultations with prominent
gurus and dancers in the field.[65] As expressed by their creators, the

---

65 An example is the Odissi Research Centre's two-volume set, *Odissi Dance
Path Finder* (1995 and 2005). Ananya Chatterjea (2004b) extensively details

purpose of these instructional texts—which generally illustrate basic conditioning moves, exercises, steps and phrases—is to create a common foundation for practitioners and delineate clear boundaries for the form. While this may be a laudable aim, these writings inevitably suppress the sub-traditions that enrich and enliven Odissi. Pedagogically, such written, filmed and digital-media materials may complement the workings of the guru-shishya parampara; at the same time, they threaten to overshadow the authority of nonconforming styles. Since the normative Odissi framework largely follows Jayantika codes, with variations based on the instructor's training, it inevitably excludes those techniques that veer from its principles. Effectively, this constitutes an absenting of the material differences palpable and submerged in Odissi's paratopic world. By narrowly regulating Odissi's representations and by keeping its circuits of power closed to an elite of authorized exponents, the Odissi community is arguably marginalizing the talents of those who can take it in imaginative new directions.[66]

Conventionally, if a museum is a space that houses historical and ethnographic artifacts, it can be argued that the the bodies of Odissi dancers, too, are turning into museums of movement: they become places that preserve fragments of gesture and emotion, representation and spectacle, history and myth, somatically *in situ* (Kirshenblatt-Gimblett 1998). This project of monumentalization is supported by state agencies, who seek to ossify classical dance in the name of perpetuating 'everlasting' tradition (Hobsbawm and Ranger 1983).

---

the issues that arise with teaching from this manual. See also the DVDs *Odissi Dance Foundations with Revital Carroll* (2011); *Fundamentals of Odissi Dance* by Dr Rohini Dandavate (2013); Gayatri Joshi's *iGurukul Odissi* at gayatri.odissi.org; and the many tutorials on Youtube.com. For a nuanced analysis that critically situates Odissi praxis in relation to a specific idiom of Odissi developed by Raka Maitra, see Kiran Kumar's *Odissi Documentation Project* (2018) at: http://www.chowk.sg/odp (last accessed 22 August 2018).

66 The importance of creatively examining Odissi's codes, its form and content, has been outlined in a series of works by Leela Venkataraman (2002), Sunil Kothari (2003), Dinanath Pathy (2007) and Alessandra Lopez y Royo (2008).

The constant challenge and promise of composing Odissi, and escaping the museological imperative, is articulated well by Kelucharan Mahapatra:

> Our temple sculptures and palmleaf manuscripts remain our primary source of material. [. . .] What life force do we bestow to make them come alive? How do we make each posture melt into the other so as to create *a continuous flow of motion?* [. . .] Each posture has a tremendous potential which we must seek out. Along with the *bhangs*, we must pay equal attention to bhav raas and hastas to form a composite unit (in Sehgal 1989: 79; emphasis added).

In essence, we might argue this *continuity of the flow*, metaphorically and materially, is what ensures the continuity of Odissi dance as aesthetic.

Classical Dance as Contemporary Dance

In the postcolonial era, Odissi moved from being performed on outdoor stages, in the halls of temple, and in public processions, to the proscenium stage. Bringing the dance into the public sphere situated it as a sophisticated form of high art functioning as national property, accessible to all—though still imbued with a rarefied aura and marked by a pristine beauty that rendered it immaculate, protected against the vulgarizing and contaminating effects of the 'popular'. Odissi thus managed a key contradiction: As a 'high art', it retained the residues of elitism; as public spectacle, it became a democratic emblem of the nation-state.

Interpellated as 'classical' and tied to the processes of nationalization and democratization, the dance exited the spheres of the ethereal and esoteric, and entered the zones of secular public performance culture. At the same time, the nature of this nationalist project can be called into question: the state accomplished its nationalist aims at the expense of the local. In earlier times, just as Odissi was a hybrid form that had accumulated diffuse meanings and influences, just as it had absorbed highly localized forms—it was now coopted by national bodies for another political purpose, assimilated into the cultural canon representing the country's supreme artistic heritage. The dance performed 'nostalgia without memory':[67] ancient times neither experienced, nor directly remembered, by the postcolonial subject, but invoked through the body of tradition. As a postcolonial project, Odissi was made to answer to the demand for a golden history by a newly emancipated public. So Odissi *classical* dance paradoxically became a *contemporary* construction: a regional body made for the national body politic.

And yet: Odissi has always carved out a paratopia, a zone of alterity—however ephemerally—in which exceptional gender practices find expression, and multiple genealogies collide and collude. Its syncretic histories militate against the idea of total determination by strategies of the state, for it has dynamically contributed to fortifying, mediating and spatializing state power. Even political regimes that exercised prohibitions against Odissi realized the potency and danger of its latently subversive epistemologies. Odissi dance performance carries within it the imprints and traces of a contested past, incongruous yet essential to what Richard Schechner (1993) calls 'the future of ritual'—regional and national, Odishan and Indian—expressed through paratopic enactments that are sometimes spectral, sometimes elliptical, and sometimes lie suppressed, but remain a vibrant presence.

---

67 The phrase is Arjun Appadurai's and describes a cultural process that has taken root in the age of globalization (1996: 30, 77–8, 82).

Conclusions

TEHAI, UNFINISHED

In analysing Odissi's history, three interrelated narratives can be identified. One: that Odissi dance constitutes a paratopia, a space of alterity, for the enactment of extraordinary genders and the expression of a regional epistemology of the body. Two: throughout its history, Odissi's relationship with the state has been a principal determinant in shaping its artistic presentations and performances of extraordinary gender. I conted this is uniquely the case with Odissi and distinguishes the tradition from other Indian classical dances. Patterns in its history do coincide with the history of other classical genres, and forge an essential commonality with those forms. Yet, Odissi, I argue, epitomizes the state's deployment of and dependence on the cultural apparatus to embody, spatialize and perpetuate its power and prestige. Three: Odissi extended its choreographies beyond the realm of the aesthetic domain to participate in the formation of state power through its heterogeneous attachments to governmentality over its history.

Indeed, no matter what its permutations and peregrinations, the association with the state has always been paramount in Odissi's past and present. Diverse regimes effectively politicized the dance at different instances: by directly providing patronage; by regulating its choreographies and rituals; by sanctioning or censuring its performances of gender. Odissi, in turn, was fundamental to the state's enactments of power.

From the pointillist to the panoramic perspective, Odissi's trajectory reiterates the theme of 'choreographies of the state,' which has a double resonance: choreographies performed *by* the state, and the choreography *of* the state by performance. Government bodies have consistently sought to regulate Odissi's performances while the state's resources have been mobilized by the corpus of classical dance. If in the earliest moments proposed for Odissi's origin, the body of the sovereign became contiguous with the body of sovereign space, with statecraft joined to stagecraft, the politics of spatialization and the politics of nationalization converge in the postcolonial scenario, with the abstracted body of the state represented by the dancing Odissi body that is now realigned from the regional to national spectacle.

The special position held by Odra-Magadhi in ancient times reflected the exceptional status of the monarch in Odisha. In the medieval period, Mahari Naach, performed by the auspicious 'brides of Jagannath', exalted the position of the king as a deified presence. With the advent of the Mughal empire, Odissi dance became contested ground, and the persistence or destruction of the dance came to signify the power of the rulers who sustained or suppressed it for ideological reasons. Gotipua dance, which developed at the time of Mughal empire and propagated the message of Gaudiya Vaishnavism, assisted in the project of reasserting the strength of Odisha's regional identity. In the colonial period, the regulation of maharis by the British Raj underscored the regime's power over the cultural affairs of its subjects, and revealed the collusion of modern reformers in bolstering the project of state intervention. The situation was reversed in the postcolonial era, when the national government appropriated Odissi into the canon of classical dance as it sought to reify the country's golden past. The dance, initially reconstructed by male gurus, has become an avenue for the production of new modes of female subjectivity at the same time that it consolidates modern gender codes and marginalizes cross-gender performance. The struggle over its identity, structures and representations continues at a time when the directives of the contemporary state, the mutation of precolonial dance traditions and the political debates surrounding Odissi's histories have indelibly transformed its praxis.

As a polychromatic genre, Odissi contains deeply contradictory narratives, displaying how a dazzling ensemble of rival discourses, both progressive and conservative, can coexist in a single perform-ance tradition. Within its dance paradigms, Odissi has enabled the enunciation of what is extraordinary, creating the possibility of promulgating what may be otherwise prohibited in mainstream life.

With its unique discourses, Odissi dance also alters our under-standing of the relationship between gender and religious agency. In many strands of contemporary critical theory, the idea remains that religious agency is often an oxymoron, that agency disap-pears as the subject conforms to religious precepts, and that non-normative gender enactments are inhibited within religious frame-works, a predicament that can only be cured by abnegating religion and embracing secularism, or at least by privatizing religion and banishing it from the public realm.[1] In contrast to these general-ized claims, with Mahari Naach and gotipua dance we have seen how a religious framework might chart a legitimate space for extraordinary gender expressions. As long as the performer inti-mated a soteriological aim, the enactment of gender difference was permitted, even extolled and regarded as honorific, an analogue for the power and exceptional position of the state sovereign. Instead, it was the self-proclaimed secular governmental forces in colonial and postcolonial India that reorganized the discourse and perception of extraordinary gender in dance as a moral and legal problematic. And even as they exerted their leverage over Odissi by disciplining it, the very act of making dance an object of inter-vention authorized it as a practice replete with power.

In conclusion, I want to argue that Odissi dance continues to hold the potential of challenging dominant norms by articulating a vision of regional difference, especially if it mobilizes its histories of extraordinary gender performances—regardless of attempts at appropriation by nationalist or conservative political forces.

1 On this, see Ashis Nandy (1995); Ruth Vanita (2002a); Talal Asad (2003); and Saba Mahmood (2004).

Because Odissi's dancing bodies bring the past into the present, they centre a set of values coeval to modernity. Given factors such as the erosion of economic and political rights among marginalized communities, the ascent of the centralized state and the rise of a homogenized discourse of gender binaries in the era of modern nationalism, performance remain one of the only arenas in which regional histories and the knowledge of the local survive. Odissi as a paratopic expression brings to prominence a system of ideals different from, yet adjacent to, the normative standard, especially around gender and place, that, by making themselves felt in corporeal terms, put into crisis the philosophies and practices of Indian postcolonial modernity. For the paratopia is what is *beside*, and *besides*, the hegemonic.

In ruminating on the end of this project, I returned then to the question of gender originally animating this work, but could not arrive at a definitive answer: Does Odissi today truly offer a space to contest or subvert those cultural conventions that restrict gender autonomy in the public sphere?

I have offered one possible response, one reading among many. As we have seen in the bodies of its histories, Odissi's real power historically lay in its ontological flexibility, its ability to resist pure fixity in favour of flux. And I want to suggest, finally, that despite all efforts to reign it in, control it, suppress it, outlaw it, or contain it, Odissi has always exceeded state mandates and mapped a domain of alterity in its difference as a space for extraordinary enactments, sustaining an enduring aesthetic and significant regional paradigm of gender. In its kinetic biographies and orientations, Odissi represents a paratopic somatic, a poetic incarnation of alterity, a sensual body, a sensual world.

A continuous flow.

NOTES ON ALLIED FORMS OF ODISHA

Bandha Nritya/Nrutya/Nritta

Bandha Nritya refers to acrobatics and contortions of the body, often based on yogic *asanas*. It finds mention in both the *Natyashastra* and *Abhinaya Chandrika,* a fact which 'testifies [to] the prevalence of acrobatic dance' historically in Indian performance (Patnaik 2006: 68). Movements include: arching the torso and joining the hands and legs, so that the body turns into a rolling circle; bringing the feet over one's shoulders, using the hands for support on the floor, doing body flips forward and backward; and balancing a chain of bodies in pyramid and other formations. Performers of Bandha Nritya in Odissi are typically young children whose limbs are supple enough to withstand the stresses of such seemingly impossible manoeuvres which obviously require a great deal of training, skill and dexterity. By the end of adolescence, Odissi dancers generally cease Bandha Nritya performance. Aloka Kanungo is one of the foremost Odissi dancers reviving the practice by incorporating elements of Bandha Nritya in her choreographies (personal conversation, February 2008). For an example, see the videotaped proceedings of the 2003 SNA conference on Odissi, in which Kanungo demonstrates her choreographic approach (Session V: Gotipua), videotape no. V-6789, Documentation Unit). See also her informative 2006–07 article in the dance annual *Attendance* on this subject; and D. N. Patnaik (2006: 67–9).

Chhau

Chhau is an open-air performance popular in Bihar, Bengal and Odisha. Cultivated by royal patrons, the form and its three subtypes—Purulia, Seraikella and Mayurbhanj—are named after the regions of Bengal and Odisha in which they took root and each exhibits a style mirroring the mores of that particular area. Embracing both sacred and secular themes, Chhau combines elements of martial arts and masked performance, choreography and drama while merging Hindu and tribal tradition. Chhau's predominantly martial origins are reflected in its very name (*chhauni* means military camp, according to Sitakant Mahapatra) as well as in its intense regime of bodywork. Once performed by all-male troupes, it is now open to women as well. Festivals celebrating the art form are abundant across India. A government dance centre to support Chhau was established in 1960; see the official website at http://seraikela.nic.in/ (last accessed on 10 July 2009) for a description of their activities. For a filmic exploration of Chhau, see Jiwan Pani's 2002 documentary *Ang Tarang: Mayurbhanj Chhau*. Additionally, the SNA has extensive performance documentation of Chhau: see, for example, SNA (2001b). For more on Chhau, see Ghose (1941); the special issue of *Marg* (1968); Deo (1973); Devi (1980: 53–5); Khokar (1984: 182–93); Mahapatra (1993); Kashyap (1997); Pani (2004: 111–18); and Chakra (2009).

Geeti Natya

Geeti Natya, a form of musical theatre in Odisha, includes dialogue, songs and choreography performed by groups of male and female performers. Like other spectacles for the stage, the costumes are elaborate, designed to hold the gaze of the beholder. Unusual among the Odishan performing arts, Geeti Natya makes limited use of dance, even though a lot of movement is used for effect; its gestures are drawn largely from folk-dance patterns. Guru Gangadhar Pradhan notably transformed Geeti Natya by his use of episodes from the epics and elaborations of *abhinaya* and incorporated its characterizations and movement vocabularies in his choreographies. See SNA (2003: reference no. V-6861, Session II).

Jatra

Jatra, a blend of dance and drama, is a folk form immensely popular in Odisha and Bengal, performed by travelling troupes once comprising only men but now all genders. Jatra is also called Geetanatya/Gananatya/Geetavinaya (musical performance) or Loknatya (folk performance). The word *jatra* (or 'yatra') generally refers to mobile events, such as processions or pilgrimage, as in the famous Rath Yatra that takes place in Puri every summer. According to Manohar Laxman Varadpande:

> [W]hen the religious singing and dancing was separated from the procession and allowed to evolve into a dramatic form progressively, the Yatra theatre came into being. Historically, the Yatra as a dramatic form owes its existence to the Krishna Bhakti cult of Bengal. The dramatic poems such as Jayadeva's *Gita Govinda* and Babu Chandidasa's *Krishna Kirtana* (fifteenth century) set the background [. . .] Apart from these religious/mythological Yatras many other Yatras based on the contemporary social and political themes emerged during the beginning of the nineteenth century (1987: 194, 197).

Best known as the form historically responsible for spreading the message of Bhakti, entertainment is its main purpose today, and in that sense it is admired for its spectacular costumes, props, stunts, music and melodramatic form. Sharmila Chhotaray observes that Jatra is

> a composite art form or as a theatre of mixed means— song and dance, acting, and recitation [. . . and] a combi- nation of multiple performative forms of other Odia folk theatre arts that emerged in different times and has emerged as the most popular form of entertainment in rural Odisha. The synthesis of syncretic popular religious practices and literature of the elite and non-elite classes, several dominant forms of Jatra emerged and eventually got shaped into a separate dramatic activity. Jatra has been capable of depicting a range of diverse and complex

stories—mythology, secular themes, humor, valour of heroic characters and melodramatic events (2013: 43).

What is also important for the world of dance is that virtually every male guru involved in the modern revival of Odissi was groomed for performance as part of a Jatra group. While Jatra thrives as a vibrant genre, it also serves as the inspiration for many other modern theatrical forms, adapted for performance in the street and on stage. On the interconnected traditions of theatre in Odisha, see Tripathy (2007). For more on Jatra in particular, see Bhattacharyya (1978); Vatsyayan (1986: 136–46); Varadpande (1987: 193–8); Pattnaik (1998); and Chhotaray (2013), and. For pictures of modern Jatra in eastern India, see the BBC profile, 'India's Changing Theatre' at: https://goo.gl/gDK5ov (last accessed on 29 June 2018).

Music and Poetry

Music and poetry are intertwined deeply in Odishan tradition. Champu, a variety of Odia music, is epitomized in a nineteenth-century anthology of 34 dazzling songs composed by celebrated poet Kavisurya Baladeva Rath. 'Mastery of *Champu-Songs* is the final test of the art of any musical aspirant in Orissa,' notes Mayadhar Mansinha (in *Marg* 1960: 44). Chhanda is a regional style of vocal music based on poetic metre. Charya, a literary form of Buddhist origin, is a kind of poem made up of a quartet of stanzas (Kothari 2001: 98). Figures in the canons of Odishan literature whose work influenced dance include the Vaishnavite poet-saint Banamali Das, known for his devotional songs; Gopal Krishna Patnaik, whose verse extols the love between Radha and Krishna; Sarala Das, author of the Odia version of the Mahabharata; and Upendra Bhanja, whose songs espoused romantic and secular themes. Odissi music has its own system of raga and *tala* that originated in the region and its proponents are advocating for classical status, based on its layering of Hindustani and Carnatic elements —on this, see Pani (1984) and Sahoo (2009).

Pala

Pala is a ballad performance of Odisha incorporating *abhinaya*. From what I saw in the SNA 2003 conference documentation, it is best described as a kind of storytelling mixed with song and theatrical elements. Demonstrations by two troupes, led by Shankarshan Das and Govind Chandra Panigrahi respectively, showed a lead *gayak* (singer/narrator) accompanied by a group of musicians (comprising of *shreepalia,* main singer; *palia,* the chorus; *bana,* the percussionist; and *palas,* cymbal-players) who reinforce the main performer's story in a dialogic and interactive performance. In her talk on this subject, Sonal Mansingh explained that *pala* means 'cultivation' or 'nourishment' which enriches one's inner life. Pala acts as a form of social satire, an edgy commentary and critique, similar to Tamasha of western India and Nautanki of northern India. Its fascinating history as a 'socio-literary-religious performance' is described in Chandrashekhar Rath's talk, 'Aesthetics of Pala' (SNA 2003). Apparently, the form traces its roots to Mughal times, when the emperor Akbar created an imaginary figure named Satya Pir (literally, 'Saint of Truth') in his quest to integrate Hinduism and Islam. Every element of the performance utopically represents the cultural synthesis of Hindus and Muslims: performers paid obeisance to the Panchadeva (five deities, including the invented Satya Pir); the costumes patched together dual religious symbols; and even the sirini (uncooked prasad, or holy food offering) was designed to appeal to Hindus and Muslims. Traditionally, Pala performers never sat down, and, while most of the movements are attached to the ground, some are aerial too. Instruments were strictly limited to the manjira (cymbals) and mridangam (drum). Pala is distinguished for introducing Odishan poetry, especially Chhandas, to the public. A chief feature of Pala is its deployment of *bhava* in service of a transformative ideal; in a successful performance, both artist and spectator should be emotionally. Perhaps it represents the precursor of the transformative ideal in Odissi as well; at the very least, it shows the significance of *rasa* and *bhava* in forms other than classical dance. Dancer Aruna Mohanty, attracted by the open-ended nature of the Pala texts and their multiple elaborations, has used the structure of Pala performance as the basis of *Barsha,* her choreographic ode to the monsoon.

For all citations here, see SNA (2003: no. V-6874, Session I). For a detailed description of Pala, see Pani (2004: 71–6).

Patachitra and Chitrapothi

Patachitra are drawings and paintings done on palm leaves, while a related art, Chitrapothi, refers to illustrations limned on cloth. These fine-art traditions are a regional specialty. Depicting landscapes, figures and themes popular in Odishan tradition, they comprise lyrical drawings, sometimes left as simple sketches but more often filled in with brightly coloured pigments and hues. Cesarone (2001) and Das (2007) have written excellent commentaries on each form while Tripathy (2007) has explored the interlinkages between traditions of *chitrakar* (visual artist) and performance. The best-loved Patachitras and Chitrapothi art serves as elaborate pictorial representations of well-known poems and narratives, such as episodes from the *Geeta Govinda, Dashavatar, Amarushatakam,* Mahabharata and Ramayana, in addition to portraying rituals of the Jagannath temple and dance postures. Many of these illustrations are grouped together in decorative scrolls and manuscripts. Rare examples of these reside in the archives of the Odisha State Museum; some are published in its 2007 Platinum Jubilee catalogue. The village of Raghurajpur, located between Puri and Bhubaneshwar, is famous for its hereditary tradition of artists specializing in these visual forms.

Prahlad Natak

Prahlad Natak is a dance drama based on a mythic story from the Puranas and the *Dashavatar* about the deity Vishnu, as the half-lion, half-human avatar Narasimha, coming to earth to save his child devotee, Prahlad, from the clutches of his father, the demon Hiranyakashipu, who was torturing his son for his obeisance to the god. When Narasimha appears, Hiranyakashipu invokes the protection of a boon he received from the gods, a talisman which seemingly assures his immortality. Yet he meets a gruesome death by evisceration at the hands of Narasimha.

A performance of *Prahlad Natak* by Krushna Chandra Sahu and group is available in a recording by the SNA (2003: no. V-6885, Session XIII). The play is a gripping event, with colourful sets and costumes, the use of dramatic make-up, masks and props, athletic movements and arresting music. Prahlad, as the protagonist, serves both as a figure of identification and a stand-in for ordinary worshippers. The dance drama expresses a Vaishnavite morality that inculcates in its followers a belief to practice their faith without fear. Sitakant Mahapatra provides a good analysis of the form, observing that, in Odishan performance we find 'rare evidence of classical-folk-tribal continuum which is hardly seen in such profusion and intensity elsewhere in the country [. . .] *Prahlad Natak*, a play composed around 1860 in Odia and attributed to Raja Ramakrishna Deva Chhotray of Jalantara, reveals this rich continuum in its literary and performative aspects' (1985: 15). He describes it as a work '[u]nusual in its combination of Oriya and Sanskrit *shlokas*, of colloquial, light, and occasionally boisterous dramatic statements with songs based on classical *ragas* and well-defined *talas*, of using both the *Sutradhara* in the pattern of Sanskrit plays and a *Gahaka* as in traditional folk-opera' (ibid.: 16). These elements make it a truly hybrid form, illustrating the unification of 'high' culture and popular culture in Odisha.

The correspondence with Odissi is revealed less in the direct mode of presentation than in the correlation of themes. The *Dashavatar* item is an important one in Odissi's repertoire, and incorporates similarly dramatic *abhinaya* in its enactment of the Prahlad (and by extension, the performer's) devotion to Vishnu. Odissi, too, is syncretic, with its many sources, and like *Prahlad Natak*, travels along the same classical–folk–tribal continuum. In Odissi, however, the story of Prahlad's rescue by Narasimha represents just one episode among the ten depicted, but the intense mood (*roudra*, or rage) and robust movements (*tandava*, or vigor) characterizing the dance sequences in the play are mirrored in the

Odissi item. *Prahlad Natak* is considered a ritual performance, and the actors are required to follow orthodox rules of purity to maintain their eligibility as exponents of the form, much like Odissi's *maharis* (ibid.: 18). For more on this tradition, see Tripathy (2007).

Sahi Jatra

Sahi Jatra is a festival dating back to the thirteenth century CE. *Sahi* translates as 'local' or 'of the area' and the most well-known Jatras of this kind occur in the temple town of Puri. Held annually in honour of Rama, customarily it lasts for 15 days. This may seem unusual since Rama is venerated mostly in northern India; however, in Odisha, Rama is considered one of the incarnations of Vishnu/Krishna/Jagannath. His fight with Ravana takes centre stage in this performance, with Durga and Kali making appearances to restore the moral order of the world. Sahi Jatra is famous for its stunning theatricality, exemplified in a presentation by Udayan Cultural Academy at the 2003 SNA conference, which featured intricate costumes, masks, jewels and props. According to scholar Devadutta Samantasinghara, Sahi Jatra usually showcases solo dance performances based on religious iconography. Many movements exhibit a similarity to Odissi's—leaps and turns, the use of *mudras*, the body's *bhangis*. Rajkumar Mohanty explains the two kinds of dances the Jatra is famous for: 'The Naga symbolises valour of the Orissan soldier, while Medha dance [. . .] preserve[s] the classical dance blended with martial stunts and techniques' (2006: n.p.).

For visuals of both the dance demonstrations and Samantasinghara's presentation, see SNA (2003: reference no. V-6884). See also Jena (2008).

Sakhi Pila, Sakhi Naach, Sakhi Nata

Sakhi Pila, also called Sakhi Naach or Sakhi Nata, resembles the gotipua style in that it involves performances by boys dressed as girls, but, according to gurus who trained in it, they are discrete forms (Majhi 2008). One principal difference is that in the former, as the name suggests, participants are considered *sakhis,* or female confidants, of Radha. Intriguingly, Sakhi Naach seems to be a variation of an old South Indian devadasi dance with erotic overtones which has otherwise disappeared. In D. N. Patnaik's characterization, Sakhi Naach is basically a crude form:

> During the closing years of the last century, the Gotipuas came to be influenced by the decadent Sakha Nacha of the southern districts of Orissa. The Sakhi Nacha which was also performed by boys in female costume was an imitation of the voluptuous dance of the *devadasis* who belonged to the adjoining Telugu regions [Andhra Pradesh]. The *Sakhi Nacha* had a lasting influence on the Gotipuas (2006: 66–7).

Dillip Kumar Tripathy sheds light on the form's inter-regional aspects, remarking that Sakhi Nata dancers 'resemble the Andhraite girls in their make-up and costume. There is hardly any difference in dress style between the Oriya and Telugu girls living in Ganjam, Gajapati, Rayagada, and Koraput districts [Southern Odisha]' (2007: 18). He also detects a northeastern influence on *Bharatalila* in particular, ultimately concluding that 'the style of presentation in dance, make-up, costume and language of Assam, Orissa and Andhra Pradesh are mutually integrated to project a unified presentation style' (ibid.). The *sakhi* role is especially vital in theatrical presentations like *Bharatalila, Radhapremalila* and *Krushnalila* (Tripathy 57–60; especially photos on these pages and p. 109). Celebrating the Bhakti ideal, performers in *lilas* express their adoration of Krishna through dance and play, extolling him as the supreme divine power.

Shabda Nritya, Shabda Swarup

Once a lively Odishan tradition, Shabda Swarup (also known as Shabda Swarapata or Shabda Nritya), now survives in the lone village of Kumbhari in Bargarh district. Mohan Khokar (1984: 180) and D. N. Patnaik (2006: 85, 93–4) have suggested that Shabda Swarup once was part of the Odissi repertoire. The dance pays homage to aspects of the deity chosen for veneration—typically

Shiva, Durga or Ganesh—while 'a Sanskrit sloka pertaining to the heroic aspects of the deity is recited in tala by the drummer who also plays out [a] synonymous rhythmic pattern' on an accompanying drum. This seems to be in keeping with the meaning of *shabda*, or 'that which is heard' (Patnaik 2006: 94).

Khokar wrote of its status as '[e]ssentially a sacred dance, intended to be performed in certain temples' (1984: 180) in the *tandava* style. Vigorous and demanding, and anchored in the Shaivite tradition, Shabda Swarup has old roots: 'Reference to the dance is seen in the Sangeet Darpana of Chatura Damodara [. . . where] the author mentions *Nrittam Sabdachali* and *nanaviddhwam shabdanrityam* (or 'various kinds of Sabda Nritya') [Patnaik 2006: 94). According to Patnaik, who chanced upon one performance, it is 'so strenuous and emotionally so intent that [the] dancer falls into a trance at the end' (ibid.). Despite its strong roots, Patnaik discussed how even in 1958, when he first witnessed it, the tradition was losing momentum and therefore was lost to Odissi's repertoire. 'It is a regrettable affair that the dance has not been improvised for the stage,' he wrote (ibid.).

In Patnaik's time, Shabda Nritya was performed by boys and associated with a village in Sambhalpur district, but now girls have taken it up as well. The connection between Shabda Nritya and Odissi was also explored at the 2003 SNA conference. In the visual documentation I saw of Bhagavata Pradhan's female troupe's performance, there is a definite relation to Odissi in several movements and postures, with its fast footwork and turns, and the use of certain body postures like Alasya (the languid pose). The footage indicates the form to be largely based on abstract choreographies, although in one sequence an ode to Chandi is included, alluding to the Shakti worship so popular in the region. Indeed, Shabda Nritya was done to *bols*; song and narrative seemed to be absent. It seems to me that much of the Sthayee composition in Odissi's repertoire borrows from Shabda Nritya. Sujata Mishra and Bharat Giri also use elements of Shabda Nritya in their dances, although its incorporation is quite subtle in their work; see SNA (2003: no. V-6884).

Texts

While scholars have unearthed many other Shastric and textual sources for Odissi, i.e. *Nartana-Nirnaya, Natya Manorama, Sangita Muktavali, Sangeeta Narayana, Sangeet Kalpalatika*, among others, the *Natya Shastra, Abhinaya Darpanam* and *Abhinaya Chandrika* are widely acknowledged as the three principal texts that have shapedthe choreographic aspects of the dance (Kothari 2001: 94–5; Patnaik 2006: 81–5, 99–109; Patnaik in Gandharva Mahavidyala 1985: n.p.). For more on historical texts related to Odissi, see Sadashiv Rath Sharma, 'Some Notes on Manuscripts of Orissi Dance' in *Marg* (1960: 20–1).

Bharatmuni's *Natyashastra* and Nandikesvara's *Abhinaya Darpanam* are considered the most authoritative among these texts, since they connect Odissi to other dances in the classical canon and provide them with a common basis. The two differ in scope: the *Natyashastra* is a treatise that covers the entire spectrum of performance—from considerations of how the stage should be constructed, to costumes and make-up to choreography—while the *Abhinaya Darpanam* is a small compendium wholly devoted to hand gestures, head, eye, and neck movements, body stances and the steps, gaits, leaps and turns to be used in dance. Its date of composition cannot be fixed with any certainty, though Manmohan Ghosh surmises it can be traced to the thirteenth century CE (see his remarks in Nandikesvara 1975: 31–5). Because of the uncertainty of the dates, we cannot definitely establish how the *Abhinaya Darpanam* relates to the *Natyashastra*, especially as the limbic gestures in each are variably catalogued and deployed. Ghosh sums up:

> The only work which gives us a clear and comprehensive idea of the Hindu stage is the *Natyashastra*. Yet for the study of history of the development of ancient Indian theatrical art, this work, though very important in many respects, is not quite sufficient in itself [. . . The *Abhinaya Darpanam*] exclusively treats of gestures in a manner rather different from the *Natyashastra* [. . .] And an important feature of our text is its treatment of items like

postures and movements etc. dependent on feet, such as
Mandala, Sthanaka, Cari, and Gati [. . .] indispensably necessary for the complete understanding of Hindu histrionic
art' (in ibid.: 1).

Maheshwara Mahapatra's *Abhinaya Chandrika* holds a special status as the only known illustrated manuscript dedicated to '*udra
nritya*' (Odissi dance). Mahapatra describes himself as court-poet
under King Narayan Deva, and this is borne out by the special
sighralipi and *karani* scripts, historically linked to royalty and used
in the composition of his Odia-language work (Das 2001: 1.*iv*). As
is often the case with these kinds of texts, determining its actual
date is a matter of debate. From the original Odia manuscript, it
seems the work was authored around 1670 CE (ibid.: *ix*n1); D. N.
Patnaik has also fixed the date to the seventeenth century CE. (Early
on, he situated the text in the twelfth century but later amended
his position, based on fresh evidence.) But after studying the
Abhinaya Chandrika and considering the historical evidence, Maya
Das has plausibly suggested 1750 as an approximate date (2001:
viii–x). Like the *Natyashastra* and the *Abhinaya Darpanam*, the
Abhinaya Chandrika considers the conventions of dance movement, but its thousand verses are concentrated on the aesthetics
of Odissi alone. Speaking of the complexity of Mahapatra's work,
Das explains:

> The *Abhinaya Chandrika* of Mahesvara Mahapatra is an
> important contribution to the field of Odissi dance. The
> author has carefully studied and made use of earlier liter-
> ature on the subject. At the same time the author has not
> followed them blindly. He boldly sets his own rules for the
> dance he understands as *Udra Nritya* and propounds his
> own theory' (2001: *iii*).

In his two-volume commentary, Das elaborates on the text's direct
relevance to Odissi, and usefully reproduces a fairly intact Sanskrit
version of the manuscript which is, nevertheless, inflected by linguistic sensibilities borrowed from its Odia-language source.

Finally, the *Shilpa Shastra*, an ancient treatise on the plastic
arts (exact date unknown), is an underanalysed influence on

Odissi, given its privileged connection to sculptural form. From this text Odissi indirectly borrows the language for several of its characteristic *bhangis*, or body bends and postures, as actualized in sculpture: Samabhanga, Abhanga, and Tribhanga/Tribhangi. References to the typical stances of the deities and other archetypal figures, their proportions, dimensions, and iconographies are drawn from the text as well as from the archaeological heritage of Odisha.

TRANSLATION OF THE HATHIGRUMPHA INSCRIPTION

*This translation is adapted from R. D. Banerji and K. P. Jayaswal,
Epigraphia Indica, Volume 20 (1929–30), pp. 71–89. I have made
minor adjustments to the text for easier reading, but the bulk of it is
reproduced exactly. Ellipses and parenthetical text are from the original,
with the exception that the latter was in parentheses and italicized. I
have highlighted performance-related text in bold.*

(Line 1) Salutations to the Arhats. Salutation all the Siddhas. By
illustrious Kharavela, the Great King, the descendant of Maha-
meghavahana, the increaser [of the glory] of the Chedi dynasty,
[endowed] with excellent and auspicious marks and features,
possessed of virtues which have reaached [the ends of] the four
quarters, overlord of Kalinga,

(Line 2) for fifteen years, with a body ruddy and handsome were
played youthsome sports; after that [by him who] had mastered
[royal] correspondence, currency, finance, civil and religious laws
[and] who had become well-versed in all [branches] of learning,
for nine years [the office of the heir apparent] was administered.
Having completed the twenty-fourth year, at that time, [he] who
had been prosperous since his infancy and who was destined to
have wide conquests as those of Vena,

(Line 3) then in the state of manhood, obtains the imperial
coronation in the dynasty of Kalinga. As soon as he is annointed,
in the first [regnal] year [he] causes repairs of the gates, the walls
and the buildings [of the city, which had been] damaged by storms;
in the city of Kalinga he instals embankments of the lake and of
other tanks and cisterns, also restores all the gardens

(Line 4) done at [the cost of] thirty-five-hundred-thousands, and [he] gratifies the People. And in the second year [he], disregarding Satakamni, despatches to the western regions an army strong in cavalry, elephants, infantry and chariots and by that army having reached the Kanha-bemna, he throws the city of the Musikas into consternation. **Again in the third year,**

(Line 5) **[he], versed in the science of the Gandharvas [i.e. music], entertains the capital with the exhibition of *dapa*, dancing, singing and instrumental music and by causing to be held festivities and assemblies;** similarly in the fourth year, the Abode of Vidyadharas built by the former Kalingan king(s), which had not been damaged before . . . with their coronets rendered meaningless, with their helmets cut in twain, and with their umbrellas and

(Line 6) *bhinjaras* cast away, deprived of their jewels all the rathikas and Bhojakas [he] causes to bow down at his feet. Now in the fifth year he brings into the capital from the road of Tanasuliya the canal excavated in the year one-hundred-and-three of King Nanda . . . having been [re-]annointed [he while] celebrating the Rajasuya, remits all tithes and cesses,

(Line 7) bestows many privileges [amounting to] hundreds of thousands on the City-Corporation and the Realm-Corporation. In the seventh year of his reign, his famous wife Vajiraghara obtained the dignity of auspicious motherhood . . . Then in the eighth year [he] with a large army having sacked Goradhagiri

(Line 8) causes pressures on Rajagaha. On account of the loud report of this act of valour, the Yavana [Greek] King Dimi[ta] retreated to Mathura having extricated his demoralised army and transport . . . [He] gives . . . with foliage

(Line 9) Kalpa [wish-fulfilling] trees, elephants, chariots with their drivers, houses, residences and rest-houses. And to make all these acceptable [he] gives at a fire sacrifice exemption [from taxes] to the caste of Brahmanas. Of Arhat . . .

(Line 10) . . . [He] causes to be built . . . a royal residence [called] the Palace of Great Victory at the cost of thirty-eight hundred thousands. And in the tenth year [he], following [the three-fold policy]

of chastisement, alliance and conciliation sends out an expedition against Bharatavasa [and] brings about the conquest of the land [or, country] . . . and obtains jewels and precious things of the [kings] attacked.

(Line 11) . . . And the market-town Pithumda founded by the Ava King he ploughs down with a plough of donkeys; and [he] thoroughly breaks up the confederacy of the T[r]amira countries of one hundred and thirteen years, which has been a source of danger to [his] Country [Janapada]. And in the twelfth year he terrifies the kings of the Utaprapatha with . . . thousands of

(Line 12) . . . And causing panic amongst the people of Magadha [he] drives [his] elephants into the Sugamgiya [Palace], and [he] makes the King of Magadha, Bahasatimita, bow at his feet. And [he] sets up [the image] 'the Jina of Kalinga' which had been taken away by King Nanda . . . and causes to be brought home the riches of Amga and Magadha along with the keepers of the family jewels of . . .

(Line 13) . . . [He] builds excellent towers with carved interiors and creates a settlement of a hundred masons, giving them exemption from land revenue. And a wonderful and marvellous enclosure of stockade for driving in the elephants [he] . . . and horses, elephants, jewels, and rubies as well as numerous pearls in hundreds [he] causes to be brought here from the Pandya King.

(Line 14) . . . [he] subjugates. In the thirteenth year, on the Kumari Hill where the Wheel of Conquest had been well-revolved [i.e. the religion of Jina had been preached, he] offers respectfully royal maintenances, China clothes [silks] and white clothes to [the monks] who [by their austerities] have extinguished the round of lives, the preachers on the religious life and conduct at the Relic Memorial. By Kharavela, the illustrious, as a layman devoted to worship, is realised [the nature of] *jiva* and *deha*

(Line 15) . . . bringing about a Council of wise ascetics and sages, from hundred [i.e. all] quarters, the monks of good deeds and who have fully followed [the injunctions] . . . near the Relic Depository of the Arhat, on the top of the hill, . . . with stones . . .

brought from many miles quarried from excellent mines [he builds] shelters for the Simhapatha Queen Sindhuja . . .

(Line 16) . . . **Patalaka . . . [he] sets up four columns inlaid with beryl** . . . at the cost of seventy-five hundred thousands; [he] causes to be compiled expeditiously the King of Prosperity, the King of Monks, the King of Religion, who has been seeing, hearing and realising blessings—

(Line 17) . . . **accomplished in extraordinary virtues, respecter of every sect, the repairer of all temples**, one whose chariot and army are irresistible, one whose empire is protected by the chief of the empire [himself], descended from the family of the Royal Sage Vasu, the Great conqueror, the King, the illustrious Kharavela.

MAJOR TEMPLES FOR THE STUDY OF ODISSI

Bhubaneshwar

TEMPLE	DATE	DYNASTY
Shatrughaneshwar	Late sixth century	Not confirmed
Parashurameshwar	Seventh century, second quarter	Sailodhbhavas
Vaitul Deul	Late eighth or early ninth century	Not confirmed
Kedar Gauri	Tenth century, second quarter	Somavamsis (Lalatendu Kesari)
Mukteshwar	Mid-tenth century	Somavamsis
Siddheshwar	Seventh, eighth or eleventh century	Not confirmed
Rajarani	Early eleventh century	Somavamsis
Brahmeshwar	Mid-eleventh century	Somavamsis (Kolavati Devi)
Lingaraj	Eleventh century, third quarter	Somavamsis/Gangas
Bhaskareshwara	Twelfth century	Not confirmed
Jameshwar	Twelfth century	Jameshwardeva
Megheshwar	Late twelfth century	Gangas (Swapneshwara)
Ananta-Vasu Deva	Late thirteenth century	Gangas (Chandrika)

Hirapur

TEMPLE	DATE	DYNASTY
Mahamaya (Yoginis)	Ninth or tenth century	Bhauma-Karas (Hira Mahadevi)

Puri

TEMPLE	DATE	DYNASTY
Jagannath (Anantavarman Chodagangadeva, Anangabhimadeva)	Late twelfth century	Gangas

Konarak

TEMPLE	DATE	DYNASTY
Surya Deul	Late thirteenth century	Gangas (Narasimhadeva)

Kalarahanga

TEMPLE	DATE	DYNASTY
Jateshwar	Late eleventh century	Kesaris (Padma-Kesari)

Niali

TEMPLE	DATE	DYNASTY
Shobhaneshwar Shiva	Late twelfth century	Nagavamsis (Vaidyanath)

Compiled from D. K. Ganguly (1984: 60); Prithwiraj Misra (2000: 13); and Thomas Donaldson (1981: 35–46 and 2001a: 48–63); and author's notes on tour with D. C. Panda (2008 and 2010).

ANTI-NAUTCH AND PURITY ASSOCIATION STATEMENTS

[From Mrs Marcus B. Fuller, *The Wrongs of Indian Womanhood* (New York: Young People's Missionary Movement, 1900), pp. 137–8.]

Text of the 1893 Appeal to Viceroy and Governor-General of India and Governor of Madras

The humble memorial of the undersigned members of the 'Hindu Social Reform Association' of Madras, and others,

MOST RESPECTFULLY SHEWETH:

That there exists in the Indian community a class of women commonly known as nautch-girls.

That these women are invariably prostitutes.

That countenance and encouragement are given to them, and even a recognized status in society secured to them, by the practice which prevails among Hindus, to a very undesirable extent, of inviting them to take part in marriage and other festivities, and even to entertainments given in honor of guests who are not Hindus.

That this practice not only necessarily lowers the moral tone of society, but also tends to destroy that family life on which national soundness depends, and to bring upon individuals ruin in property and character alike.

That this practice rests only upon fashion, and receives no authority from antiquity or religion, and accordingly has no claim to be considered a National Institution, and is entitled to no respect as such.

That a strong feeling is springing up among the educated classes of this country against the prevalence of this practice, as is evinced, among other things, by the proceedings at a public meeting in Madras, on the 5th of May, 1893.

That so keenly do your Memorialists realize the harmful and degrading character of this practice, that they have resolved neither to invite nautch-girls to any entertainments given themselves, nor to accept any invitation to entertainment at which it is known that nautch girls are to be present.

That your memorialists feel assured that Your Excellency desires to aid, by every proper means, those who labor to remove any form of social evil.

That your Memorialists accordingly appeal to Your Excellency, as the official and recognized head of society in the Presidency of Madras, and ask the representative of Her Most Gracious Majesty the Queen-Empress, in whose influence and example the cause of purity has ever found support to discourage this pernicious practice by declining to attend any entertainment at which nautch-girls are invited to perform, and thus to strengthen the hands of those who are trying to purify the social life of their community.

1899 Social Conference Resolution

In the opinion of the Conference, the Reports of all the Associations show that a healthy change is taking place, in all parts of the country, in favor of the Anti-Nautch and Purity Movements, including in the last, the condemnation of the practice of devoting girls, nominally to temple service, but practically to a life of prostitution; and it entertains no doubt that public sentiment favors both these movements, as tending to purify our personal, family, and public life; and the Conference trusts that these efforts will be continued, and that a vigilant watch will be kept by the organs of Public Opinion upon all attempts to violate this healthy sentiment.

JAGANNATH TEMPLE ACT—*RECORD OF RIGHTS* (1956)

[From *Record of Rights, Puri Shri Jagannath Temple (Administration) Act* (Orissa, Act XIV of 1952), Part 3, prepared by L. Panda, Special Officer. Published in *Orissa Gazette Extraordinary* No. 205 (in English and Odia), Monday, 3 September 1956 (Cuttack: Law Department, Government of Orissa). Translated from Odia by Kedar Mishra and edited by Anurima Banerji. For the Odia-language documents, see also Priyambada Mohanty Hejmadi and Ahalya Hejmadi Patnaik, *Odissi: An Indian Classical Dance Form* (2007: Appendix 1, pp. 116–17), and a short overview of their contents in English on pp. 29–32.]

Part III

A record-of-rights and duties of different Sevaks, Pujaris and such other persons employed for or connected with the Seva Puja and management of the Temple and its endowments as in Form D of the Appendix to the said rules.[1]

66. Panipat

67. Mandani

68. Chaka Apasar

69. Mulia Suasia

70. **Binakar**

71. Darpania

72. Kotha Suasia

73. Mahabhoi

---

1 The professional categories identified in bold are described further in this appendix. They are notable as 'defunct seva', or temple services; on this point, see S. Pati (2017).

74. **Gitagobinda**

75. **Bhitara Gauni**

76. **Sampradanijoga**

77. Dayanmali

78. **Madeli**

79. Prasad Babu, Badu Mahapatra

80. Tatua

(p. 2; emphasis added)

*

Form D excerpts (original in Odia; translations below are not exact but summarize the general contents of each section, along with further explanations where relevant):

70. Binakar (veena players; veena is a string instrument)

Musicians play during the time the deities are about to go to sleep. Seva [service] has been discontinued for past five years, due to the broken veena.

Names:

Balakrishna Binakar

Lakshyana Binakar

Artratrana Mishra (the only working artist)

Mukunda Binakar

Ramachandra Misra

Shyamsundar Misra

Qualification: This is a hereditary service done by Brahmins.

(pp. 20–1)

*

74. Gitagobinda Seva (recitation of the Gitagovinda)

No one is doing this service because the previous servitors died without inheritors. Recently Jagannath Bhallav *matha* and Raghava Das *matha* [Vaishnav monasteries] have appointed Narayana Acharya of Baselisahi Puri to do Gitagobinda service.

Service: The person entitled to do seva will be given a sari. During the time of Chandan Lagi, the person will recite Gita-gobinda inside the Bhtar Katha [the wooden barricade].

Qualification: The service is done by a Brahmin man.

(pp. 39–40)

✶

75. Bhitara Gauni/ Devadasi

Nine servitors are listed in total:

> Kundamani Devadasi
>
> Kokilaprabha Devadasi
>
> Taramani Devadasi
>
> Basanta Devadasi
>
> Parashmoni Devadasi
>
> Binodini Devadasi
>
> Srimati Devadasi
>
> Subhasini Devadasi
>
> Indumati Devadasi

All are from Baselisahi except Indumati Devadasi, who is from Markandeswara.

Rules of Service:

At Sakaldhupa [morning offerings], devadasis will dance in the jagamohan [audience hall]. After Badasingara *bhog* [evening offerings], when the god will go to his bedroom, the devadasi will sing the Gitagobinda in a place near Kalahata *dwara* [one of the doors between the Garbagriha/sanctum sanctorum and the Mukhasala/porch]. When *sayana thakur* [joint image of Jagannath and Laxmi, placed beside Jagannath during evening rituals] will come, the devadasis will sing the Gitagobinda. They will continue until *sayana thakur* leaves.

In the month of Kartik during the time of Baladhupa [early morning prayer] they will sing. During the time of Chandan Jatra—the first 21 days they will sing *bhajans* [Hindu devotional songs] and the other 21 days they will do Snan-seva [i.e. sing during the bathing service for the deities]. For 21 days they will also dance on the Chapa [boat] of Madanmohan..

During the time of Rukmini Bibaha [celebration of Rukmini and Krishna's wedding] they will sing *mangala-gana* [auspicious songs] in the Lakshmi temple. When Lakshmi comes to the Bimala temple, they also sing *mangala-gana*.

On the day of Champaka Badasi [12th day after the new moon] they accompany the bride and bridegroom [i.e. Lakshmi and Narayan].

The day Lord Jagannath comes back from Gundicha temple they will accompany Mahalakshmi, to fight with Lord Jagannath. On the first day in Gundicha temple, the devadasi will do *nata* [dance performance].

In the month of Ashwin, for Shola Puja of Bimala [a 16-day puja], they carry out a patuara [procession] during Sakaldhupa. At Bimala's bedtime they sing Malashree [popular songs for goddesses]. For 16 days, only these women can enter the Bimala temple.

In the palace, they attend the procession during Kanaka [golden] Durga Puja. On the day of Pushya Abhishekha [coronation festival] they go to Mudirastha's [designated representative of Gajapati, the Puri king] house and sing *mangalagita* [auspicious songs] for him.

In the month of Phalgun, they perform their service at the time of Bhoga. On the 14th day of Phalgun they play Holi with Mudirastha in Mahalakshmi's jagamohan.

During Navaratri, they serve Durga inside the king's palace.

They dance during Snan Yatra [bathing festival] on Snan-bedi [the deities' bathing platform].

During the time of Nabakalebara, when the new *daru* [deity] arrives for coronation, they perform *hulahuli* [ululations]. (This is their most important service.)

Salaries: Every day they receive two Badakakara, two Sarakakara, and one Tatha Arisa [different kinds of cakes]. On the days they dance, they receive two extra Mathapuri [a type of sweet].

The Bhitara Gaunis have to dance on the 1st, 3rd, 6th, 8th, 15th, 17th, 19th, 20th, and 21st days of the month. On the other days, Sampradanijogas have to dance. On the 6th and 20th days, both the groups dance.

When they die, the the fire from the kitchen of Sri Jagannath temple will be used to light their funeral pyre.

Qualifications: They are appointed by the king. They cannot marry. They should not be *byabhicharini* [licentious]. If they are licentious, their service will be stopped. They can adopt a girl from a good caste [*pani sparsa jati*]. When they become adept at dance and singing, they can become devadasis. If they have any difficulty [with the performance schedule], then the Sampradanijoga can serve as alternative. If they do not work, they do not receive their pay. Other women can be employed as devadasis.[2]

Remarks by L. Panda, Special Officer: Earlier, the devadasis had 18 bati [units] of land in a village called Usunabarapada. But nowadays the land is no longer there. Annually they were given 9.5 rupees for their food. But there is no written contract for this.

(pp. 42–5)

*

76. Sampradanijoga

The names of 14 servitors, and where they are from, are listed:

Parbati—Baselasahi

Tara—Markandeswara

Ratan—Matimandapa sahi

Dukhi—Matimandapa sahi

Mohana—Matimandapa sahi

Labanya—Balisahi

Labanyahira—Baselisahi

Shashimoni—Kundheibenta

Haripriya (listed twice)—Kundheibenta

Fakiri—Balisahi

Buli—Kundheibhenta

Kundana—Baselasahi

Hira—no place listed

(pp. 47–9)

*

78. Madali (drummer)

Names:

Gopidas—no place listed

Brundabandas—Matimandapa sahi (remark: not working now)

Rules of Service: They will play mardala [drums] at Sakaldhupa procession; and at Chandan Jatra, to and from the procession onto the boat.

Their service is equal to Bhitargaini seva.

In the month of Kartik they play mardala in the early-morning Baladhupa procession. They also play mardala in front of Snan-bedi [deities] during Snan Yatra. They also play mardala during special festivals like Shola Puja for Bimala and during Dola Yatra [Swing Festival]. In every Rath Yatra they play mardala with *kansari* [brasiers] and *ghantua* [cymbal-players].

Salaries: They are not entitled to land. Daily they are given a small pot of rice, and monthly they receive 5.5 rupees. During special festival like Sola Puja and Chandan Jatra, they receive one packet of food and 3 units of Mandua [sweet dish].

Qualifications: This is a hereditary service. When a person becomes an adult and learns to play the mardala expertly, they can be employed as madali. Their employment can be terminated if they don't show up for service; others can be hired in their place.

(pp. 57–9)

WORKS CITED

ABUL FAZ'L. 1873[1590]. *Ain-i-Akbari*, VOL. I (Henry Blochmann and Henry Sullivan Jarrett ed. and trans). Calcutta: Asiatic Society of Bengal and Baptist Mission Press.

ABHINAVAGUPTA. 1997. *Abhinavabharti* (Anupa Pande ed. and trans.). Allahabad: Raka Prakashan.

ACHARYA, Pritish. 2008. *National Movement and Politics in Orissa, 1920–29*. New Delhi: Sage Publications.

ACHARYA, Rahul. 2001. 'A Systematic Analysis of Odissi Dance'. Narthaki.com, 21 October. Available at: https://goo.gl/f6gbuE (last accessed on 2 July 2018).

———. 2002. 'Mahari: The Divine Damsels'. Boloji.com, 6 January. Available at: goo.gl/DPR7An (last accessed on 2 July 2018).

———. 2003. 'From the Mouth of a Mahari'. Narthaki.com, 24 December. Available at: goo.gl/u6FKw7 (last accessed on 2 July 2018).

——— and Parama Karuna Devi. 2008. *Puri: The Home of Lord Jagannath*. Piteipur: Jagannath Vallabha Research Center.

AGARWAL, Bina. 1990[1988]. 'Patriarchy and the 'Modernising' State: An Introduction' in Bina Agarwal (ed.), *Structures of Patriarchy: The State, the Community and the Household*. New Delhi: Kali for Women, pp. 1–28.

AHMAD, Aijaz. 1999. 'Right-Wing Politics, and the Cultures of Cruelty'. *AKBHAR* (March). Text of Ved Gupta Memorial Lecture, Delhi University, 11 February 1999. Available at: goo.gl/f9724B (last accessed on 2 July 2018)

———. 2000. *Lineages of the Present: Ideology and Politics in Contemporary South Asia*. London: Verso.

AHMED, Sara. 2015. *The Cultural Politics of Emotion*, 2nd EDN. New York: Routledge.

ALBERUNI. 1964[1030]. *Alberuni's India*, 2 VOLS (Edward Sachau trans.). Delhi: S. Chand.

ALI, Daud. 2007. 'Violence, Courtly Manners, and Lineage Formation on Early Medieval India'. *Social Scientist*, 35(9/10) (September–October): 3–21.

—— (ed.). 1999. *Invoking the Past: The Uses of History in South Asia*. New Delhi: Oxford University Press.

ALLEN, Matthew Harp. 1997. 'Rewriting the Script for South Indian Dance'. *TDR* 41(3): 63–100.

AMARU. 1984. *Amarusatakam* (Sitakant Mahapatra ed. and trans. with Dukhisyama Pattanayak). Bhubaneswar: Orissa Lalit Kala Akademi.

AMBEDKAR, B. R. 2014. *Dr. Babasahed Ambedkar: Writings and Speeches*, VOL. I, 2nd EDN New Delhi: Dr. Ambedkar Foundation.

AMBROSE, Kay, and Ram Gopal. 1983[1950]. *Classical Dances and Costumes of India*, 2nd edn. London: A. and C. Black.

AMIN, Shahid. 2005. 'Representing the Musulman: Then and Now' in Shail Mayaram, M. S. S. Pandian and Ajay Skaria (eds), *Subaltern Studies XIII: Muslims, Dalits, and the Fabrications of History*. New Delhi: Permanent Black, pp. 1–35.

ANAND, Mulk Raj. 1946. 'Planning and Dreaming'. *Marg* I(I) (October): 3–6.

ANANDHI, S. 1991. 'Representing Devadasis: "Dasigal Mosavalai" as a Radical Text'. *Economic and Political Weekly* 26(11/12) (March): 739–41, 743, 745–6.

——. 2008. 'Women's Question in the Dravidian Movement, c.1925–1948' in Sumit Sarkar and Tanika Sarkar (eds), *Women and Social Reform in India: A Reader*. Bloomington: Indiana University Press, pp. 389–403.

ANDERSON, Benedict. 1991. *Imagined Communities*, 2nd EDN. New York: Verso.

ANONYMOUS. 1912. 'Deva Dasis'. *Star of Utkal*, 16 March, pp. 126–7. Reprinted in Priyambada Mohanty Hejmadi and Ahalya Hejmadi Patnaik, *Odissi: An Indian Classical Dance Form* (New Delhi: Aryan Books, 2007), pp. 34–6, 49.

APPADURAI, Arjun. 1981. *Worship and Conflict Under Colonial Rule: A South Indian Case*. Cambridge: Cambridge University Press.

——. 1986. *The Social Life of Things: Commodities in Cultural Perspective*. Cambridge: Cambridge University Press.

——. 1996. *Modernity at Large: Cultural Dimensions of Globalization*. Minneapolis: University of Minnesota Press.

——, Frank J. Korom and Margaret A. Mills (eds). 1991. *Gender, Genre, and Power in South Asian Expressive Traditions*. Philadelphia: University of Pennsylvania Press.

APTER, Emily. 1999. *Continental Drift: From National Characters to Virtual Subjects*. Chicago: University of Chicago Press.

ARCHAEOLOGICAL SURVEY OF INDIA. 2003. *Konarak*. New Delhi: Good Earth Publications.

ARONDEKAR, Anjali. 2009. *For the Record*. Durham: Duke University Press.

ASAD, Talal. 1993. *Genealogies of Religion: Discipline and Reasons of Power in Christianity and Islam*. Baltimore: Johns Hopkins University Press.

——. 2003. *Formations of the Secular: Christianity, Islam, Modernity*. Stanford: Stanford University Press.

——. 2006. '"Modern Power and the Reconfiguration of Religious Tradition": Interview with Talal Asad by Saba Mahmood'. *SEHR*, 5(1) (Issue on Contested Polities). Available at: goo.gl/VUUoJ6 (last accessed on 2 July 2018).

ATHAR Ali, M. 1997. 'The Perception of India in Akbar and Abu'l Fazl' in Irfan Habib (ed.), *Akbar and His India*. New Delhi: Oxford University Press, pp. 215–24.

——. 2009. *Mughal India: Studies in Polity, Ideas, Society, and Culture*. New Delhi: Oxford University Press.

AWASTHI, Suresh. 2001. *Performance Tradition in India*. New Delhi: National Book Trust.

AYYANGAR, P. S. Sangapani. 1958. 'Letter to the Editor—Dance Seminar'. *Times of India*, 29 April, p. 6.

BABAJI (Sachidanda Das Babaji). 2008. Interview with author. 7 March, Puri, India.

BABB, Lawrence. 1975. *The Divine Hierarchy*. New York: Columbia University Press.

BACHELER, Otis R. 2007[1856]. *Hinduism and Christianity in Orissa: Containing a Brief Description of the Country, Religion, Manners and Customs of the Hindus*. Whitefish, MT: Kessinger Publishing.

BAGCHI, Barnita (ed.). 2012. *The Politics of the (Im) Possible: Utopia and Dystopia Reconsidered*. New Delhi: Sage India.

BAILEY, F. C. 1970. *Politics and Social Change: Orissa in 1959.* Berkeley and Los Angeles: University of California Press.

———. 1998. *The Need for Enemies: A Bestiary of Political Forms.* Ithaca: Cornell University Press.

BAKHLE, Janaki. 2005. *Two Men and Music: Nationalism in the Making of an Indian Classical Tradition.* New York: Oxford University Press.

BAKHTIN, Mikhail M. 2009. *Rabelais and His World* (Hélène Iswolsky trans.). Bloomington: Indiana University Press.

BALABANTARAY, Suresh. 2009. *Sixty Four Yogini Temple Hirapur*, 2nd EDN. Bhubaneswar: Bahi Patra.

BALLARD, Chris. 2010. 'Synthetic Histories: Possible Futures for Papuan Pasts'. *Reviews in Anthropology* 39 (15 December): 232–57.

BALLHATCHET, Kenneth. 1980. *Race, Sex, and Class under the Raj: Imperial Attitudes and Policies and their Critics, 1793–1905.* London: Weidenfeld and Nicholson.

BANERJEE, P. 1984[1978]. *The Life of Krishna in Indian Art.* New Delhi: National Museum and Publications Division, Ministry of Information and Broadcasting, Government of India.

Banerjee, Projesh. 1982. *Apsaras in Indian Dance.* New Delhi: Cosmo Publications.

BANERJEE, Sumanta. 2000[1998]. *Dangerous Outcast: The Prostitute in Nineteenth-Century Bengal.* Calcutta: Seagull Books.

BANERJEE-DUBE, Ishita. 2001. *Divine Affairs: Religion, Pilgrimage, and the State in Colonial and Postcolonial India.* Shimla: Indian Institute of Advanced Study.

———. 2000. *Religion Law and Power: Tales of Times in Eastern India, 1860–2000.* New York: Anthem Press.

——— and Saurabh Dube (eds). 2009. *Ancient to Modern: Religion, Power and Community in India.* New Delhi: Oxford University Press.

BANERJI, Anurima. 2009a. 'An Intimate Ethnography'. *Women & Performance: a Journal of Feminist Theory*, 19(1) (1 March): 35–60.

———. 2009b. 'Paratopias of Performance: The Choreographic Practices of Chandralekha' in André Lepecki and Jenn Joy (eds), *Planes of Composition: Dance, Theory, and the Global.* Calcutta: Seagull Books, pp. 346–71.

――. 2017a. 'Dance and the Distributed Body: Odissi and Mahari Performance' in Mark Franko (ed.), *Oxford Handbook on Dance and Reenactment*. New York: Oxford University Press, pp. 413–48.

――. 2017b. 'Nrityagram: Tradition and the Aesthetics of Transgression' in Violaine Roussel and Anurima Banerji (eds), *How to Do Politics with Art*. London: Routledge, pp. 88–113.

――. 2018. 'The Queer Politics of the Raj' in Urmimala Sarkar Munsi and Aishika Chakraborty (eds), *The Moving Space: Women in Dance*. Delhi: Primus Books, pp. 81–101.

――. Anusha Kedhar, Royona Mitra, Janet O'Shea and Shanti Pillai. 2017. 'Postcolonial Pedagogies: Recasting the Guru-Shishya Parampara'. *Theatre Topics*, 27(3) (November): 221–30.

BANERJI, Projesh. 1942. *Dance of India*. Allahabad: Kitabistan.

BANERJI, R. D. 1931. *History of Orissa from the Earliest Times to the British Period*, 2 VOLS. Calcutta: R. Chatterjee.

―― and K. P. Jayaswal. 1933. 'The Hathigumpha Inscription of Kharavela' in *Epigraphia Indica, Volume 20 (1929–30)*. Delhi: Archaeological Society of India, pp. 71–89.

BARBA, Eugenio and Richard Fowler. 1982. 'Theatre Anthropology'. *TDR*, 26(2) (Issue on Intercultural Performance) (Summer): 5–32.

BARTHES, Roland. 2010[1977]. *Roland Barthes by Roland Barthes* (Richard Howard trans.). New York: Hill and Wang.

BARRY, Ellen. 2015. 'Sashimani Devi, Last of India's Jagannath Temple Dancers, Dies at 92'. *New York Times* online, 23 March. Available at http://goo.gl/PW9oXN (last accessed on 2 July 2018).

BARUA, B. M. 1938. 'Hathigumpha Inscription of Kharavela', pp. 259–285. Digital copy provided by DSpace, Digital Library Initiative, University of Delhi, India. Originally printed in *Indian Historical Quarterly*, 14, article NO. 25 (1938): 459–85.

BASHAM, A. L. 1959. *The Wonder That Was India: A Survey of the Culture of the Indian Sub-Continent Before the Coming of the Muslims*. New York: Grove Press.

――. 1967. *The Wonder That Was India: A Survey of the History and Culture of the Indian Sub-Continent Before the Coming of the Muslims*, 3rd EDN. New Delhi: Rupa & Co.

BEAMES, John. 1883. 'Notes on the History of Orissa under the Mahomedan, Maratha, and English Rule'. *Journal of the Asiatic Society of Bengal*, 52(1.3–4): 231–57.

BEDI, Protima, with Pooja Bedi Ebrahim. 1999. *Timepass: The Memoirs of Protima Bedi*. New Delhi/New York: Viking.

BEHERA, K. S. and Parida, A. N. 2009. *Madalapanji: The Chronicle of Jagannath Temple (Rajabhoga Itihasa)*. Bhubaneswar: Amadeus Press.

BEHRA, Rakesh. 2008. 'Puri Sahi Jatra'. FullOrissa.com, 23 April. Accessed at: https://goo.gl/82PCfV (on 15 May 2009). Link not currently active.

BELGAUMKAR, Govind. 2007. 'Matching Ease with Elegance'. *The Hindu* online, Friday, 9 March. Available at: goo.gl/rMmHVı (last accessed on 2 July 2018).

BELL, Catherine. 1992. *Ritual Theory, Ritual Practice*. Oxford: Oxford University Press.

——. 1997. *Ritual: Perspectives and Dimensions*. Oxford: Oxford University Press.

BENCH, Harmony. 2008. 'Media and the No-Place of Dance'. *Forum Modernes Theatre*, 23(1): 37–47.

BENJAMIN, Walter. 1968. 'Theses on the Philosophy of History' in *Illuminations* (Harry Zohn trans. and Hannah Arendt ed.). New York: Harcourt Brace Jovanovich, 1968, pp. 253–64.

——. 1978. 'On the Mimetic Faculty' in *Reflections: Essays, Aphorisms, Autobiographical Writings* (E. Jephcott trans. and P. Demetz ed.). New York: Harcourt Brace Jovanovich.

BENTON, Lauren. 2000. 'Colonial Law and Cultural Difference: Jurisdictional Politics and the Formation of the Colonial State'. *Comparative Studies in Society and History*, 41(3): 563–88.

——, and John Muth. 2000. 'On Cultural Hybridity: Interpreting Colonial Authority and Performance'. *Journal of Colonialism and Colonial History* 1(1): n.p.

BERGSON, Henri. 1990. *Matter and Memory* (N. M. Paul and W. S. Palmer trans). Cambridge: MIT Press.

BERNIER, Francois. 1916[167?]. *Travels in the Mogul Empire, 1656–1668*, 2nd EDN (Archibald Constable trans. and Vincent Smith ed.). London: Oxford University Press.

BHABHA, Homi. 1994. *The Location of Culture*. London: Routledge.

Bhagavata Purana Manuscript. Orissa, India. MS.13 [17–18c.], Spencer Collection, New York Public Library.

Bhagavad Purana. 2006. (Ramesh Menon trans.). New Delhi: Rupa Books.

BHARATI, Agehananda. 1963. 'Pilgrimage in the Indian Tradition'. *History of Religions*, 3(1) (Summer): 135–67.

BHARATMUNI. 1996. *Natyashastra* (Adya Rangacharya trans.). New Delhi: Munshiram Manoharlal Publishers.

——. 2007[1967]. *Natyashastra, Ascribed to Bharata-Muni (A Treatise on Ancient Indian Dramaturgy and Histrionics)*, VOLS 1–4 (Manmohan Ghosh ed. and trans.). Varanasi: Chowkhamba Sanskrit Series Office.

BHARGAVA, Rajeev. 1994. 'Giving Secularism its Due'. *Economic and Political Weekly*, 29(28) (9 July): 1784–91.

——. 1995. 'The Secular Imperative'. *India International Centre Quarterly* ('Secularism in Crisis' issue), 22(1) (Spring): 3–16.

——. 2006. 'The Distinctiveness of Indian Secularism' in T. N. Srinivasan (ed.), *The Future of Secularism*. Delhi: Oxford University Press, pp. 20–53.

—— (ed.). 2005. *Secularism and Its Critics*. New Delhi: Oxford University Press.

BHARUCHA, Rustom. 1993. *Theatre and the World: Essays on Performance and the Politics of Culture*. New York: Routledge.

——. 1997. *Chandralekha: Woman, Dance, Resistance*. New Delhi: HarperCollins.

——. 2000. *The Politics of Cultural Practice: Thinking Through Theatre in an Age of Globalization*. Hanover: University Press of New England.

——. 2014. *Terror and Performance*. New York: Routledge.

BHASKAR. 1973. Interview-demonstration with Bhaskar. Interviewer: Walter Terry. Sound cassette. Recorded 22 July 1963 at Jacob's Pillow, Lee, Massachusetts. Item call no. *MGZTC 3-296 (60 min.), Jerome Robbins Dance Division, New York Public Library for the Performing Arts, New York, USA.

BHATTACHARJI, Sukumari. 1987. 'Prostitution in Ancient India'. *Social Scientist*, 15(2) (February): 32–61.

BHATTACHARYA, Harihar. 2005. 'Federalism and Regionalism in India: Institutional Strategies and Political Accommodation of Identity'. *Heidelberg Papers in South Asian and Comparative Politics, Working Paper No. 27* (12 May). Available at: https://goo.gl/faeDhR (last accessed on 2 July 2018)

BHATTACHARYYA, Hari Mohan. 1994. *Jaina Logic and Epistemology*. Calcutta: K. P. Bagchi and Company.

BHAVNANI, Enakshi. 1965. *The Dance in India: The Origin and History, Foundations, the Art and Science of the Dance in India—Classical, Folk and Tribal*. Bombay: Taraporevala Sons and Co. Private Ltd.

BIRCH, Edward A. 1878. *Annual Report of Hazareebagh Lock-Hospital to Cantonment Magistrate, Hazareebagh, January 8*. Included in *Reports by the Commissioners of the Patna, Presidency, Rajshahye and Cooch Behar and Chota Nagpore Divisions on the Working of the Cantonment Lock-Hospitals in their Respective Divisions for the Year 1877*. Medical Resolution, July 17, 1878, Darjeeling. By Order of Lieutenant-Governor of Bengal, Colman Macaulay, Under-Secretary to the Government of Bengal, July 24, 1878. Item no. V/24/2292, India Office Records, British Library, London, UK.

BISWAS, Sharmila. 2003–04. 'The Maharis of Orissa' in Shanta Serbjeet Singh (ed.), *Attendance: The Dance Annual of India 2003–04*. New Delhi: Ekah-Printways, pp. 58–65.

———. 2008. Interview with author. Kolkata, India, 14 February.

———. 2009. *Knowing Odissi*. Kolkata: Odissi Vision and Movement Centre.

BLOCKER, Jane. 1999. *Where is Ana Mendieta? Identity, Performativity, Exile*. Durham: Duke University Press, p. 134.

BONER, Alice, Sadasiva Rath Sarma and Bettina Bäumer. 2000[1982]. *Vastusutra Upanisad: The Essence of Form in Sacred Art*. Delhi: Alice Boner Foundation.

BOSE, Mandakranta. 1991. *Movement and Mimesis: The Idea of Dance in the Sanskritic Tradition*. Dordrecht: Kluwer Academic Publishers.

———. 1992. 'Categories of Dance: *Bandha* and *Anibandha*' in Jonathan Katz (ed.), *The Traditional Indian Theory and Practice of Music and Dance* (conference proceedings). Leiden: E. J. Brill, pp. 211–22.

———. 2001. *Speaking of Dance: The Indian Critique*. New Delhi: D. K. Printworld.

BOSE, Nirmal Kumar. 1932. *Canons of Orissan Architecture*. Calcutta: Prabasi Press.

BOURDIEU, Pierre. 1977. *Outline of a Theory of Practice* (Richard Nice trans.). Cambridge: Cambridge University Press.

BRADY, Sara. 2012. *Performance, Politics, and the War on Terror: Whatever It Takes*. New York: Palgrave Macmillan.

BRIGHENTI, Francesco. 2001. *Sakti Cult in Orissa*. New Delhi: D. K. Printworld.

BURCHELL, Graham, Colin Gordon and Peter Miller (eds). 1991. *The Foucault Effect: Studies in Governmentality*. Chicago: University of Chicago Press.

BUTLER, Judith. 1988. 'Performative Acts and Gender Constitution: An Essay in Phenomenology and Feminist Theory'. *Theatre Journal*, 40(4): 519–31.

———. 1990. *Gender Trouble: Feminism and the Subversion of Identity*. New York: Routledge.

———. 1993. *Bodies That Matter: On the Discursive Limits of 'Sex'*. New York: Routledge.

——— and Gayatri Chakravorty Spivak. 2007. *Who Sings the Nation-State? Language, Politics, Belonging*. Calcutta: Seagull Books.

C.S.R. [Sarvepalli Radhakrishnan]. 1921. 'Gandhi and Tagore'. *Calcutta Review* (October): 14–29.

CARNAC TEMPLE, SIR RICHARD. 1903[1688]. *A Geographical Account of Countries Round the Bay of Bengal, 1669–1679, by Thomas Bowrey*. Cambridge: Cambridge University Press and the Hakluyt Society.

CARROLL, Revital. 2011. *Odissi Dance Foundations with Revital Carroll*. DVD.

CARTER, Paul. 1994. *The Lie of the Land*. London: Faber and Faber.

———. 2004. *Material Thinking: The Theory and Practice of Creative Research*. Carlton: Melbourne University Publishing.

CASSELS, Nancy Gardner. 1988. *Religion and Pilgrim Tax Under the Company Raj*. New Delhi: Manohar.

CASTALDI, Francesca. 2006. *Choreographing African Identities: Negritude and the National Ballet of Senegal*. Urbana: University of Illinois Press.

CESARONE, Bernard. 2001. *Patachitras of Orissa: An Illustration of Some Common Themes*. Available at: goo.gl/au6XsL (last accessed on 2 July 2018).

CHAKRA, Shyamhari (ed.). 2010. *Odissi Annual*. Bhubaneswar: Timepass.

CHAKRABARTY, Dipesh. 2000. *Provincializing Europe: Postcolonial Thought and Historical Difference*. Princeton: Princeton University Press.

———. 2002. *Habitations of Modernity: Essays in the Wake of Subaltern Studies*. Chicago: University of Chicago Press.

CHAKRABORTHY, Kakolee. *Women as Devadasis*. New Delhi: Deept and Deep Publications, 2000.

CHAKRAVARTI, Babu M. M. 1897. 'Notes on the Language and Literature of Orissa, Parts I and II'. *Journal of the Asiatic Society of Bengal*, 66.1(4) (December): 317–48.

CHAKRAVARTI, Babu Mon Mohan. 1893. 'Uriya inscriptions of the 15th and 16th centuries'. *Journal of the Asiatic Society of Bengal* 62 (Part 1) (History, Antiquities, etc.) (1–2): 88–103. Available at: https://goo.gl/vWVqr1 (last accessed on 25 August 2018).

CHAKRAVARTI, Uma. 2018. 'The Devadasi as an Archaic Historical Artefact: Culture and Nation in a Transitional Moment' in Urmimala Sarkar Munsi and Aishika Chakraborty (eds), *The Moving Space: Women in Dance*. Delhi: Primus Books, pp. 23–47.

CHAKRAVORTY, Pallabi. 2000. 'From Interculturalism to Historicism: Reflections on Classical Indian Dance'. *Dance Research Journal*, 32(2) (Winter): 100–11.

———. 2008. *Bells of Change: Kathak Dance, Women and Modernity in India*. Calcutta: Seagull Books.

—— and Scott Kugle (eds). 2009. *Performing Ecstasy: The Poetics and Politics of Religion in India*. Delhi: Manohar.

CHANCHREEK, K. L. and Mahesh Jain. 2004. *Jaina Social Life (Ancient and Medieval India)*. New Delhi: Shree Publishers.

CHAND, Gayatri. 2012. *Guru Debaprasad Das: Icon of Odissi*. Bhubaneshwar: AB Imaging and Prints.

CHAND, Soma. 2005. 'Orissan Temple Architecture'. *Orissa Review* (July): 49–51.

CHANDRA, Bipen. 2009. *Essays on Colonialism*. New Delhi: Orient Blackswan.

CHANDRA, Sudhir. 1992. *The Oppressive Present: Literature and Social Consciousness in Colonial India*. New Delhi: Oxford University Press.

CHANDRALEKHA. 1980. 'The Militant Origins of Indian Dance'. *Social Scientist*, 9(2/3) (September–October): 80–5.

———. 2003. 'Reflections on New Directions in Indian Dance' in Sunil Kothari (ed.), *New Directions in Indian Dance*. Mumbai: Marg Publications, pp. 50–8.

CHANDRIKHA, G. 2009. 'Of Men, Women, and Morals: Gender, Politics and Social Reform in Colonial South India'. *Intersections: Gender and*

Sexuality in Asia and the Pacific, 22 (October). Available at: goo.gl/UENzNm (last accessed on 2 July 2018).

CHATTERJEE, Amal. 1998. *Representations of India, 1740–1840*. New York: St. Martin's Press.

CHATTERJEE, Amarnath (A. N). 1992. 'Gaudiya Vaisnavism' (interview) in Steven Rosen (ed.), *Vaisnavism: Contemporary Scholars Discuss the Gaudiya Tradition*. Brooklyn: FOLK Books, pp. 7–17.

CHATTERJEA, Ananya. 2004a. *Butting Out: Reading Resistive Choreographies Through Works by Jawole Willa Jo Zollar and Chandralekha*. Middletown: Wesleyan University Press.

———. 2004b. 'Contestations' in Alexandra Carter (ed.), *Rethinking Dance History*. London: Routledge, pp. 143–56.

———. 2004c. 'In Search of a Secular in Contemporary Indian Dance: A Continuing Journey'. *Dance Research Journal*, 36(2) (Winter): 102–16.

CHATTERJEE, Partha. 1986. *Nationalist Thought and the Colonial World: A Derivative Discourse*. Minneapolis: University of Minnesota Press.

———. 1993. *The Nation and Its Fragments*. Princeton: Princeton University Press.

———. 1998. 'Caste and Subaltern Consciousness' in Ranajit Guha (ed.), *Subaltern Studies VI: Writings on South Asian History and Society*. New Delhi: Oxford University Press, pp. 169–209.

———. 2008. 'Democracy and Economic Transformation in India'. *Economic and Political Weekly*, Special Article (9 April): 53–62.

———. 2010 [1991]. 'History and the Nationalization of Hinduism' in *Empire and Nation: Selected Essays*. New York: Columbia University Press, pp. 59–90.

———. 2013. *Lineages of Political Society: Studies in Postcolonial Democracy*. New York: Columbia University Press.

——— (ed.). 1997. *State and Politics in India*. Delhi: Oxford University Press.

CHATTERJEE, Ratnabali. 1992. 'The Queens' Daughters: Prostitutes as an Outcast Group in Colonial India'. Report no. R 1992: 8. Bergen: Department of Social Science and Development, Chr. Michelsen Institute.

CHATTERJEE, Santosh Kumar. 1945. *Devadasi (Temple Dancer)*. Calcutta: Book House.

CHATTERJEE, Sanjeev. 2002. *Living Dance*. USA, colour, 13 mins, VHS. Thoughtbox.

CHATTERJI, Angana P. 2009. *Violent Gods: Hindu Nationalism in India's Present, Narratives From Orissa*. New Delhi: Three Essays Collective.

CHATTOPADHYAYA, B. D. 1985. 'Political Processes and Structures of Polity in Medieval India: Problems of Perspective'. *Social Scientist*, 13(6) (June): 3–34.

———. 2010. 'Festivals as Ritual: An Exploration into the Convergence of Ritulas and State in Early India' in M. Kitts, B. Schneidmuller, G. Schwedler and E. Tounten, H. Kulke and U. Skoda (eds), *State, Power and Violence*. Wiesbaden: Harrassowitz Verlag, pp. 627–645.

——— (ed.). 2003. *Studying Early India: Archaeology, Texts, and Historical Issues*. New Delhi: Permanent Black.

CHATURVEDI, B. M. 1996. *Some Unexplored Aspects of the Rasa Theory* (P. Sri Ramachandrudu trans.). Delhi: Vidyanidhi Prakashan.

CHAULEY, G. C. 2004. *Monumental Heritage of Orissa* (*Art, Architecture, Culture and Conservation*). Delhi: Book India.

CHAWLA, Anil. 2002. 'Devadasis: Sinners or Sinned Against? An Attempt to Look at the Present Status of Devadasis'. Samarth Bharat report, 28 August. Available at: http://www.samarthbharat.com (last accessed on 2 July 2018).

CHEAH, Phen, David Fraser and Judith Grbich (eds). 1996. *Thinking Through the Body of the Law*. New York: New York University Press.

CHERIAN, Anita. 2007. 'Imagining a National Theatre: The First Drama Seminar Report'. *Sangeet Natak* 41(2): 15–49.

———. 2009. 'Institutional Maneuvers, Nationalizing Performance, Delineating Genre: Reading the Sangeet Natak Akademi Reports, 1953–1959'. *Third Frame: Literature, Culture and Society*, 2(3) (July–September): 32–60.

CHHOTARAY, Sharmila. 2013. 'Jatra Theatre as a Culture Industry: A Study of Popular Theatre from Eastern India'. *Indian Sociological Society E-Journal* 1(2)–2(1) (January–June, July–December): 43–73.

CHOUDHURY, Bidut Kumari. 1999. *Odissi Dance, Part 1*. Bhubaneswar: Chandra Sekhar Mohapatra.

CHOUDHURY, Janmejay. 2008. 'Purusottama-Jagannath and Purusottam-Puri: Its Origin and Antiquity'. *Orissa Review* (July): 5–11.

CITARASTI, Ileana. 1987. 'Devadasis of the Jagannath Temple: Precursors of Odissi Music and Dance'. *Sruti*, 33–34 (June–July): 517.

———. 2001. *The Making of a Guru: Kelucharan Mohapatra, His Life and Times*. New Delhi: Manohar.

———. 2011. 'Soldiers' Dance'. *The Telegraph* online (Calcutta edition), Monday, 29 August. Available at: goo.gl/zozY25 (last accessed on 2 July 2018).

———. 2012. *Traditional Martial Practices in Odisha*. Gurgaon: Shubhi Publications.

———. 2014. 'The Rare Documents of Jayantika'. *Nartanam* 14(4) (October–December): 16–26.

COHN, Bernard. 1967. 'Regions Subjective and Objective: Their Relation to the Study of Modern Indian History and Society' in Robert Crane (ed.), *Regions and Regionalism in South Asian Studies: An Exploratory Study; Papers Presented at a Symposium Held at Duke University, April 7–9, 1966*. Durham, NC: Duke University Press, pp. 3–37.

———. 1996. *Colonialism and Its Forms of Knowledge*. Princeton, NJ: Princeton University Press.

COLEMAN, F. M. 1899. *Typical Pictures of Indian Natives*, 6th EDN. Bombay: Times of India Office and Thacker and Co., Ltd.

CONNERTON, Paul. 1989. 'Bodily Practices' in *How Societies Remember*. Cambridge: Cambridge University Press, pp. 72–115.

COOMARASWAMY, Ananda K. 1918. *The Dance of Siva: Fourteen Indian Essays*. New York: Sunwise Turn.

———. 1985[1924]. *The Dance of Siva: Essays on Indian Art and Culture*. New York: Dover.

———. 1934. *The Transformation of Nature in Art*. Cambridge: Harvard University Press.

COORLAWALA, Uttara Asha. 1994. 'Classical and Contemporary Indian Dance: Overview, Criteria, and a Choreographic Analysis'. PhD thesis, New York University.

———. 1996. 'Darshan and Abhinaya: An Alternative to the Male Gaze'. *Dance Research Journal*, 28(1) (Spring): 19–27.

———. 2004. 'It Matters for Whom You Dance: Audience Participation in Rasa Theory'. *Dance in South Asia: New Approaches, Politics and Aesthetics* (3 March 2002). Swarthmore: Swarthmore College, pp. 61–6.

——. 2005. 'The Birth of Bharatanatyam and the Sanskritized Body' in Avanthi Meduri (ed.), *Rukmini Devi Arundale (1904–1986): A Visionary Architect of Indian Culture and the Performing Arts*. New Delhi: Motilal Banarsidass, pp. 173–194.

——. 2009. 'Dance: Of Intersecting Circles'. *Pravasi Bharatiya: Connecting India with its Diaspora*, 2(1) (January): 23–9.

CORT, John. 2001. *Jains in the World: Religious Values and Ideology in India*. New York: Oxford University Press.

CRILL, Rosemary. 1998. *Indian Ikat Textiles*. New York: Weatherhill.

——. 1994. *Introduction to Embodiment and Experience: The Existential Ground of Culture and Self*. London: Cambridge University Press, pp.1-26.

CROFT, Clare. 2015. *Dancers as Diplomats: American Choreography in Cultural Exchange*. New York: Oxford University Press.

CURTIS, L. (ed.). 1920. *Papers Relating to the Application of the Principle of Dyarchy to the Government of India, to which are Appended the Report of the Joint Select Committee and the Government of India Act, 1919*. Oxford: Clarendon Press.

DALRYMPLE, William. 2003. *The White Mughals: Love and Betrayal in Eighteenth-Century India*. New York: Viking.

DANCE RESEARCH JOURNAL (DRJ). 2016. *Dance Research Journal* 48(2) (August).

DANDAVATE, Rohini. 2013. *Fundamentals of Odissi Dance*. DVD.

DANIELSON, Dan and Karen Engle (eds). 1995. *After Identity: A Reader in Law and Culture*. New York: Routledge.

DAS, Asok Kumar. 1994. 'Akbar's Imperial Ramayana: A Mughal Persian Manuscript'. *Marg* 45(3) (March): 61–72.

DAS, J. P. 2007. *Chitra-pothi: Illustrated Palm-Leaf Manuscripts from Orissa*. New Delhi: Niyogi Books.

DAS, Maya. 2001. *Abhinaya Chandrika and Odissi Dance*, VOLS 1–2. Delhi: Eastern Book Linkers.

DAS, Vidhya. 1998. 'Human Rights, Inhuman Wrongs: Plight of Tribals in Orissa'. *Economic and Political Weekly*, 33(11) (14 March): 571–2.

DASABHUJA GOTIPUA ODISSI NRUTYA PARISAD. 2010. Dasabhuja Gotipua Odissi Nrutya Parisad website: https://goo.gl/ebrmMF (last accessed on August 2010).

DASH, Abhimanyu. 2011. 'Invasions on the Temple of Lord Jagannath, Puri'. *Orissa Review* (July): 82–9.

DATTILA. 1970. *Dattilam: A Compendium of Ancient Indian Music* (Emmie te Nijenhuis trans.). Leiden: E.J. Brill.

———. 1988. *Dattilam* (Kalamulasastra Series, VOL. 2) (Mukund Lath trans.). New Delhi: Indira Gandhi National Centre for the Arts.

DAVIS, JR., Donald R. 2007. 'Hinduism as a Legal Tradition'. *Journal of the American Academy of Religion*, 75(2) (June): 241–67.

DE CERTEAU, Michel. 2011[1984]. *The Practice of Everyday Life* (Steven Rendall trans.). Berkeley and Los Angeles: The University of California Press.

DEFRANTZ, Thomas F. 2004. *Dancing Revelations: Alvin Ailey's Embodiment of African American Culture*. New York: Oxford University Press.

DEHEJIA, Harsha. 2005. 'The Vaishnava Ethos and Shringara Bhakti' in Harsha V. Dehejia (ed.), *A Celebration of Love: The Romantic Heroine in the Indian Arts*. New Delhi: Roli Books, pp. 286–99.

——— (ed.). 2008. *A Festival of Krishna*. New Delhi: Roli Books.

DEHEJIA, Vidya. 1979. *Early Stone Temples of Orissa*. New Delhi: Vikas Publications.

———. 2009. *The Body Adorned: Dissolving Boundaries Between Sacred and Profane in India's Art*. New York: Columbia University Press.

——— (ed.). 1999. *Devi, the Great Goddess: Female Divinity in South Asian Art*. Washington, DC: Arthur M. Sackler Gallery, Smithsonian Institution / Ahmedabad: Mapin Publishing Publishing / Munich: Prestel Vergal.

DEI, Santilal. 1988. *Vaisnavism in Orissa*. Calcutta: Punthi Pustak.

DEI, Shashipriya. 1998. *Development of Temple Architecture in India: With Reference to Orissa in the Golden Age*. Calcutta: Punthi Pustak.

DELEUZE, Gilles. 1994. *Difference and Repetition* (Paul Patton trans.). New York: Columbia University Press.

———, and Félix Guattari. 1988. *A Thousand Plateaus: Capitalism and Schizophrenia* (Brian Massumi trans.). London: Athlone Press.

DELVOYE, Francoise 'Nalini'. 1997. 'The Image of Akbar as a Patron of Music in Indo-Persian and Vernacular Sources' in Irfan Habib (ed.), *Akbar and His India*. New Delhi: Oxford, pp. 188–214.

DEO, Jitamitra Prasada Singh (ed.). 2001. *Tantric Art of Orissa*. Delhi: Kalpaz Publications.

DEO, Juga Bhanu Singh. 1973. *Chhau: Mask Dance of Seraikela.* Calcutta: Eastern Zonal Cultural Centre.

DERRETT, J. Duncan M. 1968. *Religion, Law, and the State in India.* New York: Free Press.

DERRIDA, Jacques. 1982. 'Choreographies': Interview with Christie V. McDonald. *Diacritics,* 12(2) (Summer): 66–76.

———. 1987. *The Truth in Painting* (Geoff Bennington and Ian McLeod trans.). Chicago: University of Chicago Press.

DESAI, Chelna. 1988. *Ikat Textiles of India.* San Francisco: Chronicle Books.

DESAI, Devangana. 1990. 'Social Dimensions of Art in Early India'. *Social Scientist,* 18(3) (March): 3–32.

DESMOND, Jane. 1991. 'Dancing out the Difference: Cultural Imperialism and Ruth St. Denis' "Radha" of 1906'. *Signs,* 17: 28–49.

——— (ed.). 1997. *Meaning in Motion: New Cultural Studies of Dance.* Durham: Duke University Press.

DHAKY, Madhusudhan A. 1977. *The Indian Temple Forms in Karnata Inscriptions and Architecture.* New Delhi: Abhinav Publications.

DHALL, Manjusri. 1997. *The British Rule: Missionary Activities in Orissa, 1822–1947.* New Delhi: Har-Anand Publications.

DHAR, Jasobanta Narayan. 2008. 'The Story and History of Odissi Dance and Sri Geeta Govinda'. *Orissa Review* (May): 17–19. Available online at: https://goo.gl/qYyTTt (last accessed on 25 June 2018).

DILLON, Janette. 2010. *The Language of Space in Court Performance, 1400–1625.* Cambridge: Cambridge University Press.

DIMOCK Jr, Edward C. 1963. 'Doctrine and Practice among the Vaishnavas of Bengal'. *History of Religions,* 3(1) (Summer): 106–27.

———. 1966. *The Place of the Hidden Moon: Erotic Mysticism in the Vaisnava-Sahajiya Cult of Bengal.* Chicago: University of Chicago Press.

———. 1989. 'Lila'. *History of Religions,* 29(2) (November): 159–73.

———. 1991. 'On Maya'. *The Journal of Religion,* 71(4) (October): 523–37.

——— and Denise Levertov. 1967. *In Praise of Krishna: Songs from the Bengali.* New York: Doubleday.

DIRKS, Nicholas. 2001. *Castes of Mind: Colonialism and the Making of Modern India.* Princeton: Princeton University Press.

———. 2007. *The Hollow Crown: Ethnohistory of an Indian Kingdom.* Cambridge: Cambridge University Press.

———. 2008. *The Scandal of Empire: India and the Creation of Imperial Britain.* Cambridge: Belknap Press/Harvard University Press.

DISSANAYAKE, Wimal. 1996. *Narratives of Agency: Self-Making in China, India, and Japan.* Minneapolis: University of Minnesota Press.

———, Thomas P. Kasulis, and Roger T. Ames (eds). 1993. *Self as Body in Asian Theory and Practice.* New York: State of University of New York Press.

DOLAN, Jill. 2005. *Utopia in Performance: Finding Hope at the Theater.* Ann Arbor: University of Michigan Press.

DONALDSON, Thomas Eugene. 1975. 'Propitious-Apotropaic Eroticism in the Art of Orissa'. *Artibus Asiae*, 37(1–2): 75–100.

———. 1976. 'Doorframes on the Earliest Orissan Temples'. *Artibus Asiae*, 38(2–3): 189–218.

———. 1981. 'Development of the Nata-Mandira in Orissan Temple Architecture' in Joanna G. Williams (ed.), *Kaladarsana: American Studies in the Art of India.* Leiden: E. J. Brill, pp. 35–46.

———. 1982. 'Ekapada Siva Images in Orissan Art'. *Ars Orientalis*, 13: 153–67.

———. 1985. *Hindu Temple Art of Orissa*, VOLS 1–3. Leiden: E. J. Brill.

———. 1986. 'Bhiksatanamurti Images from Orissa'. *Artibus Asiae*, 47(1): 51–66.

———. 1988. 'Ganga Monarch and a Monumental Sun Temple: Thirteenth Century Orissa' in Vidya Dehejia (ed.), *Royal Patrons and Great Temple Art.* Bombay: Marg Publications, pp. 125–43.

———. 1991. 'The Sava-Vahana as Purusa in Orissan Images: Camunda to Kali/Tara'. *Artibus Asiae*, 51(1–2): 107–41.

———. 2001a. 'Bhubaneswar (Ekamra-kshetra): Temple Town and Cultural Centre' in Pratapaditya Pal (ed.), *Orissa Revisited.* Bombay: Marg Publications, pp. 48–63.

———. 2001b. *Iconography of the Buddhist Sculpture of Orissa.* New Delhi: Indira Gandhi National Centre for the Arts/Abhinav Publications.

DUBOIS, Abbé J. A. 1906[1816]. *Hindu Manners, Customs and Ceremonies*, 3rd EDN (Henry K. Beauchamp trans.). Oxford: Clarendon Press.

DUMONT, Louis. 1986. *Essays on Individualism: Modern Ideology in Anthropological Perspective.* Chicago: University of Chicago Press.

EATON, Richard. 2000. 'Temple Desecration in Pre-Modern India, Part I'. *Frontline*, 22 December, pp. 62–70.

——. 2001. 'Temple Desecration and Indo-Muslim States, Part II'. *Frontline*, 5 January, pp. 70–7.

ECK, Diana L. 1998. *Darsan: Seeing the Divine Image in India*, 3rd EDN. New York: Columbia University Press.

EISENSTEIN, Zillah. 1988. *The Female Body and the Law*. Berkeley: University of California Press.

ELLWIN, Verrier. 2001[1959]. 'Tribal Dances' in Pratapaditya Pal (ed.), *Orissa Revisited*. Bombay: Marg Publications, pp. 162–74. Reprinted from *Marg*, 13(1) (December 1959): 57-68.

EMBREE, Ainslie (ed.). 1988. *Sources of Indian Tradition*, VOL. 1. New York: Columbia University Press.

ERDMAN, Joan. 1983. 'Who Should Speak for the Performing Arts? The Case of the Delhi Dancers'. *Pacific Affairs*, 56(2) (Summer): 247–69.

—— (ed.). 1992. *Arts Patronage in India: Methods, Motives, and Markets*. New Delhi: Manohar Publications.

ERNST, Carl. 2016. *Refractions of Islam in India: Situating Sufism and Yoga*. New Delhi: Sage Publications.

ESCHMANN, Anncharlott, Hermann Kulke and Gaya Charan Tripathi (eds). 2005. *The Cult of Jagannath and the Regional Tradition of Orissa*. New Delhi: Manohar.

EZRAHI, Christina. 2012. *Swans of the Kremlin: Ballet and Power in Soviet Russia*. Pittsburgh: University of Pittsburgh Press.

FABRI, Charles Louis. 1954. Column, *The Statesman*, 5 November.

——. 1958a. 'Dance Seminar in Retrospect' (cultural report), *The Statesman*, 8 April, p. 5.

——. 1958b. 'Ballet'. *The Statesman*, 8 April, p. 5.

——. 1963. *An Introduction to Indian Architecture*. New York: Asia Publishing House.

——. 1974. *History of the Art of Orissa*. New Delhi: Orient Longman.

FANON, Frantz. 1963. *The Wretched of the Earth* (Constance Farrington trans.). New York: Grove Press.

FERGUSON, James and Akhil Gupta. 2002. 'Spatializing States: Toward an Ethnography of Neoliberal Governmentality'. *American Ethnologist*, 29(4) (November): 981–1002.

FERGUSON, Niall. 2004. *Empire: How Britain Made the Modern World*. London: Penguin.

FESTIVALS of INDIA.com. 2010. Khajuraho and Konark festival websites: https://goo.gl/TeRF45 (last accessed on 2 July 2018).

FLOOD, Finbarr B. 2009. *Objects of Translation: Material Culture and Medieval 'Hindu-Muslim' Encounter.* Princeton: Princeton University Press.

FOSTER, Susan Leigh. 1986. *Reading Dancing: Bodies and Subjects in Contemporary American Dance.* Berkeley and Los Angeles: University of California Press.

———. 1995. 'Choreographing History' in Susan Leigh Foster (ed.), *Choreographing History.* Bloomington: Indiana University Press, pp. 3–21.

———. 1997. 'Dancing Bodies' in Jane Desmond (ed.), *Meaning in Motion: New Cultural Studies of Dance.* Durham: Duke University Press, pp. 235–57.

———. 1998a. *Choreography and Narrative: Ballet's Staging of Story and Desire.* Bloomington: Indiana University Press.

———. 1998b. 'Choreographies of Gender'. *Signs,* 24(1) (Autumn): 1–33.

———. 2003. 'Choreographies of Protest'. *Theatre Journal,* 44(3) (October): 395–412.

———. 2009. 'Choreographies and Choreographers' in Susan leigh Foster (ed.), *Worlding Dance.* London: Palgrave Macmillan, pp. 98–118.

———. 2011. *Choreographing Empathy: Kinesthesia in Performance.* New York: Routledge.

——— (ed.). 1996. *Corporealities: Dancing, Knowledge, Culture, and Power.* London: Routledge.

FOUCAULT, Michel. 1984[1967]. 'Des Espaces Autres' ['Of Other Spaces'] (Jay Miskowiec trans.). *Architecture/Mouvement/Continuité* 5 (October): 46–9. Based on a lecture delivered in 1967. Available at: goo.gl/KRpkNa (last accessed on 2 July 2018).

———. 1972. *The Archaeology of Knowledge* (Rupert Swyer trans.). New York: Pantheon.

———. 1977. 'Nietzsche, Genealogy, History' in *Language, Counter-Memory, Practice: Selected Essays and Interviews* (Donald. F. Bouchard ed.). Ithaca: Cornell University Press, pp. 139–64.

———. 1979. *Discipline and Punish: The Birth of the Prison* (Alan Sheridan trans.). New York: Vintage.

———. 1980. *Power/Knowledge: Selected Interviews & Other Writings, 1972–1977* (Colin Gordon ed.). New York: Pantheon Books/Random House.

———. 1984. *The Foucault Reader* (Paul Rabinow ed.). New York: Pantheon Books.

———. 1988a. *The History of Sexuality*, VOLS. 1–3 (Robert Hurley trans.). New York: Vintage Books.

———. 1988b. *Politics, Philosophy, Cultures: Interviews and Other Writings, 1977–1984* (Lawrence D. Kritzman ed.). New York: Routledge.

———. 1993. 'About the Beginning of the Hermeneutics of the Self: Two Lectures at Dartmouth'. *Political Theory*, 21(2) (May): 198–227.

———. 2007. *Security, Territory, Population: Lectures at the Collège de France, 1977–1978* (Graham Burchell trans.). New York: Picador.

———. 2008. *The Birth of Biopolitics: Lectures at the College de France, 1978–1979* (Michel Senellart, Arnold I. Davidson, Alessandro Fontana, Francois Ewald eds and Graham Burchell trans.). New York: Palgrave Macmillan.

Fox, Richard G. 1991. *Recapturing Anthropology*. Santa Fe: School of American Research Press.

———.1996. 'Self-Made' in Wimal Dissanayake (ed.), *Narratives of Agency: Self-Making in China, India, and Japan*. Minneapolis: University of Minnesota Press, pp. 104–16.

Franko, Mark. 1993. *Dance as Text: Ideologies of the Baroque Body*. Cambridge: Cambridge University Press.

———. 1995. *Dancing Modernism/Performing Politics*. Bloomington: Indiana University Press.

———. 2002. *The Work of Dance: Labour, Movement, and Identity in the 1930s*. Middletown: Wesleyan University Press.

———. 2006. 'Dance and the Political: States of Exception'. *Dance Research Journal* 38(1–2) (Summer/Winter): 3–18.

———. 2012. *Martha Graham in Love and War*. New York: Oxford University Press.

———, and Annette Richards. 2000. 'Actualizing Absence: The Pastness of Performance' in Mark and Annette Richards (eds), *Acting on the Past: Historical Performance Across the Disciplines.* Hanover: Wesleyan University Press, pp. 1–9.

—— (ed.). 2007. *Ritual and Event: Interdisciplinary Perspectives.* New York: Routledge.

FULLER, Mrs Marcus B. 1900. *The Wrongs of Indian Womanhood.* New York: Fleming H. Revell Company.

GANDHARVA MAHAVIDYALAYA. 1985. *Angahar Festival of Odissi Dance Souvenir.* 7–10 March, Kamani Auditorium, New Delhi. New Delhi: Gandharva Mahavidyalaya.

GANDHI, Aastha. 2009. 'Who Frames the Dance? Writing and Performing the Trinity of Odissi' in Cheryl Stock (ed.), *Dance Dialogues: Conversations Across Cultures, Artforms, and Practices: Proceedings of the World Dance Alliance Global Summit,* pp. 1–11. 13–18 July, Brisbane. Queensland: Australian Dance Council, Ausdance Inc., and Queensland University of Technology, Faculty of Creative Industries. Available at: http://www.ausdance.org.au/ (last accessed on 4 December 2015).

GANDHI, Mohandas Karamchand. 1938. *Hind Swaraj, or Indian Home Rule.* Ahmedabad: Navajivan Publishing House.

GANESH, Swarnamalya. 2012. 'Research and Reconstruction of Dance Repertoire of the Nayak Period: Madurai, Tanjore and Gingee'. PhD thesis, University of Madras.

GANGULY, Dilip Kumar. 1984. *History and Historians in Ancient India.* New Delhi: Abhinav Publications.

GANGULY, Mono Mohon. 1986. *Orissa and Her Remains: Ancient and Medieval (Puri District).* New Delhi: Gian Publishing House.

GASTON, Anne-Marie. 1992. 'Dance and the Hindu Woman: Bharatanatyam Re-ritualized' in Julia Leslie (ed.), *Roles and Rituals for Hindu Women.* Delhi: Motilal Banarsidass, pp. 149–71.

GAUHAR, Ranjana. 2007. *Odissi: The Dance Divine.* New Delhi: Niyogi Books.

GELL, Alfred. 1988. *Art and Agency: An Anthropological Theory.* Oxford: Clarendon Press.

GHOSE, Akshay (ed.). 1921. 'Dramatic Performances Act (1876)' in *Laws Affecting the Rights and Liberties of the Indian People (from Early British Rule).* Calcutta: Mohun Brothers, pp. 143–7.

GHOSH, G. K. and Shukla Ghosh. 2000. *Ikat Textiles of India.* New Delhi: APH Publishing.

GHOSH, Partha S. 1998. 'The Rewriting of History'. *The Hindu* (Chennai/New Delhi), 15 July 1998.

GIERSDORF, Jens Richard. 2013. *The Body of the People: East German Dance since 1945*. Madison: University of Wisconsin Press.

GIL, José. 2006. 'Paradoxical Body' (André Lepecki trans.). *TDR*, 50(4) (Winter, T192): 21–35.

GLISSANT, Édouard. 1997. *Poetics of Relation* (Betsy Wing trans.). Ann Arbor: University of Michigan Press.

GOKHALE, Shanta. 2005. 'New Aesthetics, New Idioms'. *Sangeet Natak*, 39(3): 3–8.

GOLDMAN, Danielle. 2010. *I Want to Be Ready: Improvised Dance as a Practice of Freedom*. Ann Arbor: University of Michigan Press.

GOPINATH, Gayatri. 2005. *Impossible Desires: Queer Diasporas and South Asian Public Cultures*. Durham: Duke University Press.

GOSWAMI, A. (ed.) 1950. *Designs from Orissan Temples: An Album of Photographs* (Introduction by Km Christen. Text by D.P. Ghosh, Nirmal Kumar Bose and Y. D. Sharma). Calcutta: Thacker's Press and Directories.

—— (ed.). 1956. *Orissan Sculpture and Architecture* (Introduction and descriptive text by O. C. Gangooly; photographs by Sunil Janah [and] K.L. Kothari). Calcutta: Oxford Book and Stationery Co.

GOSWAMI, Kali Prasad. 2000. *Devadasi: Dancing Damsel*. Delhi: A.P.H. Publishing.

GOSWAMI, KRISHNADAS KAVIRAJ. 1975[1581]. *Chaitanya Charitamrita*, VOLS 1–9 (A. C. Bhaktivedanta Swami Prabhupada trans. and ed.). Bhaktivedanta VedaBase online: https://goo.gl/Hnz9Fk (last accessed on 2 July 2018).

——. 2000[1581]. *Caitanya Caritamrta of Krsnadasa Kaviraja: A Translation and Commentary* (Edward Dimock and T. Stewart trans. and ed.). Cambridge: Harvard University Department of Sanskrit and Indian Studies.

GOSWAMI, Meghali, Ila Gupta, and P.T. Jha. 2005. 'Sapta Matrikas in Indian Art and Their Significance in Indian Sculpture and Ethos: A Critical Study'. *Anistoriton*, 9 (March) (section AO51): 1–9.

GOSWAMI, Rupa. 2008. *Vidagdha Madhavam* (Sarbeshwar Dash, Bhagaban Panda and Govinda Chandra Mishra trans). Bhubaneswar: Orissa Sahitya Akademi.

——. 2003. *The Bhaktirasamrtasindhu of Rupa Gosvamin* (David L. Haberman trans.). New Delhi: Indira Gandhi National Centre for the Arts.

GOUR, Santosh. 1999. *Sakhi Pila: Boy Odissi Dancer.* New Delhi: Films Division, Ministry of Information and Broadcasting, Government of India.

GOVERNMENT OF BENGAL. 1912. Proceedings of the Bengal Legislative Council, 26 February. *Calcutta Gazette* (28 February), Part IVA. Government of Bengal: Legislative Department. Odisha State Archives, Bhubaneshwar, India.

GOVERNMENT OF INDIA. 1923. *Legislative Assembly Debates* (Official Report), Volume 3, Part 4. Delhi: Government Central Press, p. 2826.

——. 1948. 'Constituent Assembly Debates on December 3, 1948'. Article 17 discussion, *Constituent Assembly of India*, VOL. VII. Indiankanoon.org. Available at: goo.gl/rcjSYC (last accessed on 2 July 2018).

——. 1959a. 'Need for Recognising Orisi Dance as One of the Classical Dances': Demands for Grants. Lok Sabha Debates (Seventh Session), Second Series, VOL. XXVII, no. 38 (2 April), pp. 9301–64. New Delhi: Lok Sabha Secretariat.

——. 1959b. 'Odissi Dance'. Oral Answers to Questions, Lok Sabha Debates (Seventh Session), VOL. 37 (17 December), pp. 5543–5. New Delhi: Lok Sabha Secretariat.

——. 1960. 'Discussion of Cut Motions before the House: Demands for Grants'. Lok Sabha Debates (Tenth Session), Second Series, VOL. 41, NO. 36 (28 March), pp. 8449–532. New Delhi: Lok Sabha Secretariat.

——. 2000. Indian Penal Code. VakilNo1.com. Available at: goo.gl/1DefAy (last accessed on 2 July 2018).

——. 2010. Census of India. Office of the Registrar General and Census Commissioner, Ministry of Home Affairs. Available at: https://goo.gl/hn9vC9 (last accessed on 2 July 2018).

——. 2011. *Indian Penal Code, 1860.* Mumbai: Current Publications.

GOVERNMENT OF INDIA HOME DEPARTMENT. 1854. *Selections from the Records of the Government of India (Home Department). No. V: A History of the Rise and Progress of the Operations for the Suppression of Human Sacrifice and Female Infanticide in the Hill Tracts of Orissa. Compiled from*

Official Correspondence, from the Years 1836 to 1854. Calcutta: F. Carbery, Bengal Military Orphan Press.

———. 1928. *Letter and Enclosures, March 8, 1928. Correspondence between Association for Moral and Social Hygiene, London, and Government of India Offices on the Subject of Devadasi Legislation*. Item no. IOR/L/PJ/7/682: 29 May 1934–1 Februrary 1935, India Office Records, British Library, London, UK.

GOVERNMENT OF MAHARASHTRA. 1934. *Bombay Devadasis Protection Act*. Available at: https://goo.gl/zMKa4E (last accessed 29 June 2018).

GOVERNMENT OF ORISSA [ODISHA]. 1939. *Orissa Hindu Religions Endowments Act 1939*. Cuttack: Law Department, Government of Orissa. Item no. IOR/L/PJ/7/2897, India Office Records, British Library, London.

———. 1952. *Report of the Special Officer under the Puri Shri Jagannath Temple (Administration) Act (Orissa Act XIV of 1952)*. Prepared by L. Panda, Special Officer. Cuttack: Orissa Government Press. Call no. BL1227.P8A1 1961, University of Chicago Library, Chicago.

———. 1956. *Record of Rights, Puri Shri Jagannath Temple (Administration) Act (Orissa Act XIV of 1952), Part III*. Prepared by L. Panda, Special Officer. In *Orissa Gazette Extraordinary*, 205 [English and Odia], Monday, 3 September. Cuttack: Law Department, Government of Orissa. Odisha State Archives, Bhubaneshwar, India.

GOVERNMENT OF TAMIL NADU. 1947. *Madras Devadasis (Prevention of Dedication) Act*. Available at: https://goo.gl/JXyhnp (last accessed 29 June 2018).

GOVERNOR GENERAL IN COUNCIL. 1806. *Bengal Regulation IV for Levying a Tax from Pilgrims Reporting to the Temple of Jugunnath, and for the Superintendence and Management of the Temple (Passed on April 3)*. Item no. IOR/E/4/665, India Office Records, British Library, London.

GOYAL, Shankar. 1993. *Aspects of Ancient Indian History and Historiography*. New Delhi: Harman Publishing House.

GRAFF, Ellen. 1997. *Stepping Left: Dance and Politics in New York City, 1928–1942*. Durham: Duke University Press.

GREGOTTI, Vittorio. 1996. *Inside Architecture* (Peter Wong and Francesca Zaccheo trans). Cambridge: MIT Press.

GREWAL, Inderpal and Caren Kaplan. 2001. 'Global Identities: Theorizing Transnational Studies of Sexuality'. *GLQ: A Journal of Lesbian and Gay Studies* 7(4): 663–79.

GRIERSON, George Abraham (ed.). 1903–28. *Linguistic Survey of India*, VOL. 5, PART 2: *Indo-Aryan Languages. Eastern Group. Specimens of the Bihari and Oriya Languages*. Calcutta: Office of the Superintendent of Government Printing, India. Available online at https://goo.gl/ysCEGH (last accessed on 2 July 2018).

GROME, Charles. 2002[1805]. *Charles Grome's Report on the Temple of Jagannath, 10 June 1805* (K. S. Behera, H. S. Patnaik, M. P. Dash and R. K. Mishra eds). Bhubaneshwar: Orissa State Archives.

GUERNSEY, Alfred Hudson. 1878. 'Juggernaut'. *Harper's New Monthly Magazine* (July): 222–8.

GUHA, Ranajit. 1998. 'Dominance Without Hegemony and Its Historiography' in Ranajit Guha (ed.), *Subaltern Studies VI: Writings on South Asian History and Society*. New Delhi: Oxford University Press, pp. 210–309.

———. 2005. 'The Small Voice of History' in Shahid Amin and Dipesh Chakraborty (eds), *Subaltern Studies IX: Writings on South Asian History and Society*. New Delhi: Oxford University Press, pp. 1–12.

GUHA-THAKURTA, Tapati. 2004. *Monuments, Objects, Histories: Institutions of Art in Colonial and Postcolonial India*. New York: Columbia University Press.

GUPT, Bharat. 2006. *Dramatic Concepts—Greek and Indian: A Study of Poetics and Natyasastra*. New Delhi: D. K. Printworld.

GUPTA, Charu. 2002. *Sexuality, Obscenity, and Community: Women, Muslims, and the Hindu Public in Colonial India*. New York: Palgrave.

GUPTA, Ravi. 2006. 'Making Space for Vedanta: Canon and Commentary in Caitanya Vaisnavism'. *Journal of Hindu Studies*, 10(1) (April): 75–90.

GURU PANKAJ CHARAN DANCE ODISSI RESEARCH FOUNDATION (GPCDORF). Facebook site: https://goo.gl/eKWujn (last accessed August 22, 2018).

HABIB, Irfan. 2009. *Medieval India: The Study of a Civilization*. New Delhi: National Book Trust.

——— (ed.). 2005. *India: Studies in the History of an Idea*. New Delhi: Munshiram Manoharlal Publishers.

HAMERA, Judith. 2002. 'An Answerability of Memory: "Saving" Khmer Classical Dance'. *TDR*, 46(4) (Winter): 65–85.

HANNA, Judith Lynne. 1993. 'Classical Indian Dance and Women's Status' in Helen Thomas (ed.), *Dance, Gender and Culture*. New York: Macmillan, pp. 119–35.

——. 1998. 'Feminist Perspectives on Classical Indian Dance: Divine Sexuality, Prostitution, and Erotic Fantasy' in David Waterhouse (ed.), *Dance of India*. Mumbai: Popular Prakashan, pp. 193–231.

HARDING, Sandra (ed.). 2004. *The Feminist Standpoint Theory Reader*. New York: Routledge.

HARDY, Adam. 2007. 'The Dance Performed by the Temple: the Dynamics of Hindu Temple Architecture'. Lecture presented in Session 17, Shivdasani Conference. Oxford Center for Hindu Studies, 21 October.

HARPER, Katherine Anne. 1989. *The Iconography of the Sapta-Matrikas: Seven Hindu Goddesses of Spiritual Transformation*. New York: Edwin Mellen Press.

HARVIE, Jen. 2013. *Fair Play: Art, Performance, and Neoliberalism*. Basingstoke: Palgrave Macmillan.

HASAN, Zoya. 1994. *Forging Identities: Gender, Communities, and the State in India*. Boulder: Westview Press.

HATANAKA, Kokyo. 1996. *Textile Arts of India*. San Francisco: Chronicle Books.

HAWLEY, John Stratton. 1992. 'Krishna and the Performing Arts' (interview) in Steven Rosen (ed.), *Vaisnavism: Contemporary Scholars Discuss the Gaudiya Tradition*. Brooklyn: FOLK Books, pp. 77–100.

—— and Mark Juergensmayer. 1988. *Songs of the Saints of India*. New York: Oxford University Press.

HELLIER-TINOCO, Ruth. 2011. *Embodying Mexico: Tourism, Nationalism, and Performance*. New York: Oxford University Press.

HESS, Ron. 1985. *Given to Dance*. USA, 57 min, colour, DVD.

THE HINDU. 1958. 'Dance Patterns of Orissa', *The Hindu Weekly Review*, 6 (14 April): 15.

——. 2009. 'Mahari Dance Show on August 31', Saturday, 29 August. Available at: goo.gl/1uip2r (last accessed on 2 July 2018).

HIRSCHL, Ran. 2008. 'The Judicialization of Politics' in Gregory A. Caldeira, R. Daniel Keleman, and Keith E. Whittington (eds), *The Oxford Handbook of Law and Politics*. Oxford: Oxford University Press, pp. 119–141.

HOERNLE, A., F. Rudolfe and Herbert A. Stark. 1906. *A History of India*, 3rd EDN. Cuttack: Orissa Mission Press.

HORNECK, Anthony. 1704. *The Great Law of Consideration: or, a Discourse, wherein the Nature, Usefulness, and Absolute Necessity of Consideration, in Order to a Truly Serious and Religious Life, is Laid Open*, 8th EDN. London: S. Holt.

HOBSBAWM, Eric. 1983. 'Introduction: Inventing Traditions' in Eric Hobsbawm and Terence Ranger (eds), *The Invention of Tradition*. New York: Cambridge University Press, pp. 1–14.

HOLDREGE, Barbara. 1998. 'Body Connections: Hindu discourses of the Body and the Study of Religion'. *International Journal of Hindu Studies*, 2(3) (December): 341–86.

HUGHES, Jenny. 2011. *Performance in a Time of Terror: Critical Mimesis and the Age of Uncertainty*. Manchester: Manchester University Press.

HUNTER, W. W. 1886. *Imperial Gazetteer of India*, VOL. 10, 2nd EDN. London: Trubner and Co.

———. 1908–31. *Imperial Gazetteer of India, 1840–1900*. Oxford: Clarendon Press.

———. 2005[1872]. *Orissa*, VOLS 1 and 2. Elibron Classics.

HUSAIN, Iqbal. 1997. 'Akbar's Farmans—A Study in Diplomatic' in Irfan Habib (ed.), *Akbar and His India*. New Delhi: Oxford University Press, pp. 66–78.

HYDE, Alan. 1997. *Bodies of Law*. Princeton: Princeton University Press.

INDEN, Ronald. 1990. *Imagining India*. Oxford: Basil Blackwell.

———. 2006. Text and Practice: Essays on South Asian History. New Delhi: Oxford University Press.

INDIRA GANDHI NATIONAL CENTRE FOR THE ARTS. 2010. Indira Gandhi National Centre for the Arts website. Available at: http://ignca.nic.in (last accessed on 2 July 2018).

CENTRE FOR CULTURAL RESOURCES AND TRAINING. 2004. *Bandha Dance* (*Gotipua Dancers, Orissa*). DVD, colour, 28 mins. India.

INVIS MULTIMEDIA. 2003. *Odissi*. DVD, colour. India.

INDIAN COUNCIL FOR CULTURAL RELATIONS (ICCR). 1965. *Toward Understanding India*. Bombay: Bhatkal Books.

INDIANKANOON.org. 2010. Online database of Indian laws, court and tribunal judgments and law journals. Available at: https://www.indiankanoon.org (last accessed on 2 July 2018).

INDIAN STATUTORY COMMISSION. 1930. *Indian Statutory Commission, Volume 16: Selections from Memoranda and Oral Evidence by Non-Officials* (*Part I*). London: His Majesty's Stationery Office.

IYER. L. A. K. 1927. 'Devadasis in South India: Their Traditional Origin and Development'. *Man in India* 7(47): 47–52.

IYER, Raghavan. 1986. *Parapolitics: Toward the City of Man*. New York: Concord Grove Press.

JACKSON, Naomi and Toni Shapiro Phim (eds). 2008. *Dance, Human Rights, and Social Justice: Dignity in Motion*. Lanham: Scarecrow Press.

JACKSON, Shannon. 2011. *Social Works: Performing Art, Supporting Publics*. New York: Routledge Press.

JACOBI, Hermann. 1968[1884]. *Jaina Sutras, Part One* (translated from Prakit). New York: Dover Publications. Availavle online at: goo.gl/kbkVCB (last accessed on 2 July 2018).

———. 1986[1895]. *Jaina Sutras, Part Two* (translated from Prakit). New York: Dover Publications. Available online at: goo.gl/y1Pai7 (last accessed on 2 July 2018).

JAENICKE, Dieter. 1997. 'Dancing Forbidden'. *Ballett international/Tanz aktuell* [English EDN] (April): 38–43.

JAGANNATH TEMPLE. 2017. Official website of Jagannath temple, Puri, India: http://jagannath.nic.in/?q=home (last accessed on 2 July 2018).

JAGANNATHA TERCAPANCHANANA. 1874[1796]. *A Digest of Hindu Law, On Contracts and Successions*, VOL. 1 (Henry Thomas Colebrooke trans.), 4th EDN. Madras: Higginbotham and Co.

JAKOBSEN, Janet and Ann Pellegrini (eds). 2008. *Secularisms*. Durham: Duke University Press.

JAMESON, Fredric. 1992. *Postmodernism, or the Cultural Logic of Late Capitalism*. Durham: Duke University Press.

———. 2005. *Archaeologies of the Future: The Desire Called Utopia and Other Science Fiction*. New York: Verso.

JANMOHAMED, Abdul R. 1985. 'The Economy of Manichean Allegory: The Function of Racial Difference in Colonialist Literature'. *Critical Inquiry* 12(1) (Autumn): 59–87.

JAYADEVA. 2004. *The Gitagovinda of Jayadeva: Love Song of the Dark Lord* (Barbara Stoler Miller trans.). Delhi: Motilal Banarssidas.

———. 2005. *Sri Jayadev's Geeta Govindam Astapadis: English Translation* (Kshirod Prosad Mohanty trans.). Cuttack: Sansar Press.

———. 2006. *The Gita Govinda of Sri Jayadeva* (A. K. Tripathy and P. C. Tripathy trans). New Delhi: Publications Division.

JAYAMKONDAR. 1920[eleventh–twelfth century CE]. *Cayankontar Kalinkattup parani: kata cankirakam* [Tamil]. Chennai: T. Celvakesavaroya Mudali.

——. 1928[eleventh–twelfth century CE]. *Cayankontar Kalinkattup parani: kata cankirakam* [Tamil]. Chennai: T. Celvakesavaroya Mudali.

——. 2001[eleventh–twelfth century CE]. *Kalingathu Parani* [Tamil]. *Project Madurai.* Web version prepared by P. R. Sivakumar, P. K. Ilango and Dr. K. Kalyanasundaram. Available at: https://goo.gl/91vb59 (last accessed on 22 August 2018).

JAYALAKSHMI, N. S. (Jaya teacher). 2012. Interview with author. Chennai, 16 November.

JEANES, Rosemary A. 1982. 'Tradition and Learning in the Odissi Dance of India: Guru-Sisya-Parampara'. MA thesis, York University.

JEEVANANDAM, S., and Rekha Pande. 2012. 'Devadasis and Gift Giving in Medieval India'. *Zenith: International Journal of Multidisciplinary Research* 2(5) (May): 181–91.

JENA, Mona Lisa. 2008. 'A Street Play Named Sahi Jatra', KalingaTimes.com. Accessed at: http://www.kalingatimes.com/variety/news_20080413-Sahi_Yatra.htm (on 15 May 2009). Link currently not active.

JENKINS, Ron and Ian Watson. 2002. 'Odissi and the ISTA Dance: An Interview with Sanjukta Panigrahi' in Ian Watson (ed.), *Negotiating Cultures: Eugenio Barba and the Intercultural Debate.* Manchester: Manchester University Press, pp. 67–75.

JOHNSON, Greg. 2002. 'The Situated Self and Utopian Thinking'. *Hypatia,* 17(3) (Summer): 20–44.

JORDAN, Kay K. 2003. *From Sacred Servant to Profane Prostitute: A Study of the Changing Legal Status of the Devadasis, 1857–1947.* New Delhi: Manohar.

JOSHI, Gayatri. iGurukul Odissi website: gayatri.odissi.org (http://gayatri-odissi.org/odissi-fundamentals/ (last accessed on 3 July 2018).

JOSHI, P. C. 1983. 'Culture and Cultural Planning in India'. *Economic and Political Weekly,* 18(51) (17 December): 2169–74.

JOSHI, Rama and Joanna Liddle. 1985. 'Gender and Imperialism in British India'. *Economic and Political Weekly,* 20(43) (26 October): 72–8.

KAKTIKAR, Aadya. 2011. *Odissi Yaatra—The Journey of Guru Mayadhar Raut.* New Delhi: SAB.

KALA VIKASH KENDRA. 1958. *Dance and Music of Orissa, Souvenir* (Kavichandra Kalicharan Pattanaik, Upendra Mitra, Gorachand Misra and Nilmadhab Bose eds). Cuttack: Kala Vikash Vendra. Item call no. *MGZR, Odissi clippings file, Jerome Robbins Dance Division, New York Public Library for the Performing Arts, New York City.

——. 1959–63. *Folk Dance and Music of Orissa Bulletins, 1–6*, Bulletin 2: Sundargarh (6 November 1960) (Biswanath Shaw comp.). Cuttack: Kala Vikash Kendra. Item call no. *MGS (Hindu), Jerome Robbins Dance Division, New York Public Library for the Performing Arts, New York City.

——. 2010. Kala Vikash Kendra website: http://odissikvk.com/organisation.htm (last accessed on 2 April 2010).

KALI, Devadatta. 2010. *Devimahatmyam: In Praise of the Goddesss*. Delhi: Motilal Banarsidass.

KALIA, Ravi. 1994. *Bhubaneshwar: From a Temple Town to a Capital City*. Carbondale: Southern Illinois University Press.

KANT, Shashi. 2000. *The Hathigumpha Inscription of Kharavela and the Bhabru Edict of Ásoka: A Critical Study*, 2nd EDN. Delhi: D. K. Printworld.

KANUNGO, Aloka. 2006–07. 'Bandha Nritya'. *Attendance: The Dance Annual of India 2006–07, Traditions of East*: 70–85.

KANUNGO, Pralay. 2003. 'Hindutva's Entry into a Hindu Province: Early Years of RSS in Orissa'. *Economic and Political Weekly*, 38(31) (2–8 August): 3293–303.

KAPUR, Ratna. 2005. *Erotic Justice: Law and the New Politics of Postcolonialism*. Portland: Glasshouse Press.

KAR, Durga Prasad, and Kar, Padmalaya. 2006. *The Weaving Art of Orissa*. Bhubaneswar: Mahalakshmi Publication.

KASHYAP, Prakiti. 1997. 'Chhau'. *Ballett International* (July): 39–41.

KASULIS, Thomas P., Roger Ames and Wimal Dissanayake (eds). 1993. *Self as Body in Asian Theory and Practice*. Albany: State University of New York Press.

KAUTILYA. 1976. *Arthasastra*, 8th EDN (R. Shamasastry trans.). Mysore: Mysore Printing and Publishing House.

KAVIRAJ, Sudipta. 1988. 'A Critique of the Passive Revolution', *Economic and Political Weekly*, 23(45–47), (November): 2429–33, 2436–41, 2443–44.

———. 1991. 'On State, Society and Discourse in India' in J. Manor (ed.), *Rethinking Third World Politics*. London: Longman.

———. 1999. 'The Imaginary Institution of India' in Partha Chatterjee and Gyanendra Pandey (eds), *Subaltern Studies VII: Writings on South Asian History and Society*. New Delhi: Oxford University Press, pp. 1–39.

———. 2010a. *Imaginary Institution of India*. New York: Columbia University Press.

———. 2010b. *The Trajectories of the Indian State: Politics and Ideas*. Ranikhet: Permanent Black.

KEITH, A. Berridale (ed.). 1922. *Speeches and Documents on Indian Policy, 1750–1921*, VOL. I. London: Oxford University Press.

KERSENBOOM, Saskia C. 1998. *Nityasumangali: Devadasi Tradition in South India*. Delhi: Motilal Banarsidass.

KESSLER, Rochelle. 2005. 'Adorning the Beloved: Krishna Lila Images of Transformation and Union' in Harsha V. Dehejia (ed.), *A Celebration of Love: The Romantic Heroine in the Indian Arts*. New Delhi: Roli Books, pp. 187–92.

KHAN, Ahsan Raza. 1997. 'Akbar's Initial Encounters with the Chiefs: Accident vs Design in the Process of Subjugation' in Irfan Habib (ed.), *Akbar and His India*. New Delhi: Oxford University Press, pp. 1–14.

KHAN, Iqtidar Alam. 1997. 'Akbar's Personality Traits and World Outlook—A Critical Appraisal' in Irfan Habib (ed.), *Akbar and His India*. New Delhi: Oxford, pp. 79–96.

KHOKAR, Ashish. 2010. 'Guru Deba Prasad Das: Guru of Global Odissi', *Narthaki.com*, 6 November. Available at: goo.gl/DPTR8F (last accessed on 2 July 2018).

———, and Mohan Khokar. 2011. *The Dance Orissi*. New Delhi: Abhinav Publications.

KHOKAR, Mohan. 1984. *Traditions of Indian Classical Dance*, 2nd EDN. Delhi: Clarion Books.

———. 1985. 'In Praise of Passion'. *The Splendours of Indian Dance*. New Delhi: Himalayan Books, pp. 54–63.

———. 1987. *Dancing for Themselves: Folk, Tribal and Ritual Dance of India*. New Delhi: Himalayan Books.

———. 1998. 'The Tradition of Goti Pua', *The Hindu* folio, special issue with *Sunday Magazine, Dance* (27 December). Available at: goo.gl/MkTpxh; full special issue available at: goo.gl/GSr5zZ (last accessed on 2 July 2018).KHOKAR, Mohan and Ashish Khokar. 2011. *The Dance Orissi*. New Delhi: Abhinav Publications.

KIMURA, Masaaki and Akio Tanabe (eds). 2006. *The State in India: Past and Present*. New Delhi: Oxford University Press.

KINSLEY, David. 1986. *Hindu Goddesses: Visions of the Divine Feminine in the Hindu Religious Tradition*. Berkeley: University of California Press.

KIRSHENBLATT-GIMBLETT, Barbara. 1990. 'Performance of Precepts, Precepts of Performance' in Richard Schechner and Willa Appel (eds), *By Means of Performance: Intercultural Studies of Theatre and Ritual*. Cambridge: Cambridge University Press, pp. 109–17.

———. 1998. 'Objects of Ethnography'. *Destination Culture: Tourism, Museums, and Heritage*. Berkeley: University of California Press, pp. 17–78.

———. 2004. 'The Museum—A Refuge for Utopian Thought' [English version]. German translation may be found in Jörn Rüsen, Michael Fehr and Annelie Ramsbrock (eds), in *Die Unruhe der Kultur: Potentiale des Utopischen*. Velbrück Wissenschaft.

KISHWAR, Madhu. 1985. 'Gandhi on Women'. *Economic and Political Weekly*, 20(41) (12 October): 1753–8.

———. 1989. Introduction, in Ruth Vanita and Madhu Kishwar (eds), *Women Bhakta Poets*. New Delhi: Manushi Trust, pp. 3–8.

———. 1994. 'Codified Hindu Law: Myth and Reality'. *Economic and Political Weekly*, 29(33) (13 August): 2145–61.

———. 2002. *Religion at the Service of Nationalism and Other Essays*. Delhi: Oxford University Press.

KLAIC, Dragan. 1992. *The Plot of the Future: Utopia and Dystopia in Modern Drama*. Ann Arbor: University of Michigan Press.

KOLB, Alexandra (ed.). 2011. *Dance and Politics*. New York: Peter Lang.

KORITZ, Amy. 1997. 'Dancing the Orient for England: Maud Allan's The Vision of Salome' in Jane Desmond (ed.), *Meaning in Motion: New Cultural Studies of Dance*. Durham: Duke University Press, pp. 133–52.

KOSAMBI, D. D. 2002. *Combined Methods in Indology and Other Writings* (Brajadulal Chattopadhyaya ed.). New Delhi: Oxford University Press.

———. 2008. *An Introduction to the Study of Indian History*. Bombay: Popular Prakashan.

KOTHARI, Sunil. 1969. 'The Chhau Dances'. *The World of Music* 11(4): 38–55.

———. 1967. 'The Gotipua Dancers of Orissa'. *Illustrated Weekly of India*, 88(45) (10 December)10: 19–21.

———. 1970. 'Sabdaswarapata Dance.: The Tandava Aspect of Odissi'. *Sangeet Natak* 18 (October–December): 31–8.

———. 1974. 'Odissi Dance' in Sonal Mansingh, Souvenir Programme, Bombay, 22 September 1976.   Reprinted from the *Quarterly Journal of the National Centre for the Performing Arts, Bombay* 3(2): 37–49. Item call. no. *MGZB, Jerome Robbins Dance Division, New York Public Library for the Performing Arts, New York City.

———. 1982. 'Enactment of Gita Govinda in Neo-classical Dance Forms'. *Journal of the Department of Dance, Rabindra Bharati University, Calcutta,* 1: 1–10.

———. 1990. *Odissi: Indian Classical Dance Art.* Bombay: Marg Publications.

———. 2000. 'The State of Classical Dance Today' in Pratapaditya Pal (ed.), *Reflections on the Arts in India.* Mumbai: Marg Publications, pp. 133–43.

———. 2001. 'Odissi: From Devasabha to Janasabha' in Pratapaditya Pal (ed.), *Orissa Revisited.* Bombay: Marg Publications, pp. 93–104.

———. 2003. *New Directions in Indian Classical Dance.* Bombay: Marg Publications.

———. 2007. Interview with author. New Delhi, August 23 and September 5.

———. 2015. 'The Celestial Beauty'. *The Hindu,* 11 June. Available at: goo.gl/M7rPFt (last accessed on 2 July 2018).

—— and Bimal Mukherjee (eds). 1995. *Rasa: The Indian Performing Arts in the Last Twenty-Five Years.* Calcutta: Anamika Kala Sangam.

KOWAL, Rebekah, Jens Giersdorf and Randy Martin (eds). 2017. *The Oxford Handbook of Dance and Politics.* New York: Oxford University Press.

KRAMRISCH, Stella. 1983. *Exposing India's Sacred Art: Selected Writings of Stella Kramrisch* (Barbara Stoler Miller ed.). Philadelphia: University of Pennsylvania Press.

———. 2007. *The Hindu Temple,* VOLS 1–2. New Delhi: Motilal Banarsidass Publishers.

KRAUT, Anthea. 2015. *Choreographing Copyright: Race, Gender, and Intellectual Property Rights in American Dance*. New York: Oxford University Press.

KUGLE, Scott. 2007. *Sufis and Saints' Bodies: Mysticism, Corporeality, and Sacred Power in Islam*. Chapel Hill: University of North Carolina Press.

KULKE, Hermann. 1978. *Devaraja Cult*. Ithaca: Cornell University Press.

———. 1981. 'King Anangabhima III, the Veritable Founder of the Gajapati Kingship and of the Jagannatha Trinity at Puri'. *Journal of the Royal Asiatic Society of Great Britain and Ireland* 1: 26–39.

———. 1994. *Religion and Society in Eastern India*. Bhubaneshwar: Eschmann Memorial Fund.

———. 2006. 'The Integrative Model of State Formation in Early Medieval India: Some Historiographic Remarks' in Masaaki Kimura and Akio Tanabe (eds), *The State in India: Past and Present*. New Delhi: Oxford University Press, pp. 59–81.

———. 2010. 'Yayati Kesari Revisited: Ramachandra of Khurda and the Yayati Kesari Legend of Puri' in Peter Berger, Roland Hardenberg, Ellen Katner and Michael Prager (eds), *The Anthropology of Values: Essays in Honor of Georg Pfeffer*. Delhi: Pearson, pp. 400–11.

——— and Burkhard Schnepel (eds). 2001. *Jagannath Revisited: Studying Society, Religion and the State in Orissa*. New Delhi: Manohar.

KULSHRESHTHA, Sushma and A. C. Sarangi. 2001. *Abhinaya-Chandrika and Odissi Dance*, VOLS 1–2. New Delhi: Eastern Book Linkers.

KUMAR, Kiran. 2018. Odissi Documentation Project. Chowk Productions website. Available at: http://www.chowk.sg/odp (last accessed 22 August 2018).

LALIT KALA AKADEMI. 1981. *The Blue God*. New Delhi: Lalit Kala Akademi.

LALITHA, Vakulabharanam. 2011. *Women, Religion and Tradition: The Cult of Joginis, Matangis and Basvis*. Bhopal: Indira Gandhi Rashtriya Manav Sangrahalya

LARASATI, Rachmi Diya. 2013. *The Dance That Makes You Vanish: Cultural Reconstruction in Post-Genocide Indonesia*. Minneapolis: University of Minnesota Press.

LAURIE, William Ferguson Beatson. 1852. *The Idol-Shrine: Or, the Origin, History, and Worship of the Great Temple of Jagannath*, 2nd EDN. Madras: Pharoah and Co., at the Atheneum Press, Mount Road.

LEFEBVRE, Henri. 1991. *The Production of Space* (Donald Nicholson-Smith trans.). Malden: Blackwell.

LELE, Jayant (ed.). 1981. *Tradition and Modernity in Bhakti Movements.* Leiden: E. J. Brill.

LEONARD, Karen. 2013. 'Political Players: Courtesans of Hyderabad'. *Indian Economic and Social History Review,* 50(4): 423–48.

LEPECKI, André. 2004. 'Inscribing Dance' in André Lepecki (ed.), *Of the Presence of the Body: Essays on Dance and Performance Theory.* Middletown: Wesleyan University Press, pp. 124–39.

———. 2006. *Exhausting Dance: Performance and the Politics of Movement.* New York: Routledge, 2006.

LEVINE, Philippa. 1996. 'Rereading the 1890s: Veneral Disease as "Constitutional Crisis" in Britain and British India'. *The Journal of Asian Studies,* 55(3) (August): 585–612.

———. 2000. 'Orientalist Sociology and the Creation of Colonial Sexualities'. *Feminist Review,* 65 ('Reconstructing Femininities: Colonial Intersections of Gender, Race, Religion, and Class' issue) (Summer): 5–21.

———. 2003. *Prostitution, Race & Politics: Policing Venereal Disease in the British Empire.* New York: Routledge.

LINDA, Mary F. 1990. 'The Kalinga Temple Form'. *Ars Orientalis,* 20: 87–111.

LINGAT, Robert. 1993. *The Classical Law of India* (J. Duncan M. Derrett trans.). Delhi: Munshiram Manoharlal.

LOPEZ Y ROYO, Alessandra. 2007a. 'The Reinvention of Odissi Classical Dance as a Temple Ritual' in Evangelos Kyriakidis (ed.), *The Archeology of Ritual.* Los Angeles: Cotsen Institute of Archaeology, UCLA, pp. 155–81.

———. 2007b. *Performing Konarak, Performing Hirapur: Documenting The Odissi Of Guru Surendranath.* UK, 35 mins, colour, DVD. London: SOASIS/AHRC Research Centre for Cross-Cultural Music and Dance Performance.

———. 2008. *ReConstructing and RePresenting Dance: Exploring the Dance/Archaeology Conjunction.* E-book published online by Stanford Humanities Lab, Stanford University, Palo Alto, California. Available at: http://humanitieslab.stanford.edu/117/Home (last accessed on 15 May 2009). Link currently inactive.

[LOPEZ Y ROYO] IYER, Alessandra. 1993. 'A Fresh Look at Nritta (Or Nritta: Steps in the Dark?)'. Dance Research,11(2) (Autumn): 3–15.

LORENZEN, David (ed.). 1995. *Bhakti Religion in Northern India*. Albany: SUNY Press.

LOS ANGELES COUNTY MUSEUM OF ART (LACMA). 1984(?). Interview with Sanjukta Panigrahi by Nancy Mason Hauser. VHS, colour, 18 mins.

LOWEN, Sharon. 2001. *The Dancing Phenomenon: Kelucharan Mohapatra*. New Delhi: Roli Books.

———. 2004. *Odissi*. New Delhi: Wisdom Tree.

———. 2005. *The Performing Arts of India: Development and Spread Across the Globe*. Gurgaon: Shubhi Publications.

———. 2007. Interview with author. New Delhi, 25 August.

———. 2014. 'Remembering Oriya Girl Sanjukta Panigrahi, Dancer of India'. *Deccan Chronicle* online, 24 October. Available at: goo.gl/C1WNqf (last accessed on 2 July 2018).

LYON, Andrew (ed.). 1873. 'Contagious Diseases. Act No. XIV of 1868 Act' in *The Law of India, Vol. II: The Miscellaneous Laws*. Bombay: Thacker, Vining & Co., pp. 194–200.

MAHANIDHI SWAMI. 2008. *Prabhupada at Radha-Damodara*: Solitary Years of India's Greatest Saint. N.p.: Mahanidhi Swami. Ebook.

MAHANTY, Surendra and Orissa Sahitya Akademi. 1982. *Souvenir, Orissa Sahitya Akademi Silver Jubilee*. Bhubaneswar: Orissa Sahitya Akademi.

MAHAPATRA, Kedarnath (ed.). 1996. *A Descriptive Catalogue of Sanskrit Manuscripts of Orissa*, VOL. 2. Bhubaneshwar: Orissa Sahitya Akademi.

MAHAPATRA, Kelucharan. 1983. 'Our Art Is Our God'. Interview with Ulrich Tegeder and Madhavi Mudgal. *Ballett International* 6(3) (March): 16–17, 50. Item no. *MGZA 83-696, Jerome Robbins Dance Division, New York Public Library for the Performing Arts, New York City.

MAHAPATRA, Ratikant. 2008. Interview with author. Bhubaneshwar, India, 23 February.

MAHAPATRA, Sitakant. 1979a. 'Preserving the Purity of Odissi Dance'. *Times of India*, Sunday, 25 February, p. 8. Item call no. *MGZR Odissi clippings file, Jerome Robbins Dance Division, New York Public Library for the Performing Arts, New York City.

———. 1979b. *Gestures of Intimacy*. Calcutta: United Writers.

——. 1985. 'Prahlada Nataka: A Window on a Syncretic Performative Tradition'. *National Centre for the Performing Arts Quarterly Journal* 14(1) (March): 15–25.

——. 1991. *Tribal Wall Paintings of Orissa*. Bhubaneswar: Orissa Lalit Kala Akademi.

—— (ed.). 1993. *Chhau Dance of Mayurbhanj*. Cuttack: Vidyapuri.

MAHMOOD, Saba. 2005. *The Politics of Piety: The Islamic Revival and the Feminist Subject*. Princeton, NJ: Princeton University Press.

MALLIA, Chitta Ranjan. 2013. 'Gotipua Dance Tradition in Odisha: An Overview'. *Odisha Review* (October): 55–9.

MALLIK, Basanta Kumar. 2004. *Paradigms of Dissent and Protest: Social Movements in Eastern India*. New Delhi: Manohar.

MANI, Lata. 1998. *Contentious Traditions: The Debate on Sati in Colonial India*. Berkeley and Los Angeles: University of California Press.

MANNING, Susan. 1993. *Ecstasy and the Demon: Feminism and Nationalism in the Dances of Mary Wigman*. Berkeley: University of California Press.

MANSFIELD, P. T. 1929. *Bihar and Orissa District Gazetteer: Puri*, REV. EDN. Patna: Government Printing, Bihar and Orissa.

MANSINGH, Sonal. 1997a. 'Dancing on Poisonous Snakes'. *Ballett International/Tanz Aktuell* [English EDN] (July): 38.

——. 1997b. 'Odissi'. *Ballett International/Tanz Aktuell* [English EDN] (July): 36–7.

MANU 1869[1796]. *The Institutes of Hindu Law, or the Ordinances of Manu*, 3rd EDN (William Jones and Graves Chamney Haughton trans; Standish Grove Grady ed.). London: W.H. Allen.

MANU AND BHRIGU. 2003. *Manusmriti* (M. N. Dutt trans. and R.N. Sharma ed.). Delhi: Chaukhamba Sanskrit Pratishthan.

MARG. 1960. *Volume 13(2)—Orissi Dance* (March).

——. 1968. *Volume 22(1)—Chhau Dances of India* (December).

MARGLIN, Frédérique Apffel. 1985a. 'Types of Oppositions in Hindu Culture'. *Journal of Developing Societies* 1(1): 65–83.

——. 1985b. *Wives of the God-King: The Rituals of the Devadasis of Puri*. New Delhi: Oxford University Press.

——. 1990. 'Refining the Body: Transformative Emotion in Ritual Dance' in Owen Lynch (ed.), *Divine Passions: The Social Construction of Emotion in India*. Berkeley: University of California Press, pp. 212–36.

——. 1992. 'Jagannath Puri' (interview) in Steven Rosen (ed.), *Vaisnavism: Contemporary Scholars Discuss the Gaudiya Tradition*. Brooklyn: FOLK Books, pp. 207–17.

——. 2008. *Rhythms of Life: Enacting the World with the Goddesses of Orissa*. New Delhi: Oxford University Press.

MARTIN, Randy. 1998. *Critical Moves: Dance Studies in Theory and Politics*. Durham: Duke University Press.

MASSAD, Joseph. 2002. 'Re-orienting Desire: The Gay International and the Arab World'. *Public Culture* 14(2): 361–85.

——. 2008. *Desiring Arabs*. Chicago: University of Chicago Press.

MASSUMI, Brian. 2002. *Parables for the Virtual: Movement, Affect, Sensation*. Durham: Duke University Press.

MATANGA Muni. 1992 & 1994[sixth century CE]. *Brhaddesi of Sri Matanga Muni* [Brihaddeshi], VOLS 1–2 (Prem Lata Sharma trans. and ed.). Delhi: Indira Gandhi National Centre for the Arts, and Motilal Banarsidass.

MATSUDA, Mari J. 1996. *Where Is Your Body? and Other Essays on Race, Gender, and the Law*. Boston: Beacon Press.

MATTSON, Rachel. 2004. 'The Seductions of Dissonance: Ragini Devi and the Idea of India in the US, 1893–1965'. PhD thesis, New York University, New York.

MAURY, Curt. 1969. *Folk Origins of Indian Art*. New York: Columbia University Press.

MAUSS, Marcel. 2006[1935] 'Techniques of the Body': *Techniques, Technology, and Civilisation* (Nathan Schlanger trans. and ed.). Oxford: Berghahn Books.

——. 2000. *The Gift* (W. D. Halls trans.). New York: W. W. Norton.

MAYO, Katherine. 1927. *Mother India*. New York: Harcourt, Brace and Company, Inc.

MEDURI, Avanti. 1988. 'Bharatanatyam—What Are You?' *Asian Theatre Journal*, 5(1): 1–22.

——. 1996. 'Nation, Woman, Representation: The Sutured History of the Devadasi and Her Dance'. Ph.D. Thesis, Graduate School of Arts and Sciences, New York University.

MELZER, Sara E. and Kathryn Norberg (eds). 1998. *From the Royal to the Republican Body: Incorporating the Political in Seventeenth- and Eighteenth-Century France*. Berkeley: University of California Press.

MEDURI, Avanti (ed.). 2005. *Rukmini Devi Arundale, 1904–1986: A Visionary Architect of Indian Culture and the Performing Arts*. Delhi: Motilal Banarsidass.

MEHTA, Pratap Bhanu. 2004. 'World Religions and Democracy: Hinduism and Self-Rule'. *Journal of Democracy*, 15(3) (July): 108–21.

MEFTAHI, Ida. 2016. *Gender and Dance in Modern Iran: Biopolitics on Stage*. New York: Routledge.

MENON, Nivedita. 2004. *Recovering Subversion: Feminist Politics Beyond the Law*. Urbana: University of Illinois Press, 2004.

MENON, Ramesh. 2011[2007]. *Bhagavata Purana*, VOLS 1–2. New Delhi: Rupa.

MILLER, David M. and Dorothy C. Wertz. 1976. *Hindu Monastic Life: The Monks and Monasteries of Bhubaneswar*. Quebec: McGill-Queen's University Press.

MINAI, Cassidy. 2013. 'Odissi Dance in Odia Films'. *Cinemanrityagharana.blogspot.com*, 28 November. Available at: goo.gl/cHDGC2 (last accessed on 29 June 2018).

MIRZA NATHAN [Alaudin Isfahan]. 1936. *Baharistan-I-Ghaybi: A History of the Mughal Wars in Assam, Cooch Behar, Bengal, Bihar and Orissa During the Reigns of Jahangir and Shahjahan*, VOLS. 1 and 2 (M. I. Borah trans.). Gauhati: Government of Assam and Department of Historical and Antiquarian Studies, Narayani Handiqi Historical Institute.

MISHRA, D. B. 2006. 'Glimpses of Performing Art Heritage in Orissan Inscriptions'. *Orissa Review* (May): 23–9. Available at: http://magazines.odisha.gov.in/Orissareview/may2006/engpdf/22-29.pdf (last accessed on 15 May 2009).

MISHRA, Hari Ram. 1964. *Theory of Rasa in Sanskrit Drama with a Comparative study of General Dramatic Literature*. Chhatarpur: Vindhyachal Prakashan.

MISHRA, K. C. 1984. *Cult of Jagannath*. Calcutta: Firma KLM.

MISHRA, Kailash Pati. 2006. *Aesthetic Philosophy of Abhinavagupta*. Varanasi: Kala Prakashan.

MISHRA, Pankaj. 2005. 'More Trouble Than It Is Worth'. *Common Knowledge* 11(3) (Fall): 432–44.

MISHRA, Purna Chandra. 2013. 'Mahari Tradition of Sri Jagannath Temple'. *Odisha Review* (July): 49–53.

MISRA, Prithwiraj. 2000. 'Shiva and His Consorts: The Yoginis of Hirapur'. *Manushi*, 118: 13–18.

MITTER, Partha. 1994. *Art and Nationalism in Colonial India, 1850–1922.* Cambridge: Cambridge University Press.

MITRA, Rajendra Lal. 2007[1875]. *Antiquities of Orissa*, VOLS 1–2. Bhubaneswar: Amadeus Press.

MOHANTY, A. B. (ed.). 1960. *Madalapanji* [Odia]. Cuttack: Prachi Samiti.

MOHANTY, Bansidhar (ed.). 1995. Silpa Ratnakara. Bhubaneswar: Orissa Lalit Kala Akademi.

MOHANTY, Chandra Talpade. 1991. 'Under Western Eyes' in Chandra Talpade Mohanty, Ann Russo and Lourdes Torres (eds), *Third World Women and the Politics of Feminism.* Bloomington: Indiana University Press, pp. 51–80.

MOHANTY, Gopinath, et al. (eds). 2008. *Cultural Heritage of Orissa, Volume 10: Puri District, Part 1.* Bhubaneswar, State Level Vyasakabi.

MOHANTY, Kumkum. 2010. 'Steps to Success'. *The Telegraph*, Monday, 9 August. Available at: goo.gl/dEgrhg (last accessed on 2 July 2018).

MOHANTY, Nivedita. 1982. *Oriya Nationalism: Quest for a United Orissa, 1866–1936.* New Delhi: Manohar.

MOHANTY, Prafulla Kumar. 2002. *State Formation in Ancient Orissa.* Kolkata: Punthi Pustak.

MOHANTY, Sachidananda (ed.). 2005. *Early Women's Writings in Orissa, 1898–1950.* New Delhi: Sage Publications.

———. 2008. *Gender and Cultural Identity in Colonial Orissa.* Hyderabad: Orient Longman.

MOHANTY, Surendra. 1982. *Lord Jagannatha: The Microcrosm of Indian Spiritual Culture.* Bhubaneswar: Orissa Sahitya Akademi.

MOHANTY HEJMADI, Priyambada. 1990. 'The Trinity of Odissi'. *Sangeet Natak*, 96 (April–June): 3–18.

———. 2012. Interview with author. Bhubaneshwar, India, 14 March.

———. 2017. Interview with Tapati Chowdurie. Narthaki.com, 11 June. Available at: goo.gl/o6JWnA (last accessed on 2 July 2018).

———, and Ahalya Hejmadi Patnaik. 2007. *Odissi: An Indian Classical Form.* New Delhi: Aryan Books International.

MOHAPATRA, Ghanshyam. 1971. *Odissi Dance*. India, 21 min. colour, 16mm film (1 reel). Konark Films PVT Ltd. Dance director: Guru Kelucharan Mahapatra. Music: Raghunath Panigrahi. English narration by Ritha Devi.

MOHAPATRA, Ramesh Prasad. 1984. *Jaina Monuments of Orissa*. Delhi: D. K. Publications.

MOHAPATRA, Rupashree. 2012. Interview with author. Puri, India, 4 December.

MORE, Thomas. 1965[1516]. *Utopia* (Paul Turner trans.). London: Penguin.

MORRIS, Gay and Jens Giersdorf (eds). 2016. *Choreographies of 21st Century Wars*. New York: Oxford University Press.

MUBAYI, Yamini. 2005. *Altar of Power: The Temple and the State in the Land of Jagannath, Sixteenth to Nineteenth Century*. New Delhi: Manohar.

MUKHERJEE, Binode Behari. 1988. *Abanindranath Tagore* (Kshitis Roy trans.). New Delhi: National Gallery of Modern Art.

MUKHERJEE, Mithi. 2010. *India in the Shadows of Empire: A Legal and Political History, 1774–1950*. New Delhi: Oxford University Press.

MUKHERJEE, Prabhat. 1979. *History of the Chaitanya Faith in Orissa*. New Delhi: Manohar.

———. 1981. *The History of Medieval Vaishnaism in Orissa*. New Delhi: Asian Educational Services.

MUÑOZ, José. 1999. *Disidentifications: Queers of Colour and the Performance of Politics*. Minneapolis: University of Minneapolis Press, 1999.

———. 2009. *Cruising Utopia: The Then and There of Queer Futurity*. New York: New York University Press.

MURALIDHAR Rao, D. 1995. *Vaastu Shilpa Shastra*. Bangalore: SBS Publishers.

NAIR, Janaki. 1994. 'The Devadasi, Dharma and the State'. *Economic and Political Weekly* 29(50) (10 December): 3157–9, 3161–7.

———. 1996. *Women and Law in Colonial India: A Social History*. New Delhi: Kali for Women.

NAIR, Sreenath (ed.). 2015. *The Natysastra and the Body in Performance*. Jefferson: McFarland and Company.

NANDA, Chandi Prasad. 2008. *Vocalizing Silence: Political Protests in Orissa, 1930–42*. New Delhi: Sage.

NANDIKESVARA. 1917. *The Mirror of Gesture, Being the Abhinaya Darpana of Nandikesvara* (Anand Coomaraswamy and Gopala Kristnayya Duggirala trans). Cambridge, MA: Harvard University Press.

———. 1936. *The Mirror of Gesture, Being the Abhinaya Darpana of Nandikesvara* (Anand Coomaraswamy and Duggirala Gopalakrishna trans). New York: E. Weyhe.

———. 1957. *Abhinayadarpanam*, 2nd EDN (Manmohan Ghosh trans.). Calcutta: Firma K.L. Mukhopadhyaya.

———. 1975. *Abhinayadarpanam*, 3rd EDN (Manmohan Ghosh trans.). Calcutta: Manisha Granthalaya.

NANDY, Ashis. 1989. 'The Political Culture of the Indian State'. *Daedalus*, 118(4) (Fall): 1–26.

———. 1994. *The Illegitimacy of Nationalism*. Delhi: Oxford University Press.

———. 1995. 'An Anti-Secularist Manifesto'. *India International Quarterly* 22(1) (Spring): 35–64.

———. 1997. 'The Twilight of Certitudes: Secularism, Hindu Nationalism, and Other Masks of Deculturation'. *Alternatives: Global, Local, Political* 22(2) (April–June): 157–76.

———. 2015. *The Intimate Enemy: Loss and Recovery of Self under Colonialism*, 2nd EDN. New Delhi: Oxford University Press.

———. 2002. 'Unclaimed Baggage'. *The Little Magazine* 3(2): 14–19. Available at: http://www.littlemag.com/faith/ashis.html (last accessed 3 September 2018).

NARAYAN, Shovana. 1998. *Kathak: Rhythmic Echoes and Reflections*. New Delhi: Roli Books.

———. 2003. *Performing Arts in India: A Policy Perspective*. New Delhi: Kanishka Publishers.

———. 2004a. *Indian Theatre and Dance Traditions*. New Delhi: Harman Publishing House.

———. 2004b. *Kathak*. New Delhi: Wisdom Tree.

———. 2007. *Krishna in Performing Arts*. Gurgaon: Shubhi Publications.

NARAYANAN, Mundoli. 2006. 'Over-Ritualization of Performance: Western Discourses on Kutiyattam'. *TDR* 50(2) (Summer, T190): 136–53.

NARAYANAN, Vasudha. 1999. 'Brimming with Bhakti, Embodiments of Shakti: Devotees, Deities, Performers, Reformers, and Other Women of Power in the Hindu Tradition', in Feminism and World Religions, eds. Arvind Sharma and Katherine K. Young. Albany: SUNY Press.

NARTANAM. 2015. Volume 15(1)—*Folk Dances of Odisha* (January–March).

NAYAK, Smritilekha. 2008. 'Dance and Architecture: Body, Form, Space, and Transformation'. M.Arch. thesis, University of Maryland.

NEEDHAM, Anuradha and Rajeshwari Sunder Rajan (eds). 2007. *The Crisis of Secularism in India*. Durham: Duke University Press.

NELSON, Christopher T. 2008. *Dancing with the Dead: Memory, Performance, and Everyday Life in Postwar Okinawa*. Durham, NC: Duke University Press.

NESS, Sally Ann. 2008. 'The Inscription of Gesture: Inward Migrations in Dance' in Carrie Noland and Sally Ann Ness (eds), *Migrations of Gesture*. Minneapolis: University of Minnesota Press, pp. 1–30.

NEVEU KRINGELBACH, Hélène. 2013. *Dance Circles: Movement, Morality, and Self-Fashioning in Urban Senegal*. New York: Berghahn Books.

NEVILLE, Pran. 1996. *Nautch Girls of India: Dancers, Singers, Playmates*. New Delhi: Variety Book Depot.

NGUGI wa Thiong'o. 1998. *Penpoints, Gunpoints, and Dreams: Towards a Critical Theory of the Arts and the State in Africa*. Oxford: Clarendon Press.

———. 2007. 'Notes Towards a Performance Theory of Orature'. *Performance Research* 12(3) (September): 4–7.

NIETSCHZE, Friedrich. 2004[1873]'.On the Use and Abuse of History for Life' (Ian Johnston trans.). Available at: http://www.mala.bc.ca/~johnstoi/Nietzsche/history.htm (last accessed on 15 May 2009).

NISSHANK. 1958. 'A Survey of the Dance in India'. *Times of India*, 15 August, pp. 18–19.

NORA, Pierre. 1989. 'Between Memory and History: Les Lieux des Memoires'. *Representations*, 26 (Spring 1989): 7–25.

NORMAN, Dorothy. 1957. 'Folk Art in Orissa, India'. *College Art Journal* 16(2) (Winter 1957): 1000–108.

NRUTYAYAN. 2012. Website on Guru Deba Prasad Das dance style. Nrutyayan.com (last accessed on 2 July 2018).

O'SHEA, Janet. 2007. *At Home in the World: Bharata Natyam on the Global Stage*. Middletown: Wesleyan University Press.

ODISSI RESEARCH CENTRE. 1995. *Odissi Dance Path Finder*, VOL. 2. Bhubaneshwar: Odissi Research Centre.

———. 2005. *The Odissi Dance Path Finder*, VOL. I, 3rd EDN. Bhubaneshwar: Odissi Research Centre.

OLDENBURG, Veena Talwar. 1990. 'Lifestyle as Resistance: The Case of the Courtesans of Lucknow'. *Feminist Studies* 16(2) ('Speaking for Others/Speaking for Self: Women of Color' issue) (Summer): 259–87. Available at: goo.gl/TQuXZM (last accessed on 2 July 2018).

OMAR, Aref. 2008. 'The Origin of Odissi'. *New Sunday Times, Sunday People* (10 May). Available at: https://goo.gl/g2Irv6 (last accessed on 22 August 2018).

ORISSA STATE MUSEUM. 2006. *The Orissa Historical Research Journal* 48(2). Bhubaneshwar: Orissa State Museum.

———. 2007a. *Descriptive Catalogue of Illustrated Manuscripts* (Platinum Jubilee Publication). (Bhagyalipi Malla comp. and ed.). Bhubaneshwar: Orissa State Museum.

———. 2007b. *The Orissa Historical Research Journal*, 48(3 and 4) (Platinum Jubilee Special Issue). Bhubaneshwar: Orissa State Museum.

———. 2008a. *Flora and Fauna in Palmleaf Panorama: A Selection from Orissa State Museum*. Bhubaneswar: Orissa State Museum.

———. 2008b. *Passion on Palmleaf: A Collection from Orissa State Museum*. Bhubaneswar: Orissa State Museum.

———. n.d . *Illustrated Palmleaf Manuscripts of Orissa: A Selection from Orissa State Museum*. Bhubaneswar: Orissa State Museum.

ORISSA LALIT KALA AKADEMI. 1992. *Rangarekha*. Bhubaneswar: Orissa Lalit Kala Akademi

ORR, Leslie C. 2000. *Donors, Devotees, and Daughters of God: Temple Women in Medieval Tamil Nadu*. Oxford: Oxford University Press.

OZOUF, Mona. 1988. *Festivals and the French Revolution* (Alan Sheridan trans.). Cambridge: Harvard University Press.

PAES, Domingo and Fernao Nunes. 1900[1510]. *A Forgotten Empire (Vijayanagar): A Contribution to the History of India* (Robert Sewell trans. and ed.) London: Swan Sonnenschein and Co., Ltd.

PAL, Pratapaditya (ed.). 2001. *Orissa Revisited*. Mumbai: Marg Publications.

——— (ed.). 2009. *Goddess Durga: The Power and the Glory*. Mumbai: Marg Publications.

PALLASMAA, Juhani. 2005. *The Eyes of the Skin: Architecture and the Senses*. West Sussex: John Wiley & Sons, Ltd.

PANDA, D. C. 2000. *Kalingara Mandira Sthapatya* [Odia]. Bhubaneswar: Art Centre.

———. 2003. *Bharatiya Samskruti O Murtikalare: Hindu Devadevi* [Odia]. Bhubaneswar: Art Centre.

———. 2006. *Kalingara Mandira Gatrare: Devadevi Murti* [Odia]. Bhubaneswar: Art Centre.

PANDA, Namita. 2011a. 'Danseuse Steps in to Revive Mahari'. *The Telegraph*. 19 May. Available at: goo.gl/bkZjqq (last accessed on 2 July 2018)

———. 2011b. 'Dancers Pay Tribute to Guru: Danseuse Rupashree Mohapatra visits Sashimani Devi, the Last Living Devadasi of Jagannath Temple'. *The Telegraph*, 6 September. Available at: goo.gl/39Sg7T (last accessed on 2 July 2018).

PANDA, Sasanka S. 2004. 'Durga Worship in the Upper Mahanadi Valley'. *Orissa Review* (October): 66–80.

PANDA, Shishir Kumar. 1991. *Medieval Orissa: A Socio-Economic Study*. New Delhi: Mittal Publications.

———. 1995. *The State and the Statecraft in Medieval Orissa Under the Later Eastern Gangas (A.D. 1038–1434)*. Calcutta: K. P. Bagchi Publications.

PANDARIKA VITTHALA. 1994[sixteenth century CE]. *Nartana-Nirnaya of Pandarika Vitthala*, VOL. 1 (R. Sathyanarayana trans. and ed.). Delhi: Motilal Banarsidass.

———1996[sixteenth century CE]. *Nartana-Nirnaya of Pandarika Vitthala*, VOL. 2 (R. Sathyanarayana trans. and ed.). Delhi: Motilal Banarsidass.

———. 1998[sixteenth century CE]. *Nartana-Nirnaya of Pandarika Vitthala*, VOL. 3 (R. Sathyanarayana trans. and ed.). Delhi: Motilal Banarsidass.

PANDE, Alka. 2005. 'Myriad Moods of Love' in Harsha V. Dehejia (ed.), *A Celebration of Love: The Romantic Heroine in the Indian Arts*. New Delhi: Roli Books, pp. 45–53.

PANDE, S. C. (ed.). 2009. *The Concept of Rasa, With Special Reference to Abhinavagupta*. Shimla: Indian Institute of Advanced Study.

PANI, Jiwan. 1972. 'Abhinaya in Odissi Dance'. *Sangeet Natak* 24: 39–43.

———. 1984. 'The Tradition of Odissi Music'. *National Center for Performing Arts Quarterly Journal* 13(1) (March): 31–7.

———. 1985. 'The Tradition of Maahaari Dance'. *National Center for Performing Arts Quarterly Journal* 14(3) (September): 24–8.

———. 1995. 'The Experience of Rasa Through Indian Art Dances' in Bimal Mukherjee and Sunil Kothari (eds), *Rasa: The Indian Performing*

Arts in the Last Twenty-Five Years, Volume 1: Music and Dance. Calcutta: Anamika Kala Sangam, 1995, pp. 149–56.

——. 2002. *Ang Tarang: Mayurbhanj Chhau.* India, 41 mins, colour, DVD. Sangeet Natak Akademi.

——. 2004. *Back to the Roots: Essays on Performing Arts of India* (Reba Pani comp.). New Delhi: Manohar.

PANI, Subas. 2004. *Blue Hill: Hymns to Lord Jagannatha* (translations from Oriya and Sanskrit). Delhi: Rupa.

PANIGRAHI, Krishna Chandra (K. C.). 1961. *Archeological Remains at Bhubaneshwar.* Calcutta: Orient Longman.

——. 1984. 'The Authenticity of the Madala Panji and Methods of Assessing its HIstorical Correctness' in Daityari Panda and Sarat Chandra Panigrahi (eds), *The Cult and Culture of Lord Jagannath.* Cuttack: Rashtrabhasha Samavaya Prakashan.

——. 2008. *History of Orissa (Hindu Period).* Cuttack: Kitab Mahal.

PANIGRAHI, Ramesh P. 1998. *Perspectives on Odissi Theatre.* Bhubaneswar: Orissa Sangeet Natak Akademi.

PANIGRAHI, Sanjukta. 1988. 'Dance Is Bliss'. Interview with K. K. Gopalakrishnan. *Mirror* (July): 36–7.

——.1993. Interview with Barnali Sen. *The Telegraph Weekend,* 10 April, p. 8.

——. 1997[1995]. 'The Rediff Special: Sanjukta Panigrahi'. Interview with *Savvy Magazine,* reprinted on Rediff.com. Available at: goo.gl/u14VS4 (last accessed on 2 July 2018).

PANIGRAHI, Sri Nilamadhab (ed.). 1995. *Sangitarnavachandrika by Nilakanth.* Bhubaneswar: Orissa Sangeet Natak Akademi.

PANIKKAR, K. N. 2001. 'Outsider as Enemy: The Politics of Rewriting History in India'. *Frontline,* 18(1) (6–19 January), online edition. Available at: goo.gl/cGwt24 (last accessed on 2 July 2018).

——. 2007. *Colonialism, Culture and Resistance.* New Delhi: Oxford University Press.

PANIKKAR, Shivaji K. and Abha Sheth (eds). 2003. *Art of Ancient India: Contextualizing Social Relations.* Conference proceedings, 'Theorizing India's Pre-modern Visual Culture: Issues of Class, Caste, Gender, and Sexualities', 13–15 February, Department of Art History and Aesthetics, Maharaja Sayajirao University of Baroda.

PANIKKAR, Shivaji K. and Gary Smith. 1997. *Saptamatrka Worship and Sculptures: An Iconological Interpretation of Conflicts and Resolutions in the Storied Bramanical Icons*. New Delhi: D. K. Printworld.

PANINI. 1891–98. *The Ashtadhyayi of Panini* (Srisa Chandra Vasu trans.), BOOK IV (1896). Benares: Sindhu Charan Bose. Available at: goo.gl/aJQzbQ (last accessed on 2 July 2018).

PARASHMONI DEVI. 2012. Interview with author. Puri, India, 3 and 4 December.

———. 2014. Performance at Jagannath temple. Puri, India, 23 December.

PARGTER, F. E. 1987. 'Ancient Countries in Eastern India'. *Journal of the Asiatic Society of Bengal*, 66.1(2) (March): 85–112.

PARIDA, A. N. 1999. *Early Temples of Orissa (From the Sixth Century A.D. to the End of Somavamsi Rule)*. Delhi: Commonwealth Publishers.

PARKER, Kunal. 1998. ' "A Corporation of Superior Prostitutes": Anglo-Indian Legal Conceptions of Temple Dancing Girls, 1800-1914'. *Modern Asian Studies* 32(3): 559–633.

PATHY, Dinanath. 2007. *Rethinking Odissi*. New Delhi: Harman Publishing House.

PATHY, Soubhagya, Rahul Acharya, Chittaranjan Bairisal and Harsa Kumar Satapathy. 2005. 'The Costumes of the Sutra Odissi Dancers of Malaysia: A Dialogue with Textual and Substantial Evidences'. Narthaki.com, 28 September. Available at: goo.gl/si45ZY (last accessed on 2 July 2018).

———. 2006. 'Sanjukta Panigrahi: The Pioneer'. *Angarag* 2 (Autumn): 10–19.

PATI, Biswamoy. 1992. 'Dialectics of Transition: Orissa, 1943–50'. *Economic and Political Weekly* 27(7) (15 February): 353–64.

———. 1995. 'Of Devadasis, "Tradition", and Politics'. *Economic and Political Weekly* 30(43) (28 October): 2728.

———. 1997. 'Between "Then" and "Now": Popular Memory in Orissa'. *Economic and Political Weekly* 34(4) (14–20 June): 1391–1394.

———. 2001. *Situating Social History: Orissa (1800–1997)*. New Delhi: Orient Longman Limited.

PATI, Surendranath. 2017. 'The Defunct "Sevas" in the Sri Mandira Puri'. *Odisha Review* (June): 135–6.

PATNAIK, Dhirenda Nath (D. N.). 1971. *Odissi Dance*. Bhubaneshwar: Orissa Sangeet Natak Akademi.

——. 1990. *Odissi Dance*, 2nd EDN. Bhubaneshwar: Orissa Sangeet Natak Akademi.

——. 1998. *Folk Theatre of Orissa*. Bhubaneshwar: Orissa Sangeet Natak Akademi.

——. 2001. 'Odissi Dance—Past and Present'. *Nartanam* 1(2) (April–June): 7–13.

——. 2006. *Odissi Dance*, 3rd EDN. Bhubaneswar: Orissa Sangeet Natak Akademi.

——. 2008. Interview with author. Cuttack, India, 4 March.

PATNAIK, Kali Charan [Kalicharan Patnaik / Kalicharan Pattanaik / Kalicharan Pattnaik / Kavichandra Kalicharan Pattanaik]. 2006a[1954–55?]. 'Odissi Dance: Series 1, Kavi Chandra Kali Charan Patnaik' (Soubhagya Pathy ed. and trans.). *Angarag* 1 (Spring): 67–78.

——. 2006b[1954–55?]. 'Odissi Dance: Series 2, Kavi Chandra Kali Charan Patnaik' (Soubhagya Pathy ed. and trans.). *Angarag* 2 (Autumn): 129–34.

——. 2013[1958a]. 'Odissi Dance'. *Sangeet Natak, Papers from the First Dance Seminar* (1958) 47(1–4): 202–14.

——. 1958b. 'Odissi Music'. *Journal of the Music Academy, Madras* 29: 83–91.

——. 1958c. 'Odissi Nritya'. *Journal of the Music Academy, Madras* 29: 92–5.

——. 1967. 'Gitagobinda in Odissi Dance'. Pamphlet in Geet Govind Celebrations proceedings, 18–20 March. Sangeet Natak Akademi archives, New Delhi, India.

PATNAIK, Lal Mohan. 1941. *Resurrected Orissa*. Cuttack: L.M. Patnaik.

PATNAIK, Napoleon. 2012. Interview with author. Dimirasena, Odisha. 16 March.

PATNAIK, Nityanand. 2000. *Sacred Complex of Orissa*. New Delhi: Gyan Publishing House.

PATNAIK, Satyndra. 1987. *Brahmanical Religion in Ancient Orissa*. New Delhi: Ashish Publishing House.

PATNAIK, Tandra. 2005. *Sunya Purusa: Bauddha Vaisnavism of Orissa*. New Delhi: D. K. Printworld.

PATTANAYAK, Subhas Chandra. 2005. 'A Nasty Trick Played in the Guise of Odissi Dance Research'. Orissamatter.com, 9 October. Available at: https://goo.gl/pzFbNz (last accessed on 3 July 2018).

PATRA, K. M. 1971. *Orissa Under the East India Company*. New Delhi: Munshi Manoharlal.

PECHILIS PRENTISS, Karen. 1999. *The Embodiment of Bhakti*. New York: Oxford University Press.

PEGG, James. 1832. *India's Cries to British Humanity*, 3rd EDN. London: Simpkin and Marshall.

———. 1847. *A Voice from India: The British Connection with Idolatry and the Government Grant to the Temple at Juggernarta and Numerous Other Temples in India*. London: John Snow.

———. 1848. *The Government Grant to Juggernaut's Temple*. London: Ward and Co.

PENNER, James. 2014. 'On Aggro Performance: Audience Participation and the Dystopian Response to the Living Theater's Paradise Now'. *Comparative Drama*, 48(1–2) (Spring & Summer): 75–92.

PHELAN, Peggy. 1993. 'The Ontology of Performance: Representation Without Reproduction' in *Unmarked: The Politics of Performance*. London: Routledge, pp. 146–66.

———. 1996. 'Feminist Theory, Poststructuralism and Performance' in Carol Martin (ed.), *A Sourcebook on Feminist Theatre and Performance: On and Beyond the Stage*. New York: Routledge, pp. 157–83.

PILLAI, G. Shankara. 1991. 'Spatial Relationship in Ritual and Performance' in Kapila Vatsyayan (ed.), *Concepts of Space: Ancient and Modern*. New Delhi: Abhinav Publications, pp. 437–9.

PINNEY, Christopher. 1997. *Camera Indica: The Social Life of Indian Photographs*. Chicago: University of Chicago Press.

———. 2004. *Photos of the Gods*. London: Reaktion Books.

POLLUX. 1955a. 'Social Whirl'. *Times of India*, 30 January, p. 10.

———. 1955b. 'Social Whirl'. *Times of India*, 13 February, p. 10.

———. 1959. 'Social Whirl'. *Times of India*, 22 February, p. 8.

POOVAIAH, Sita. 1950. 'The Art and Science of Indian Classical Dancing and Its Social Bearings'. PhD thesis, University of Bombay. Item call no. *MGS (Hindu) 77-663, Asia Dance Project, Jerome Robbins Dance Division, New York Public Library for the Performing Arts, New York City.

POOVEY, Mary. 1995. *Making a Social Body: British Cultural Formation, 1830–1864*. Chicago: University of Chicago Press.

PRAHARAJ, Gopal Chandra. 1931–40. *Purnachandra Oriya Bhashakosha* [Oriya, Bengali, Devanagari, and Roman Alphabets]. Cuttack: Utkal Sahitya Press. Online version published jointly by the University of Chicago Digital South Asia Library, Srujanika, and the US Department of Education, April 2012. Available at goo.gl/BzJHXa (last accessed on 2 July 2018).

PRAJA MANDAL. 1946–47. File 387-P(S)/1946 Praja Mandal Propaganda against the Rulers in Orissa States. Propaganda for Separation of Sambalpur from the Provice of Orissa (correspondence). Item no. IOR/R/1/1/4510, India Office Records, British Library, London.

PRASAD, A. K. 1991. *The Devadasi System in Ancient India: A Study of Temple Dancing Girls*. Delhi: H. K. Publishers.

PRASAD, Pushpa. 1997. 'Akbar and the Jains' in Irfan Habib (ed.), *Akbar and His India*. New Delhi: Oxford University Press, pp. 97–108.

PREVOTS, Naima. 1998. *Dance for Export: Cultural Diplomacy and the Cold War*. Middletown: Wesleyan University Press.

PRICKETT, Stacey. 2013. *Embodied Politics: Dance, Protest, and Identities*. Alton: Dance Books.

PRASAD, Dr Rajendra. 1992[1955]. 'The Role of the Arts' in *Dr. Rajendra Prasad: Correspondence and Select Documents, Volume 17: Presidency Period, January 1954 to December 1955* (Valmiki Choudhary ed.). New Delhi: Allied Publishers, pp. 459–60.

PROSAD, Kshirod. 2006. *Compilation of Odissi Dance Theory*. Cuttack: Kala Vikas Kendra.

PROTEVI, John. 2009. *Political Affect: Connecting the Social and the Somatic*. Minneapolis: University of Minnesota Press.

PUAR, Jasbir. 2007. *Terrorist Assemblages: Homonationalism in Queer Times*. Durham: Duke University Press.

———. 2013. 'Rethinking Homonationalism'. *International Journal of Middle Eastern Studies* 45: 336–9.

PURKAYASTHA, Prarthana. 2014. *Indian Modern Dance, Feminism, and Transnationalism*. Basingstoke: Palgrave Macmillan.

PURUSOTTAMA MISRA. 2009[seventeenth century CE]. *Sangitanarayana* (Mandakranta Bose trans. and ed.). Delhi: Motilal Banarsidass.

PUTCHA, Rumya S. 2013. 'Between History and Historiography: The Origins of Classical Kuchipudi Dance'. *Dance Research Journal* 45(3): 1–20.

———. 2015. 'Dancing in Place: Mythopoetics and the Production of History in Kuchipudi'. *Yearbook for Traditional Music* 47: 1–26.

QURESHI, Regula Burckhardt. 2006. 'Female Agency and Patrilineal Contraints: Situating Courtesans in Twentieth-Century India' in Martha Feldman and Bonnie Gordan (eds), *The Courtesan's Arts: Cross-Cultural Perspectives*. New York: Oxford University Presa, pp. 312–31.

RAGHAVAN, Venkatarama. 2010[1940]. *The Number of Rasa-s*. Chennai: Adyar Library and Research Centre.

RAGINI DEVI. 1928. *Nritanjali: An Introduction to Hindu Dancing*. New York: Oriental Publishers.

———. 1958. 'Odissi, Classical Dance of Orissa'. Excerpt reprinted from *Sunday Standard* (India), 27 April 1958, in *Bulletin* (Institute of Traditional Cultures, Madras), pp. 206–07.

———. 1980[1962]. *Dances of India*. New York: Arno Press.

———. 1990. *Dance Dialects of India*. New Delhi: Motilala Banarsidass.

———. 2002. *Dance Dialects of India*, 3rd REVD EDN. New Delhi: Motilal Banarsidass.

RAJA PANDA. 2012. Interview with author, 28, 29 and 30 June. Puri, India.

RITHA DEVI. 1987. *Vibrant Sculpture / Frozen Dance*. USA, 29 mins, colour, video. Ritham Chhanda (Eternal Rhythm) Dance Academy.

———. 1988. *Satvam Rajas Tamas*. USA, 123 mins, colour, VHS.

———. 2003a. Lecture-Demonstration on Mahari Repertoire. Sundaram Tagore Art Gallery, New York City, 28 June.

———. 2003b. Interview with author. New York City, 19 August.

———. 2008. 'Sixty Years of Odissi'. *Nartanam: A Quarterly Journal of Indian Dance* 7(4) (November 2007–January 2008): 23–36.

RAHMAN [REHMAN], Indrani. 1958. Odissi performance by Indrani Rahman and interview with Philip Garston Jones, ATV. Midland Montage: 27.11.1958: Indian Classical Dance. Media Archive for Central England (MACE), University of Lincoln, UK. Available at: https://goo.gl/UFCz4B (last accessed on 22 August 2018).

———. 1961. *Indrani and Company*. US, black-and-white, 22 mins, video. Performance recorded at Human Rights Day Concert, United Nations General Assembly Hall, New York, December 10. Item call no. *MGZIC 9-4794, 1 video cassette, Jerome Robbins Dance Division, New York Public Library for the Performing Arts, New York City.

———. 1968. Interview with Indrani and interview with Henry H. Crapo (sound recording). Item call no. *MGZTL 4- 2401, 1 sound disc (ca. 24 mins). Jerome Robbins Dance Division, New York Public Library for the Performing Arts, New York City.

———. 1975. Interview with Indrani by Genevieve Oswald in New York City on Dec. 11, 1975 (sound recording). Item call no. *MGZTL 4-391, 2 sound discs (ca. 98 min.), Jerome Robbins Dance Division, New York Public Library for the Performing Arts, New York City.

———. 1976 [1975]. Interview by Genevieve Oswald in New York City on 11 December 1975 (transcript; dated 9 May 1976). Item call no. *MGZMT 5-391, Dance Oral History Project, Jerome Robbins Dance Division, New York Public Library for the Performing Arts, New York City.

———. 1986. *Conversations on the Dance: Indrani and Madhur Jaffrey*. 14 April, Bruno Walter Auditorium, Lincoln Center, New York City (sound recording). Item call no. *MGZTC 3-922, 1 sound cassette (75 min.), Jerome Robbins Dance Division, New York Public Library for the Performing Arts, New York City.

RAHMAN, Sukanya. 2004. *Dancing in the Family: An Unconventional Memoir of Three Women*. New Delhi: Rupa.

———. 2009. 'Remembering Indrani: September 19, 1930–February 5, 1999'. Narthaki.com, 16 December. Available at: goo.gl/4FvviM (last accessed on 2 July 2018).

RAJAMANNAR, P. V. 2013[1958]. 'Inaugural Speech'. *Sangeet Natak* (Papers from the First Dance Seminar), 47(1–4): 1–10.

RAJENDRAN, C. 2016. 'The Sacred and the Profane: Gleanings from the Discourses of Dance Traditions of Ancient India' in Maratt Mythili Anoop and Varun Gulati (eds), *Scripting Dance in Contemporary India*. London: Lexington Books, pp. 3–10.

RAJGURU, S. N. 1958. *Inscriptions of Orissa (300–700 A.D.)*, VOL. I, PART 2. Bhubaneshwar: Orissa State Museum and Orissa Sahitya Akademi.

———. 1960. *Inscriptions of Orissa (c.600–1100 A.D.)* VOL. 2. Bhubaneshwar: Orissa State Museum and Orissa Sahitya Akademi.

———. 1961. *Inscriptions of Orissa (c.1045–1190 A.D.)* VOL. 3, PART 2. Bhubaneshwar: Orissa State Museum and Orissa Sahitya Akademi.

——. 1966. *Inscriptions of Orissa*, VOL. 3, PARTS 1–2. Bhubaneshwar: Orissa State Museum and Orissa Sahitya Akademi.

——. 1972. *History of the Gangas*, PART 2. Bhubaneswar: Orissa State Museum.

——. 1992. *Inscriptions of the Temples of Puri and Origin of Sri Purusottama Jagannatha*, VOL. I, PART I. Puri: Shri Jagannath Sanskrit Vishvavidyalaya.

RAMANUJAN, A. K. 1989. 'Talking to God in the Mother Tongue'. *Manushi* 50–2 (January–June): 9–14.

——. 1999. *The Collected Essays of A. K. Ramanujan* (Vinay Dharwadker ed.). New Delhi: Oxford University Press.

RAMASWAMY, Krishnan, Antonio de Nicolas and Aditi Banerjee (eds). 2007. *Invading the Sacred: An Analysis of Hinduism Studies in America*. New Delhi: Rupa.

RAMBERG, Lucinda. 2014. *Given to the Goddess: South Indian Devadasis and the Sexuality of Religion*. Durham: Duke University Press.

RAMUSACK, Barbara N. 2003. *The Indian Princes and Their States*. Cambridge: Cambridge University Press.

RANBIR, Durga Charan. 2015. 'Mission Odissi'. Interview with Tapatie Chowdurie. *The Hindu* online, 8 January. Available at: https://goo.gl/PspUup (last accessed August 22, 2018).

RAO, Maya. 2012. Interview with author. Bangalore, 10 November.

RAO, Velcheru Narayana and Sanjay Subrahmanyam. 2008. 'An Elegy for Niti: Politics as a Secular Discursive Field in the Indian Old Regime'. *Common Knowledge*, 14(3): 396–423.

RATH, Bijaya Kumar and Satyendra Patnaik. 2008. *Orissa: History, Art and Culture*. Delhi: Sundeep Prakasha.

——, and Kamala Ratnam (eds). 1995. *The Forgotten Monuments of Orissa*. New Delhi: Publications Division, Ministry of Information and Broadcasting, Government of India.

RATH, Jayanti. 2007. 'Kharavela: The Great Philanthropic Emperor'. *Orissa Review* (April): 40–1.

RATH, Shyam Sundar. 2005. *Martial Arts: A Critical Analysis of Orissa*. Delhi: Kapaz Publications.

RATH, Tarini Charan. 1920. 'Ramananda Raya'. *Journal of the Bihar and Orissa Research Society* 6 (September): 448–53. Archival Reference no. J1-14/21, Odisha State Archives, Bhubaneshwar, India. Available at:

https://catalog.hathitrust.org/Record/009017421 (last accessed 22 August 2018).

RATNAKA, Pooja. 2009. 'God's Little Dancers: The Gotipua Tradition of Orissa'. *Craft Revival Quarterly* (May). Available at: goo.gl/uSYLSY (last accessed on 2 July 2018).

RAUT, Madhumita. 2007. *Odissi: What, Why, and How . . . Evolution, Revival, and Technique.* Delhi: B. R. Rhythms.

RAUT, Mayadhar. 2007. Interview with author. New Delhi, 24 September.

RAY, Amita. 1990. 'Calcutta and the Early Growth of the Bengal School of Painting'. *Marg* 41(4) (June): 51–64.

RAY, Aniruddha. 1997. 'Middle Bengali Literature: A Source for the Study of Bengal in the Age of Akbar' in Irfan Habib (ed.), *Akbar and His India.* New Delhi: Oxford, pp. 225–42.

RAY, B. C. 1981. *Orissa Under the Mughals: From Akbar to Alivardi, a Fascinating Study of the Socio-Economic and Cultural History of Orissa.* Calcutta: Punthi Pustak.

RAY, Dipti. 2007. *Prataparudradeva, the Last Great Suryavamsi King of Orissa (AD 1497 to AD 1540): The Great Suryavamsi King of Orissa 1497 to 1540.* New Delhi: Northern Book Centre.

RAY, Himanshu Prabha. 2007. *Sacred Landscapes in Asia: Shared Traditions, Multiple Histories.* New Delhi: Manohar.

REDDY, K. Santhaa. 2002. 'Devadasis: Time to Review History'. Samarthbharat.com, 12 April. Available at: goo.gl/koxfBu (last accessed on 2 July 2018).

REDDY, Muthulakshmi. 1920(?). 'A Paper Against Dedication of Girls to Temples'. SUBJECT FILE NO. II, PART 3, pp. 533–9, Muthulakshmi Reddy Papers, Nehru Memorial Museum and Library.

———. 1935. 'The Peril in Our Streets'. *Indian Social Reformer* (February): 23–5.

REED, Susan. 2010. *Dancing the Nation: Performance, Ritual, and Politics in Sri Lanka.* Madison: University of Wisconsin Press.

RIG VEDA. 1896. Ralph T. H. Griffith trans. Sacred-texts.com. Available at: goo.gl/FMPpsj (last accessed on 2 July 2018).

RISLEY, Herbert and W. Crooke. 1999[1915]. *The People of India.* New Delhi: Asian Educational Services.

RIVAZ, H. T. 1889. *The Bengal Regulations, the Acts of the Governor-General in Council, and the Frontier Regulations Applicable to the Punjab, Volume*

1: *Containing Bengal Regulations, and Acts from 1834 to End of 1872*. Lahore: W. Ball and Co.

ROACH, Joseph R. 1996. *Cities of the Dead: Circum-Atlantic Performance*. New York: Columbia University Press.

ROSEN, Steven J. 2005. 'Sri Radha: The Supreme Nayika of Gaudiya Vaishnavism' in Harsha V. Dehejia (ed.), *A Celebration of Love: The Romantic Heroine in the Indian Arts*. New Delhi: Roli Books, pp. 230–5.

ROSS, Janice. 2015. *Like a Bomb Going Off: Leonid Yakobsen and Ballet as Resistance in Soviet Russia*. New Haven: Yale University Press.

ROUSSEL, Violaine and Anurima Banerji (eds). 2017. *How to do Politics with Art*. London: Routledge.

ROUT, Kartik Chandra. 1988. *Local Self-Government in British Orissa, 1869–1935*. Delhi: Daya Publishing House.

ROWE, Nicholas. 2010. *Raising Dust: A Cultural History of Dance in Palestine*. London: I. B. Tauris.

ROY, Ratna. 2004 [2002]. 'Mahari Dance: An Alternative Narrative in Orissi—A Feminist Analysis' in *Dance in South Asia: New Approaches, Politics and Aesthetics* (Proceedings, 3 March). Swarthmore: Swarthmore College, pp. 55–9.

———. 2006. 'Politics of Representation: The Portrayal of the Female in Guru Pankaj Charan Das's Pancha Kanya Dance Dramas'. *Manushi*, 153: 34–41.

———. 2007. 'The Mahari Tradition'. *Ragavani: Ragamala's Quarterly Journal of South Asian Music and Dance* (Spring, 22 June). Available at: https://goo.gl/7rKJDp (last accessed on 15 May 2009). Link currently inactive.

———. 2009. *Neo Classical Odissi Dance*. New Delhi: Harman Publishing House.

ROY BURMAN, J. J. 1996. 'Hindu-Muslim Syncretism in India'. *Economic and Political Weekly* 31(20) (18 May): 1211–15.

———. 2002. 'Concepts of Syncretism: An Introduction' in *Hindu–Muslim Syncretic Shrines and Communities*. New Delhi: Mittal Publications, pp. 5–34.

RUBIN, Gayle. 1992. 'Thinking Sex: Notes for a Radical Theory of the Politics of Sexuality' in Carol Vance (ed.), *Pleasure and Danger: Exploring Female Sexuality*, 2nd EDN. London: Pandora Press, pp. 267–318.

SACK, Daniel. 2015. *After Live: Possibility, Potentiality, and the Future of Performance*. Ann Arbor: University of Michigan Press.

SAHOO, Itishree. 2009. *Odissi Music: Evolution, Revival, and Technique*. Delhi: B. R. Rhythms

SAHU, Bhairabi Prasad. 1997. *Cultural History of Orissa (1435–1751)*. New Delhi: Anmol Publications.

——. 2001. 'Brahmanical Ideology, Regional Identities and the Construction of Early India'. *Social Scientist* 29(7–8) (July–August): 3–18.

SAHU, N. K. 1984. *Kharavela*. Bhubaneswar: Golden Jubilee Publications.

——. 1996. 'Jainism in East India' in Shyam Singh Shashi (ed.), *Encyclopaedia Indica: India, Pakistan, Bangladesh*. New Delhi: Anmol Publications, pp. 602–42.

SAID, Edward. 1978. *Orientalism*. New York: Vintage.

SANGARI, Kumkum. 1995. 'Politics of Diversity: Religious Communities and Multiple Patriarchies'. *Economic and Political Weekly* 30(51–2) (1995): 3287–312, 3381–90.

—— and Sudesh Vaid (eds). 1989. *Recasting Women: Essays in Indian Colonial History*. New Delhi: Kali for Women.

SANGEET NATAK AKADEMI (SNA). 1956. *SNA Bulletin 4* (March). SNA archives, New Delhi, India.

——. 1958a. *SNA Bulletin 8*, Dance Seminar Number (April). SNA Archives, New Delhi, India.

——. 1958b. *SNA Bulletin 9* (July). SNA archives, New Delhi, India.

——. 1959. *SNA Report 1953–58*. SNA archives, New Delhi, India.

——. 1961. *SNA Bulletin 18* (April). SNA archives, New Delhi, India.

——. 1961. 'Mahari Dancers of Puri Temple'. *Bulletin of Institute of Traditional Cultures, Madras, Part 1*: 164–5. Excerpt reprinted from *Sangeet Natak Akademi Bulletin*, 9 July 1958.

——. 1989. Performance excerpts of Sanjukta Panigrahi at SNA Annual Awards Ceremony, Ravindralaya, Lucknow, Uttar Pradesh, October 1. VHS videocassette, 50 mins, Hindi/English, Reference no. V-563, Documentation Unit, SNA, New Delhi, India.

——. 1987a. 'Pankaj Charan DasInterview in Hindi and Demonstration'. Special Documentation of Eminent Artists, SNA Studio, 22 March. VHS videocassette, 58 mins, Hindi, Reference no. VHS V-297, Documentation Unit, SNA, New Delhi, India.

——. 1987b. 'Priyambada Hejmadi Mohanty (Odissi Dance)'. Performance excerpts from SNA Awards Ceremony, Bhubaneshwar, Odisha, 22 February. VHS videocassette, Oriya/Hindi/English, 27 mins, Reference no. V-289, Documentation Unit, SNA, New Delhi, India.

——. 2000. 'Gotipua Songs of Birabar Sahoo and Group'. Rabindra Mandap, Bhubaneshwar, Orissa, 22 September. VHS videocassette, Reference no. V-5482, Documentation Unit, SNA, New Delhi, India.

——. 2001a. 'Pradakshina—Celebrating the 75th Birth Anniversary of Guru Kelucharan Mahapatra'. 5–6 July, Kamani Auditorium, New Delhi. Reference no. V-5873, Documentation Unit, SNA, New Delhi, India.

——. 2001b. 'Seraikella Chhau'. Jiwan Pani Memorial Festival, India International Center (IIC), New Delhi, 7 November. VHS videocassette, Reference no. VHS-6031, Documentation Unit, SNA, New Delhi, India.

——. 2003. 'Proceedings of Symposium and Workshop on Performing Art Tradition of Orissa with Reference to Odissi Dance, 11–14 May 2003, Toshali Sands, Puri (Orissa)'. VHS videocassettes, total time 34:12 hours, English/Oriya/Hindi, Reference nos. V-6874 to V-6886, Documentation Unit, SNA, New Delhi, India.

——. 2007. 'Nritya Sanrachna—Festival of Choreographic Work'. Performance excerpts of Madhavi Mudgal's choreographies, Pragjyoti Auditorium, Guwahati, Assam, 15 March. VHS videocassette, 53 mins. English/Hindi, Reference no. V-8473. Document Unit, SNA, New Delhi, India.

——. 2007. *Indian Drama in Retrospect.* New Delhi: Hope India Publications.

——. 2010. Sangeet Natak Akademi website: http://www.sangeet-natak.org/ (last accessed on 2 July 2018).

——. 2013[1958]. *Sangeet Natak, Papers from the First Dance Seminar, 1958* 47(1–4).

——. 2014[1958]. 'Programme of the Dance Seminar'. *Sangeet Natak, Papers from the First Dance Seminar, 1958* 48(1–4): 115–20.

SARKAR, Sumit. 2002. *Beyond Nationalist Frames: Postmodernism, Hindu Fundamentalism, History.* Bloomington: Indiana University Press.

——. 1998. *Writing Social History.* Delhi: Oxford University Press.

SARKAR MUNSI, Urmimala. 2014. 'A Century of Negotiations: The Changing Sphere of the Woman Dancer in India' in Subrata Bagchi (ed.), *Beyond the Private World: Indian Women in the Public Sphere*. Delhi: Primus Books, pp. 293–312.

——, and Bishnupriya Dutt. 2010. *Engendering Performance: Indian Women Performers in Search of an Identity*. New Delhi: Sage.

SARMA, M. Nagabhushana. 2008'. 'Old Moorings and New Pastures'— Dance Scenario in Post-Independent India: An Overview'. *Nartanam: A Quarterly Journal of Indian Dance* 7(4) (November 2007–January 2008): 5–22.

SARMA, M. Nagabhushana (ed.). 2010. *Nartanam: A Quarterly Journal of Indian Dance* 10(3) (July–September). Mumbai: Kuchipudi Kala Kendra.

SASIDHARAN, Keerthik. 2017. 'True Authorship is Often a Mirage'. *The Hindu*, 17 December. Available at: https://goo.gl/tyD7sJ (last accessed 18 Auguest 2018).

SAVARKAR, Vinayak Damodar. 1969[1923]. *Hindutva: Who Is a Hindu?* 5th EDN. Bombay: Veer Savarkar Prakashan.

——. 1971. *Six Glorious Epochs of Indian History* (S. T. Godbole trans. and ed.). Bombay: Bal Savarkar and New Delhi: Rajdhani Granthagar.

SAXENA, Monika. 2006. 'Ganikas in Early India: Its Genesis and Dimensions'. *Social Scientist* 34(11–12) (December): 2–17.

SAXENA, Sushil Kumar. 2006. *Swinging Syllables: Aesthetics of Kathak Dance*. New Delhi: Sangeet Natak Akademi.

SCHARFE, Hartmut. 1989. *The State in Indian Tradition*. Leiden: E. J. Brill.

SCHECHNER, Richard. 1977. 'Water the Fruits, Not the Roots'. Paper presented at Anamika Kala Sangam's Chhau Dance Festival, Calcutta, India, 4 February. Copy from the private collection of Richard Schechner, New York, USA.

——. 1985. *Between Theater and Anthropology*. Philadelphia: University of Pennsylvania Press, 1985.

——. 1993. *The Future of Ritual: Writings on Culture and Performance*. New York: Routledge.

——. 2001. 'Rasaesthetics'. *TDR* 45(3) (Fall): 27–49.

——. 2004. 'Restoration of Behaviour' in *Over, Under, and Around*. Calcutta: Seagull Books, pp. 101–86.

——, and Willa Appel (eds). 1990. *By Means of Performance: Intercultural Studies of Theatre and Ritual*. Cambridge: Cambridge University Press.

——, Phillip Zarrilli, Sanjukta Panigrahi and Kelucharan Mahapatra. 1988. 'Collaborating on Odissi: An Interview with Sanjukta Panigrahi, Kelucharan Mahapatra, and Raghunath Panigrahi'. *TDR* 32(1) (Spring): 128–38.

——, and Carol Martin. 1970s–present. Private collection of primary materials on Odissi and Chhau dance traditions. New York, USA.

SCHEDULED CASTES AND SCHEDULED TRIBES RESEARCH AND TRAINING INSTITUTE. 2004[1990]. *Tribes of Orissa*. Bhubaneswar: Scheduled Tribes and Scheduled Castes Development Department, Government of Orissa.

SCHMIDT, Jochen. 1997. 'From Temple to Stage'. *Ballett International/Tanz Aktuell* [English edn] (July): 26–9.

SCHNEIDER, Rebecca. 2011. *Performing Remains: Art and War in Times of Theatrical Reenactment*. New York: Routledge.

SCHNEPEL, Burkhard. 1995. 'Durga and the King: Ethnohistorical Aspects of Politico-Ritual Life in a Southern Orissan Jungle Kingdom'. *Journal of the Royal Anthtropological Institute*, 1(1) (March): 145–66.

——. 2002. *The Jungle Kings: Ethnohistorical Aspects of Politics and /Ritual in Orissa*. New Delhi: Manohar.

SCHNEPEL, Cornelia. 2009. 'Bodies Filled with Divine Energy: The Indian Dance Odissi'. *Paragrana* 18: 188–99.

SCHWARTZ, Susan L. 2004. *Rasa: Performing the Divine in India*. New York: Columbia University Press.

SCHWEIG, Graham M. 2002. 'Humility and Passion: A Caitanyite Vaishnava Ethics of Devotion'. *Journal of Religious Ethics* 30(3) (Fall): 421–44.

——. 2007[2005]. *Dance of Divine Love: India's Classic Sacred Love Story. The Rasa Lila of Krishna*. Delhi: Motilal Banarsidass.

SCOLIERI, Paul. 2013. *Dancing the New World: Aztecs, Spaniards, and the Choreography of Conquest*. Austin: University of Texas Press.

SCOTT, James. 1998. *Seeing Like a State: How Certain Schemes to Improve the Human Condition Have Failed*. New Haven: Yale University Press.

SECRETARY OF STATE FOR INDIA IN COUNCIL. 1909. *Imperial Gazetteer of India, Volume 4: Administrative*. Oxford: Oxford University Press.

SEN, Amartya. 2005. *The Argumentative Indian: Writings on Indian Culture, History, and Identity*. London: Penguin.

SEN, Geeti. 2005. 'The Raas Lila: The Enchantment with Innocence' in Harsha V. Dehejia (ed.), *A Celebration of Love: The Romantic Heroine in the Indian Arts*. New Delhi: Roli Books, pp. 209–14.

—— (ed.). 2003. *India: A National Culture?* New Delhi: India International Centre and Sage.

SEN, Sudipta. 2002. *A Distant Sovereignty: National Imperialism and the Origins of British India*. New York: Routledge.

SEHGAL, Rashme.1989. 'Kelucharan Mahapatra: The Living Legend'. *The India Magazine of Her People and Culture* (August): 74–84.

SENAPATI, Nilamani, N. K. Sahu and Premananda Tripathy. 1966. *Orissa District Gazetteers, Volume 12: Bhubaneswar*. Orissa Government Press.

SENAPATI, Rabindra Mohan. 2004. *Art and Culture of Orissa*. New Delhi: Government of India, Publications Division.

SETHI, Arshiya. 2015. 'A Moment in History: Story of Three Dancers'. *Nartanam* (1954, Inter-University Youth Festival special issue) (July–September): 11–51.

SHAH ALAM II. 1765. 'Firmaun from the Mogul for the Northern Sircars' (No. IV), in *Treaties and Grants from the Country Powers, to the East India Company, Respecting their Presidency of Fort. St. George, on the coast of Choromandel; Fort William, in Bengal; and Bombay, on the Coast of Malabar, from the Year 1756 to 1772*, pp. 25–6. Item no. IOR/A/2/20, India Office Records, British Library, London.

SHAH, Natubhai. 1998. *Jainism: The World of Conquerors*, VOL. I. East Sussex: Sussex Academic Press.

SHAH, Purnima. 2002. 'State Sponsorship of the Arts in India: The Appropriation of the National and Regional'. *Dance Chronicle*, 25(1) (2002): 125–41.

SHAH, Hasan. 1993[1790]. *The Dancing Girl: A Novel by Hasan Shah* (Qurratulain Hyder trans.). New York: New Directions.

SHAHANI, Kumar. 1991. *Bhavantarana*. Odiya. 63 mins. Colour. Starring Kelucharan Mahapatra and Sanjukta Panigrahi.

SHANKAR, Jogan. 1990. *Devadasi Cult: A Sociological Analysis*. New Delhi: Ashish Publishing House.

SHARMA, Aparna. 2015. *Documentary Films in India*. New York: Palgrave Macmillan.

SHARMA, Aradhana and Akhil Gupta (eds). 2006. *The Anthropology of the State: A Reader*. London: Wiley-Blackwell.

SHARMA, Arvind. 2002. 'On Hindu, Hindustan, Hinduism and Hindutva'. *Numen*, 49(1): 1–36.

SHARMA, Avinash. 2015. '800-year-old Devadasi Tradition Ends; Lord Jagannath's Last Human Wife Dies at 92'. *OneIndia News*, Friday, 20 March. Available at: https://goo.gl/gp66Vc (last accessed on 28 August 2018).

SHARMA, Jyotirmaya. 2003. *Hindutva: Exploring the Idea of Hindu Nationalism*. New Delhi: Viking.

SHARMA, R. S. 1983. *Perspectives in Social and Economic History of Early India*. New Delhi: Cosmos.

———. 1991. *Aspects of Political Ideas and Institutions in Ancient India*, 3rd EDN. New Delhi: Macmillan.

———. 2001. *Early Medieval Indian Society: A Study in Feudalisation*. Hyderabad: Orient Longman.

SHARMA, Ruchika. 2016. 'The Indian Nautch Girl in Early Colonial Travel Writing' in Maratt Mythili Anoop and Varun Gulati (eds), *Scripting Dance in Contemporary India*. London: Lexington Books, pp. 11-25.

SHASHIMONI DEVADASI. 2003. 'From the Mouth of a Mahari'. Interview and translation from Odia by Rahul Acharya, 24 December. Available at: Narthaki.com, and at: goo.gl/MbSANC (last accessed on 2 July 2018).

———. 2008. Interview with author. Puri, India, 7 March.

SHASTRI, J. L. (ed.). 1970. *Ancient Indian Tradition & Mythology: [Purāṇas in translation]*. Delhi: Motilal Banarsidass.

SHAY, Anthony. 2002. *Choreographic Politics: State Folk Dance Companies, Representation, and Power*. Middletown, CT: Wesleyan University Press.

SHAW, Miranda Eberle. 1995. *Passionate Enlightenment: Women in Tantric Buddhism*. Princeton: Princeton University Press.

SHEA MURPHY, Jacqueline. 2007. *The People Have Never Stopped Dancing*. Minneapolis: University of Mineapolis Press.

SHREE JAGANNATH TEMPLE MANAGING COMMITTEE. 1971. *Shree Jagannath Temple Manual* (P. Tripathy ed.) [English and Odia]. Puri: The Temple.

Item no. BLL01012497846, Asia, Pacific and Africa Collections T33931, British Library, London.

SHRIRAM BHARATIYA KALA KENDRA. 2010. http://thekendra.com/ (last accessed on 2 July 2018).

SIEGEL, Lee. 1978. *Sacred and Profane: Dimensions of Love in Indian Traditions as Exemplified in the Gitagovinda of Jayadeva*. Delhi: Oxford University Press, 1978.

———. 2009. *Gitagovinda: Love Songs of Radha and Krishna*. New York: Clay Sanskrit Library, New York University Press and the JJC Foundation.

SIEGEL, Marcia. 1973. *At the Vanishing Point: A Critic Looks at Dance*. New York: Saturday Review Press.

SIKAND, Nandini. 2016. *Languid Bodies, Grounded Stances. The Curving Pathway of Neoclassical Odissi Dance*. New York: Berghahn Books.

SINGER, Milton. 1956. 'Cultural Values in India's Economic Development'. *Annals of the American Academy of Political and Social Science*, 305 (Agrarian Societies in Transition) (May): 81–91.

SINGH, A. K. 1993. 'Socialism and Mixed Economy' in Nirmalya Bhushan Das Gupta, J. L. Raina, H. M. Jauhari and B. M. Jauhari (eds), *Nehru and Planning in India: Proceedings of the National Seminar on Pandit Jawaharlal Nehru Planning Commission and Planned Development in India*. New Delhi: Concept Publishing, pp. 93–100

SINGH, Gulbahar. n.d. *Gotipua*. DVD, colour, 32 mins, India. New Delhi: Indira Gandhi National Center for the Arts.

SINGH, Shanta Serbjeet. 2007. Interview with author. New Delhi, 10 September.

——— (ed.). 2003–04. *Attendance: The Dance Annual of India 2003–04*. New Delhi: Ekah-Printways.

SINGH, Tarlok. 1993. 'Jawaharlal Nehru and the Planned Development of India' in Nirmalya Bhushan Das Gupta, J. L. Raina, H. M. Jauhari and B. M. Jauhari (eds), *Nehru and Planning in India: Proceedings of the National Seminar on Pandit Jawaharlal Nehru Planning Commission and Planned Development in India*. New Delhi: Concept Publishing, pp. 29–35.

SINGH, Upinder. 1994. *Kings, Brahmanas, and Temples in Orissa: An Epigraphic Study AD 300–1147*. New Delhi: Munshiram Manoharlal.

SIRCAR, D. C. 1996. *Indian Epigraphy*. Delhi: Motilal Barsidass.

SMITH, Caron. 2005. 'The Gopis as a Collective Heroine in the Bhagavata Purana' in Harsha V. Dehejia (ed.), *A Celebration of Love: The Romantic Heroine in the Indian Arts*. New Delhi: Roli Books, pp. 39–43.

SMITH, Neil. 1992. 'Contours of a Spatialized Politics: Homeless Vehicles and the Production of Geographical Scale'. *Social Text* 33: 54–81.

SONEJI, Davesh. 2004. 'Living History, Performing Memory: Devadasi Women in Telugu-Speaking South India'. *Dance Research Journal* 36(2) (Winter): 30–49.

———. 2012. *Unfinished Gestures: Devadasis, Memory, and Modernity in South India*. New York: Oxford University Press.

——— (ed.). 2010. *Bharatanatyam: A Reader*. New York: Oxford University Press.

——— and Indira Peterson (eds). 2008. *Performing Pasts: Reinventing the Arts in Modern South India*. New York: Oxford University Press.

SPEAR, Percival. 1990. *A History of India, Volume 2: From the Sixteenth to the Twentieth Century*. London: Penguin.

SPELLMAN, John W. 1964. *Political Theory of Ancient India: A Study of Kingship from the Earliest Times to c.A.D. 300*. Oxford: Clarendon Press.

SPINK, Walter. 2005. 'The Quest for Krishna' in Harsha V. Dehejia (ed.), *A Celebration of Love: The Romantic Heroine in the Indian Arts*. New Delhi: Roli Books, pp. 30-37.

SPIVAK, Gayatri Chakravorty. 1996. 'How to Teach a Culturally Different Book' (1991) in Donna Landry and Gerald M. McLean (eds), *The Spivak Reader: Selected Works of Gayatri Chakravorty Spivak*. New York: Routledge, pp. 237–66.

———. 2001. 'Moving Devi'. *Cultural Critique*, 47 (Winter): 120–63.

———. 2009. *Nationalism and the Imagination*. Kolkata: Seagull Books.

SRI GOPAL. 2005. 'Mahari Tradition Revisited'. *Nartanam* 5(1) (January–March): 60–6.

SRINIVAS, M. N. 1952. *Religion and Society Amongst the Coorgs of South India*. Oxford: Clarendon Press.

———. 1989. *The Cohesive Role of Sanskritization and Other Essays*. New Delhi: Oxford University Press.

SRINIVASAN, Amrit. 1985. 'Reform and Revival: The Devadasi and Her Dance'. *Economic and Political Weekly*, 20(44): 1869–76.

———. 1988. 'Reform or Conformity? Temple 'Prostitution' and the Community in the Madras Presidency' in Bina Agarwal (ed.), *Structures of Patriarchy*. New Delhi: Kali for Women, pp. 175–98.

—— (ed.). 2007. *Knowledge Tradition Text: Approaches to Bharata's Natyasastra*. New Delhi: Sangeet Natak Akademi and Hope India Publications.

SRINIVASAN, Priya. 2007. 'The Bodies Beneath the Smoke or What's Behind the Cigarette Poster: Unearthing Kinesthetic Connections in American Dance History'. *Discourse in Dance* 4(1): 7–48.

——. 2009. 'The Nautch Women Dancers of the 1880s: Corporeality, U.S. Orientalism, and Anti-Immigration Laws'. *Women and Performance* 19(1) (March): 3–22.

——. 2012. *Sweating Saris: Indian Dance as Transnational Labour*. Philadelphia: Temple University Press.

SRINIVASAN, Doris M. 2006. 'Royalty's Courtesans and God's Mortal Wives: Keepers of Culture in Precolonial India' in Martha Feldman and Bonnie Gordan (eds), *The Courtesan's Arts: Cross-Cultural Perspectives*. New York: Oxford University Press, pp. 161–81.

SRJAN.COM. 2016. 'Milestones in Guru Kelucharan Mohapatra's Life'. Srjan.com. Available at: https://goo.gl/12qtCy (last accessed 22 August 2018).

STAAL, J. F. 1963. 'Sanskrit and Sanskritization'. *The Journal of Asian Studies* 22(3) (May): 261–75.

STARZA, O. M. 1993. *The Jagannatha Temple at Puri: Its Architecture, Art and Cult*. Leiden: E. J. Brill.

STEWART, Tony. 1992. 'The Biographies of Sri Chaitanya and the Literature of the Gaudiya Vaisnavas' (Interview) in Steven Rosen (ed.), *Vaisnavism: Contemporary Scholars Discuss the Gaudiya Tradition*. Brooklyn: FOLK Books, pp. 101–25.

——. 1997. 'When Rahu Devours the Moon: The Myth of the Birth of Krsna Caitanya'. *Journal of Hindu Studies*, 1(2) (August): 221–64.

STHAPATI, V. Ganapati. 2002. *Indian Sculpture & Iconography: Forms and Measurements*. Pondicherry and Ahmedabad: Sri Aurobindo Society and Mapin Publishing.

STIRLING, Andrew. 1825. 'An Account, Geographical, Statistical and Historical of Orissa Proper, or Cuttack'. *Asiatic Researches*, 15: 163–338.

STOLER MILLER, Barbara. 1986. *The Bhagavad Gita: Krishna's Counsel in Time of War*. New York: Bantam Books.

——. 2004. *The Gita Govinda of Jayadeva: Love Song of the Dark Lord*. Delhi: Motilal Banarsidass.

STRATHERN, Marilyn. 1988. *The Gender of the Gift: Problems with Women and Problems with Society in Melanesia*. Berkeley: University of California Press.

STRYKER, Susan. 2008. *Transgender History*. Berkeley, CA: Seal Press.

SUBRAMANIAM, V. 1972. 'Unity and Diversity in India: The Strength of the Indian Union'. *The Roundtable: The Commonwealth Journal of International Affairs* 62(248): 509–18.

———. (ed.). 1980. *The Sacred and the Secular in India's Performing Arts: Ananda K. Coomaraswamy Centenary Essays*. New Delhi: Ashish Publishing House.

SUGANDHI, Namita. 2003. 'Context, Content and Composition: Questions of Intended Meaning and the Asokan Edicts'. *Asian Perspectives* 42(2) (Fall): 224–46.

SUNDER RAJAN, Rajeshwari. 2000. 'Women Between Community and State: Some Implications of the Uniform Civil Code Debates in India'. *Social Text* 18(4): 55–82.

———. 2003. *The Scandal of the State: Women, Law, and Citizenship in Postcolonial India*. Durham, NC: Duke University Press.

SURESH, Vidya Bhavani. 2004. *What is Odissi?* Chennai: Skanda.

SUTTON, Amos. 1833. *A Narrative of the Mission to Orissa (The Site of the Temple of Jugurnauth)*. Boston: Free-Will Baptist Connexion.

SWAPNASUNDARI. 2005. *The World of Kuchipudi Dance*. Gurgaon: Shubhi Publications.

SWARO, Dasarathi. 1990. *Christian Missionaries in Orissa: Their Impact on 19th Century Society*. Calcutta: Punthi Pustak.

SWINDLEHURST, Albert. 1918. 'Hindu Law and Its Influence'. *Yale Law Journal* 27(7) (May): 857–77.

TAGORE, Abanindranath, and Rani Chanda. 2003[1944]. *Jorashankor Dhare* [Beside Jorashanko; Bengali]. Kolkata: Visva-Bharati.

TAMBE, Ashwini. 2009. *Codes of Misconduct: Regulating Prostitution in Late Colonial Bombay*. Minneapolis: University of Minnesota Press.

TANDON, Rekha 2016, 'Odissi: A Dance of Sculpture I and II' in Routledge Performance Archive, Taylor and Francis. Available at: goo.gl/FfW4Yj (last accessed on 2 July 2018).

TARLEKAR, G. II. 1991. *Studies in the Natyasastra*, 2nd EDN. Delhi: Motilal Banarssidas.

TAYLOR, Diana. 2003. *The Archive and the Repertoire: Performing Cultural Memory in the Americas*. Durham, NC: Duke University Press.

TEGEDER, Urlich. 1985. '. . . .because they have no shadows!' *Ballett International* 8(8) (August): 18–23.

———. 1983. 'Our Art is God'. *Ballett International* 6(3) (March): 16–17.

THE TELEGRAPH. 2011. 'Mahari Comes Alive on Stage'. *The Telegraph*, Thursday, 26 May. Available at: goo.gl/YAGkZC (last accessed on 2 July 2018)

THAPAR, Romila. 1978. *Ancient Indian Social History*. New Delhi: Orient Longman.

———. 1989. 'Epic and History: Tradition, Dissent and Politics in India'. *Past and Present* 125 (November): 3–26.

———. 1990. *A History of India*, VOL. I. London: Penguin.

———. 2000a. *Cultural Pasts: Essays in Early Indian History*. New Delhi: Oxford University Press.

———. 2000b. *History and Beyond*. New Delhi: Oxford University Press.

———. 2001. *Early India*. Berkeley and Los Angeles: University of California Press.

———. 2002. *The Penguin History of Early India From the Origins to AD 1300*. New Delhi: Penguin.

———. 2007. 'Secularism, History, and Contemporary Politics in India' in Anuradha Needham and Rajeshwari Sunder Rajan (eds), *The Crisis of Secularism in India*. Durham, NC: Duke University Press, pp. 191–207.

———, Harbans Mukhia, Bipan Chandra and Sudhir Chandra. 1970. 'Communalism and the Writing of Indian History'. *Economic and Political Weekly* 5(19) (May 9): 770–4.

THAROOR, Shashi. 1997. 'Unity, Diversity, and Other Contradictions' in *India: From Midnight to the Millenium*. New York: Harper Perennial.

THIELEMANN, Selina. 2002. *Divine Service and the Performing Arts in India*. New Delhi: A. P. H. Publishing Corporation.

THOMSON, Susan Jean. 1989. *Seraikela Chhau Dance and the Creation of Authority: From Princely State to Democracy*. PhD thesis, Harvard University.

THORNTON, Edward. 1857. *Gazetteer of the Territories of the East-India Company, and of the Native States on the Continent of India*. London: W. H. Allen and Co.

TIMES OF INDIA. 1927. 'Central Legislature: Dedication of Hindu Girls to Temples, Debate in the Council of State'. *Times of India*, 13 September, p. 11.

——. 1954a. 'Inter-University Youth Festival: Bombay Student Wins Prize'. *Times of India*, 6 November, p. 13.

——. 1954b. 'Inter-University Youth Festival: Govt. Foresight Hailed'. *Times of India*, 9 November, p. 8.

——. 1955. 'Engagements'. *Times of India*, 17 February, p. 3.

——. 1958. 'Dr. Rajamannar Opens Dance Seminar'. *Times of India*, 31 March, p. 7.

——. 1995a. 'Move to Revive Devadasi System in Puri'. *Sunday Times of India*, 10 September, p. 1.

——. 1995b. 'Five Women Appear for Devadasi Interview'. *Times of India*, 13 September, p. 9.

——. 1995c. 'Puri Devadasis Decline to Take Aspirants under Their Wing'. *Times of India*, 15 September, p. 9.

TOEPFER, Karl. 1997. *Empire of Ecstasy: Nudity and Movement in German Body Culture, 1910–1935*. Berkeley: University of California Press.

TRIPATHI, Chandra Dhar. 2008. *Kamarupa-Kalinga-Mithila: A Politico-Cultural Alignment in Eastern India, History, Art, Traditions*. New Delhi: Indian Institute of Advanced Study / Aryan Books.

TRIPATHY, Ajit Kumar. 2009. 'Jayadeva and Gitagovinda'. *Orissa Review* (Special issue) (July): 1–34. Available at: https://goo.gl/jeuyAH (last accessed on 3 October 2016).

TRIPATHY, Dilip Kumar. 2007. *Visual and Performing Arts in South Orissa: An Interface*. New Delhi: Harman Publishing House.

TRIPATHY, Paramananda (ed.). 1971. *Shree Jagannath Temple Manual* [Odia and English]. Puri: Jagannath Temple.

TRIPATHY, Snigdha. 1997. *Inscriptions of Orissa, Volume 1: Circa Fifth to Eighth Centuries A.D.*). New Delhi: Indian Council of Historical Research and Motilal Banarsidass.

TURNER, Victor. 1995[1969]. *The Ritual Process: Structure and Anti-Structure*. Chicago: Aldine Transaction.

VANCE, Carol (ed.), *Pleasure and Danger: Exploring Female Sexuality*, 2nd EDN. London: Pandora Press.

VANITA, Ruth. 2002a. 'Whatever Happened to the Hindu Left?' Comment in *Seminar* #512, States of Insecurity: A Symposium on Emergency

Laws, Human Rights and Democracy (April). Web edition. Available at: https://goo.gl/rFr9My (last accessed 22 August 2018).

——. 2005. 'Born to Two Mothers, the Hero Bhagiratha, Female–Female Love, and Miraculous Birth in Hindu Texts'. *Manushi* 146: 22–33.

—— (ed.). 2002b. *Queering India: Same-Sex Love and Eroticism in Indian Culture and Society.* New York: Routledge.

——, and Salim Kidwai (eds). 2000. *Same-Sex Love in India: Readings from Literature and History.* New York: St. Martin's Press.

VARADPANDE, Manohar Laxman. 1987. *History of Indian Theatre: Loka Ranya Panorama of Indian Folk Theatre*, VOL. 2. New Delhi: Abhinav Publications.

——. 1983. *Religion and Theatre.* New Delhi: Abhinav Publications.

VARLEY, Julia. 1998. 'Sanjukta Panigrahi: Dancer for the Gods' (David Korish and Roxana Avila trans.). *New Theatre Quarterly* 14(55) (August): 249–73.

VASHISHTHA, Neelima. 2004. '*Jorasankor Dhare*: on Abanindranath Tagore's Personality and Works of Art'. *Studies in Humanities and Social Sciences*, 11(2) (Winter): 105–28.

VASUDEV, Gayatri Devi (ed.). 2009. *Vastu: Astrology and Architecture* (Papers presented at the First All IndiaSymposium on Vastu, Bangalore, 3–4 June 1995). Delhi: Motilal Banarsidass.

VATSYAYANA. 1962. *The Kamasutra of Vatsyayana* (Sir Richard F. Burton trans.). New York: E. P. Dutton.

VATSYAYAN, Kapila. 1963. 'Notes on the Relationship of Music and Dance in India'. *Ethnomusicology*, 7(1) (January): 33–8.

——. 1967. 'The Theory and Technique of Classical Indian Dancing'. *Artibus Asiae*, 29(2–3): 229–38.

——. 1972. *Some Aspects of Cultural Policies in India.* Paris: UNESCO.

——. 1974. *Indian Classical Dance.* New Delhi: Publications Division, Ministry of Information and Broadcasting, Government of India.

——. 1976. *Traditions of Indian Folk Dance.* New Delhi: Indian Book Company.

——. 1977. *Classical Indian Dance in Literature and the Arts*, 2nd EDN. New Delhi: Sangeet Natak Akademi.

——. 1982a. *Dance in Indian Painting.* Atlantic Highlands: Humanities Press.

———. 1982b. *Guru–Shishya Parampara: The Master–Disciple Tradition in Classical Indian Dance Music.* London: Arts Council of Great Britain.

———. 1983. *The Square and the Circle of the Indian Arts.* Atlantic Highlands: Humanities Press.

———. 1986. *Traditional Indian Theatre: Multiple Streams.* New Delhi: National Book Trust.

———. 1992. *Indian Classical Dance*, 2nd EDN. New Delhi: Publications Division, Ministry of Information and Broadcasting, Government of India.

———. 1995. 'The Future of Dance Scholarship in India'. *Dance Chronicle* 18(3): 485–90.

———. 1996. *Bharata: The Natyasastra.* New Delhi: Sahitya Akademi.

———. 1997. *Indian Classical Dance*, 3rd EDN. New Delhi: Publications Division, Ministry of Information and Broadcasting, Government of India.

———. 2007a. *Classical Indian Dance in Literature and the Arts*, 3rd EDN. New Delhi: Sangeet Natak Akademi.

———. 2007b. *Incredible India: Arrested Movement, Sculpture and Painting.* New Delhi: Wisdom Tree.

———. 2007c. 'Aesthetic Theories Underlying Asian Performing Arts' in Himanshu Prabha Ray (ed.), *Sacred Landscapes in Asia: Shared Traditions, Multiple Histories.* New Delhi: Manohar, pp. 19–25.

—— (ed.) 1991. *Concepts of Space: Ancient and Modern.* New Delhi: Indira Gandhi National Centre for the Arts and Sterling Publishers.

—— (ed.). 1996. *Concepts of Time: Ancient and Modern.* New Delhi: Indira Gandhi National Centre for the Arts and Sterling Publishers.

—— (ed.). 2006. *The Cultural Heritage of India, Volume 7: 'The Arts', Part 1.* Calcutta: The Ramarishna Mission Institute of Culture.

VENKATARAMAN, Leela. 2002. *Indian Classical Dance: Tradition in Transition.* New Delhi: Roli Books.

———. 2005. 'Heroine by Chance'. *The Hindu*, Sunday Magazine, 23 January 2005. Available at: https://goo.gl/ApbQsQ (last accessed on 29 June 2018).

———. 2007. Interview with author. New Delhi, 25 September.

———. 2015a. 'The Dancer Who Lived on Society's Edge'. *Times of India*, 30 March. Available at: goo.gl/D1JFyb (last accessed on 2 July 2018).

———. 2015b. 'Pre-1952 Odissi: Priyambada Mohanty Hejmadi'. *Nartanam* 15(3) (1954, Inter-University Youth Festival special issue) (July–September): 56–62.

VERMA, Som Prakash. 1997. 'Painting Under Akbar as Narrative Art' in Irfan Habib (ed.), *Akbar and His India*. New Delhi: Oxford University Press, pp. 149–73.

VIDYARTHI, Govind. 1958. 'With the Daughters of Urvasi and Rambha'. *Sangeet Natak Akademi Bulletin* 9 (July): 1–3.

VIJAISRI, Priyadarshini. 2004. *Recasting the Devadasi: Patterns of Sacred Prostitution in Colonial South India*. Delhi: Kanishka Publishers.

———. 2005. 'Small Speeches, Subaltern Gender: Nationalist Ideology and Its Historiography' in Shahid Amin and Dipesh Chakraborty (eds), *Subaltern Studies IX: Writings on South Asian History and Society*. New Delhi: Oxford University Press, pp. 83–125.

VIJAYSREE, C., Meenakshi Mukherjee, Harish Trivedi and T. Vijay Kumar (eds). 2007. *Nation in Imagination: Essays on Nationalism, Sub-Nationalisms and Narration*. Delhi: Orient Longman.

VOLKOFF, Alex. 'Speaking with Her Eyes and Fingertips'. *Tehran Journal* (1 May): n.p. Item call no. *MGZR, Odissi clippings file, Jerome Robbins Dance Division, New York Public Library for the Performing Arts, New York City.

VON GLASENAPP, Helmuth. 1999. *Jainism: An Indian Religion of Salvation* (Lala Sunder Lal Jain Research Series) (Shridhar B. Shrotri trans.). Delhi: Motilal Banarsidass.

WADE, Bonnie C. 1998. *Imaging Sound: An Ethnomusicological Study of Music, Art, and Culture in Mughal India*. Chicago: University of Chicago Press.

WAGNER, R. 1991. 'The Fractal Person' in Marilyn Strathern and M. Godelier (eds), *Big Men and Great Men: Personifications of Power in Melanesia*. Cambridge: Cambridge University Press, pp. 159–73.

WALKER, Frank Deaville. 2006[1922]. *India and Her Peoples*. Edinburgh: Hesperides Books.

WALKER, Margaret. 2016. *India's Kathak Dance in Historical Perspective*. New York: Routledge.

WARD, William. 1815[1811]. *A View of the History, Literature, and Religion of the Hindoos: Including a Minute Description of their Manners and Customs, and Translations from Their Principal Works*, VOL. 2, 2nd EDN. Digital excerpts courtesy of Center for the Study of the Life and Work of William Carey (1761–1834, William Carey University, Hattiesburg, Mississippi. Available at: goo.gl/mQPvin (last accessed on 2 July 2018).

———. 1823. *All Religions and Religious Ceremonies, Part II: A View of the History—Religion—Manners and Customs of the Hindoos, Together with the Religion and Ceremonies of Other Pagan Nations.* Hartford, CT: Oliver D. Cooke and Sons.

Webb, George. 2003[1807]. *George Webb's Report on the Temple of Jagannath, 19 December 1807* (K. S. Behera, H. S. Patnaik, M. P. Dash and R. K. Mishra eds). Bhubaneshwar: Orissa State Archives.

White, Hayden. 1978. *Tropics of Discourse: Essays in Cultural Criticism.* Baltimore: Johns Hopkins University Press.

———. 1990. *The Content of the Form: Narrative Discourse and Historical Representation.* Baltimore, MD: Johns Hopkins University Press.

———. 2010. *The Fiction of Narrative: Essays on History, Literature, Theory, 1957–2007.* Baltimore, MD: Johns Hopkins University Press.

Whitehead, Judith. 1995. 'Bodies Clean and Unclean: Prostitution, Sanitary Legislation, and Respectable Femininity in Colonial North India'. *Gender and History* 7(1) (April): 41–63.

———. 1998. 'Community Honor / Sexual Boundaries: A Discursive Analysis of Devadasi Criminalization in Madras, India, 1920–1947' in James E. Elias, Vern L. Bullough, Veronica Elias and Gwen Brewer (eds), *Prostitution: On Whores, Hustlers, and Johns.* New York: Prometheus Books, pp. 91–106.

———. 2001. 'Measuring Women's Value: Continuity and Change in the Regulation of Prostitution in Madras Presidency, 1860–1947' in Himani Bannerji, Shahrzad Mojab and Judith Whitehead (eds), *Of Property and Propriety: The Role of Gender and Class in Imperialism and Nationalism.* Toronto: University of Toronto Press, pp. 153–81.

Williams, Patrick, and Laura Chrisman (eds). 1994. *Colonial Discourse and Postcolonial Theory: A Reader.* New York: Columbia University Press.

Williams, Raymond. 1986. 'The Uses of Cultural Theory'. *New Left Review* 1(158) (July–August): 19–31.

———. 1977. *Marxism and Literature.* Oxford: Oxford University Press.

Wulff, Donna. 1986. 'Religion in a New Mode: The Convergence of the Aesthetic and the Religious in Medieval India'. *Journal of the American Academy of Religion* 54(4) (Winter): 673–88.

WRIGHT, Elaine. 2008. *Muraqqa: Imperial Mughal Albums from the Chester Beatty Library* (exhibition catalogue). Alexandria: Art Services International.

YAMIN, Mohammed. 2009. *Impact of Islam on Orissan Culture*. New Delhi: Readworthy Publications.

ZARRILLI, Phillip. 1984. ' "Doing the Exercise": The In-Body Transmission of Performance Knowledge in a Traditional Martial Art'. *Asian Theatre Journal* 1(2) (Autumn): 191–206.

———. 1998. *When the Body Becomes All Eyes: Paradigms, Discourses and Practices of Power in Kalarippayattu*. New Delhi: Oxford University Press.

INDEX